A POLITICAL ECONOMY OF MEDICINE

A Political Economy of Medicine: Great Britain and the United States

J. Rogers Hollingsworth

The Johns Hopkins University Press
Baltimore and London

© 1986 The Johns Hopkins University Press
All rights reserved
Printed in the United States of America

The Johns Hopkins University Press
701 West 40th Street
Baltimore, Maryland 21211
The Johns Hopkins Press Ltd., London

The paper used in this publication meets the minimum requirements of
American National Standard for Information Sciences—Permanence of
Paper for Printed Library Materials, ANSI Z39.48-1984.

Library of Congress Cataloging-in-Publication Data

Hollingsworth, J. Rogers (Joseph Rogers), 1932–
     A political economy of medicine, Great Britain and the United States.

     Bibliography: p.
     Includes index.
     1. Medical care—Great Britain—History.   2. Medical care—United
States—History.   3. Medical policy—Great Britain—
History.   4. Medical policy—United States—History.   I. Title.
[DNLM: 1. Delivery of Health Care—history—Great Britain.
2. Delivery of Health Care—history—United States.   3. Economics,
Medical—history—Great Britain.   4. Economics, Medical—history—
United States.   5. Health Policy—history—Great Britain.   6. Health
Policy—history—United States.   7. Politics—history—Great Britain.
8. Politics—history—United States. W 84 FA1 H7p]
RA485.H65   1986   362.1′0941   86-2720
ISBN 0-8018-3262-4 (alk. paper)

for
Ellen Jane

Contents

List of Tables and Figures

FIGURES

Preface

This is a comparative study that confronts the problem of why the U.S. medical delivery system differs from that in Great Britain. A major thesis is that differences in power among key groups shaped the changing structure of the system—particularly the methods of payment for services. The study also addresses the problem of how differences between the two countries in group conflict and in their system structures led to different system performances. By focusing on group power and conflict, changes in structure, and system performances—all in a comparative fashion—the study differs markedly from the existing literature.

Part I of the study is historical in nature, concerned with explaining why there was so much variation in the evolving structure of the medical delivery systems between Great Britain and the United States during the period between 1890 and 1970. Part II focuses on how differences in structure led the two systems to perform differently between the end of World War II and the mid-1970s.

A basic assumption of the study is that a comparative perspective will sharpen our understanding of the evolution and performance of each system. Even though the historical analysis consists of two case studies, there is an effort to raise common questions and to abstract from the two cases the dimensions along which they differed in order to move the analysis to a more theoretical level. And the study attempts to do this in part III.

I am, of course, indebted to many scholars who have written extensively about the histories of these two systems. Brian Abel-Smith, Odin Anderson, Frank Honigsbaum, Rudolph Klein, Almont Lindsey, Charles Rosenberg, Paul Starr, Rosemary Stevens, and Morris Vogel are only a few whose work has been especially helpful. At the same time, my attempt to undertake a comparative study within a conceptual framework that is theoretically oriented dictates the selective aspects of the histories of the two countries that I analyze, and for this reason some of my concerns are often at variance with the excellent scholarship that has preceded mine. My concluding set of observations (chap. 7) departs rather substantially from the previous literature on the two systems, as the analysis takes the first steps toward the development of a theory of how the relative power of various groups influences the structure and performance of medical delivery systems. Because the theoretical discussion is constructed primarily from an analysis of only two cases, however, it must, of necessity, be somewhat tentative.

The study engages in two types of analysis: internal and comparative. The internal analysis is presented in part I, and the concerns are with the historical development of each system. While the analysis focuses on a common set of concerns about the two countries, the distinctive histories require that they receive separate treatment. The purpose in providing the detailed case studies is not to uncover new information about the two medical delivery systems. Rather, it is to provide the empirical basis for the generalizations and theory construction that are presented in part III.

The comparative analysis takes place in part II. It is an effort to demonstrate how differences in the distribution of power and in the structure of the two systems influenced differences in their behavior. Finally, the purpose of the entire study is to provide the materials for moving to the theoretical type of analysis presented in part III.

Neither internal nor comparative analysis is inherently superior to the other. Indeed, they complement each other. The internal analysis permits one to focus on each case in some depth, on unique events and personalities, distinctive organizations, and social processes that are country-specific in nature. With comparative analysis, one is concerned with how variation between systems explains some difference in the systems. In the comparative style of research, however, the analysis lacks the depth that the internal strategy permits. Internal analysis emphasizes the configurative-idiosyncratic aspects of separate cases, while comparative analysis places much less emphasis on the context within which events occur.

The two case studies in part I are presented in a configurative style, with an emphasis on much that was unique in each system, though the analysis does focus on a common set of problems:

1. How influential was the working class vis-á-vis the capitalist class and medical providers in shaping the system through which medical care would be provided?
2. How did each nation solve the problem of financing medical care?
3. How were medical education, specialties, and research organized in each system?
4. How autonomous was the role of the state in shaping the medical delivery system in each country, and to what extent did the relative power of the working and capitalist classes and medical providers shape state policy in each system over time?
5. Why were services provided in the public, for-profit, and/or the voluntary sectors, and with what consequences?

The historical analysis of the two case studies attempts to integrate two theoretical paradigms for the period between 1890 and 1970: (1) a political-economy or a group conflict paradigm, and (2) a social structural paradigm. With the group conflict paradigm, the analysis demonstrates how differences in the structure and performance of the two systems resulted from differences in the distribution of power among the working class (i.e., lower-income consumers), upper-income consumers, and providers (i.e., physicians, hospital administrators, etc.). With the social structural perspective, the concern is to understand why the two systems have differed in the extent to which (1) they have been in the public or private sector, (2) the state dimensions of the systems have been centralized or decentralized, and (3) the systems have had different levels of specialization.

Many medical histories have focused primarily on medical technology and changes in styles of medical therapy. In contrast, this study focuses much more on the social relations in which medical systems are embedded and the influence of power relationships on the structure of a national medical system. It seeks to analyze how a society's power relationships and the structure of a medical system interact to influence the performance of the system.

Most medical histories have devoted little attention to the state. But in all highly industrial societies, the state has become increasingly involved not only in the delivery of medical services but also in the governance of the entire economy. Some of the most exciting literature in the social sciences during the past two decades has focused on the role of the state in twentieth-century capitalist societies (Offe 1972; 1974; 1975; Block 1980; Skocpol 1981; Carnoy 1984; Alford and Friedland 1985). And, responding to the insights of this literature, this study is very much concerned with the reasons for and the consequences of the differences in the role of the state in the two systems.

The historical case studies suggest that the present-day variation between the two systems was very much shaped by the way that power was distributed between providers and consumers at the end of the nineteenth century. If one is to understand differences in contemporary medical delivery systems, a historical explanation is necessary, for organizations and practices tend to persist once they become institutionalized and people become socialized into different ways of doing things. Early on, relationships between physicians and patients became institutionalized: providers became accustomed to certain forms of payment, which set limits on the type of changes that could subsequently occur; and patients became accustomed to certain forms of organization, and this, too, placed constraints on subsequent changes. In other words, existing arrangements structure future predispositions and in turn influence later events. As a result, social policy is an inherently historical process, in which groups have little choice but to build upon previous efforts to deal with similar problems. And if one is to understand social institutions, the analysis must be historical in nature.

Some may argue that, historically, variation between the two medical systems resulted from differences in ideologies in the two countries. While these have existed, they have been outweighed by ideological similarities.

Moreover, ideological differences had little impact on the variation in the structural evolution and performance between the two medical systems.

Being capitalist societies at approximately the same stages of development, the two countries by the early part of the twentieth century shared a common ideology about the nature of illness and how to cope with it. In all societies, ideology plays an important role in determining the nature and definition of disease, medical knowledge, and medical practice. Of course, historically there has not been simply one ideology in these two societies. However, the dominant ideology defined disease as a biological, individual phenomenon. Largely for this reason, research on and the treatment of disease in the two countries has tended to be more concerned with cure and treatment than with prevention. The unit of analysis has been more the individual than the collective. And by emphasizing an individual therapeutic response, such an ideology has absolved the economic and political environment from the responsibility for disease. Even though much disease is caused by the social and economic conditions in the two societies, the medical delivery systems of Britain and the United States have tended to legitimate the existing social order, for the majority of people in the two countries have believed that the problem of illness can be solved by working at the level of the individual rather than by restructuring the society. By focusing on the microcausality of disease, medical science in the two societies has tended to minimize the macrocausality, to deemphasize the role of the social and economic structure. It is in this sense that the two societies have shared a common ideology about disease and treatment. Preventive activities in both countries have focused at the individual level on such things as immunization, proper diet, and adequate exercise and at the societal level on such things as water treatment, sewage systems, and clean air programs. But in neither country has there been much concern with the relationship between disease and a society's stratification system. As a result, neither country has attempted to alter states of health by reshaping the society's dominant social institutions.

Rather than differences in ideology about disease and method of treatment, it has been differences in the distribution of power among key groups that has been instrumental in bringing about differences in the organizational structure in the medical delivery systems between the two countries. And these differences are discussed at some length in chapters 1 and 2.

The comparative analysis in part II demonstrates how the relative power of groups and the different structures in the two systems influenced their behavior or performance during the period following World War II. Of course, the performance of the two systems was influenced by more than the differences in the relative power of groups and the structure of the two systems. For example, within each country, changes in the level of medical expenditures were influenced by changes in the gross national product and technological complexity as well as by increases in the quantity of care demanded and supplied. But these changes have occurred in both systems. It is only by pursuing a comparative perspective that one can begin to understand how variation in group conflict and structure between the two systems influenced variation in system performance.

There are several categories in which the behavior or performances of the two systems is compared. First they are compared in terms of equality. To what extent did the systems differ in the degree to which social classes and income groups had access to medical facilities? How equitably were medical resources distributed across regions? How did variation between the two systems influence differences in levels of health across social classes and income groups in each country? Second, they are compared in terms of innovativeness: while there are a number of strategies by which one may analyze the innovativeness of a system, the analysis here addresses the question of how differences in the organizational structure of the two systems influenced differences in the speed with which various types of medical technology diffused throughout the two countries. Third, the two systems are compared in terms of expenditures on medical care: how did the organizational structure of the systems influence the amount that the societies spent on medical care? And finally, the analysis deals with the question of how variation in the organizational structure and levels of funding of medical research influenced differences in research styles.

The definition of a medical delivery system is one that is somewhat arbitrary and is best established with an eye to the purpose of the analysis. In this study, the concerns are with the power of groups and with the structure and performance of a national medical delivery system, and these concerns dictate a particular set of boundaries for the system. Specifically, a medical delivery system is defined as being composed of those individuals, groups, and organizations that extract resources from the environment and allocate them for medical treatment. Governments, social insurance systems, private insurance organizations, physicians, philanthropists, foundations, hospitals, clinics, and patients are part of the system, as are organizations that conduct research for medical treatment. Because the study is concerned with the medical delivery system of each country but not with the entire health services, there is no systematic effort to analyze public health services. Insofar as the study is concerned with health, it focuses only on the impact of the medical delivery system on health and not on the myriad of other forces—distribution of income, education, housing, food, and a host of other considerations—that influence levels of health.

In order to engage in comparative analysis, one needs comparable data, but the closer the analysis comes to the present, the more difficult it is to obtain comparable data on some of the key concepts in the study. Primarily for this reason, most of the analysis does not extend beyond the mid-1970s.

This study by no means attempts to be a comprehensive history of the medical systems in the two countries during the past century. For example, there are many policy issues and controversies that are deliberately ignored in order to emphasize the driving forces that have structured change and performance in the two systems. The analysis is also selective in another respect. I have based much of my study of the British system on data for England and Wales. Styles of policy making and the organization of medical services in Northern Ireland and Scotland have occasionally differed from those in England and Wales. Because of limitations of space, however, I have focused much of the study prior to 1948 on England and Wales, particularly for matters in the private sector. The analyses of equality of access and equality in levels of health also rely primarily on data for England and Wales. On the other hand, when dealing with central government problems, which were nationwide, my analysis has been broader than England and Wales. For purposes of demonstrating why specific types of structures emerged and how group conflict and structure influence system performance, moving back and forth from the more limited focus on England and Wales to the centralized British state is a matter of no consequence as far as the theoretical findings of this study are concerned.

Acknowledgments

Over the years, several of my colleagues at the University of Wisconsin have contributed immeasurably to the conceptualization of this book. Jerry Hage some years ago suggested that there would be substantial payoff from borrowing theoretical insights from the literature on complex organizations and by applying them to a total societal level of analysis. I have done this in the following study as I attempt to assess how changes in the structure of the British and American medical delivery systems influenced changes in their behavior. To him, I am deeply indebted for helping me to become aware of how the theoretical literature for one level of analysis may be transferred to another level. Bob Alford suggested, in a number of stimulating conversations, that one should try to understand the preference of specific groups both over time and across countries, a suggestion that has also proven to be very valuable. I believe that this aspect of the present study is quite novel in the social science literature. Later, the stimulating seminars on class analysis of Erik O. Wright and Ivan Szelenyi helped to sharpen my perspective on how group and class conflict shape the way that social service systems behave. Bob Hanneman, now of the University of California at Riverside, has always been available to discuss concepts, history, and measurement problems—whatever was necessary in order to sharpen my perspective on the subject at hand.

A number of my colleagues graciously read the entire manuscript and made critical comments that were helpful in clarifying theoretical, methodological, and historical arguments. They are Odin Anderson, Steve Feierman, Lisa MacPherson, Ted Marmor, Jerry Marwell, Charlie Rosenberg, Rosemary Stevens, Morris Vogel, and Erik O. Wright. In addition, my colleagues in the History of Medicine Department at the University of Wisconsin kindly invited me to present some of my work to the History of Medicine Workshop, an experience that was very valuable in helping to clarify my understanding of the process of medical innovations. Nobel laureates Baruch Blumberg and Howard Temin graciously shared their views about medical research with me in several stimulating conversations.

Early in the project, several of my students (Steve Johnson, Ralph Coates, Fred Burkhard, and Jody Davis) provided invaluable assistance in collecting and analyzing data for various tables. Frank Monfort assisted in the computer analysis of mortality data in chapter 5. Later, Dan Bailey carried out innumerable tasks that aided in bringing the manuscript to completion. Sandy Heitzkey, Jane Mesler, and Anita Olson, and other staff members of the University of Wisconsin History Department, in their usual graceful and efficient manner, typed several drafts of the manuscript.

Financial support for this and related projects was provided by the Graduate Research Committee and the Institute for Research in Poverty at the University of Wisconsin; the National Science Foundation under grant SOC 76–17318; the German Marshall Fund; the Law, Science, and Medicine Program and the Program on Non-Profit Organizations, both of Yale University; the Woodrow Wilson International Center for Scholars; the Commonwealth Fund; the Rockefeller Foundation Study and Conference Center in Bellagio, Italy; and the Rockefeller Foundation for a grant in order to use the Rockefeller Archives.

The librarians of the University of Wisconsin have been continually helpful, especially Elizabeth Hewitt, Priscilla Neill, and Ruth Sanderson. I also wish to thank the librarians at Yale University, the New York Academy of Medicine, and the Department of Health and Social Security in London.

Three people who deserve special mention are Lee Benson, Walter Lincoln Palmer, and the late Walter Johnson. Lee Benson has had dozens of conversations with me about the possibility of integrating history with the social sciences, avoiding the narrow specialization that characterizes so much of present scholarship, and moving history to a more theoretical level of analysis. In writing this study, I have attempted to attain all three goals. It was Walter Lincoln Palmer, a great physician and medical educator, who did much to introduce me to the inner world of medical education, while Walter Johnson many years ago helped me to understand how fun and stimulating the study of American history could be. Without knowing it, all three played a direct role in the development of this study.

As the above comments imply, I am especially grateful to the University of Wisconsin for providing me the freedom, the opportunity, the resources, and the stimulating environment to carry out this study. Much of my education has occurred at this university, which has a remarkably stimulating interdisciplinary environment.

The person who has assisted me the most in this project, from beginning to end, has been my wife, Ellen Jane Hollingsworth. She has been my constant companion and collaborator. I owe her far more than words can express for her advice and editorial assistance, and, as a small token of my love and appreciation, I dedicate this book to her.

List of Abbreviations

AFDC	Aid to Families with Dependent Children
AMA	American Medical Association
BMA	British Medical Association
CT	computed tomography
DRG	diagnostic related groups
FDA	Food and Drug Administration
FRCS	Fellow of the Royal College of Surgeons
GDP	gross domestic product
GNP	gross national product
HCFA	Health Care Financing Administration
HMC	Hospital Management Committee
HMO	Health Maintenance Organization
MRC	Medical Research Council
MRCP	Member of the Royal College of Physicians
NHI	National Health Insurance
NHS	National Health Service
NIH	National Institutes of Health
RHB	Regional Hospital Board
UGC	University Grants Committee

Part One
System Structure

Introduction

The following two chapters focus on the evolution of the medical delivery systems of England and Wales and of the United States from the late nineteenth century until approximately 1970. Focusing on a single country, each chapter begins with an analysis of the medical delivery system at the end of the nineteenth century. At that time, each system was quite decentralized and uncoordinated, with most services embedded in the for-profit and nonprofit sectors.

By 1970, the two systems had been fundamentally transformed. The system in England and Wales was concentrated primarily in the public sector and had become more centralized than any other in Western Europe or North America. Virtually all hospitals had become nationalized, and every citizen had access to hospital care without having to be concerned about paying for services. Most doctors were paid by the state, though the nature of the payment varied, depending on whether one was a general practitioner or engaged in hospital practice. While some citizens had private medical insurance so that they could "jump the queue" in the event that hospitalization was necessary, in general most relied on the public sector for most of their care.

By 1970, the medical delivery system of the United Stated differed in each of these respects. Concentrated very much in the private sector, the U.S. system was more decentralized than any in North America or Western Europe. While the federal government owned a few hospitals, for the most part the hospital system was very decentralized and fragmented: there were local public hospitals, voluntary nonprofit hospitals, and for-profit hospitals. Most medical care was provided on a fee-for-service basis, though the number of health maintenance organizations (HMOs) was increasing. However, citizens could not be as unconcerned about medical costs as in England and Wales, for even though Medicare and Medicaid had come into existence during the mid 1960s, millions of Americans were still without any form of medical insurance or third-party coverage. Being badly coordinated, the U.S. system was spending a much higher percentage of gross national product (GNP) on medical care than was the case in Britain, and yet the U.S. population had much less equality of access to medical care.

A major theme in the following two chapters is that differences in the relative power of the working class and medical providers produced two rather different medical delivery systems. Historically, the working class has been very fragmented in the United States because of racial, ethnic, and religious cleavages. Moreover, the sheer size and complexity of the U.S. economy has meant that there has been very little solidarity among the

working class. While there has not been a high degree of class consciousness within the working class of England and Wales, in the late nineteenth
century and subsequently, it was able to mobilize much more power—
particularly in regard to medical care—than its U.S. counterpart. For example, the working class of England and Wales, through membership in
friendly societies in the late nineteenth and early twentieth centuries, was
able to shape the circumstances under which nonhospital care was delivered. Partly as a result, medical care became more accessible to lower-
income groups there than in the United States.

Of course, there were other reasons why the working class was able to
mobilize political power more effectively in England and Wales than in the
United States. At the turn of the century, the United States was still very
much an agricultural country, with slightly more than 40 percent of its
labor force in agriculture, as compared to 15 percent in Great Britain. In
the United States, only 28 percent of the labor force was engaged in manufacturing, mining, and construction, but in Britain, the figure was 54 percent. And because the British political system was smaller but more centralized, it was easier for the working class there to organize a labor party, to
mobilize political power, and to shape national policy than in the United
States, where the political system was very large, fragmented, and decentralized (Hollingsworth 1982; Cronin 1984; Cronin and Schneer 1982;
Winter 1983).

Meantime, the power of the medical profession has historically been
much weaker in England and Wales than in the United States. This was in
part because the medical profession of England and Wales has long been
more rigidly stratified than that in the United States. By the end of the
nineteenth century, there were in England and Wales basically two types of
practitioner, who were differentiated very much in terms of their relationship with the prestigious voluntary hospitals of the day. On the one hand,
there were the general practitioners, who practiced mostly outside the hospitals, and on the other the physicians and surgeons who had hospital connections. In the United States, however, the division between the hospital-
and nonhospital-based physicians never developed to the same degree
throughout the country as in England and Wales and elsewhere in Europe.
As a result, the medical profession historically has been much more united
in the United States than in England and Wales and the U.S. profession has
been more influential.

Historically, in both countries the medical profession has been more
powerful in shaping medical policies and the performances of the medical
system than has the working class. However, their relative power has
differed: the working class has been more powerful in England and Wales
than in the United States, while the reverse is true of the medical profession.

Over time, these differences between the two countries contributed to quite distinct methods of financing medical care and different levels of specialization, access to medical care, commitment to primary care and to biomedical research, and coordination of various parts of medical delivery systems. The power of groups is not automatically translated into specific types of policies, however. Rather, the state plays an important role in translating the power of specific groups into public policy. Indeed, it has become increasingly important in the histories of the medical systems of both countries, but far more so in England and Wales than in the United States.

The following analysis suggests that the state mediates among various interest groups with conflicting positions; conflict among specific groups contributes to the expansion of the state's role. Rarely are the demands of the working class and other groups incorporated into state policy in their original form. In this sense, the state as a mediator of group conflict is a player with some autonomy. But across countries, it is dissimilarity in the power of key groups that does much to explain differences in specific types of policies.

In the following two chapters, analysis focuses on the processes by which groups influenced and interacted with such structural features as changes in the distribution of medical services between the public and private sectors, an increasingly autonomous state, and changes in the levels of specialization, particularly as exemplified in medical education and research. By 1970, the interplay of the forces of group conflict and social structure had produced in the two countries two strikingly different medical delivery systems.

1
The Medical Delivery
System of England and Wales,
1890–1970

The development of medical delivery systems in the twentieth century has been strongly influenced by the structure of the individual system and the distribution of power among groups at the end of the nineteenth century. For this reason, this chapter begins by analyzing the system's structure in the late nineteenth and early twentieth centuries in England and Wales. It is concerned with showing the dominant arrangement for delivering medical care: the very strong private sector; the fragmented and uncoordinated nature of medical care delivery; the divisions in the medical profession; the challenges posed by specialization; the traditions in education and research; and the power of consumers. The analysis will then turn to the pressures for changes with the system, forces ultimately culminating in the creation of the National Health Service (NHS) in 1948.

There was in the late nineteenth century a fragmented set of power arrangements that would shape the future of both nonhospital and hospital care. The medical delivery systems of England and Wales and of the United States were decentralized and inegalitarian, with a great deal of variation in the access of social classes to care. In parts of the United States, but especially in England and Wales, one set of institutions was, in theory, for "the undeserving poor," or paupers, another for the "deserving poor," and yet another for the middle and upper classes. In both countries, the medical system was highly privatized, and public responsibility for medical services was limited. Medical technology was very unevenly distributed from region to region, as well as among institutions even within the same city.

While the various parts of the medical delivery system affected one another, the voluntary hospitals in England and the groups that dominated them were by far the most prestigious and one of the most important parts of the system. Within the hospital sector, the behavior of voluntary hospitals was constrained by the values and preferences of upper-income groups and the nation's elite physicians and surgeons. In contrast, most of the public sector hospitals were designated to serve the pauper class, but because their patients had virtually no political influence, they played little role in shaping the behavior of Poor Law institutions (Gilbert 1966; Abel-Smith 1964; Hollingsworth and Hollingsworth 1983; 1985).

By focusing initially on the different institutional arrangements for providing medical care in England and Wales during the late nineteenth and early twentieth centuries and on the medical schools that trained practitioners, one can better understand which groups dominated the system and benefited most from changes in medical science and technology, how the technology was financed, and how medical education was interrelated in complex ways with the structure of the delivery system. The following discussion focuses first on the medical care of the most decentralized sector, that is, the private sector, which in 1890 was far more important in terms of size than the public sector, though the latter was growing rapidly.

THE PRIVATE SECTOR

Hospitals

Voluntary General Hospitals

It has been only during the past century that hospitals have become important institutions for treating the ill. During most of the nineteenth century, they were primarily for the sick poor—those who could not receive proper care at home. Essentially, there had been two types of institution in England and Wales for treating the ill: public workhouses for paupers and voluntary hospitals. And it was the rigid class structure in Britain that gave rise to these two systems.

Voluntary hospitals became the elite institutions for providing care, historically to the "deserving poor." Dependent for their income on charitable contributions, voluntary hospitals were limited in the speed with which they could adapt to changing medical technology by the willingness of the wealthy to provide money. In short, the behavior of the voluntary hospitals was very much constrained by the preferences of the well-to-do. Because they had historically tended to exclude the destitute from care and because the middle and upper classes received care at home, the beneficiaries of access to hospital care had been the "deserving poor."

With the passage of time, the large voluntary hospitals increasingly provided enormous benefits to an important interest group—the elite physicians and surgeons—and the behavior of these hospitals began to reflect their value preferences as well. Historically, the physicians and surgeons of London had provided medical care in the large voluntary hospitals without payment. They supported themselves from the sizable fees they charged well-to-do patients whom they treated in their offices on Harley and Wimpole streets, and who provided contributions to finance the voluntary hospitals. Thus the doctors who accepted positions in these hospitals were making charitable contributions to the poor, but by doing so they were also generating the good will of their wealthy clients or patrons.

Though the voluntary hospitals had been established to serve the needs of the deserving poor, some of the larger and more prestigious ones had long performed another important function: that of teaching institution. The doctors on the medical school faculties received compensation from medical students. The position of teacher increased their status and was a good investment, in that students in later years referred their wealthy patients to their former teachers. Unlike the situation in Germany and the trend that was later to develop in the best centers in the United States, medical teaching was done by hospital staff, not by university professors (Abel-Smith 1964: 18; C. Newman 1957; Peterson 1978; Poynter 1961).

Eventually, two archetypal medical doctors emerged. In the large voluntary hospitals there were physicians and surgeons, many of whom were graduates of Oxford or Cambridge and had upper-class connections. The few hospital positions were virtually monopolized by a small elite within the medical profession, who had little incentive to create new positions. Because they treated patients in the hospitals without fees and were held in high esteem as teachers, the hospital consultants gained enormous legitimacy and generated widespread trust as brilliant medical practitioners. And yet by 1910, the hospital consultant in England and Wales was beginning to be slightly anachronistic. Even though medical technology was rapidly changing and new medical specialties were developing, the typical hospital consultant was not a specialist but a generalist who was not engaged in scientific or medical research. In 1900, it was rare for specialty departments to exist in the great teaching hospitals. Each consultant, having considerable autonomy over his practice, simply had his own number of allocated beds and treated patients with a wide assortment of ailments. Because most consultantships went to the doctors who already enjoyed high social status, specialization was not such an important variable in determining who the medical elite of England and Wales were (Stevens 1966: 31–34).

The other archetype doctor in England and Wales was the general practitioner, who was commonly excluded from the large voluntary hospitals and thus tended to treat poorer patients outside the hospital, and who was much more concerned about the source of his income than the consultant with his wealthy patients. Over time, permanent and serious splits developed between consultants and general practitioners that over the longer run weakened the power of the medical profession vis-à-vis consumers. Moreover, these divisions were to have profound effects on the subsequent structure of the medical delivery system in England and Wales.

In accordance with the preferences of the hospital-based doctors, certain types of cases were excluded from access to the voluntary hospitals. Doctors—especially in the teaching hospitals—wished to treat the unusual or the spectacular case and preferred to concentrate their energies on curable cases that would demonstrate their skills, not their shortcomings (Great Britain, Metropolitan Hospitals 1892, vol. 13). Constrained by the value preferences of the upper-income groups, who financed large voluntary hospitals as well as the doctors who worked in them, the general voluntary hospitals also tended to exclude most types of infectious diseases—even though these were among the major killers in the population, especially among the poor. Thus these hospitals became institutions for the treatment of designated types of acute cases (Abel-Smith 1964: 13–15, 24, 44–45, 185–86; Webb and Webb 1910: 151–52).

When the large voluntary hospitals had been viewed as exclusively for the deserving poor, most of the income had come from wealthy patrons who were willing to help the poor. But as higher standards for the treatment of various forms of acute care were developed, this type of hospital encountered difficulty in raising the money necessary to meet the increased costs. Changes in technology slowly altered medical practice in them, affected who had access to them, and on a modest scale changed the financing of hospital care. For example, surgery increasingly became more complex and sophisticated. As a result, surgeons insisted on new operating rooms and new equipment. As surgery became more frequent in the hospitals, the number of patients treated and discharged increased (Abel-Smith 1964: 32, 189). Consequently there was a rise in the costs of managing hospitals.

When the wealthy failed to provide adequate funds, hospitals turned increasingly to patient fees. In addition, two national organizations were established to raise funds from more varied sources: the Hospital Sunday Fund, which raised money from the middle classes through the churches, and the Hospital Saturday Fund, which collected small weekly contributions from the skilled working classes. In return, the contributors expected assurance of hospital care when and if they needed it. Despite the fund-raising activities of these two organizations, the donations, endorsements, and special appeals fell far short of the necessary funds. As a result, the voluntary hospitals increasingly faced the question of charging patients for care. This was a delicate matter, and those who managed hospitals feared that, if they began to charge middle-class patients who could afford to pay for services, the wealthy patrons might think that the hospital was no longer dependent on them, and charitable contributions might decline. Furthermore, there was some fear that payment from patients might cause the consultants to demand a fee for their services, thus creating a further strain on the hospitals.

Nevertheless, large voluntary hospitals slowly began to set aside a separate set of beds for paying patients. Some hospitals asked some patients to make contributions toward the total cost of their care, while others asked them to pay a flat rate in addition to paying the doctor on the hospital staff. By the end of the century, some form of payment by patients had been introduced into the large voluntary hospitals. Eventually the wealthy also demanded hospital services. Thus those in England and Wales were no

longer serving only the deserving poor, although the overwhelming majority of patients were still nonpaying. By admitting the well-to-do to the best
hospitals and charging them fees for services, however, England and Wales
were no longer operating most elite hospitals entirely on a charitable basis
(Abel-Smith 1964: 134–37, 140–50, 189). Even so, the behavior of the large
voluntary hospitals continued to reflect the value preferences of the elite
consultants and upper-income groups.

Specialized Hospitals

As the large general hospitals in the voluntary sector excluded many diseases from their concern, other types of institutions in both the public and
private sectors responded to unmet needs. During the nineteenth century,
throughout the country, a number of specialized private hospitals came
into existence, in reaction not only to changes in medical technology but
also to the structure and behavior of the general voluntary hospitals. Probably no factor was of greater importance in stimulating the development of
the private specialized hospitals than the fact that many young doctors
found their futures blocked in the general hospitals. It was not unusual for
a physician in a London hospital to wait for twenty years before becoming
a consultant. As a result, a number of younger doctors established specialized hospitals that concentrated on types of treatment usually neglected by
the general hospitals (Stevens 1966).

   The specialized hospitals were an interesting example of how the source
of funding placed constraints on an organization's behavior. While there
were a few exceptions, the private specialized hospitals of England tended
to serve the rich and the middle class. As a result, those diseases that were
most common among the poor (tuberculosis and other types of infectious
diseases) were generally not treated by these hospitals. Instead, specialized
hospitals for children, midwifery, eye diseases, orthopedics, and diseases of
the skin became common. Most of these charged fees for their services,
though, when the poor did receive care there, they paid either nothing at all
or only a token fee (Great Britain, Metropolitan Hospitals 1892, vol. 14).

   For some years, there was considerable institutional competition between the general and specialized hospitals in the private sector. Initially,
the medical elite of the general hospitals tended to ridicule their junior
colleagues for moving to the specialized hospitals, for charging fees, for
becoming specialists, and for treating diseases that were inappropriate for
gentlemen. At the turn of the century, most of the medical elite of the
general hospitals resented specialization as a matter of principle, but they
were even more upset when the special hospitals attracted some of their
wealthy patients, especially when a few of them made generous contribu-

tions to the hospitals (Great Britain, Metropolitan Hospitals 1890, 12: 233–34, 251–53; 1890–91, 13: 430–46, 504).

Because it was possible to demonstrate the efficaciousness of specialized medical technology and because wealthy patients increasingly gravitated to the specialist hospitals, the large voluntary hospitals eventually had no alternative but to develop specialized departments and appoint specialists as consultants. Even so, for some years the medical elite in the best voluntary hospitals continued to look down on specialization and to treat specialists as being on the fringe of medical practice. For this reason, the special hospitals in England and Wales, especially in London, became the basic centers for specialist training and research, instead of the prestigious teaching hospitals, which remained general hospitals.

Outpatient Services

The outpatient clinics of the large general hospitals were originally quite modest in size, but over time they grew as the demand for medical care increased. By the turn of the century, hundreds of thousands of patients received care in the outpatient departments of large general hospitals. Around 1890, more than one million outpatients were treated in all of London's hospitals, and in 1906, almost two million outpatients were responsible for more than five million attendances in London's hospitals (Steele 1891: 267; Braun 1909: 10).

General Practitioners

Competition with the Voluntary Hospitals

The increasing urbanization and expansion of the middle class were accompanied by rising demands for medical care outside the hospitals, especially care provided by general practitioners. For all practical purposes, general practitioners were excluded from practicing in the prestigious general hospitals. Even so, they began to expand their medical practice around the turn of the century.

The world of the general practitioner was competitive. Not only did they compete among themselves for patients on a fee-for-service basis, but the most intense competition—resulting in serious cleavages—was with the physicians who practiced in the large voluntary hospitals. As the size of the outpatient clinics in the voluntary general hospitals expanded, general practitioners argued that many patients who could afford to pay for care were receiving free treatment and that outpatient clinics were wrongfully luring patients from themselves. They believed that a person able to pay a fee for service had no right to receive free treatment in a hospital outpatient clinic and that, when hospitals permitted patients to receive free care, the fees of private practitioners were driven down. Because the majority of general hospitals provided free care around 1900, general practitioners in London argued that they were being pauperized by the outpatient activities of the large voluntary hospitals (Great Britain, Metropolitan Hospitals 1892, 14: xxxviii–xxxix). The general practitioners also alleged that consultants and specialists in these stole patients they referred for consultation, and as a result, many general practitioners became increasingly reluctant to refer patients to consultants for fear that they would never get them back (Great Britain, Poor Laws 1909, 37: 255–57).

These antagonisms had become especially bitter by the end of the nineteenth century and reflected the basic differences of opinion between doctors in the metropolitan areas who had hospital-based appointments and those who did not. These divisions, as well as those between generalists and specialists, do much to differentiate the medical profession in England and Wales from that in the United States (Abel-Smith 1964: 102–18).

Contract Practice in Friendly Societies

The provision of nonhospital medical care by friendly societies was one of the most important means of organizing British medical care and was also one of the features most different in the historical development of medical delivery in Britain and the United States. Basically, through the friendly societies, consumers were able to influence the mechanisms for the delivery of general practitioner services. From this base, consumers remained significant in the development and evolution of the medical delivery system, exerting considerable influence in structuring it to suit their preferences.

For a small sum of money, members of friendly societies were assured of receiving the care of a general practitioner during times of illness. The doctors who provided these services worked on a contract basis and were paid a set fee for each person on their list. With the passage of time, it was the friendly society, rather than the general practitioner, that dictated the conditions under which more and more outpatient services were provided. In this type of arrangement, the provider exercised less professional autonomy and dominance over the system than would have been the case had remuneration been on a free-for-service basis (Abel-Smith 1965).

Friendly societies were workingmen's organizations that had been in existence since the eighteenth century, but their numbers reached unprecedented heights in the early twentieth century. At that time, there were approximately 24,000 registered societies in Britain with about five and three-quarters million members, most of whom were skilled workers (Gilbert 1966: 165; Great Britain, Poor Laws 1909, 37: 258). The societies provided no services for the families of members, and they attempted to screen out those who suffered from physical defects. Approximately one-half of the adult males in Great Britain were members of the societies, some of which were very large, two having over 700,000 members, and several over 50,000 (Great Britain, Poor Laws 1909, 37: 870).

With the passage of time, however, the financial condition of the friendly societies caused them to turn to the central government for assistance in maintaining their medical benefits. The basic financial problem that confronted the societies during the late nineteenth century resulted from the fact that their actuarial tables were based on the assumption that a sizable portion of their membership would die before middle age and therefore would never make any claim for sickness benefits. Mortality rates for middle-aged adult males improved in the late nineteenth century, but increased longevity was not accompanied by less sickness. As more members survived and lived longer, the demand for medical and sickness benefits increased, thus placing considerable strains on the friendly societies' resources. It was the recognition of these financial problems that eventually caused the societies to support a national health insurance scheme—something to which they were opposed as long as they believed their organizations to be solvent.

The most serious problems for the friendly societies in the late nineteenth century were with the general practitioners and were intensified by increasing financial difficulties. For a number of reasons, there was considerable resentment among many doctors who had contracts with friendly societies: they could be dismissed by a society secretary; they had little bargaining power with the society; some doctors' appointments were obtained as a result of bribery and corruption; and doctors had little opportunity to set their own fees. Moreover, many doctors were upset that patients had no choice in the selection of a doctor and that doctors could not refuse to treat someone on a contract list; indeed they had to treat all the people on a list or risk losing the contract to someone who would. Many doctors believed that some people joined friendly societies merely as a means of qualifying for low-cost medical care and thus forced general practitioners to charge lower fees to compete. It was concern over these issues and the resulting cleavages between the general practitioners and the friendly societies that the National Health Insurance Act would later attempt to resolve (Honigsbaum 1979). Whatever the faults of the friendly societies, they clearly exemplified the power of consumer groups over medical professionals.

In a service as large as that provided by the societies, there was great variation in the quality of care. Many members complained that they received only perfunctory treatment unless the doctor also was able to charge fees for treating other members of the family. There were numerous accusations that the friendly society doctor supplied only the most inexpensive medicine and treatment. In fact, it was not uncommon for a member, when ill, to incur additional expense to receive care from another general practitioner rather than rely on the society's contract practitioner. For these reasons, the friendly society doctor was generally held in low esteem both in and outside the medical profession (Honigsbaum 1979; Gilbert 1966: 288–318).

THE PUBLIC SECTOR

The private sector had not been able to meet all of the medical needs of the country, and its limitations influenced the public sector provision of medical care. These two sectors were interdependent in that the inadequacies of each generated responses from the other. In general, the services of the public sector were addressed to a different set of clients from those of the private sector. The basic public institutions were those provided by the Poor Law (i.e., "outdoor relief," the workhouse, and the Poor Law Infirmary), as well as the public infectious diseases hospitals.

For the most part, the public sector was organized around a set of Poor Laws that reflected the view that poverty demonstrated a personal failing and alms were likely to contribute to the shortcomings of the poor. There was a widely held view among taxpayers that recipients of Poor Law relief should be stigmatized by temporarily losing their rights as citizens. The poor were to be treated as though they were outcasts from the rest of the society, a group to be tolerated, perhaps pitied, but despised. They were assumed to be guilty of sin, of laziness and improvidence. The stamp of pauperism was to be clear upon all who received Poor Law medical relief. And in an effort to minimize the number of those receiving outdoor care (i.e., relief outside the workhouse), a means test was rigorously enforced. An assumption of the Poor Law was that people should be deterred from applying for state aid, and therefore a condition of receiving it was that the recipient live in the workhouse, where one would be clearly branded a pauper and impelled to reform. The rules were not intended to apply to the aged and the sick, however, who were to be eligible to receive outdoor relief. If they could not manage at home, the sick might also receive relief in the workhouses. But in theory, it was anticipated that they would be accommodated separately so that they would be immune from the punitive aspects of the workhouse that the able-bodied poor were to experience (Abel-Smith 1964: 46–47; Gilbert 1966: 13–14, 21).

Because paupers were severely stigmatized, they had little political power with which they might influence the type of care available to them. At a later date, those who were dependent on public services had some impact on service quality, but until the World War I period, the major groups who exerted pressure to improve the quality of the Poor Law facilities were the doctors and social workers involved, and these pressures were not sufficient to be of great consequence early in the century. The situation with regard to the Poor Law, with users unrepresented and ignored, was rather different from the pattern prevailing among upper-, middle-, and skilled working-class people. Receiving services in the private sector, those groups expected to influence the provision of care and usually did so.

The Poor Law

Outdoor Relief

At the level of the central government, the Local Government Board—established in 1871—administered grants to local government authorities and established the guidelines for administering Poor Law medical relief to the poor. At the local level, domiciliary treatment of the sick poor was under the control of a board of guardians in each of the 646 "unions" (i.e., districts) into which England and Wales were divided. The Local Government Board mandated that each board of guardians appoint a district medical officer, who was to provide medical care to the sick poor in their homes or in dispensaries. By 1910, there were approximately 3,700 district medical officers, or about one-sixth of the doctors practicing in the entire country. Operationally, the system was decentralized, with each local board of guardians controlling the administration of medical relief within its district. The districts varied greatly in size, population, the salary paid to the district medical officers, their work-load, and the quality of care provided to the sick poor. Salaries for most of the medical officers were very low, the usual figure being approximately £100 per annum, out of which most had to provide their own drugs, medicines, dressings, and bandages. As a result, much of the care provided by district medical officers was rather perfunctory in nature (Great Britain, Poor Laws 1909, 37: 249, 268–69, 282–83, 859).

The quality of outdoor Poor Law medical relief varied greatly between those districts that had a dispensary (a place for consultations between doctor and patient, where the expense for medicine was paid by the guardians and not by the doctor) and those that did not (Webb and Webb 1910: 26–27, 40–41). Where there were dispensaries, the work conditions for medical officers and the quality of medical care were somewhat better, but as a rule, dispensaries existed only in the metropolitan areas (Abel-Smith 1964: 28, 31, 90; McVail 1909: 126–39). Overworked, underpaid, and confronted with numerous patients who were to be treated under the most adverse of circumstances, the district medical officer could do little to diagnose and treat illnesses according to the standards by which medicine was being practiced in the prestigious voluntary hospitals. Still, the point is that local public authorities assumed some role in the delivery of health services, however miserly the administration and low the quality.

Many people were reluctant to apply for outdoor relief because of the dread of being stigmatized as paupers and losing certain rights as citizens. The stigma was felt less strongly in large urban areas, where there were shifting populations, than in small towns and villages, where almost everyone knew everyone else and local feelings and traditions were strong. However, throughout the country many individuals, whether suffering from chronic or acute illness, preferred to suffer until they were in great agony or near death rather than seek Poor Law relief and be classed as paupers (Great Britain, Poor Laws 1909, 37: 252–54, 936–37; McVail 1909: 147; Webb and Webb 1910: 46–51).

Workhouses and Infirmaries

Usually, the sick poor preferred to receive outdoor treatment, but those who had no one to care for them and who thought that there was no institution in the voluntary sector accessible to them often sought aid in the workhouse. Each of the 646 districts had a workhouse, and it was there that most of the sick poor sought relief from both acute and chronic illness. Almost every workhouse had a sick ward, separating those who were ill from those who were not. Of course, there was great variability in the quality of the workhouses, especially between urban and rural districts. However, the conditions were often so awful that many people refused to enter them until they were almost in a "moribund state" (Webb and Webb 1910: 76, 89).

The *British Medical Journal* (1895: 1231) reported after a careful survey that numerous workhouses had no hot or cold water, children's wards, surgical supplies, or means of isolating patients, had inadequate or nonexistent privacy for lying-in women, and were greatly overcrowded. The *Journal* summarized its findings by noting that there was "an absence of all intelligent appreciation of the needs of the sick." None of the 300 rural workhouses had a medical officer in full-time residence. Rather, the guardians usually appointed a part-time doctor, who was able to visit patients only irregularly and infrequently. Because the workhouse medical officer was required to pay for medicine from his meager salary, the patients received the most simple types of remedy. Moreover, many of the rural workhouses, for reasons of economy, had no trained nurse, and many had no night nurse, trained or untrained. Where workhouses had no salaried nurse, pauper nurses cared for the patients (Webb and Webb 1910: 96–97; McVail 1909; Great Britain, Poor Laws 1909, 37: 273, 859–62).

In general, the urban workhouses tended to improve during the late nineteenth century. By 1900, many of them had a resident medical officer, trained salaried nurses, medicine financed by the boards of guardians, and new wings built to accommodate the ill. Nevertheless, most urban work-houses were overcrowded, lacked modern medical facilities, and had an inadequate supply of nurses and doctors.

In a few urban districts, the guardians constructed a new and independent Poor Law Infirmary. Compared with the best hospitals of the day, these infirmaries provided care of a medium quality. They had their own staff of doctors and nurses and had no pauper nurses or attendants. By 1910, the type of hospital equipment available in some of these institutions did not differ greatly from that provided in the best voluntary hospitals. Rather, the difference between the two types of institution resulted from the lower proportion of doctors, specialists, and nurses in the infirmaries. And although the newer infirmaries were housed in modern buildings containing up-to-date medical and surgical facilities, their staffs were generally inferior to those found in the best voluntary hospitals, and their salaries were somewhat lower (Great Britain, Poor Laws 1909, 37: 246–47, 863–64; McVail 1909: 48–50). Most of the staff were greatly overworked and, in contrast to the doctors in the voluntary hospitals, had much less control over the patients who were admitted, as the infirmary was required to admit every case recommended by a relieving officer.

Despite the progress that the infirmaries represented, Poor Law medical services were poorly distributed over the country. Ranging from the hospitals with the best physical equipment that money could buy to workhouses that were filled with filth and vermin and totally unsuited for humans, Poor Law medical facilities were increasingly a subject of political controversy, and the demands for reform would last for many years.

Another problem, one that would persist in the delivery of medical services in England and Wales to the present, was poor communication, at this period between the medical officers who provided domiciliary care and the doctors who provided institutional treatment for the sick poor. Both were under the control of the Local Government Board and the various boards of guardians, but they were for all practical purposes two distinct types of service. Once a patient entered a medical institution, his doctor on the outside had no communication with the one inside about the patient's care, and when the patient was discharged, there again was no communication about the type of care received while under confinement (Webb and Webb 1910: 125–26).

Infectious Diseases Hospitals

The development of public hospitals for infectious diseases reveals a great deal about the institutional innovation in the area of medical care. As the voluntary hospitals failed to treat most infectious diseases, the public sector responded to the widespread demand for facilities for isolating and caring for patients with them. As the Poor Law machinery, with the Local Government Board and local boards of guardians, was already in existence, the government responded by placing infectious diseases hospitals under the Poor Law statutes.

With the passage of time, however, the technicalities of the Poor Laws and the needs of society came into conflict. When epidemics broke out, these asylum hospitals responded by admitting patients who were not paupers, though patients who had the financial ability were expected to make some payment for their care. By the end of the nineteenth century, the infectious diseases hospitals in London were permitted to admit all patients suffering from infectious diseases and were denied the authority to charge a fee for the care. This, of course, represented an important precedent for the future of the delivery of medical services in England and Wales. Even though such hospitals were financed by Poor Law rates, their services became free and available to all citizens of London (Abel-Smith 1964: 122–30).*

Thus England and Wales still had one type of delivery system for the elderly and infirm poor, another for the working classes, and a separate one for the upper middle class and the wealthy. The most prestigious type of medical care at the turn of the century centered primarily on the large voluntary hospitals, which had long served the "deserving poor," but which increasingly provided care for paying patients. The elite consultants, who made the large voluntary hospitals their operational base, were primarily generalists and had little interest in specialization and even less in chronic cases and paupers. Care from voluntary hospital outpatient clinics was widespread and often led to serious disagreements between hospital-based doctors and general practitioners. The private system was thus riven by cleavages among hospital consultants, specialists, and general practitioners. Although the elite of English society, through social ties to consultants and donations to voluntary hospitals, had established an important role in shaping the medical delivery system, a sizable segment of the working class had, through friendly societies, played an important role in shaping the way by which an array of services was delivered by general practitioners.

A wholly separate system, but similarly fragmented, existed in the public sector for paupers. Whether the poor were served by domiciliary arrangements, dispensaries, workhouses, or infirmaries, the system was widely

---

* The asylum hospitals were operated under the authority of the metropolitan asylums boards. They were administered by a body made up of representatives of the boards of guardians and financed by the Poor Law authorities. Originally built only for paupers, they eventually became, for all practical purposes, public health institutions (Webb and Webb 1910: 108, 157; Ayers 1971).

used. Coordination between outdoor relief doctors and institutionally based providers was minimal. Overall, the resources of providers, paupers, or any single group for bringing about change were very modest. But several groups channeling their energies toward certain kinds of change were able to create sufficient flexibility to bring about system changes, as the development of a national health insurance system in the early part of the century demonstrated.

THE NATIONAL HEALTH INSURANCE PLAN

The British adopted a national health insurance plan in 1911, something the Americans have avoided to the present day. Why did they do this so early in the century?

As medical care became more expensive and as the demand for it increased, its financing became the most important medical issue facing the nation in the early part of the century. Changes in medical technology and their consequences for the financing of care were important forces for altering the British medical system throughout the first four decades of the twentieth century, and one of the most important changes that took place was the development of the National Health Insurance (NHI) system in 1911.

The NHI plan—primarily a scheme for financing nonhospital medical care and cash sickness benefits—did much to shape the delivery of medical services for a sizable segment of the British public. It resolved many problems concerning the financing and accessibility of medical care for almost one-third of the population: The National Health Insurance Act emerged as it did in 1911 because of three organized interest groups—the friendly societies, the insurance companies, and the doctors.

In Great Britain the friendly societies represented a sizable segment of the consuming public that was organized to obtain medical and sickness benefits. In the United States, where industrialization developed somewhat later and where there was considerable racial and ethnic hostility among the population, trade unions and consumer groups that might have shaped medical legislation were much weaker. Thus American doctors, who did not have the intense cleavages evidenced in Britain between hospital- and nonhospital-based doctors, were in a better position to dictate the conditions under which medical care would be provided. In Britain, however, considerable consumer power was already organized on the subject of nonhospital medical care, and this fact, combined with the divisions within the medical profession, does much to explain the difference in the historical development of health delivery in the two countries.

Britain's friendly societies rather than its trade unions shaped the specific provisions of the National Health Insurance Act. Although the power of the trade unions was fragmented into many different organizations and their concerns were primarily with wages and the conditions of employment, they operated as a lobby of some modest consequence for the NHI program. In contrast, the concerns of the friendly societies were much more narrowly focused and much better articulated. The societies were essentially a consumer group with narrow interests, focusing on medical benefits. Whereas the British trade unions at the turn of the century had approximately 1.6 million members, the friendly societies had more than 5 million (Gilbert 1966: 162, 177). Even though there were many different friendly societies, for several reasons they had considerable political clout. Their long history provided them with considerable legitimacy, gave them the opportunity to develop extensive political contacts with other groups in British society, and permitted them to generate considerable support among their membership. Their history and huge membership made them a highly visible force in British politics, which in itself was an element of power.

The friendly societies were facing serious financial problems by 1908. Many were paying out more in medical and sickness benefits than they were receiving from their members and were thus on the verge of bankruptcy. When Lloyd George proposed his system of national health insurance, he had potential allies as long as he satisfied the concerns of the friendly societies. They were very much opposed to a highly centralized, state-operated system, and preferred a state-mandated scheme that they would administer. Moreover, they believed it essential that they dictate the circumstances under which the doctors provided services. Their leaders argued that a national health insurance system must be administered not for monetary profit but by nonprofit organizations (among which the friendly societies were prominent).

However, a number of the concerns of the friendly societies ran counter to the interests of the insurance companies, a very powerful interest group. Whereas the societies had been primarily concerned with keeping their members out of the poorhouse and with providing a death benefit, the insurance companies of Britain had approximately 30 million death benefit policies in effect and were understandably anxious that the government not provide a death benefit as part of a national health insurance program. The industry was powerful, not only because of the almost £300 million of insurance in force, but also because it employed almost 100,000 people, 70,000 of whom were door-to-door sales agents who had weekly contact with almost every working-class home in the country. In effect, the industry's sales force constituted a small army with considerable potential political clout with their customers. The insurance companies demanded that they, along with the friendly societies, become the agents for administering a substantial portion of the health insurance program. (For a discussion of the insurance industry, see Gilbert 1966: 289–447.)

But without the support of the nation's doctors, the NHI plan had no hope of success. Many general practitioners had long worked for friendly societies by contract and been compensated on a capitation basis. As the financial problems of the societies became more acute, however, the conditions of the doctors' contracts became increasingly objectionable to much of the medical profession. For several years after 1905, the British Medical Association (BMA) published reports and generated discussion about the undesirable conditions under which general practitioners worked for friendly societies (McCleary 1932: 73–83; Honigsbaum 1979; R. Jones 1981: 22–26).

By 1900, the BMA had become outspoken on matters involving a broad range of medical services. Since the elite of the medical profession identified most strongly with the Royal College of Physicians and the Royal College of Surgeons and only weakly with the BMA, by the turn of the century, the BMA had become primarily a professional organization for defending the interests "of the average, often underprivileged, general practitioner" (Stevens 1966: 22). Although 55 percent of the doctors on the medical register in Britain were members of the BMA in 1910, very few members were consultants or specialists (Eckstein 1960: 44–45; Little 1932).

The doctors demanded that several cardinal points be incorporated into the NHI plan. First, reacting to their conflicts with the friendly societies, they demanded that patients be permitted to choose their own doctors and that the doctor have the right of refusing service to a patient. This of course was in contrast to the practice of the friendly societies, whereby the doctor was required to treat all patients covered by a contract. Second, the doctors demanded that there be an upper income limit on those who were entitled to medical benefits, to prevent provision of free services to those who could afford to pay. Third, they argued that the medical benefits under a national health insurance scheme should not be administered by the friendly societies but by local insurance committees, which the doctors hoped to dominate. Furthermore, they insisted that they should have adequate representation in the administration of all other aspects of the program (H. Levy 1944: 17). In sum, the general practitioners viewed the NHI program as a means of enhancing their professional autonomy and increasing their income (P. Jones 1981).

As professionals are generally fearful of being compensated in a manner that departs from their past experience, the hospital-based doctors— especially the consultants—insisted that the NHI scheme not apply to hospital care. They were anxious to maintain their traditional privileges and

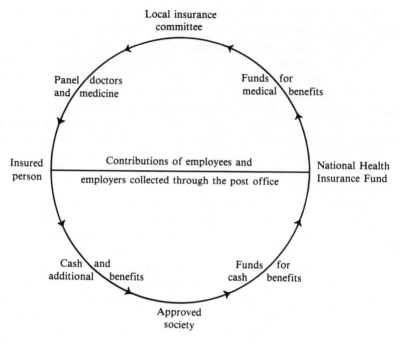

Fig. 1. The National Health Insurance Plan (*source:* Herbert 1939: 91, modified)

status and feared that the government might end up regulating admissions to hospitals and the type of care administered to patients. The hospital-based consultants also believed that, if the hospital patient load increased as a result of the NHI plan, there would be more hospital-based doctors and a decline in the monopoly position that the "honoraries" exercised in the hospital.

The NHI plan provided two broad types of benefits—medical and cash—and, although it was state regulated and mandated, it was administered primarily in the private nonprofit sector. Parliament achieved an amazing success in incorporating into legislation the major views of each of the powerfully organized groups that had lobbied on the issues. Because the scheme ultimately evolved into and placed constraints on the nature of the NHS, which came into existence in 1948, some discussion of its organizational structure is desirable (see figure 1).

The machinery to administer the program was quite cumbersome, as cash and medical benefits were treated separately. The cash benefits were administered by what was called an approved society and the medical benefits by local insurance committees. By law, all manual workers between the ages of 16 and 65 and nonmanual workers—with a few exceptions— earning below £160 annually were required to participate (the maximum salary was raised to £250 in 1919). Contributions were made on a uniform rate, with workers paying four-ninths, employers three-ninths, and the state two-ninths, a payment scheme that was quite common in Europe during the interwar years (McCleary 1932; H. Levy 1944).

Virtually every NHI-insured person was expected to join an approved society, most of which were organized by trade unions, friendly societies, and insurance companies. Individuals paid their money to the Post Office, the money was remitted to the Ministry of Health, and the cash benefits then circulated to insured individuals via the approved societies. The ordinary benefits of the approved societies were to be cash benefits for sickness, disablement, and maternity and were to be the same for all individuals regardless of their level of income.

The administration of the medical benefits was equally complex. The doctors, wishing to become independent of the friendly societies and trade unions but not wanting to be under the control of the central government, had demanded that medical benefits be administered through local insurance committees, which were private and decentralized mechanisms for dispensing medical services. The committees varied in size from twenty to forty members. By statute, three-fifths of a committee's members represented insured persons (technically these were representatives of the approved societies), and one-fifth were appointed by the county or county borough councils. The remaining members were representatives of the medical profession, "chemists" (pharmacists), or women. This arrangement represented a compromise, which freed the doctors from the direct control of the approved societies (dominated by trade unions), friendly societies, and insurance companies. At the same time, the doctors failed to dominate the local medical insurance committees. And while one must not exaggerate the influence of consumers in those committees, they were a force to be reckoned with, and it was the influence of the consuming public over the administering of medical benefits that did much to differentiate the British and U.S. medical delivery systems (Abel-Smith 1965).

Every insured person was entitled to the services of a general practitioner in any part of Great Britain. Individuals were free to choose any doctor, and doctors in turn were free to refuse to serve any individual. Participating doctors received compensation on a capitation basis, just as those who had earlier entered into a contract arrangement with the friendly societies had. Free drugs were also a statutory benefit for the insured, as each participating doctor was at liberty to prescribe medication (Lindsey 1962: 10–11).

Although the system was called National Health Insurance, it was very much a private system. The traditional friendly society system of providing benefits had been significantly expanded, thus permitting insurance companies to participate in the scheme. The central government regulated the scheme, but the approved societies and the local insurance committees remained in the private sector. The general practitioners participating in the program were not public employees.

Because the act provided insurance coverage for almost one-third of the population, its influence on medical delivery was considerable. Its inadequacies generated dissatisfaction and caused people to search for alternatives, which eventually led to the implementation of the NHS in 1948. Perhaps the most important inadequacies were inequities in access to the system and in its benefits. Because the basic goal of the system was to prevent pauperism of workers rather than to improve the general health of the population, it did not cover most of the population. True, the enactment of the NHI plan suddenly provided benefits for more than 10 million people who previously were without them from either trade unions or friendly societies. With the exception of a maternity benefit for the confinement of the wife of an insured man, the plan did not provide coverage for dependents. Nor did it provide coverage for the country's middle and upper classes, an omission that was eventually to become politically important (McCleary 1932).

For those who were covered by NHI, the types of available medical technology and services were very limited. Most of the medical services were those of the general practitioner. In this sense, the British system was unlike national health insurance in Germany at that time, where all types of medical service were provided the insured and where well over 80 percent of the doctors participated (McCleary 1932: 54). In Britain, however, there was no general coverage for surgery or any other type of treatment in hospitals, for convalescent or nursing home care, for ambulatory specialist diagnosis or treatment, or for diagnostic techniques involving x-ray, urinalysis, or blood examination. In other words, the NHI scheme increased the number of people covered, but it did not significantly alter the type of benefits that trade unions and friendly societies had traditionally provided in their contracts with the doctors. By 1938, throughout Britain almost 17 million people were covered by the insurance plan, and approximately 16,000 doctors were active in it. Those private practitioners who did not participate generally limited their practice to the well-to-do (H. Levy 1944: 123–31; Brend 1917: 179; Honigsbaum 1979).

It is difficult to evaluate the quality of care provided by the NHI plan. Overall, the system meant better medical care for the entire nation, for at least 10 million people were now covered who previously were not and who were generally toward the lower end of Britain's pay scale. However, many instances of slipshod treatment were recorded, a fact that indicates considerable variation in the quality of care.

The economic incentive of the practitioner was an important factor influencing the quality of care. Some doctors used their NHI involvement as a means of gaining the dependents of their insured patients for their practice. If the insured could afford to pay medical fees for his family, there was an incentive for the practitioner to take considerable care with his patients, as with insured patients who insisted on paying the doctor an additional fee (Brend 1917: 181).* Because participating physicians were paid a flat fee for each patient and not on a fee-for-service basis, there was no incentive for doctors to provide excess service and thus drive up the costs. Though the system was not designed with an intent to contain medical expenditures, its fundamental structure tended to place constraints on escalating costs.

Despite its shortcomings, the overall effect of the NHI system was positive. It did help to protect the working classes against destitution resulting from ill health. The program encouraged doctors to locate in some of the more densely populated neighborhoods of industrial cities, areas that had previously been underserved. Thus the system provided not only more equitable access to care, but easier access.

On the other hand, the decentralized and very fragmented NHI system was somewhat inefficient. In 1933, the International Labor Organization revealed that 17 percent of the costs of the NHI system was spent on administering the program, whereas in Germany, Sweden, Switzerland, and France administrative costs ranged between 7 and 10 percent of the total program. Given that the NHI system basically provided a modest cash and a very limited medical benefit, its decentralized structure was one of the world's most expensive governmental medical insurance programs to administer (H. Levy 1944: 289–301; Great Britain, Royal Commission on National Health Insurance 1926).

While the decentralized and private character of the approved societies meant that modest benefits varied greatly from one approved society to another, the NHI system did much to develop a more egalitarian medical delivery system than that which was emerging in the United States at the same time.

INCREASING PUBLIC PROVISION OF MEDICAL SERVICES

The NHI scheme was only one of several public programs developed in Britain prior to World War II. Slowly, the public sector assumed more and more responsibilities in the provision of medical care both in and out of hospital. Many of these responsibilities were carried out at the local level, where mechanisms for coordination were weak. And despite the increased

---

* Those covered by the NHI plan were called "insured persons" or "panel patients" when they were receiving medical care. See Honigsbaum 1979: 9.

responsibility borne by the public sector in providing medical services, the private sector remained critical both in defining the modes of care and in delivering it.

Over a period of several decades, a wide variety of public authorities became involved in providing medical services to select groups in the population. They began incrementally with a skeletal and rather patchwork set of medical services to specific target groups, but over time they gradually added more and more components to their programs. It was symptomatic of the fragmented care that each service was usually given by a separate practitioner and often provided benefits for separate members of a family: the NHI system (1911–48) insured workers; the public medical services for expectant and nursing mothers, infants, and schoolchildren; and the Poor Law service (Titmuss 1958: 173). Not only were these services uncoordinated, but the activities of each also placed severe constraints on the activities of the others. Despite the shortcomings of these services, slowly one group after another was guaranteed access to medical care through some form of collective provision—a situation quite unlike that in the United States.

Perhaps the public nonhospital medical care programs that best reflected these characteristics were those involving schoolchildren, and the school program of greatest importance was that which evolved from the Education Act of 1907, establishing medical inspection of children in state schools. Technically, the central government via the minister of health was responsible for the inspection and treatment of schoolchildren, but in fact the responsibility was delegated to the local authorities, which also had the authority for inspecting children who were in voluntary secondary schools (Political and Economic Planning 1937: 120).

Even though the Education Act mandated school medical inspection of children, for several years there was a serious problem of what to do about the large number identified as having some form of medical defect. The local authorities eventually responded, and by 1914, more than three-fourths of the local education authorities were providing medical treatment for schoolchildren. Later, these services were greatly expanded and improved, with all of the education authorities providing some form of medical and dental treatment (Political and Economic Planning 1937: 119–21; Gilbert 1966: 126, 156).

Other legislative steps that enlarged public provision of medical services involved maternity benefits. Once the state was providing medical services for the breadwinner, via the NHI plan, and for schoolchildren, a natural development was the provision of care for mothers. Under the Maternity and Child Welfare Act (1918), the central government encouraged the local authorities to provide ante- and postnatal clinics, a system of home visiting, infant welfare centers, and funds for midwives. Because the local authorities had considerable latitude in determining the types of service they provided, these services varied enormously from area to area (Political and Economic Planning 1937: 90–91), but by 1937, approximately 50 percent of English expectant mothers received some antenatal care (Herbert 1939: 134). In 1936, the Midwives Act authorized local governments to provide a complete maternity service under the control of local authorities. In response, former voluntary and public arrangements for midwifery services were combined, and a publicly supported, full-time salaried midwifery service was developed (ibid.: 137).

Many local authorities followed up a birth by home health visiting, whereby a nurse provided some supervision in the home for nursing mothers and newly born infants. In 1936, almost one-third of all expectant mothers in England and Wales received some home health visiting, and more than 95 percent of all children born in England and Wales received at least one health visit by the local authorities during the first year of life (Political and Economic Planning 1937: 106; McCleary 1932: 36). Moreover, many local authorities provided milk and food during both pregnancy and lactation (Political and Economic Planning 1937: 98). In addition, the state, at the local level, provided infant welfare centers, which numbered more than 2,500 by the 1930s. Providing medical care to more than 60 percent of the nation's young children in the 1930s, these centers became an important part of the nation's medical services.

As long as the demand for hospital medical care was relatively limited, class based, and/or made by a particular group, the private sector tended to have the capacity to respond to it. But as medical technology became increasingly complex and efficacious, there was a substantial increase in demand by all social classes. And the greater the homogeneity of demand for medical care across social classes (i.e., the less the demand was heterogeneously based), the more the pressures grew for the public sector to respond. More specifically, the public sector grew in response to the inadequacies of the private sector to meet all the society's demands. Many public institutions, hitherto reserved almost exclusively for the poor, were placed under different public auspices and operated as general hospital facilities for all local residents.

Most public general hospitals prior to 1929 were inextricably associated with the Poor Law, but most medical services provided under the Poor Law were inadequate. In recognition of this, Parliament, in the Local Government Act of 1929, reorganized the Poor Law. To increase the efficiency and quality of the public facilities the act abolished the boards of guardians and transferred their functions to the county and county borough councils, where Poor Law services were to be administered by public assistance committees. Each governing authority was then free to transform facilities for the sick into public hospitals (Political and Economic Planning 1937:

250). The hope was that this would greatly change the character of public hospitals and increase the number of beds available to the general public. However, the local authorities were given a great deal of discretion, and thus change in the public hospital sector was very uneven across the country (Bruce 1966: 227).

After 1930, in and about London and in a few other areas, there was considerable progress in developing a comprehensive and coordinated public general hospital system; elsewhere, changes occurred much more slowly. A variety of factors slowed the progress of local authorities in upgrading Poor Law facilities for the use of the general public, the most important being the economic depression of the 1930s.

The transition of public hospitals from the governing authority of the boards of guardians to local authorities represented an important shift in that local government became further involved with health services. The newly authorized public general hospitals were, however, quite unlike the voluntary general hospitals. The medical staff of public hospitals exercised less authority, enjoyed less freedom, and had fewer opportunities for pecuniary gain. Whereas the "honorary" in the voluntary hospital had an allotment of beds and decided whether a patient would or would not be admitted, the public hospitals were required to admit all patients coming to them. Although the increase in the number of local authority hospitals required an increase in the number of hospital staff, public hospitals had fewer staff than the voluntary ones. Unlike the latter, which relied heavily on an honorary staff, which was generally unpaid, the former attempted to recruit a full-time, salaried, usually younger medical staff and to engage visiting consultants from the prestigious voluntary hospitals, whose role was generally to perform specialized surgery (Political and Economic Planning 1937: 17, 251–53; Abel-Smith 1964: 360, 375–78; Herbert 1939: 122–25; Hollingsworth and Hollingsworth 1983; 1985).

Even though the differences between the public and voluntary hospitals were narrowing over time, there was considerable persistence in the differences between the two systems in their type of patients. The public hospitals had a virtual monopoly of the treatment of infectious diseases, provided most of the maternity services, and received transfers of incurable, postoperative, and various chronic cases from voluntary hospitals. In London and other large cities, however, they were relatively well equipped and did treat acute cases. After the Local Government Act of 1929, the stigma of public hospitals as pauper institutions began to disappear, with the result that they acquired more legitimacy and use and slowly began to be used for more acute cases (Hollingsworth and Hollingsworth 1983; 1985).

VOLUNTARY HOSPITALS DURING THE INTERWAR PERIOD

The years between the world wars were a period of considerable travail for the voluntary hospitals of England and Wales. Accepted by most citizens as the dominant providers of inpatient services, and carrying large outpatient loads, the hospitals found themselves more pressed than ever before. Greatly improved technology, which attracted more and more patients, was very expensive.

Increasingly, hospitals sought to incorporate advances in neurosurgery, orthopedic, plastic, and thoracic surgery, and diagnostic radiology. Moreover, there were substantial advances in such nonclinical areas as biochemistry, bacteriology, and endocrinology, which had important clinical implications. The clinical effects of these advances tended to center in the hospital, a fact that led an ever larger proportion of the population in Western nations to turn to the hospital for complex medical care. To incorporate these developments in medical specialties usually meant expanding hospital staffs and more costly equipment. The financing of changes in the complexity of medical technology was thus probably the most important problem that the hospitals—especially those in the private sector—faced during the interwar period.

Many voluntary hospitals were engaged in deficit financing after World War I. Parliament provided a £500,000 grant to assist them in getting their accounts in order, but one grant was not adequate to solve their financial problems. British hospitals also received income from various approved societies—approximately £200,000 annually for special cases of NHI patients—and the local governments made modest contributions to them as payments for patients who were transferred from local government hospitals. Voluntary hospitals also resorted to energetic fund-raising appeals, relying on lotteries, dances, bazaars, dinners, and boxing matches (Abel-Smith 1964: 323–24).

But the major change in financing occurred as a result of direct and indirect payments by patients. In England, there was a substantial increase in the percentage treated in voluntary hospitals who had insurance—in 1921, approximately 25 percent of all patients treated in voluntary hospitals had insurance, and by 1938, 36 percent did (Abel-Smith 1964: 385). In 1935, there were approximately 10 million people—mostly middle class—who were covered by a wide assortment of plans that provided payment for treatment in either public or private hospitals (Great Britain, Royal Commission on Workman's Compensation 1945: 1080–81; H. Levy 1944: 162). Also, by the late 1920s, the large voluntary hospitals had added a number of private paying beds to accommodate the upper-income groups. Indeed, by 1929 London had more than 1,000 private paying beds (Abel-Smith

1964: 339). But most consultants continued to do their inpatient work without fees.

By 1938, the sources of voluntary hospital income had become quite varied, a fact that was a sharp change from the almost exclusive dependence on the charitable contributions of the late nineteenth century. Voluntary hospitals received between 40 and 50 percent of their income from patients paying on their own behalf or from payments by local authorities on behalf of patients.

During the interwar years, some parts of the country had an oversupply of hospitals while others had critical shortages. At the outbreak of World War II, almost half of the nation's 700 voluntary hospitals had fewer than 30 beds, and in many of the small general practitioner–dominated cottage hospitals, a low quality of patient care was provided. Most cottage hospitals had inadequate equipment, and their staff often attempted to carry out surgery that was beyond their competence (Abel-Smith 1964: 406; Hollingsworth and Hollingsworth, 1983; 1985).

Between the two wars, there had been modifications in the outpatient as well as in the inpatient services of voluntary hospitals. After the introduction of the NHI plan, there had initially been a decrease in the number of people treated in the outpatient clinics. But as hospital insurance became more widespread in response to voluntary hospital decisions to charge patients, there was an increase in the number of outpatients. This led to serious problems with the BMA over the types of patient and medical practitioner who should have access to the hospital outpatient clinics (Abel-Smith 1964: 327, 333; Honigsbaum 1979).

The nonhospital-based doctor took the view that the more patients there were attending the outpatient clinics, the less money there would be for the nonhospital-based private practitioners. To prevent people from being treated in the hospital outpatient departments, the BMA tried unsuccessfully to restrict the purchase of hospital insurance and to limit the hospital outpatient clinics to those who were referred there by a private practitioner. The hospitals, in contrast, were in financial difficulty and wished to increase their revenue from hospital insurance policyholders. As a result, outpatient departments increased the number of patients throughout the interwar years and caused an intense and lingering dispute between the general practitioners and the doctors practicing in the hospital. The outside practitioner accused the hospitals of caring little for the well-being of patients and only wishing to have their money. In turn, the hospitals blamed the general practitioners for unnecessarily referring NHI patients, who paid nothing for outpatient clinic services.

No longer were the outpatient clinics of the voluntary hospitals primarily for the deserving poor. The increasing costs of medical technology had encouraged them to cater to the middle-class, paying patient despite the almost unanimous opposition of the nonhospital-based medical profession and its spokesman, the BMA (Honigsbaum 1979).

MEDICAL EDUCATION AND RESEARCH

Like many other aspects of the medical delivery system in England and Wales, medical education was also very much influenced by the pervasive class system. That is, while the working class may have influenced the method of delivery of certain types of outpatient services, medical education reflected the preferences of prestigious consultants and their upper-class clients. For this reason, there were always real limits on the extent to which the working class could influence the medical delivery system of England and Wales.

The medical education and research systems provide the knowledge base for the delivery of medical services. In both Britain and the United States, the dominant approach to the study of disease has been microcasual in nature. That is, the dominant medical paradigm has focused on bacteria, parasites, and viruses as the cause of disease, and two basic strategies have emerged for dealing with disease.

With one strategy, collective action or government intervention was designed to promote sanitation policies and quaratine procedures that would improve the environment. With the other strategy, when individuals were afflicted by various types of organisms, doctors and hospitals were to be available in order to provide treatment. Hence, throughout Western Europe and North America, there emerged a curative strategy that focused on providing treatment when an individual became ill.

In many respects, the dominant strategy in medical education has been consistent with the basic ideology in the two societies concerning class relationships. A main concern of the medical system has been with restoring people to health so that they could become gainfuly employed. It is partly for this reason that in both societies the treatment of chronic diseases has long received much lower priority than that of acute illness. Insofar as the chronically ill can become gainfully employed individuals, the medical system has given chronic illness high priority. On the other hand, those with chronic illness who cannot be transformed into highly productive individuals have tended to receive low priority. It is in this context that geriatrics has historically had low status in medical education in both countries (McKeown 1975; 1976).

Of course, there is another paradigm that historically has received little concern in medical education in Britain and the United States. This is the macrocausal approach to disease, the position that many diseases are a manifestation of a society's power relations. For example, Marx, Engels, and Rudolph Virchow held the view that disease is the result of oppressive power relations and that, in order to maximize a society's health, it is necessary to improve the living and working conditions of the working class. But rather than adopting a social approach to medicine in capitalist societies, medical educators have viewed illness primarily as a biological phenomenon. And the particular biological approach to health reflects the bourgeois ideology that has been dominant in British and American medical education during the last century (Navarro 1976; 1980).

Even though there have been common approaches to disease, medical education has been organized in significantly different ways in Britain and the United States. And these differences have influenced variation in the levels of specialization and styles of medical research in the two societies. Indeed, differences in the ways that medical education was organized at the turn of the century ultimately were of considerable importance in shaping differences in evolution between the two medical systems.

If we are to understand the history of medical education, research, and specialization in the two societies during the twentieth century, however, we must focus some attention on the status of the medical profession in each country at the turn of the century. Historically, the relative status and power of the medical profession in England and Wales and the United States are somewhat paradoxical. In the late nineteenth century, the medical profession in England and Wales enjoyed much more status than its counterpart in the United States. Because consumers were better organized in England and Wales and because the profession was seriously divided between general practitioners and hospital-based doctors, however, the English and Welsh profession in the early twentieth century and later had to share more power with consumers. In contrast, consumers were poorly organized in the United States, where, as a result, the potential power of the medical profession vis-à-vis consumers was greater. In the late nineteenth and early twentieth centuries, it was educational reform that permitted the U.S. profession to upgrade its power and status relative to those of any in the world. The U.S. medical schools enjoyed so little legitimacy in the late nineteenth century that a veritable revolution in medical education was possible—a revolution that transformed the status and power of the American medical profession. It is for this reason that medical education is such an integral part of the history of the U.S. medical system in the twentieth century. In England and Wales, however, medical education enjoyed much more legitimacy at the beginning of the twentieth century, a fact that limited the potential for change in its institutional structure. Ironically, it was the very backwardness of U.S. medical education in the late nineteenth century that permitted a revolution to occur and that in the long run permitted the best centers of U.S. medical education to attain a high level of excellence. And while medical education is a key part of the English and

Welsh system, its importance in transforming the delivery system has been much less than in the United States.

Medical education in England developed as an apprentice system. It had first developed outside the hospitals, but later, as hospitals were established, students "walked" the wards with the physician or surgeon with whom they were studying. At first, the hospitals provided for no preclinical or extraclinical instruction, but over time, more formal medical instruction was established within the hospitals.

By the beginning of the twentieth century, two types of English medical school had emerged. There were the twelve hospital schools in London, most of which had no more than a casual affiliation with the University of London. And elsewhere in England there were medical schools that were more formally part of a university.

The London hospital type medical school had historically been grafted onto existing hospitals, although the voluntary hospitals had not originally been designed to meet the needs of medical education. As a result, London medical education adapted to the established practices of the prestigious voluntary hospitals. As these schools were quite autonomous, most of the doctors who taught there were without university appointments (G. Newman 1918; C. Newman 1957; McKeown 1976b; Great Britain, University Education 1912: 142–43).

The provincial medical schools had a somewhat similar origin, but in their case a stronger affiliation with a university did exist, and as a result, some of the preclinical faculty were serious researchers rather than medical practitioners who simply did some part-time basic science instruction, as was the case in most of the London schools. The clinical teachers in the provincial university medical schools, however, were generally local practitioners and were part-time teachers and relatively independent of the university, just like their London colleagues (Peterson 1978).

While English medical education was more homogeneous and distinctly higher in quality than that which existed in the United States at the turn of the century, English medical schools, in the opinion of the leading medical educators of the day, were clearly inferior to those in Germany, which had rapidly become the envy of the elite of the medical world (A. Flexner 1925: 67–69; G. Newman 1918: 67–69). The German medical schools attained their level of excellence largely because historically they were tightly integrated into a university structure rather than being independent hospital schools. By the end of the nineteenth century, German medical professors had full-time university appointments, applying all of their energies to teaching, research, and care of patients. Moreover, the German schools were highly differentiated, being specialized into clinics of internal medicine, surgery, psychiatry, obstetrics and gynecology, ophthalmology, dermatology, and pediatrics. Each clinic was headed by a professor, was as well equipped as any in the world, and consisted of wards, lecture theaters, examining rooms, libraries, and laboratories for pathology and research. Each professor had a staff of full-time and part-time assistants and devoted as much time to research as to teaching. For the medical teacher in Germany, the laboratory was indispensible to clinical activity, for the university hospital was primarily a research and teaching institution. The clinician and the basic scientist enjoyed essentially the same status and were in frequent communication with one another (Great Britain, University Education 1911: 305–22).

In England, however, the traditions of clinically oriented medical education based in voluntary hospitals were so strong and so legitimate that there was little effort to follow the German pattern. As a result, the English medical system did not develop the research and specialization dimensions increasingly found in Germany and, later, in the United States. The emphasis was on clinical teaching rather than scientific research. The English model was designed to train practicing doctors, so most instruction took place at the bedside of a patient, with the emphasis on the immediate, technical problem but with very little discussion of the etiology of a disease. There was little theoretical or discursive instruction. Most of the teaching faculty of the London medical schools were very much isolated from scientific developments that were taking place within the universities, and they saw very little of doctors at other hospitals (Great Britain, University Education 1911: 350; A. Flexner 1912).

Some English medical schools provided only preclinical training, some only clinical instruction, and some both preclinical and clinical instruction. In equipment and resources for preclinical training, however, the English schools lagged far behind the best in the world. In some, there were a few excellent full-time men in the preclinical sciences—especially at Oxford, Cambridge, and King's College and University College in London (Hearnshaw 1929; Bellot 1929). In most of the medical schools, however, the preclinical sciences were taught not by a basic scientist but by a clinician. The preclinical sciences in most London schools were weak, for they had evolved from a traditional hospital structure that had made no provision for such instruction. Bacteriology and pathology laboratories often had inadequate facilities, usually tucked away in some corner of the hospital, and there was rarely any equipment for biochemistry (Great Britain, University Education 1912: 136; 1911: Cmd. 5911, 273–274; A. Flexner 1912: 12–14, 27, 116, 143).

The clinical staff of the hospital and university medical schools were basically the elite of the medical profession. The highest-ranking teachers in English hospitals were consultants, but one became a consultant not because of scientific achievement but—generally around age forty—after spending many long and faithful years in the hospital, rising from house officer through registrar, and assistant physician or surgeon. Those who finally attained the rank of consultant often held an arts degree from either Oxford or Cambridge and had studied medicine at the school to which they later were consultants. In addition to the basic degree or diploma that qualified one to be a practitioner, prospective consultants tended to receive higher degrees. For example, the Royal College of Physicians granted the Member of the Royal College of Physicians (MRCP) diploma. Similarly, surgeons aspiring to the rank of consultant were expected to attain the status of Fellow of the Royal College of Surgeons (FRCS). Eventually, the FRCS or the MRCP became virtual prerequisites for the rank of consultant (Clark 1964; Stevens 1966).

Consultants were not chosen from among those who had made some important contribution to the theoretical literature, though some made distinguished contributions to scientific knowledge. The emphasis in filling an opening for a consultantship was not on whether the individual was one of Britain's finest clinicians but on congeniality and collegiality (A. Flexner 1912: 190–94; Peterson 1978: 135–65). Once they became consultants, most clinicians left behind any semblance of a laboratory or scientific state of mind as they attempted to fraternize with earls, marquises, cabinet members, and other notables. Most English consultants, as has been suggested above, were generalists. Though most large voluntary hospitals by 1910 had specialized departments, the elite physicians and surgeons of these hospitals viewed specialized fields as threats to their authority and status (Peterson 1978: 274; A. Flexner 1925: 207, 216, 239–42; G. Newman 1918).

Like any system of medical education, the English system had advantages and disadvantages. Clearly, the English medical student had substantial opportunity to acquire bedside experience in the hospital wards. Deemphasizing large lecture halls, which were commonly used in the German universities, the English system, with its heavy emphasis on bedside clinical training, tended to produce relatively good general practitioners. Far more so than was the case in Germany, it brought the medical student into extensive contact with patients in the wards, thus providing extensive training in the diagnosis and nursing of illness. The English system helped students to understand pain and suffering and to empathize with patients. Probably no other country surpassed England in providing bedside teaching (Great Britain, University Education 1912: 137–41; Newman 1918: 74).

The medical faculty of English medical schools by the 1920s were very much smaller than those in the United States, and, as a result, ultimately had much less specialization (Rockefeller Foundation, vol. 17).

Most consultants were so busy with their private practice, visiting the wards, and teaching that they lacked the energy or time for systematic reading or research. And even the assistant physician was usually untrained in research and rarely trained to consult the literature on his subject. His outlook tended to be entirely practical, for he was preparing himself to be a practitioner of medicine, not a teacher or a researcher. As a consequence, the young house officer's preliminary scientific training tended to be wasted (Great Britain, University Education 1911: 2; 1912: 141).

During the 1920s, in addition to being less exposed to specialization than their U.S. and German counterparts English medical students were not trained in the use of an array of complex technology. For example, laboratory methods, other than urine examinations, were not used in a majority of hospital ward cases—even in the better teaching hospitals; and x-rays and blood examinations were relied upon much less frequently than in the United States. This was because it was assumed that most would eventually become general practitioners and would have to rely on more ordinary methods of physical examinations (Rockefeller Foundation, vol. 17).

Another serious shortcoming of English medical education was common to medical schools in all western societies. As was noted above, the practice in teaching hospitals was generally to focus on acute illness, with little attention to the destitute, the elderly, or those suffering from infectious diseases. As a result, medical schools tended to exclude from the student's training some of the most common medical problems of the day. Perhaps the greatest weakness in medical education was the deemphasis on preventive medicine and public health in English medical schools in the early part of the century. True, there was some teaching of hygiene at such London hospital schools as St. Thomas's, St. Bartholomew's, Guy's, and Charing Cross, but there was an almost complete lack of emphasis on preventive medicine in the standard syllabus or examinations (Brand 1965: 110). Moreover, the following subjects were generally neglected: principles of epidemiology, the etiology of disease, principles of health insurance, mental health, parasitology, immunology and problems relating to vaccination, industrial medicine, venereal diseases, and the impact of poverty on health. Furthermore, most medical students received very inadequate training in obstetrics and gynecology. Nevertheless, infant and maternal mortality rates were extremely high, tuberculosis and many other infectious diseases were very common, and rickets and other diseases resulting from malnourishment were widespread.

Medical education, on both sides of the Atlantic, was primarily concerned either with the cure of disease or with caring for those who were ill but relatively unconcerned with the cause and prevention of the disease. Medical students had very little training in the relationship between occupations on the one hand and physical disability, fatigue, and sickness on the other, despite the fact that there was already considerable literature that had established definite links between disease and various occupations (G. Newman 1918: 85–101). Undoubtedly the training of medical schools would have been more relevant to the needs of the society had they focused to a considerable extent on the treatment of tuberculosis, venereal and other infectious diseases, the detection and management of mental illness, and chronic problems involving geriatrics, instead of excluding most of these problems from the medical hospital (Great Britain, Poor Laws 1909, 37: 277–78).

Whereas England was in the forefront of medical discoveries in the first one-third of the nineteenth century, by 1900, it was clearly lagging behind Germany in scientific productivity and creativity. And it was the differences in the organization of medical science and medical education that caused England to lag behind (Geison 1978: 31; Sharpey-Shafer 1919: 297, 208; Cardwell 1957). Joseph Ben-David argues that it was the competitive, decentralized, and well-financed university structure that explains why German science was so creative and productive during this period. True, the two leading English universities, Oxford and Cambridge were not in a structural sense highly centralized, but Ben-David contends that English medical science was retarded by the rigid class structure, which kept researchers and potential innovators "in their place" through a set of traditions that were internalized among men interested in medical science. The net effect was a homogenized and, for all practical purposes, centralized or elite set of values that retarded competitiveness and hence English scientific progress. Progress was also limited by shortages of funds (Ben-David 1960; 1971). Moreover, the study of medical technology enjoyed less prestige in the more traditional English universities than in the newer ones of Germany. Given Ben-David's emphasis on the structural conditions conducive to scientific discoveries, it is remarkable that English science has performed as well as it has during the twentieth century.

Thus the weakness of preclinical fields meant that the English system was not as committed to training medical scientists as the German and, later, U.S. medical schools. Also, in the long run, this has deterred the English from investing as much of their national resources in biological and medical research, as well as medical specialization, as the Americans have. One reason that twentieth-century medical practitioners in the United States would turn in such large numbers to specialization and/or medical research was to increase their status and income, to differentiate themselves from one another. In England, however, the differentiation between the hospital-based doctor and the outside general practitioners, the consultant and the nonconsultant, meant that severe constraints were placed on the ability and incentive of English doctors to specialize and to conduct research. Consultantship meant, in the early part of the century, that medical men could gain high status and income without having to become highly specialized or to engage in research. In the long run, the structural constraints on research and specialization in English medical training has had an unintended effect: it has meant that England has not had the acute short-age of primary care physicians and excess number of specialists expe-rienced by the United States.

Though the U.S. system of medical education had been revolutionized during the first two decades of the twentieth century, there were only mod-est changes in the English system, which, as a result, remained fundamen-tally different from what became the dominant pattern in the United States and in Germany. There the universities have tended to occupy a key posi-tion in the management of the medical schools. Moreover, the major teach-ing hospitals have tended to be attached to a university and the various hospital departments have been in the charge of a university professor. In London—the center of English medical education—medical education continued during the interwar period to be very much influenced by its development as an adjunct of the great voluntary hospitals rather than as an extension of universities. True, the undergraduate medical schools in other parts of England followed different patterns, varying somewhat in their connections with universities.

By 1939, all medical schools in England and Wales, with the exception of the West London Hospital Medical School, had become university medical schools, but there was considerable variation in the relationship between them and their respective universities. Most of the provincial universities had medical schools that were integrated into the university structure, along lines similar to the system in the United States. But the medical schools in London, though schools of the University of London, were much more closely associated with their parent hospitals. Prior to the NHS, the London teaching hospitals were managed by governing bodies that were relatively independent of the university and on which had virtu-ally no representation.

During the years after 1920, the pattern of staffing in teaching hospitals and undergraduate medical schools hardly changed (*Great Britain*, MOH 1944). While many of the junior staff held full-time salaried positions, most senior members of the clinical faculty continued to hold part-time posi-tions, as most of them were actively engaged in private practice. Since the senior clinical faculty also held honorary appointments on the staffs of several widely scattered, nonteaching hospitals, they taught at the medical school for only a few hours a week. Moreover, their teaching appointments continued to be honorary ones, with virtually no salary from either the medical school or the teaching hospital. Of course, the clinical teachers gave their time generously under the circumstances, but these were not conditions that made for much cohesion and integration in medical school teaching programs. Prior to the Goodenough Report on Medical Educa-tion in 1944, there were only eleven full-time clinical professors in all of England's medical schools. Under these circumstances, it is understandable why there was much less clinical research in the better medical schools in comparison with those of Germany and the United States.

The organization of the training of medical specialists was also very different in England. Postgraduate education had evolved in an unstructured and haphazard environment. There was hardly any rational policy to coordinate it and no single process by which one acquired it. Historically, not only was there no overall responsibility for postgraduate training, but many organizations were involved, and in a very uncoordinated manner: the special hospitals and institutes of London, the royal colleges, and, to a modest extent, the undergraduate medical schools (Revans and McLachlan 1967: 7; Stevens 1966: 174).

In London it was generally agreed that postgraduate medical education should remain outside the twelve undergraduate medical schools and their parent hospitals. Of course, there had historically been some modest link between these medical schools and postgraduate training, but nothing like the major training of specialists that one has observed in the twentieth century in such U.S. university medical schools as that at Johns Hopkins, Harvard, Yale, Columbia, Pennsylvania, Chicago, and many more.

During the interwar period, much of the postgraduate training of English medical specialists took place in special hospitals that had developed because of the reluctance of the better general hospitals to provide facilities for newly developing specialties. As a result, the special hospitals remained independent and generally unattached to the general teaching hospitals and were not engaged in undergraduate teaching. Because of London's large size and great wealth, however, a number of the special hospitals eventually became very distinguished institutions (Great Britain, Royal Commission on Medical Education, 1965–68: 182). Eventually, many outstanding consultants at general hospitals competed for privileges on the staffs of various special hospitals. Because these positions were either unpaid or inadequately paid, consultants could give only a fraction of their time to special hospital work, and only a small part of that could be devoted to the training of postgraduates or to research. Very few had the time to conduct any research or to train the developing postgraduate specialist to do so.

In 1935, there was a modest break with this tradition with the establishment of the Royal Postgraduate Medical School, which was associated with the Hammersmith Hospital. However, the hospital was relatively isolated from the center of London, and it remained a separate entity from the special hospitals that were scattered around London. For years after the establishment of the school, there was pressure on the special hospitals to establish links with it, but the hospitals were reluctant to do this for fear of losing their identity and autonomy.

The awarding of postgraduate degrees and diplomas has been far more complex, unsatisfactory, and confusing in Britain than in the United States. The British have had many more types of postgraduate diplomas, and there has been considerably more variation in their quality, even in the same subject. Nor have they been very successful in defining a specialist. Historically, they have had considerable difficulty in designating a degree or diploma that automatically certified that one deserved to be so labeled. By 1940, excluding the diplomas of the royal medical colleges, there were several dozen different postgraduate medical diplomas (Stevens 1966: 177).

Following World War I, the royal medical colleges held their position as the professional leaders in medicine, but they had few, if any, direct links with postgraduate training in the hospitals. While the Royal College of Obstetricians and Gynecologists had been established in 1929 as a specialist college, the Royal College of Physicians and the Royal College of Surgeons were still generalist in nature. The former included all areas of medicine, while the latter covered all surgical specialties, including anesthesiology. Each college had one diploma, the MRCP for physicians, and the FRCS for surgeons (Stevens 1966: 106), each of which was a generalist, not a specialist, postgraduate diploma. The examinations of the colleges were designed not so much to test the training and performance of the applicant but to select the doctors best suited eventually to become consultants. Indeed, both colleges stressed that the passing of these examinations did not signify the completion of postgraduate training but only indicated that the candidate was prepared to continue his education.

In general, English medical schools during the twentieth century have enjoyed much less prestige than has been the case with medical schools in the United States. There one of the leading universities, the Johns Hopkins University, gained much of its prestige and influence as a result of the excellence of its medical school. And while the Hopkins experience was unique in the United States, the excellence of their medical schools has done much to uplift the prestige and legitimacy of many U.S. universities. In England and Wales, however, medical schools have rarely enjoyed the same ranking in the university hierarchy, and this is in part a result of the fact that the medical profession there has been somewhat less influential.

In both countries prior to 1948, there was little centralized control over medical education. The General Medical Council by the early part of the twentieth century had brought about some convergence in the curriculum of medical schools. The consultant, being clinically oriented, was the model that English education emphasized. Thus emphasis on nonclinical training was modest. As the importance of specialty training was downplayed, there was little systematic effort to coordinate it or to provide routinized courses of training—very much in contrast to the United States, which by 1940 had a well-institutionalized system for certifying training in various medical specialties.

The medical delivery system that prevailed in Great Britain on the eve of World War II was considerably different from that at the beginning of the twentieth century. The state had assumed much responsibility in response to the increased demand for more access to medical care. The nature of public involvement with medical care was extremely important in shaping both the contours of the medical profession and the structures for delivering services.

In sharp contrast to the U.S. system, the British adopted a national health insurance system as early as 1911. Its adoption symbolized important differences from the U.S. system, many of which resulted from the difference in the power of consumers between the two societies. The British consumers historically were better organized in their labor unions and friendly societies and thus played a significant role in shaping the nature of medical services. Because national health insurance occurred in Great Britain before the existence of a complex medical technology, the state established an administrative and financial structure that encouraged large numbers of doctors to engage in general practice. In those countries that developed national health insurance late (e.g., Sweden and Canada) or not at all (e.g., the United States), the governments did not have the financial and administrative structure to provide the incentive for a large proportion of its medical profession to engage in nonhospital-based general practice. It is this historical process that helps to explain why such a large portion of the British medical profession has practiced exclusively outside the hospital.

The NHI system, by providing economic security for general practitioners, helped to perpetuate and strengthen the cleavage in the British medical profession between general practitioners and the hospital-based doctors. And because of their divisions British doctors were less powerful in shaping the conditions under which medical services were provided than their colleagues in the United States, where the medical profession was more united and more powerful politically.

While the NHI system did much to generate equality of access to general practitioner care, it nevertheless had many inequities. Moreover, there were many gaps in service, as it did not cover dependents and many in the work force with relatively high incomes. Thus the British government responded by providing alternative services for many of those not covered by the NHI system. And while the rather decentralized system was badly administered and there was variation from area to area, it did provide much better access to medical care than that which existed in the United States.

The history of the British medical delivery system suggests that technology influences structure, for once there was a technology that was believed to be efficacious, the behavior of private and public hospitals began to converge. Even so, there were distinct differences between the public and private sectors throughout the interwar period. For example, the voluntary hospitals continued to be dominated by upper-income groups and elite physicians, while the public hospitals were somewhat more responsive to a broader constituency. While the large voluntary hospitals faced serious financial problems between the two world wars, they tended to provide higher-quality services and to have better staffs than public hospitals of comparable size. Moreover, they remained less egalitarian than public sector hospitals. Voluntary hospitals had more professional staff and money per bed, so that medical innovations diffused more rapidly than among public hospitals of the same size. In addition, large voluntary hospitals were more adaptive to medical innovations because they were more research oriented and had larger teaching facilities than public hospitals of comparable size (Hollingsworth and Hollingsworth 1983; 1985).

Nevertheless, the public general hospitals were rapidly being upgraded between the two world wars as public pressures mounted for governmental assistance. And while the public hospitals continued to be overcrowded and had fewer nurses and physicians per bed than voluntary hospitals, the difference in the level of technological complexity between the two types of hospital was narrowing with the passage of time.

Even though there remained substantial private services in Britain by 1939, the public sector in medical services had grown far more rapidly since 1911 than in the United States. British consumers, being more homogenous ethnically and better organized than U.S. consumers, would continue to exert powerful pressures for the state to play an even larger role in the British medical delivery system. But as long as the public sector was decentralized, the potential to remove regional inequities and to coordinate hospital services within and across regions was very limited.

The number of nurses, doctors, specialists, and hospital beds in England and Wales had increased both absolutely and in proportion to the population between 1911 and 1938 (see table 1; Pinker 1966: 61; Jewkes and Jewkes 1961: 9–10, 25, 53). Moreover, the working conditions of doctors had greatly improved after 1911. For example, the medical journals at the turn of the century had complained bitterly about the low standards of living, fee splitting, bribery and commissions among doctors, and the overcrowded offices of general practitioners; but the development of the NHI system had caused these conditions to diminish (Webb and Webb 1910: 253; Little 1932: 328).

Table 1 Medical Professionals and Hospital Beds per 100,000 Population, England and Wales and the United States, 1911–1941

	Doctors		Specialists (per 100 Doctors)		Nurses		Hospital Beds	
	England & Wales	United States	England & Wales	United States	England & Wales	United States	England & Wales	United States
1911	65	164	5.2	3.6	235	284	547	470
1921	66	142	7.0	9.6	329	336	595	770
1931	77	132	7.8	17.0	329	403	N.A.	790
1941	88	132	8.2	23.5	465	417	637[a]	990

Source: Hollingsworth and Hanneman 1983.
[a] 1938 data.

Despite these changes, there were still many inadequacies in medical care in England and Wales in 1938. These shortcomings led to considerable dissatisfaction both within the medical profession and without and generated pressures that eventually resulted in the development of the NHS, which was enacted in 1946 and implemented in 1948. There remained, in the judgment of most competent observers, a critical shortage of beds in relation to needs—despite the fact that then, as well as now, providers of medical care had little ability to measure need. Most voluntary hospitals had been built during the nineteenth century and in many respects were very much out of date and lacking in amenities (Hollingsworth and Hollingsworth 1983; 1985).

But the condition of the public general hospitals was much worse. Most of them were converted Poor Law institutions, and outside large cities, many had inadequate operating rooms and x-ray departments (Titmus 1950; Hollingsworth and Hollingsworth 1983; 1985).

There was a grossly inequitable distribution of specialists and consultants, which, during the interwar years, was determined more by the opportunities for doctors to earn a high income than by medical needs of an area. Specialists were heavily concentrated in medical school centers, while many counties did not have any gynecologists, thoracic surgeons, dermatologists, pediatricians, or psychiatrists. Moreover, there was also an uneven distribution of general practitioners. A resort town like Harrogate had an oversupply, whereas the working-class areas in neighboring cities were very much in need of doctors. In 1938, Kensington had seven times as many practitioners as South Shields, a ratio that was common across a great deal of the country. In many parts of the country—especially small towns—both private and public hospitals permitted general practitioners to carry out surgery for which they were inadequately trained (Hollingsworth and Hollingsworth 1983; 1985).

The inadequacies of medical services in England and Wales did not affect every group and region in the same way, of course. The working classes were covered by NHI for the services of a panel doctor, but their dependents were still not covered. In theory, anyone who was sufficiently poor could receive medical care in a voluntary or local authority hospital without payment—though in practice, the stigma attached to receiving free care acted to discourage a large proportion of low-income people from seeking it. And as the discussion above suggests, the medical care provided by local authorities left a great deal to be desired. The middle classes were also poorly served by the medical system prior to the NHS. They were not covered by NHI, and their coverage by private health insurance was very inadequate. As Harry Eckstein has written, "it was the middle class which bore the principal burden of neglect. It received no concessions at all in the finance of its medical requirements and it was forced, by indirect means, to subsidize the medical coverage of the rest of the population" (1958: 9). In other words, the middle class paid for its own medical services (on a sliding scale), and paid more of the costs for hospital, consultant, and specialist services than did lower-income groups (Jewkes and Jewkes 1961: 20–21; Watkin 1978: 10).

PRESSURES AND PROPOSALS FOR CHANGE

Because of the widespread dissatisfaction with medical services, there were numerous pressure groups, commissions, and reports between the wars that focused on means of addressing some of the problems described above. A few of the reports were socialist in origin, but most were not. Regardless of their ideological perspective and origin, they did much to generate a national dialogue about the delivery of medical services and contributed to the organization of the NHS in 1946.

One of the earliest groups advocating a fundamental change in the medical delivery system was the State Medical Service Association (the forerunner of the Socialist Medical Association). Reflecting labor's demands for a higher standard of living, the association argued that medical care should be free and available to everyone without any type of means test. Unlike upper-income groups, which generally emphasized the importance of curative medicine, it was labor and organizations sympathetic to labor such as the State Medical Service Association that insisted that medical education and research should be reorganized so that curative and preventive medicine would be integrated. Moreover, the association believed that hospitals should be nationalized and all doctors paid on a salary basis, with general practitioners sharing the hospital work with specialists and consultants (Murray 1971: 1–19; Navarro 1978: 14–24; Moore and Parker 1918: 85–87; Watkin 1975: 111–13).

Many of these views were expressed by a Labour party report entitled *The Organization of the Preventive and Curative Medical Services and Hospital and Laboratory Systems under a Ministry of Health.* The British medical establishment responded in 1920 with a report by the Ministry of Health's Consultative Council under the chairmanship of Lord Dawson of Penn. The document is popularly known as the Dawson Report and the Council is better known as the Dawson Commission (Watkin 1975: 112; 1978: 12). The Dawson Report was one of the most forward-looking and influential documents to emerge on British medical care during the interwar period. It made several major arguments about the inadequacy of medical services: that their organization deprived the nation of the benefits of some of the most important advances in medical technology, that advances in the organization of medical delivery had not kept pace with advances in scientific knowledge, and that the distribution of medical services was very much outdated (Eckstein 1958: 115; Great Britain, MOH 1920).

According to the report, these shortcomings could be remedied only by a reorganization of the delivery of medical services that would merge preventive and curative medicine. Because the Dawson Commission believed that the general practitioner should provide the coordination for integrating communal and individualized medicine it recommended that much of the system should revolve around this central figure. The commission also recommended that the country be divided into regions, each of which would contain primary and secondary health centers, coordinated under a single authority. Primary health centers would bring general practitioners together with specialists and consultants and would result in a useful intellectual exchange. The secondary centers were to be general hospitals staffed by consultants and specialists, who would treat more complicated cases referred from the primary centers. The services of the primary and secondary centers were to be available to *all* citizens. Within each region, primary health centers would be based on secondary health centers, and each secondary center would in turn have direct links with a teaching hospital having a medical school. In this way, the commission hoped that academic influence and spirit of inquiry would permeate the system of secondary and primary medical centers (Forsyth 1966; J. Ross 1952; Eckstein 1958; Stevens 1966; Lindsey 1962). The Dawson Commission essentially sidestepped the issue of the method of compensating the doctors. It believed that patients should make some contribution to the cost of their treatment and therefore endorsed in principle the idea of medical insurance. Moreover, the commission rejected the idea of nationalizing the voluntary hospitals.

Because the Dawson Commission had focused special attention on the financial difficulties of voluntary hospitals, the Ministry of Health appointed another commission in 1921, under the chairmanship of Viscount Cave, to explore solutions to those financial problems. The Cave Commission reported that the financial condition of the voluntary hospitals was so poor that only state assistance could maintain them (Lindsey 1962: 15).

These issues were broadened several years later when the Royal Commission on National Health Insurance reported in 1926 on the shortcomings of the NHI system. In particular, this commission advocated such additional insurance benefits as specialist treatment and laboratory services and stressed the desirability of providing coverage to dependents and others who received no protection under NHI. Even so, the commission, believing that such a move would undermine the independence of the voluntary hospitals did not recommend the extension of benefits to cover inpatient hospital care.

Societal militancy increased during the depression following the Wall Street crash of 1929. In response, the State Medical Service Association merged with the Socialist Medical Association, which in turn became closely associated with the Labour party; in fact, it became the author of the party's health policy. The Labour party demanded fundamental changes in the British medical system: it should be free and open to all; it should be nationally supervised, regionally planned, and locally administered, with regional health centers linked to general and teaching hospitals; and curative and preventive medicine should be integrated (Navarro 1978: 26–27; Murray 1971: 20–34). As the depression deepened, the Socialist Medical Association became both more active and vocal. Later, D. Stark Murray (1971: 38) would observe that most of the ideas of the Socialist Medical Association were incorporated into the NHS.

But as the socialists became more militant, conservative forces continued to respond with changes of their own. Conservative forces in the medical establishment seemed to recognize that some changes of their choosing might prevent the more far-reaching reform proposed by the socialists (Navarro 1978). In 1929, the BMA advocated extending NHI to dependents of insured persons and other designated groups not previously covered and providing maternity and consultant services for those who were covered (Watkin 1975: 121). The association issued a report in 1938 asserting that everyone should have access to a general practitioner and endorsed the idea of hospital regions in which all the hospitals (either voluntary or public) would be well equipped to handle specialized and complex cases (ibid.: 121–26).

One of the most important reports prepared by medical providers was that issued in 1942 by the Medical Planning Commission, a body that had been established in 1940 by the BMA, the royal colleges, the Scottish medical corporations, and even members of the Socialist Medical Association. Given the broad representation of the medical profession on this commission, its report reveals a great deal about the thinking among elite doctors concerning the desirability for fundamental changes in the delivery of medical services. In many respects, the commission echoed the views of the Dawson Report of twenty years earlier, by arguing that changes in the organization of medical practice had not kept pace with changes in medical knowledge, that the direction for reforms should be through the development of hospital regions, and that the transition of general practice should be from a decentralized, individualistic type of service to a more centralized, less competitive, corporate work situation (Forsyth 1966: 118). In addition, the report argued that medical need, not economic status, should determine access to medical care: that the rich should not receive better care than the poor (Lindsey 1962: 28–29). To achieve this goal, the report proposed that the NHI program be extended to cover at least 90 percent of the British population, but that hospitals should continue to charge patients according to their ability to pay. In order to promote a more integrated and efficient general practice service, the report advocated a collective form of service, with general practitioners working from health centers sponsored by local authorities. Ideally, the local health centers would be closely linked with the regional system, thus achieving a medical service that would integrate curative and preventive medicine (Navarro 1978: 32).

These reports were all fuel for a national policy debate that gradually involved more and more groups. There was an emerging consensus, both within the medical profession and without, that the coverage of the NHI system was too restricted and that some type of substitute financing mechanism was necessary in order to provide medical care for a large portion of the population. An assumption shared by all of the interwar reports was that changes in medical technology and the costs of financing access to it dictated important changes in the structure of the delivery system. However, there were serious differences among various professional groups concerning the direction that some of the changes should take. In general, the profession was divided over which medical services should be under local government control, which should be tied to the central government, and which should be retained to the private sector. Moreover, there was much disagreement about the future status of the voluntary hospitals and the compensation of the hospital-based doctor.

More than anything else, it was the experiences of World War II that alerted the overwhelming majority of the British people to the serious inadequacies in the medical delivery system and convinced both the public and the medical professionals that substantial changes were possible. In preparation for heavy civilian casualties from air raids, the British government established the Emergency Medical Service under the Ministry of Health in 1939.

Some hospitals were taken over entirely by the emergency service in order to make more beds available. The net effect of the service was a great deal of overcrowding in hospitals, the premature discharge of many patients, and the construction of "hutted" annexes to many existing hospitals (J. Ross 1952: 76–77; Stevens 1966: 70–71; Eckstein 1958: 88–89; Titmuss 1950: 194–95).

As changes imposed by the war, especially overcrowding, made the public increasingly aware of the shortcomings of the existing medical delivery system, pressures increased for permanent changes. Moreover, as many voluntary hospitals became accustomed to accepting large sums of money from the central government during the war, it became difficult for them to confront the possibility of returning to financial uncertainty once the war was over.

At the beginning of the war, it was apparent to the planners within the Emergency Medical Service that the shortcomings of the medical system were far more serious than most well-informed professionals had imagined. Unfortunately, the decentralized hospital system, the lack of uniform record keeping among hospitals, and the poor inventory of the nation's hospital facilities had meant that hitherto most members of the medical profession had not known a great deal about most of the small voluntary hospitals, of which there were several hundred. During the war, however, the centralized collection of information about hospitals made it increasingly apparent to the medical profession that many hospitals suffered from inadequate income and deteriorating physical plants. Within a very short period, the central government, through the Ministry of Health and the Emergency Medical Service, upgraded the physical facilities of numerous hospitals by providing surgical equipment, new operating rooms, x-ray rooms, kitchens, blankets, beds, and clothing. Indeed, the service demonstrated that, with a centralized organization, the quality of hospital care could be upgraded throughout the country within a relatively short time. It also demonstrated that centralized government authority had the potential to bring coordination and rationality into what had hitherto been a disorganized, inefficient, and competing set of hospitals (ibid.: 83, 480; Eckstein 1958: 89–90).

Perhaps one of the most important consequences of the Emergency Medical Service was the effect that it had on the thinking of two influential groups. During the war, participating doctors administered medical care and many upper-middle- and upper-class citizens received it in types of hospitals different from those they were used to. The medical elite was very active in the development and implementation of Emergency Medical Service policy from the beginning, for the first time shaping a medical service for the entire country. Numerous consultants left their private practices and accepted government salaries at only a fraction of their former earnings, working in hospitals far removed from their elegant offices. By the time the war ended, many consultants and specialists had become accustomed to the idea of working on a salaried basis in voluntary hospitals and had become convinced that government planning was necessary in order to bring about a more equitable distribution of medical resources throughout the country. Consultants who had never worked in a hospital other than a teaching one now had an opportunity for the first time to observe the inadequacies of medical facilities in much of the country, and as a result many vowed to rectify the system.

As middle- and upper-income people entered public hospitals for the first time, they saw firsthand the relics of old workhouses, the conditions under which the poor and the elderly received medical care, the physical deterioration and inadequate facilities of provincial hospitals. As the well-to-do intermingled with those who were less fortunate, the privileged classes became more sensitive to the problems of poverty, old age, and chronic disease. In sum, the war did much to soften temporarily the class rigidities of British society and to generate a collective conscience that began to focus more systematically on the means of reshaping medical delivery in the postwar period.

In October 1941, the minister of health reflected much of the nation's mood by announcing that the government would create a national hospital service after the war. For at least two years civil servants within the Ministry of Health had been studying policy options for changing the British medical system, proposing solutions of a wide-ranging nature that would be acceptable to the major actors in the medical area (Klein 1983b: 1–30). By 1941, support for more equitable access to and distribution of medical services coordinated by public authorities was provided by leaders in the medical profession, of all major political parties, and of almost every other group in British society. The critical question was the precise shape that the changes would take.

The expectations of a new system were intensified in 1942 when the Beveridge Report on social insurance was published. Vague insofar as it only outlined the government's specific proposals on medical care, the report was important in that it placed medical care squarely within the context of social policy. It stated the government's intention of providing a program that would "ensure that for every citizen there is available whatever medical treatment he requires" and that would be available to all without a means test (Beveridge 1942).

The government began serious consultations with doctors, officials from public and voluntary hospitals, and other interested parties about the structure of a national health service and in February 1944 issued a white paper designed to focus discussion on the type of new medical system. The white paper demonstrated the government's belief that radical changes would fail and that the new service had to be carefully built on past experience. It assumed that doctors and patients must retain their freedom to participate or not and that the program was to be administered jointly by central and local authorities, with due regard for democratic processes (Lindsey 1962: 33–34). Voluntary hospitals would come under the program only on a voluntary basis, but because there were such strong financial incentives for them to participate, it was assumed that most would join the scheme (Stevens 1966: 71).

According to the white paper, all participating general practitioners were to practice under a contract with the Central Medical Board, which would try to bring about a more equitable geographical distribution of general practitioners. Drawing on the Dawson Report of 1920, the white paper placed considerable emphasis on the establishment of health centers for grouped general practice, though doctors were to have the option of continuing in separate or individual practice. The white paper was somewhat vague in its plans for specialists and consultants, though the consultants were to be compensated on a salary basis and were to have hospital-based appointments.

As Rudolph Klein observes, the importance of the white paper derives from the fact that it was a compromise document that sought to reconcile a host of conflicting aims of policy and to minimize opposition from each of the major interest groups (consultants, general practitioners, consumers, and civil servants, as well as leaders of the Conservative and Labour parties) (1983b). The white paper quickly won widespread approval in Parliament and was generally received with enthusiasm in the larger society.

Overall, the medical profession was very much in favor of most of the substantive changes proposed by the white paper, but at the same time, it was very fearful of being subjected to control by the government. With the document's proposals to provide a free and comprehensive medical service and a free and complete hospital service for everyone, doctors were in substantial agreement. The profession also endorsed by a vote the idea that there be large administrative areas for hospitals, that the government regulate the geographical distribution of general practitioners in the country, that doctors no longer be permitted to sell their private practices, and that there be local health centers for both preventive and curative care in which groups of general practitioners might practice (Murray 1971; Hart 1972b: 572).

Even though the medical profession was very much in favor of most of the substantive issues proposed by the white paper, some doctors viewed with alarm its proposal that local authorities supervise and manage the hospitals. As Harry Eckstein has observed, "the doctors did not fear nationalization as much as municipalization" (1958: 149), for they tended to associate local government involvement in medical care with Poor Law workhouses, underfinanced and poorly equipped hospitals, and medical institutions that offered little opportunity for professional advancement and recognition.

The general practitioners had an entirely different set of concerns. They were fearful that the government intended eventually to move them into local health centers in which remuneration would be salaried. Whereas a salary was not objectionable to consultants because of their wartime experience, general practitioners were anxious to preserve their compensation on a capitation basis. Moreover, they feared that if their practice became located primarily in local group health centers, they would become mere minor civil servants and it would be difficult to retain their professional autonomy. The medical profession, divided between general practitioners on the one hand and consultants and specialists on the other, was able to emphasize negative positions on specific issues in the white paper, but internal divisions meant that it had great difficulty in generating a positive program of its own.

Over a period of several months in 1945, Aneurin Bevan, the new Labour minister of health, carried out extensive consultations with the medical profession, voluntary hospitals, local authorities, trade unions, dentists, and other concerned groups. In response to the medical profession's opposition to local authority control of hospitals, Bevan was quite willing to propose larger regions. Moreover, he was willing to make certain that the doctors be guaranteed substantial representation in the administration of the new program, that a capitation scheme of payment be preserved for general practitioners, and that the local authorities retain their control over domiciliary services. After many months of careful consultation with all major interests and extensive planning, Bevan finally submitted to Parliament the government's plan for a national health service in March 1946, and it was approved without much difficulty in November 1946.

To achieve his success, Bevan had courted the elite of the royal colleges, and they in turn had supported his program. He is quoted as having said that he "choked [the consultants'] mouths with gold" (Hart 1973: 1196). Believing that the leaders of the royal colleges were more astute and powerful than members of the BMA, Bevan structured the program so that consultants and the teaching hospitals would continue to receive favored treatment, whereas the general practitioner would continue to work outside the hospital with a much lower status. There is little doubt that the hospital-based doctors had been highly successful in their negotiations with Bevan. For example, he adopted in essence their positions on the following issues: conditions of service and pay, permission to continue with private practice but with access to NHS hospital beds, a high degree of control over appointments and promotions, and control over the merit award system that the NHS established (Navarro 1978: 41–42; Gill 1971: 348).

The National Health Service

Even though the NHS brought about changes in the British medical delivery system, it is apparent that it was an outgrowth of or evolution from earlier arrangements in the delivery of medical care. As Almont Lindsey suggests, the new program was a compromise among conflicting structures of the past, imperatives of the present, and the hopes of the future (1962: 450). A major goal of Bevan and other government planners had originally been to develop a highly rationalized and coordinated national health delivery system. In this respect, the NHS failed, for the system was not well integrated, and there was poor communication among key elements of the system. The NHS represented the rationalization of three traditional parts of the total medical delivery system: (1) the general medical services, controlled by local executive councils and providing general practitioner, dental, optical, and pharmaceutical services; (2) hospital services, which tended to be arranged on a regional basis; and (3) local authority services, which provided domiciliary services (i.e., midwifery, maternity, child welfare, and home nursing care, as well as ambulance and certain types of preventive health services).

General Medical Services

The NHS provided for "free" general medical services under the authority of local executive councils. Basically, the work of the councils was to keep records and dispense payments, as their policy-making role was very limited. The councils were essentially the same organizations that had functioned as the local insurance committees under the NHI program.

Most general practitioners continued, as before, to provide medical services on a capitation basis and to be excluded from the hospitals. All patients, as under the NHI program, were free to choose their own general practitioners, though each doctor was at liberty to refuse a patient. Moreover, a patient was free to transfer to another doctor, and each doctor could remove a patient from his list if he chose to do so. Doctors were also permitted to treat patients privately on a fee-for-service basis, but very few patients sought this option. In order to protect the quality of service, individual general practitioners were not permitted to have more than 3,500 persons on their list, though in most years the average tended to be somewhat less than 2,500. Overall, the income of the general practitioner improved substantially as a result of the NHS, just as participation in the NHI system represented an improvement over what had existed before 1911 (Titmuss 1858; Navarro 1978: 42).

Over the years, general practitioners have operated like small businessmen. While preserving their autonomy, they were free to practice privately, could adjust the size of their practice to suit themselves, and could work in industry or for an insurance company. But in general, such doctors were quite isolated, lacking the close contact with professional colleagues available to those who worked in hospitals or health centers, and conducted very little research. There were no mechanisms for certifying the standard of work by general practitioners. Moreover, their earnings depended on the quantity of patients seen rather than the quality of care provided, though if the quality was perceived to be very low, they ran the risk of losing patients (Great Britain, NHS 1979: 73–82, 89, 231, 288).

As the level of technological complexity and specialization increased in recent decades, the distance between the status of the general practitioner and that of the hospital-based doctor tended to widen. Thus the consultants in the teaching hospitals remained the most influential doctors in the medical system—as before the introduction of the NHS—and the general practitioner the least influential.

A major idea behind the NHS was to coordinate, rationalize, and equalize the distribution of general practitioners across the country. The Medical Practices Committee was created as a government agency whose major responsibility was to make periodic surveys of the country in order to regulate the distribution of doctors.

At the local level, the executive councils also administered the services of pharmacists, opthalmologists, and dentists, though these were subject to less control than the general practitioners. Their participation in the NHS was also voluntary, but unlike the general practitioners, they could practice wherever they wished (Eckstein 1958: 203). Moreover, there was no limit to the number of people to whom they could provide services, and they were compensated on a fee-for-service basis, though the government did attempt to regulate their fees.

Hospital Services

Structure

The second basic pillar of the NHS was hospital services, and it was here that the NHS made the most radical departure from what had existed prior to 1948. The government nationalized throughout Britain 1,143 voluntary hospitals with approximately 90,000 beds and 1,545 municipal hospitals with about 390,000 beds. The nationalization did not include old people's homes, or many nursing homes and convalescent homes, but it did include general, mental, and tuberculosis hospitals, as well as those for chronic diseases. Within NHS hospitals, everyone was entitled to care without charge. Within a relatively short time, the NHS upgraded former Poor Law hospitals into very acceptable hospitals, many of which acquired for the first time fully trained specialists and ancillary staff as well as up-to-date diagnostic equipment (Hart 1971: 406).

The government divided England and Wales into 14 (later 15) hospital regions, each of which was to be affiliated with a university with one or more medical schools. Each hospital region was to operate under the control of a regional hospital board, members of which were not elected but appointed by the minister of health. Some regions contained as many as 250 hospitals, whereas others had fewer than 100, and some covered large areas of the country, whereas others did not (Stevens 1966: 170). Indeed, there was much variation among regions, the largest having more than 4.5 million people and more than 65,000 hospital beds, and the smallest approximately 1.5 million people and about 14,000 beds (Lindsey 1962: 244–45).

Significantly, the NHS provided the teaching hospitals with a preferred status by treating them differently. Although each region was based on a teaching hospital, the teaching hospitals were nevertheless excluded from the regional organization. Each was administered by a separate board of governors directly responsible to the minister of health, who would appoint the governors from among representatives of the university, the senior staff of the hospital, and the local authorities.

Whereas the teaching hospitals were administered directly by the board of governors in a two-tier system operating under the minister of health, the administration of nonteaching NHS hospitals was more complex. Under the regional hospital boards (RHBs) there were hospital management committees (HMCs), which had the task of coordinating the large number of hospitals operating within a region. Many small hospitals were grouped together in an effort to assure that they would provide similar services to those provided by the large hospitals with hundreds of beds. HMCs had the responsibility of supervising day-to-day activities such as maintaining equipment and physical facilities, purchasing supplies, and appointing personnel other than medical specialists and dentists (Lindsey 1962: 247). Ideally, they were to standardize hospital services across the country.

The function of the RHB was to plan for the distribution of specialists and hospitals under their jurisdiction, to determine and supervise the allocation of money to individual hospitals, and to supervise the staffs of hospitals. Significantly, these boards employed all the specialists working in the hospitals except those who were still primarily engaged in training. The purpose of this was to prevent the specialists from being too attached to an individual hospital when they could serve several. This procedure assured small hospitals of having access to the same medical specialties as the larger ones and was designed to equalize the quality of hospitals.

The members of the RHB and HMCs were, in theory, to come from all walks of life, with doctors prohibited (after 1957) from constituting more than one-fourth of the membership (Lindsey 1962: 245), though in fact, medical representation and corporate interests tended to dominate the RHB (Robson 1973: 421–22; Eckstein 1958: 188). Most of the work of the RHBs and HMCs was conducted by their committees and by salaried officials attached to them. Because these officials were full-time, they were able to shape the decisions of the hospital boards and management committees. For all practical purposes, the real running of the hospitals was executed by a professional staff rather than by representatives from the community.

The management of the teaching hospitals was less affected by the NHS, as they were permitted to continue their privileged position in the medical delivery system. After the nationalization of the hospitals, the endowment of each nonteaching hospital was brought under national control and placed in a central fund from which money was then allocated to RHBs and HMCs in proportion to the number of beds they controlled. In this, as in many other matters, the teaching hospitals were given special treatment and status, as they were permitted to retain their endowment, a factor that assured that they would continue to behave differently from the nonteaching hospitals.

While the hospitals, consultants, and the royal colleges initially engaged in some sulking about the NHS, they soon accepted the system, for they recognized that their privileged status was enhanced by it. The large voluntary hospitals had not been in a viable financial position in 1945, and nationalization meant that they would now offer secure and well-paid jobs, have sizable support staffs and wide-ranging diagnostic equipment and departments, and exclude general practitioners. For the consultants, the NHS provided better work conditions, enhanced their power over the nation's medical resources, and provided the opportunity for private beds and private practice in government facilities. Because of the centralized nature of the medical delivery system, the royal colleges emerged with enhanced influence over the entire system (Klein 1983a; 1983b).

Consultants

Whereas consultants formerly had an appointment in and attachment to a single hospital, under the NHS they were expected to serve in various hospitals in a broad geographical area. The exact type of work that consultants were to do in the various hospitals was arranged among themselves, the local doctors, and other professionals in specific hospitals (Stevens 1966: 190). To prevent the nepotism and favoritism that had characterized appointments at the consultant level earlier in the twentieth century, applications for consultant positions were accepted from candidates throughout the country once a RHB announced a vacancy and advertised it, and an individual could become a consultant only when and where the Ministry of

Health and the board designated an opening. In this respect, the consultant had less choice about location than the general practitioner (ibid.: 189).

The salary of the medical specialists was nationally based, subject to no variation across specialties, regions, or localities. Of course, there were salary increments over time for advances in rank. Consultants were not required to work full-time, however, as they were compensated primarily for the time they spent in the hospital. Indeed, most consultants did not accept full-time appointments; for example, more than two-thirds of the consultants worked on a part-time basis in 1959 (Lindsey 1962: 337). There had long been a widespread feeling among specialists that part-time service carried high prestige and status—a carryover from the days when consultants worked on a part-time honorary basis in the hospitals. Most consultants, therefore, entered into part-time contracts with their RHBs. Although consultants examined the outpatients referred to them, they had a staff of junior and senior doctors who assumed a substantial portion of the medical care for which the consultants were responsible.

Because the consultants were employed by the RHB rather than the individual hospital, in some respects they enjoyed much more professional autonomy than their U.S. counterparts. The British medical leaders have often argued that the rigorous screening procedures for selecting their consultants have rendered quality controls less necessary than in a large country such as the United States in which the senior medical staff of a hospital has been subject to less national screening and competition. Whereas extensive procedures for peer review of physicians engaged in hospital practice have emerged in the United States, in contrast, there were few formal procedures in Britain for disciplining consultants who performed inadequately or even for determining whether they performed satisfactorily (Stevens 1966: 191–96). Once an RHB appointed an individual to the rank of consultant (at an average age of 37), the person had a tenured appointment until retirement at age 65. In addition to their salary, consultants were also permitted to receive income from other sources for practice.

At any rate, the consultants, by being employed at the regional rather than at the hospital level, retained much of their independence. They were allocated a specified block of beds but were not subject to much control by the HMCs or their colleagues in the hospitals in which they worked. As Rosemary Stevens comments, "consultants continue[d] to behave as if they were still independent professional men, voluntarily donating their services" (Stevens 1966: 192).

Distiction Awards. In response to the concern that a salaried service might not provide sufficient incentives to consultants to practice high-quality medicine, the NHS made distinction awards to consultants, the stated goal being "to stimulate effort and encourage initiative." The number of consultants receiving awards was technically to be determined by the minister of health, but recipients were actually determined by the elite of the medical profession—usually by a committee that included the presidents of the English and Scottish royal colleges.

One study concluded that 43 percent of the people who became consultants received a distinction award at some point in their career. Because of the awards, the salaries of specialists varied considerably under the NHS, despite public pronouncements about the egalitarian salary scale in the system. Moreover, the distribution of the awards was quite uneven across the medical specialties throughout Britain. For example, in 1964, 60 percent of internists, thoracic surgeons, cardiologists, neurologists, and neurosurgeons received awards as compared to no more than 13 percent of those in geriatrics, anesthesiology, and psychiatry. Part-time consultants received more awards than full-time consultants, and those in teaching hospitals more than those in nonteaching hospitals. These trends had hardly changed by 1979. Once a distinction award is made, the consultant receives the annual financial reward for life (Stevens 1966: 213; Great Britain, NHS 1979: 235–37).

Private Practice. All part-time consultants were permitted to engage in private practice, a factor of considerable symbolic importance. It was a tradition they insisted on preserving. Moreover, it represented an additional source of income for those specialists who chose to work part-time in the NHS.

The extent of private practice, however, has been somewhat difficult to determine. Because the government permitted a small number of pay beds to remain in the hospitals after 1948, one crude indicator of the extent of private practice was the frequency with which these beds were used. Throughout Britain, pay beds were approximately 1 percent of all staffed NHS hospital beds, but over time only about one-half of these were utilized at any one point (Great Britain, NHS 1979: 291). In general, consultants were not permitted to admit private patients to beds other than pay beds. Nevertheless, a high percentage of the consultants who were permitted to treat private patients did so. In 1964, part-time consultants accounted for 69 percent of all of those employed by the entire NHS, and their incomes were higher than their full-time colleagues, not only because many part-timers received distinction awards but also because of the extra income received from private practice (Mencher 1967; Gill 1971: 350).

The fact that hospital provident societies provided, throughout Britain, private medical insurance for almost 1 million people in 1959 suggests that a sizable number of people wanted the opportunity to have private care in private nursing homes, private hospitals, and in NHS hospitals (Lindsey 1962: 278–79). By the late 1970s, approximately 2.5 million citizens had purchased private medical insurance, and the membership in such plans was growing at a rate of approximately 10 percent a year. Most of the private insurance was purchased to provide consumers with swifter treatment by their choice of physicians and hospitals, and with a private hospital room and other amenities. The purpose was not primarily to obtain a higher quality of care, as most of the physicians who treated private patients also practiced in the NHS. However, one of the basic motives in acquiring private service was to avoid long waiting periods for elective surgery. And yet the British private sector was responsible for less than 3 percent of the total expenditures on medical care by 1979. Basically, more and more citizens were requesting that their employers provide some form of private medical insurance in case it were needed, but all but a small fraction of medical services were still being provided by the NHS (Spivack 1979; Klein 1979). When confronted with a serious illness, almost all citizens still opt for NHS services.

Local Authority Services

The executive councils and the RHBs were concerned primarily with providing curative and supportive care to patients, whereas a major function of the local health authorities, the third major part of the NHS, was to provide preventive care. As the local authorities lost the municipal hospitals to the national government, their basic role was to continue their traditional public health functions, most of which dealt with preventive services. Some activities that had long been optional now became mandatory, but the local authorities were able to carry out their functions more efficiently because of the availability of more funds. In each county, the chief public health officer, the medical officer of health (a position that had been in existence for more than a hundred years), was aided by a sizable number of specialists in many different areas: midwives, home visitors, home nurses, speech therapists, doctors, and dentists—to mention but a few.

One of the chief local government health activities continued to be home visiting for mothers and children. In 1949 there were approximately 10 million home visits, and in 1960 almost 12 million (Lindsey 1962: 364–69; Great Britain, NHS 1979: 76). Distinct from home visiting was the activity of district nurses who did many types of home nursing, generally under the supervision of a general practitioner. By 1960, there were approximately 10,300 district nurses and almost 23 million home visits. As hospital care became increasingly costly, patients were discharged early, on the assumption that they would receive care from district nurses, and as the service expanded, some patients were kept out of the hospitals altogether (Lindsey 1962: 373).

The domiciliary midwife service was another important local authority service. Under the NHS a sizable portion of all births continued to take place in the home, and a midwife was present at virtually all domiciliary confinements. In a high percentage of cases, a midwife conducted the delivery without a doctor's presence. In addition, midwives were active in the local authority prenatal clinics and in family planning and genetic counseling (Great Britain, NHS 1979: 77).

With the passage of time, community services for the elderly have become increasingly important. There has continued to be an expansion in the number of home nurses for the elderly, meals on wheels, and other types of home assistance. Because of constraints on resources, however, throughout the period since 1948 there has been a lack of communication and coordination between employees of the NHS and local authorities. For example, since the NHS is funded centrally, local authorities have had incentives to push as much care onto the NHS as possible. And because of financial pressures, local authorities have not been able to develop social services as fully as they would like. Despite the shortcomings of the system, however, the British have provided far more extensive home visiting to the elderly than anything yet developed in the United States. And it is partly for this reason that a larger percentage of the elderly throughout Britain have been able to avoid going into old people's homes.

Some of the local authority services would not have functioned had it not been for the large number of volunteers and voluntary organizations that contributed their time. Volunteers were particularly active in the domiciliary service and in the local clinics. The British Red Cross, the League of Friends, the Order of St. John, and the Women's Voluntary Service are among the organizations that were especially active. The volunteers, the district nurses, and others who aided in providing nursing care in the home did much to assist patients to remain at home rather than be removed to a hospital, convalescent institution, or nursing home. Evening and night services were also helpful for the elderly and the chronically ill. All of these services, as distinct from services in institutions, were very important in keeping the costs of the NHS low relative to those in other countries.

CONCLUDING OBSERVATIONS

All the forces making for the emergence of the NHS are somewhat difficult to unravel. Certainly the shift to the NHS did not come about overnight but was the result of a political process that had taken place over several decades. To understand the process, it is important to understand that the Labour party and its friends played an important role throughout the interwar period in shaping the agenda for changes in the structure of the medical delivery system, and it was this agenda to which various conservative groups and the elite of the medical profession were continuously pressured to respond.

Despite many coherent plans for change that developed between 1918 and 1948, the system that was implemented in 1948 was not a fully integrated or highly rationalized program of medical care. Yet the British did manage to develop a far more coherent and rational system than the Americans have yet achieved. Moreover, the British did achieve a system with a relatively high degree of coordination—given the size and complexity of the system.

The NHS is an excellent example of how traditional practices and structures persist despite serious efforts to reshape a system. Probably no country in the world has produced so many wise reports for improvements in the delivery of medical services as has Great Britain. And yet the structures that emerged in 1948 were basically a variation on those that existed before the NHS. Indeed, the histories of the British and U.S. medical delivery systems are testimony to the argument that once institutional arrangements come into existence, it is very difficult for a society to engage in any later radical restructuring. Probably the most important change that occurred was the nationalization of the voluntary hospitals, which resulted in a much more centralized medical delivery system. But as with the steel and other industries after World War II, pressure for nationalization may have come from the left, but in the final analysis, the change occurred because of the consent of the nation's economic and social elites. And in this instance the elite of the medical profession consented because they feared that the country could not continue to finance the hospital system in the same fashion as it had before 1948.

The NHS did not bring about an integration of curative and preventive health centers as the Dawson Commission and others had advocated, and local health services continued to be poorly financed. Meantime, the cleavages and poor communication between the hospital-based doctors and the general practitioners continued. And while the NHS did much to upgrade the quality of a very high percentage of hospitals, it singled out the prestigious teaching hospitals for special treatment.

In recent years, Theda Skocpol and several other scholars have argued that policy intellectuals and state officials are critical actors in the shaping of social policy and that an important task of the analyst is to assess their role at critical junctures in the history of welfare policies (Block 1980; Orloff and Skocpol 1984; Skocpol 1981). In the case of the NHS, both groups were important in that they attempted to harmonize the proposals of existing powerfully organized groups. Bevan drew on the advice of Sir Wilson Jameson, the chief medical officer, and others within the Ministry of Health who sought "practical solutions" to the situation. While the Ministry of Health at the end of World War II was a bureaucracy with a long tradition and considerable legitimacy, its powers to mold the nation's medical system in some autonomous or independent fashion were quite limited, if for no other reason than that it had a long tradition of being involved in local affairs and of keeping its most influential medical officers far removed from the formulation of national policy (Abel-Smith 1964: 475). Nevertheless, civil servants did engage in extensive meetings with representatives of the medical profession in an effort to devise means of reconciling alternative positions. And their role in developing an acceptable consensus among conflicting groups was important. If policy intellectuals and civil servants did not set the agenda for change, without their work in achieving concessions from groups with differing priorities, the NHS could hardly have emerged with as much legitimacy as it did at the time of its creation.

As a minister, Bevan's chief task was to use the power of the state to conciliate all of the critical actors: local authorities, medical officers within his ministry, general practitioners, the royal colleges, dentists, pharmacists, public hospitals, teaching and nonteaching voluntary hospitals, the Socialist Medical Association, and the Labour party. Because there had long been widespread public discussion about the shortcomings of the nation's medical services, there was a strong consensus, built upon the horrors of war, that all citizens should have access to medical facilities without regard for their ability to pay. Just as citizens were able to look to the state for safe water supplies, highways, and educational facilities, there had emerged a consensus that people should also be able to look to the state for medical and dental facilities. Operating within this consensus, Bevan's goal was to build on the past, to expand existing facilities, and to provide them with a more secure financial basis. In sum, the state's role was primarily one of conciliation and channeling forces for change. Because of the broad national consensus on the major issues, Bevan was able to bring some of the nation's most aristocratic and reactionary groups into harmony with those that were very left oriented. And it was because the NHS emerged from such a national consensus that it has long enjoyed widespread popular support (Abel-Smith 1964: 487; Klein 1983b).

With the NHS, the British system had become one of the most centralized in a democratic country. And with a high degree of centralization and coordination, it was now possible for it to engage in relatively effective cost controls through prospective funding. Moreover, it was able to promote greater equality of access to services across social classes and groups. But as the analysis will later demonstrate, the greater centralization and coordination did place constraints on the modernization and innovativeness of the system.

One of the most striking differences between the evolution of the British and U.S. systems has been that, while the status and power of medical providers have been considerable in both, lower-income consumers have a much stranger tradition of shaping the structures and policies in the British than in the U.S. system. For this reason, the medical needs of lower-income consumers have received more attention in Britain than in the United States. The consuming public still exerts more influence in the British system, but the relative power and influence of the hospital-based doctors have increased substantially under the NHS. No doubt the increasing complexity of medical technology has provided specialists and consultants with greater prestige, as it has in most other countries, but the centralized structure of the NHS has made it easier for the British medical elite to penetrate the political system and to influence medical policy. In Britain, the medical profession has become increasingly successful in determining which issues will and will not be placed on the policy agenda in setting limits on the power of the state (Klein 1983b).

Britain was one of the few countries that adopted a national health insurance system very early in its history (1911), at a time when hospital-based technology was relatively unimportant, and the administrative and financial structure encouraged large numbers of doctors to engage in general practice. Significantly, the adoption of this type of decision at an early date provided financial security for general practitioners and helped to counteract the trend toward specialization. By 1948, when the NHS came into existence, a very large proportion of Britain's medical profession was still engaged in general practice. By limiting the number of specialist posts available in hospitals, the NHS was able to place considerable constraints on the percentage of doctors who specialized. Moreover, the minister of health, working with regional hospital boards and the Advisory Committee on Consultant Establishments, was in a strategic position to influence the distribution of doctors across different specialty fields (Stevens 1966: 228).

Because the NHS has been in a position to limit the number of available specialty positions and because patients gained access to a specialist primarily as a result of a referral from a general practitioner, the general practitioner has had a more important role in the NHS than in the U.S. system. This helps to explain why, in the middle 1960s, approximately 70 percent of Britain's medical profession was engaged in general practice and 30 percent in specialty practice.

On the other hand, the United States did not develop national health insurance early or any other mechanism that would have provided the incentive for a large proportion of its profession to engage in nonhospital-based general practice. As medical technology shifted more toward the hospital, there has been a great deal of incentive, in countries that did not develop a national health insurance system early, for doctors to specialize. For example, the specialist–general practitioner ratio in the United States at times has been almost the reverse of that in Britain. In the middle 1960s, approximately 65 percent of all U.S. doctors were specialists, and 35 percent were general practitioners. It is not surprising that historically patients in the United States have bypassed the general practitioner and have gone directly to the specialist, without any type of referral.

In short, the timing of national health insurance in various western countries helps to explain the variation in the financial and administrative structures that have placed constraints on the specialist–general practitioner ratio. And even though the NHI scheme died in Britain with the introduction of the NHS in 1948, the establishment of local executive councils and RHBs provided a financial and administrative structure that placed effective constraints on the number of specialists in the system. In the United States, however, where the constraints on the number of specialists are due more to the marketplace than to government regulation, the function and number of specialists is very different. (Heidenheimer and Layson 1979).

In contrast to the more market-oriented U.S. medical system, the NHS has meant that for all citizens, the ability to obtain treatment was divorced from the ability to pay. While it was very much shaped by the previous history of the British medical system, it nevertheless was a major innovation in a worldwide context. It was the first system in a market-oriented society to provide universal access to medical care without a method of financing based on insurance principles and to represent a strong commitment to the principles of rationality, efficiency, and equity. The reason that such a system could emerge in Britain and not in the United States was that historically power was distributed differently among key interest groups in the two societies.

The working class and various policy intellectuals were key actors in bringing about the NHI system in 1911, for both groups kept up pressures for a public system covering the whole of the population. For example, it was the desire of the working class for affordable access to hospitals that helped lead to the creation of public general hospitals after 1929, just as its earlier wishes for maternity and schoolchildren's services had led local authorities to deliver screening, home visiting, and medical services. Gradually, the public responsibilities for health had increased in Britain, with incremental movement away from local authorities and toward central administration and oversight. The NHS reflected the role of consumer power in that, after 1948, no one was to be without access to minimum medical care.

Providers have been less influential in the NHS than in the U.S. system, where they have been much more important in determining the level of spending allocated to medical care and the location of resources are to be located. Nevertheless, the medical profession of Britain has been able to exert considerable influence in shaping the public agenda for medical policy and retain clinical autonomy over the treatment of illness. However, it has been severely constrained in its professional activities by the limited resources of the NHS (Klein 1983b).

In a publicly dominated system such as the NHS, most patients receive less than optimal treatment. Constrained by limited resources, the NHS has been committed to providing, for all citizens, a minimum level of care, a term that it has historically defined as the services that most people use most of the time and/or the services necessary to treat diseases that are common for certain age groups. On the other hand, those who have wanted a second opinion, the services of a world famous surgeon, or access to the latest expensive technology more often than not have had to go outside the system and use the private sector. Whether in the financing of public education or public medical services and whether in Britain or the United States, limited budgets force governments increasingly to provide minimum rather than optimal services. It is the private sector in both countries, shaped by upper-income groups and elite providers, that historically has been able to provide for a limited portion of the population. But to understand why the private sector has remained dominant in the United States, one must understand that the distribution of power has been fundamentally different from that in Britain.

2
The Medical Delivery
System of the United States,
1890-1970

Like the historical development of its counterpart in England and Wales, the evolution of the U.S. medical delivery system was very much constrained by the social structure in which it was integrated. Specifically, the way in which power was distributed in each society set limits on the autonomy of the medical profession and shaped the types of relations that would develop among state actors, the medical profession, the working class, and upper-income groups. Moreover, the class structure in each society helps to explain historically which diseases would be the most subject to treatment, which diseases would receive the most immediate and expensive attention, and which groups in the society would have the most access to medical care. And in both societies, the way in which the system (including medical education) was organized and financed at the time when technology became a highly salient issue very much constrained the type of organizational arrangements that would exist subsequently.

There are three characteristics of American society that deserve special emphasis if one is to understand the unique contours of the medical delivery system, but unless one views the history of that system within a comparative perspective, one is unlikely to comprehend these traits. The first characteristic is the relatively open and fluid class structure that historically has existed in the United States, which has resulted in a more egalitarian medical profession than that of England and Wales. Of course, the U.S. medical system, like any other, has had its own stratification system, but U.S. practitioners have always treated one another in a more egalitarian way. Whereas in England and Wales, doctors who dominated the hospitals formed a social elite, professional democracy has been more widespread in the United States among all doctors. Americans have historically tended to address any medical practitioner, with egalitarian abandon, as "Dr. So-and-so," whereas the British distinguish between a specialist (addressed as "Mr." or "Ms.") and any other doctor (addressed as "Dr."). The U.S. medical profession, unlike its European counterpart, has been less willing to deny hospital privileges to classes of practitioner on the grounds that their training was deficient (Shryock 1967; Stevens 1971; Kaufman 1976; Kett 1968).

In the American colonies, local conditions required that every practitioner be the functional equivalent of a druggist, surgeon, physician, and midwife. During this period, the overwhelming majority of doctors received their training by apprenticeship or simply pretended to have received medical training. There were virtually no elaborate training facilities that led to the rigid type of stratification system among practitioners that existed in England. And while there have been sharp divisions in the medical profession in the United States, they have never been as great as in England and Wales. As a result, American practitioners have been able to exert more dominance over medical affairs than their counterparts on the other side of the Atlantic. (This is not to deny that British doctors are the most influential group shaping the policies of the NHS.)

The second characteristic that has shaped the structure of the medical delivery system is the commercial and business spirit of Americans. Throughout the history of the United States, foreign observers have been struck by the extent to which a large proportion of physicians have viewed their practice as a business enterprise and by the way the desire to accumulate wealth has influenced the medical profession. And therefore it should be no surprise that the profit motive is more important in shaping the contemporary structure of the medical delivery system in the United States than in any other advanced capitalist society.

In the nineteenth century, foreign observers noted that successful medical practitioners in the United States were those who made money, whereas in England and Wales they were those who had a close relationship with the upper class and aristocracy. The elite doctor of that period in Germany was the scientific investigator; in the United States, however, there was little prestige to be gained from scientific research, and even the doctor who could afford to engage in it found it necessary to accumulate money from practice as a means of gaining a good professional reputation. Compared with the practice of medicine in nineteenth-century Germany, or even in England and France, U.S. practice was very commercialized and narrowly practical—very much business oriented (Bonner 1963; Shryock 1947a).

The third characteristic that has historically differentiated U.S. medical delivery system from those in most European countries has been the lack of a sense of community. Because of the ethnic, racial, and religious differences that have chracterized much of their history, Americans have been less concerned with the well-being of their fellow citizens than have Europeans, who live in societies that are relatively homogeneous in ethnic, linguistic, and religious characteristics. The European countries that are relatively homogeneous tended to provide more hospital and medical assistance for the poor at an earlier date and to have had more governmentally financed medical services for all citizens than the United States. A society with as many ethnic and religious differences and as little working-class consciousness as U.S. society tends to deemphasize communal and maximize individual responsibility for medical needs. And in such a system, medical care tends to be consumed much more in the private than in the public sector. Under these conditions, prosperous ethnic leaders have been able to assist those who are less fortunate within their social group—and indeed this is what has occurred in the past. Because of the greater racial and ethnic heterogeneity in U.S. society, the voluntary sector became quite pervasive.

In general, the greater the homogenization of demand for medical services, the greater the likelihood that the public sector will respond and provide services that are relatively homogeneous throughout the society. But the greater the heterogeneity of demand, the greater the likelihood that medical services will be provided in either the for-profit or the nonprofit voluntary sector and that the services will be quite heterogeneous to various social classes and groups and across geographic regions. Hence, in the United States, a very large country with considerable ethnic and racial heterogeneity, it was difficult for consumers to mobilize political power in order to demand that the state provide medical services. As a result, the public sector did not develop on the same scale as in the more homogeneous societies of Scandinavia and England and Wales. Rather, ethnic and racial heterogeneity in the United States gave rise to a delivery system that developed in the private sector. As a consequence, in the early part of the twentieth century, various ethnic and religious groups were already establishing hospitals and dispensaries for serving the already ethnically fragmented society. And as medical technology became more complex and efficacious in the twentieth century, it tended to evolve largely in the decentralized for-profit and ethnically fragmented voluntary sectors (Hollingsworth and Hollingsworth, forthcoming).

Because the system in the United States would develop more in the private sector than those of most European countries, there would continue to be much greater variation in services across and within regions. And because consumers were more weakly organized than in most western countries, the U.S. medical profession was to be much more successful in determining the conditions under which medical services would be provided. And for this reason, the medical profession was to be relatively successful in attaining its policy preferences.

THE PRIVATE SECTOR

Early Medical Practice

The structure and culture of American society, which varied from area to area, placed real limits on the nature of medical practice in the late nineteenth century. While there was considerable diversity in the practice of medicine in England, there was much more in the United States. In England there were public health and Poor Law doctors who served one set of patients. General practitioners tended to provide nonhospital services to the working class and to work in cottage hospitals, while elite consultants tended to serve well-to-do patients and to work in prestigious hospitals. But there was no such neat set of institutions that differentiated U.S. practitioners from one another. Instead, the much more differentiated marketplace, which varied from place to place, gave rise to a more varied type of medical practice. Social and economic settings gave rise to very heterogeneous patterns of medical services.

Despite the egalitarian tendencies in U.S. medicine relative to that in Europe, there was a well-stratified system of medical practitioners in every large city. In every major metropolitan area, there was an elite group of physicians—just as in London—who attempted to separate themselves from the rank and file of the profession. As in London, a great deal of elitism tended to revolve around one or several of the city's best medical schools. In New York, for example, the elite practitioners generally held appointments at either the College of Physicians and Surgeons, the Medical College of New York University, or the Bellevue Hospital school. The more prestigious practitioners generally joined together in elite medical societies and held a sizable portion of the consulting and attending positions in New York's better hospitals and dispensaries. In most large cities, there were also large, less prestigious medical societies to which other doctors might belong (Stern 1945: 20; Billings 1876: 363–65; Rosenberg 1967; 1977a; 1979; 1982).

Competition was intense among practitioners in the late nineteenth century, and one way of coping with the competition in the cities was to develop a specialized practice. But specialization required several conditions. First, specialization is generally based on new discoveries, and often on the development of new instruments. And in the late nineteenth century, new discoveries were occurring with sufficient frequency to meet this condition. Specialization also required a sizable number of patients needing specialized knowledge, and for this reason, new specialties in the United States, as in England, tended to develop primarily in large urban areas.

Finally, specialization required specialized societies in order to facilitate the exchange of knowledge among practitioners. As the nineteenth century neared an end, more and more local specialty societies were created in large cities, and in many instances these tended to become the community's elite societies. Meantime, national specialty societies emerged, designed not only to advance and recognize specialized knowledge but also to restrict competition and enhance status.

Even though most American specialists in the late nineteenth century were largely self-trained, they succeeded in acquiring higher status and earning higher fees than general practitioners (Rosenberg 1967). But the status system was different from that in England, where the elite doctors were the consultants in London's teaching hospitals, who tended to be generalists and frown upon specialization.

Because the medical profession in the United States was much more commercially oriented than that in Britain or several other European societies, the incentives and tendencies for it to specialize were much stronger. This is not to suggest that the pursuit of commercial gain was the only consideration motivating doctors to specialize. In both England and the United States they did so because of the honor accorded to those who were learned and the intellectual satisfaction derived from mastering a complex body of knowledge. But the commercial spirit was much more pervasive in the United States.

While specialists tended to have shorter hours and conduct much of their practice in a private office, most late nineteenth-century private practitioners were engaged in family practice and tended to treat patients in their homes. And in the age before the telephone and automobile, the number of patients who could receive care in a given day was relatively small. A high proportion of doctors spent much of their time simply traveling from one patient to another. As a result of the time required, more doctors were needed to serve the population than would later be the case when transportation and communication improved (Starr 1982).

While "regular" practitioners in large cities tended to treat middle- and upper-class patients in their homes, the type of care that the urban poor received was very different. The poor in large cities received a crude form of what today might be called public medicine, but what in the late nineteenth century was known as medical charity. Most service of this type was provided by the private charity dispensaries, which were scattered in many parts of the cities. The most common type of dispensary had one young salaried resident physician. Most dispensaries had extraordinary demands made on them, often treating thousands of cases annually, though their budgets and staffs were small. With funds provided mostly by private charities, dispensaries provided an array of outpatient services, such as vaccination, extraction of teeth, and minor surgery. In certain respects, the dispensaries served the same function as the outpatient clinics of the large voluntary hospitals in English society. Socially conscious Americans helped to finance medical services that were designed for the "deserving poor": those who worked hard and attempted to support themselves, except when they were in bad health. As in England, the charity hospital and dispensary were not to be used by the morally depraved and the "undeserving." Rather, public almshouses in the United States, like the Poor Law workhouses in England, were to serve the prostitute, the drunkard, the lunatic—and even the chronically ill. Just as the elite physicians of London used their consulting hospital positions in order to broaden their experience and prestige, so elite physicians in the largest U.S. cities also acted as consultants to dispensaries in order to accumulate specialty experience, which in turn enhanced their prestige. And with the passage of time, a few medical schools established their own dispensaries or made special relationships with public hospitals as a means of providing clinical experience for medical students as well as faculty (Rosenberg 1967; 1974b; Vogel 1975: 124–25; M. Davis 1927; Davis and Warner 1918).

Whereas much of the working class in Britain was organized into friendly societies, which contracted with general practitioners to provide general nonhospital services on a capitation basis, there was very little that was comparable in the United States. As a result, working-class people had to make arrangements for themselves, either seeking out a practitioner in private practice and paying for each visit or gravitating to a dispensary.

Like the general practitioners of England, who insisted that free hospital outpatient clinics were not carefully administering a means test and were depriving them of fee-paying patients, many general practitioners in New York, Philadelphia, and other large cities protested that many patients who received medical services at free dispensaries were quite capable of paying private physician fees. Indeed, experience in both countries demonstrates that, when free services are supposed to be dispensed on the basis of a means test at the same time as most outpatient care is provided on a fee-paying basis, serious tensions will develop between those who manage the free clinics and their colleagues who practice on a fee-for-service basis on the outside.

In the small towns and rural parts of the United States, practitioner services were structured somewhat differently in that there were less specialization and fewer hospitals and dispensaries and that the doctors generally had less formal training. The Kansas surgeon Arthur E. Hertzler wrote that, when he was a young boy in Kansas during the latter part of the nineteenth century, "most of the doctors had never attended a medical school. Most of them had 'read medicine' with some active doctor but many just bought a book." In the Deep South and in parts of the trans-Mississippi West, many doctors owned and managed a "drugstore" as well as practicing medicine. Some doctors were manufacturers and distributors of patent medicines, while others were also teachers, editors, merchants, and postmasters. Because there were often few demands for the services of a doctor in small villages, it was there that many doctors had some occupation in addition to practicing medicine. In most hamlets, the citizenry believed that doctors were largely self-taught and were therefore little concerned with where the doctor had studied or received his training. A doctor was simply a person who practiced medicine, and as long as he brought people relief from suffering, no questions were asked about his educational background (Bonner 1959: 11; Hertzler 1938: 34; Wheeler 1933).

The country and village doctor of the late nineteenth century led a rugged and demanding life. Frequently on call—day or night—doctors often traveled great distances to visit a patient. "Strength, patience, good humor, and courage" were the characteristics of a successful country doctor (Bonner 1959: 15). Because the doctor had only a primitive technology with which to treat patients, his main concern was less with curing illness than with providing comfort for the patient and in relieving the mental suffering of a family. And because he often traveled great distances and had relatively few other patients competing for his time, the country doctor, once having arrived at a patient's home, often spent considerable time tending the patient (Bonner 1959; Hertzler 1938; Wheeler 1933).

Hospitals

Changes in hospitals in the late nineteenth and early twentieth centuries were shaped by two broad factors. First, the increasing urbanization, combined with the decline in the size of families, meant that many who were ill could no longer be adequately treated at home. And while some have taken the view that this led to an expansion of hospitals before there was any technological reason for the change, this is a bit of an exaggeration, for technological innovations and scientific advances such as anesthesia, antisepsis, and increasing anatomical and physiological knowledge were also factors of considerable importance in expanding the demand for more hospitals. By the turn of the century, the hospital in the United States, as in England, was becoming a more appropriate place for treating surgical patients than the home (Rosenberg 1977a; 1979; Rosner 1982; Starr 1982).

The unique characteristic of U.S. hospitals was the extent to which general service hospitals were concentrated in the private sector. Not only were voluntary hospitals far more numerous than public ones, but proprietary hospitals at the turn of the century were the most common type. Public provision of general services was distinctly in the minority.

Hospitals were a veritable patchwork of services and qualities, with virtually no integration or coordination. Although in some communities there were efforts by groups to find out whether a new hospital was needed, for the most part hospitals began and operated in relative isolation from one another (even if they were in physical proximity).

Finally, U.S. hospitals were very much reflections of the structure and culture of the community in which they were located. Ethnic hospitals functioned in ethnic enclaves. Catholic and Jewish hospitals were founded to serve religious preferences and motives. In communities too poor for voluntary groups to mobilize capital, proprietary hospitals supplied services, and in metropolitan areas, where the problems of poverty and population density were vast, public hospitals grew to immense size. Overall, diversity and variety are keys to thinking about medical services delivered in hospitals.

Meantime, hospitals were dissimilar from those in England and Wales in that there were fewer centers of excellence, in that the proprietary form of ownership and the ethnic-based hospital were commonplace, and in that most doctors serving in them were based outside the hospital in private practice.

Proprietary Hospitals

The quintessential proprietary hospital in the early twentieth century originated as a result of two forces: lack of local capital, and physician preference. The former refers to the difficulties many small communities had in locating capital sufficient to fund a hospital. Even though hospitals founded at the beginning of the twentieth century were small and inexpensive by today's standards, they required sufficient capital to provide a building with some specialized facilities and to fund a nursing staff. Often there simply was not enough local capital to meet even these modest requirements. In such situations, voluntary hospitals did not emerge to meet local health needs. Meantime, the concept of government responsibility for social services was ill developed, and urban governments supplied only minimal services, such as police, fire protection, and schools. In larger cities, there was some public responsibility for indigent hospital services, but this was less common in small towns and villages. Thus, for many smaller communities, if there were to be hospitals, they would have to be through arrangements that were highly privatized: they would have to be proprietary.

The second force leading to the early and prolific development in proprietary hospitals was physician preference. Doctors often preferred to group their more seriously ill patients in one location. A hospital built next-door to the doctor's office seemed to many physicians something that would permit more efficient practice as well as provide a genuine social service. Doctors, too, were more likely to recognize that communities needed a hospital and feel the absence of one in their professional lives.

For some doctors in larger cities, there was an additional pragmatic motive for founding and administering their own hospitals. They did not have hospital privileges at the existing hospitals, and thus, if they directed their patients to a hospital, they were in effect sending patients to another doctor. By founding their own hospital, they could be sure of keeping patients who required hospitalization, not losing them to another physician (Lynaugh 1982).

Often these two forces—lack of capital and physicians preference—were combined. It was the local doctor who most clearly perceived the need for a hospital and who came to see that, if he did not create one, no one else would. Communities through public action might support a school, but the demand for hospital care was so low that there was often a general unwillingness for public authorities to support a hospital, especially in newer communities.

Proprietary hospitals were seen by some commentators as developing in the time before a community realized its civic responsibilities and needs for providing acute care. The intense community poverty that prevented the emergence of hospitals sponsored by community groups was particularly notable in the southeastern United States and in rural areas in general. Much the same phenomenon occurred in the states of the Pacific, where newness was more of a factor than poverty. The proprietary hospital thus filled community, patient, and physician needs at low cost, developing in places in which there was neither enough capital nor perceived need for voluntary or government hospitals to originate. The proprietary form of hospital could be organized quickly and cheaply and thus fill a gap in the market in a flexible and responsive manner. That same flexibility and responsiveness permitted it to close if local supports became too meager.

There is very little evidence that proprietary hospitals were lucrative sources of income for their owners. No doubt some proprietors hoped to benefit substantially from their investments, but there is no firm evidence that such results ensued. Rather, one can argue that the considerable turnover among proprietary hospitals indicates a certain lack of financial success.

During the 1930s and 1940s proprietary hospitals were not very enduring. As with for-profit firms in general, the process of dissolution for proprietary hospitals was not very difficult or cumbersome. One simply closed the facility. There were no trustees to consult, no public authorities that had to approve. Because these hospitals tended to be small, there was not much pressure in most communities to keep them open in order to fulfill community responsibilities.

The proprietary hospitals were especially hard-pressed by the Depression of the 1930s. As thousands of Americans who had previously relied on proprietary hospitals for care were unable to pay their medical bills, hundreds of proprietary hospitals closed, though some were taken over by the voluntary and public sectors.

The decline in the number of proprietary hospitals was not continuous everywhere, however. After World War II new constellations of population developed rapidly in California, Texas, and Florida. As in earlier decades, new communities often lacked the social, economic, and political infrastructure necessary to create a voluntary or public hospital. Usually, however, there was some demand—even if modest—for some type of hospital to provide acute care. The newness of these areas meant that for-profit hospitals were quick to develop, confident that there would be enough paying patients to keep the facility open and to reward the investors.

Beginning in 1965, however, the policies of the federal government, through the Medicare and Medicaid programs, revitalized the proprietary hospital industry. During the 1970s the share of all general hospital beds that were for-profit began to increase rapidly, after having fallen for several successive decades. By 1983 there were more beds in the proprietary sector than ever before. While some observers have taken the view that the strength of the proprietary sector is due to the fact that for-profit organizations always enjoy more vitality than nonprofit ones—particularly government institutions—the proprietary hospital sector would probably have continued its long-term decline had it not been for the infusion of federal money into the sector. First. Medicare and Medicaid agreed to reimburse proprietary hospitals—like public and voluntary hospitals—for interest on debt service as well as for costs of depreciating plant and capital equipment. Second, Medicare reimbursement guaranteed for-profit hospitals a reasonable return on equity as part of the hospital cost base. Because public and voluntary hospitals did not receive a return on equity, Medicare provided proprietary hospitals with certain distinct advantages. While the return on net equity has varied over time, occasionally it has been as high as 20 percent.

Meantime, there were other incentives that had a positive effect on the financial affairs of proprietary hospitals. Whereas voluntary hospitals enjoyed incentives such as relief from corporate taxation, ability to receive tax-deductible gifts, and no obligation to distribute profits to shareholders, for-profit hospitals had other advantages. For example, various types of federal and state taxes were allowable costs under the Medicare program, and the advantages of tax-exempt nonprofit hospitals over for-profit hospitals were thus reduced. And while voluntary non-profit hospitals were able to float tax-exempt bonds, and thus to acquire higher bond ratings and pay lower rates of interest than they would otherwise, tax-exempt financing was also available under limited circumstances to investor-owned hospitals under the so-called small issue exemption. Investor-owned hospitals were also able to raise capital by issuing stock, a strategy unavailable to public and voluntary hospitals. Finally, lower taxes and milder regulatory climates in southern states were incentives to proprietary hospitals.

Voluntary Hospitals

The origins of the voluntary hospital have been well documented elsewhere in rich detail, so that it is necessary here only to indicate the bare outlines of the circumstances leading to the founding of the earliest ones (Rosenberg

1977a; 1979; Vogel 1980; Starr 1982). Briefly, voluntary hospitals were usually created by outstanding local leaders who believed that some facility should be provided for the "deserving poor" and for travelers who had no place of succor when ill (Rosner 1982). Doctors were often quite active in propelling the idea of establishing a hospital (Starr 1982). Sometimes founders had motives related to religious obligation, in that they saw the provision of a hospital as an expression of their service to a higher being.

The original concept of the voluntary hospital was that its services would be free to patients and that it would serve a public function in the sense of providing a needed service for those in the city who needed assistance (Vogel 1980). Although the hospital might serve public functions, it was firmly controlled by the private philanthropists who created it and whose control over resources endowed them with control over policy. Private sources provided the basic capital and made up almost the whole of the operating budget, since few patients paid for services. Medical staff was chosen by the private governors of the hospital, who also made the decisions about the kinds of cases suitable for admission. Patients who were contagious, vagrant, or morally suspect were not welcome in most voluntary hospitals. Nor were the mentally and chronically ill. Lay corporations and boards of trustees were in clear authority over the medical profession in typical early voluntary hospitals (Rosenberg 1979; Larrabee 1971: 107). The model of paternalism was strong (Starr 1982), carrying implications for patients, staff, and hospital sense of mission.

At the time the earliest voluntary hospitals were established in the United States, a hospital could offer little in the way of curative services. The risk of infection was great and the mortality from surgery so high that hospitals were used only as a last resort by patients. As in England, the middle classes, who could summon medical care to come to them, made virtually no use of hospitals. As was suggested above, however, conditions were changing by the late nineteenth century.

Social and economic conditions at the turn of the century gave rise to an incredible spurt of hospital construction and creation, manifest in the voluntary sector. Underlying this expansion was a massive influx of diverse immigrant groups into the United States, many of whom maintained a distinct social identity. They founded churches specific to their faiths, published newspapers in their own languages, and often founded hospitals and schools for themselves. The older the community, and the more established the immigrant group, the greater the chance that the ethnic or religious minority would have generated wealth that could be tapped to create institutions like hospitals.

Many voluntary hospitals were founded primarily to serve special groups and not, as the earliest hospitals had been, for the common good and the destitute. Ethnic-based hospitals, unlike early philanthropic ones, were often created by people who thought they might use them. Moreover, many streams of immigrants found that existing hospitals were cold and unfriendly places in which their native languages were not understood or spoken. Immigrant doctors were not recognized, and immigrant patients could not receive medical services from "their own people." Thus the increasing pluralism of the U.S. population led to the creation of large numbers of new voluntary hospitals to service special populations. In many instances, hospitals took the names of particular ethnic groups. There could be no question that the German hospital was mainly for German immigrants or that Dublin Hospital was for Irish ones. In hospitals orienting their care toward particular ethnic groups, it was more likely that immigrant doctors could have staff appointments and that immigrant patients would not be treated like outcasts because of their ethnic backgrounds or language preferences. Hospitals, often with only a few beds, were sited in ethnic enclaves, very accessible to the local population. Some religious and/or ethnic-based hospitals made it a firm policy that patients of all backgrounds would be admitted, while others made much less of a point about their general availability.

As vast numbers of voluntary hospitals were created in the early twentieth century, ethnicity was only one of several factors associated with the creation of new institutions. Religious pluralism sometimes led to the founding of hospitals. Indeed, the role of churches in administering hospitals was notable. By 1928, church-sponsored hospitals numbered 841, with over 100,000 beds. Although there were more independent nonprofit hospitals than church nonprofit ones, the latter provided more beds and had more capital investment.

In sum, voluntary hospitals in the early twentieth century came into being in response to the greatly increased perception of need, the heterogeneity of population, and the availability of capital. These forces led to the creation of hundreds of hospitals across the country. Obviously, arrangements varied enormously, given the diversity of communities and interests. In some communities, business and civic leaders recognized the desirability of having a local hospital and undertook a subscription campaign to purchase a building. In another variant of this model, city governments helped to create a nonprofit hospital board (on which the mayor served), and there was a general expectation that the new hospital would carry a mission of broad social responsibility. Not all areas of the country participated in this process, however. In the mountain and western states, population density was so low that there was a low demand for hospital care. Towns were too new and raw for civic consciousness to be strong.

The southeastern states were also extremely short of hospitals. The South, traditionally short of capital, was not very urbanized, and there were serious problems of locating hospitals so as to draw enough paying patients. As in the mountain and western states, patients had to travel great distances.

The reasons for the persistence of and increase in the voluntary sector are complex, of course. Perhaps the key factor has been the ability of voluntary hospitals to obtain new sources of income. Second, the voluntary hospital has redefined its target group. After 1900, the prototypical hospital deemphasized its provision of free care to the needy and began to appeal more directly to paying white-collar patients. David Rosner has suggested that as the proportion of the needy who were of white Anglo-Saxon stock declined, the philanthropists and hospitals lost interest in charity work. Immigrant poor were less appealing (1982).

Initially, voluntary hospitals were dependent upon philanthropy for their operating budgets as well as for capital, but philanthropy had obvious limits in terms of the number of patients it could and would support. Moreover, as patient care required more expensive technology, the impact of the philanthropic dollar changed (Rosner 1979). To put the issue more pointedly, the more complex the technology in hospitals, the higher the costs. Patients began using higher-cost services, recovering more quickly, and beng discharged, so that other patients could enter. This was in marked contrast with earlier times, in which patients tended to have long stays while bodies sought to heal themselves.

Voluntary hospitals, by the first decade of the twentieth century, were recognizing that their traditional role of serving the "deserving poor," with philanthropists paying the bill, was outmoded. Middle-class people, sensitive to the benefits of hospitalization, were turning to the hospitals in increasing numbers as the inadequacies of home care became more evident. To serve these needs, hospitals had to find new sources of income. The main source to which voluntary hospitals addressed themselves was the patient, who increasingly paid for at least part of the care received.

Although voluntary hospitals became increasingly dependent on patients for their revenues in the early part of the twentieth century, a few city governments nevertheless established the precedent of paying a per diem amount to voluntary hospitals for treating patients on a means tested basis. In other words, a precedent had been established upon which the society would build in the 1960s with the inauguration of the Medicaid program: state authorities would certify that certain classes of indigent patients were eligible to receive care and the state would reimburse the hospital.

Although the role of philanthropy in the voluntary hospital declined as the twentieth century progressed, for many years it remained substantial. Paul Starr (1982) has suggested that many nonprofit hospitals persisted because the ethnic and religious groups associated with their founding were disinclined toward merger. Such groups were concerned that the people they wanted to protect ("their clientele") would be disregarded unless their hospitals, often inefficiently small, continued to operate. Since hospitals were not expected to make money, there was no clear standard for deciding to close them. Having enough hospital beds was, for most of the twentieth century, a very compelling concern.

For doctors, the voluntary hospital tended to become an adjunct of their private practice. And as this occurred, the nineteenth-century tendency for doctors in large urban areas to provide services gratuitously for most of their hospital patients became a thing of the past. In contrast to Europe, where hospital based doctors tended more and more to be employees of hospitals, the American voluntary hospital became a free workshop for the doctor's private business.

Public Hospitals

Public hospitals for acute care in the United States, as in England and Wales, grew out of quite different circumstances from those that gave rise to voluntary hospitals and proprietary hospitals. Initially, public authorities in the United States created social service institutions with the idea of protecting society from those who were handicapped or dangerous. The mentally ill, it was reasoned, should be kept from becoming a nuisance to society. Likewise, the very poor, those who seemed perennially dependent and unable to care for themselves, were provided a minimal existence in almshouses provided by the state. The public purse might be opened, begrudgingly, to care for people at a very low standard if private systems could not be found or if the people posed some threat or embarrassment. But the pattern of provision was mean, and care had far less emphasis than custody.

Almshouses were administered by different authorities in various parts of the country—in New England by the towns and elsewhere, more often than not, by counties (Warner 1904: 100). Public authorities in the nineteenth century usually left to voluntary groups the provision of health services for the "deserving poor" (including ethnic and religious minorities). Acute care for the general population was to come from the private sector. But in the long run, city and county governments, with their almshouses, inevitably found themselves in the acute care area, albeit reluctantly. After all, in crowded almshouses, people fell ill, babies were born, and chronic diseases were commonplace. Almshouses found it necessary to appoint doctors and make some provision for nursing, however unenthusiastically these actions were undertaken.

In many early public institutions, there was often a lack of differentiation in the treatment facilities between those needing acute care and those with chronic or mental illness. Over time, as public institutions grew larger, it was deemed desirable to distinguish the acute from other cases. In large institutions, there were enough acute cases to merit a separate facility. And thus institutions that had not been intended for acute services began to provide them, but for the most part only to stigmatized classes. Public authorities were making no effort to run a general acute care facility; rather, what they offered was a minimal service facility for those who could not make their way into the normal societal institutions.

Almshouses might spawn hospitals and change their names, but the stigma of the almhouses remained after the cosmetic alterations. One after another of the metropolitan and urban areas of the United States reluctantly recognized their obligation to provide some health services for those who were not served by the voluntary sector. Of course, there was a kind of circularity in such provision. Once public authorities recognized an obligation to provide medical care for the destitute, voluntary hospitals felt even less obligation to admit them. If there were public facilities, voluntary hospitals were more free to engage in patient dumping, so that pressure for public hospitals to grow was continuous. New York City elaborated a network of hospitals for acute care—a network with units varying in size and function. The public hospital system included hospitals famous for teaching and research, on one hand, and those little better than custodial facilities on the other. Other cities chose a different solution—one huge municipal or county hospital, rather than a set of hospitals. In some cities, there were separate public hospitals for blacks—for example, the Kansas City Hospital, founded in 1930. Although conditions were very far from ideal, the founding of a public hospital did reveal some public sense of responsibility for citizens who had no access to voluntary hospitals.

In discussing public hospitals, it is necessary to be sensitive to their environmental setting. Large metropolitan areas tended to have large public hospitals that had the almshouse as their origin and public appropriations as their source of support. Over time, they began to collect modest sums from patients, but the expectation was that the tax base would underwrite the hospital budget. The clientele was limited primarily to the indigent, and only in emergencies were nonindigent patients admitted. Sometimes municipal statutes stipulated care to the indigent only, to exclude those who could pay from treatment in the public facilities.

The histories of large public hospitals are filled with stories of grotesquely crowded wards, of neglected patients waiting hours for care, of poor food and dirty linens. For example, in 1873, the Philadelphia Hospital had a capacity of 500 beds but had a thousand patients, and the stench of patients poorly cared for was almost unbearable. As late as 1914, many patients at Charity Hospital in New Orleans were kept two to a bed (Dowling 1982: 78).

Outside metropolitan areas, public hospitals were usually of a quite different stripe. They were created by local authorities with the expectation that patient fees would fund the services (McNerney 1962: 9). The responsibility of the public authority was to provide the capital for creating the hospital and to pay the costs for welfare patients who used the facility. But the paying patient, much as in the voluntary hospital, was the major source of the operating budget.

Public hospitals varied by region in the extent to which they were fundamentally for the indigent. For example, serving the poor was more common in the northeastern public hospitals, whereas those in the Southwest were much more involved with paying patients (Belknap and Steinle 1963: 35).

One might ideally classify public hospitals by the percentage of the patients who were indigent. By 1915, the larger the city, the more likely it was that there would be multiple hospitals, with voluntary ones for paying patients and public ones primarily for the indigent. In such circumstances, private hospitals often refused charity cases with the argument that there were special hospitals created for them, and such facilities should be used. In smaller communities, the public hospital might well be the only one, in which case it was likely to be overwhelmingly dependent on patient fees and open to everyone.

In public hospitals, especially those designated for the indigent, there was, as opposed to conditions in voluntary hospitals, more mixing of acute care patients with senile and chronic cases. Whereas voluntary hospitals sometimes had clear policies against admission of some kinds of ailments, restrictions were uncommon in public hospitals, as they were recognized as institutions of last resort. Thus the state was assuming responsibility for those for whom no private system, paying or voluntary, did.

Obtaining their mandate from public authorities and oriented toward the much less fortunate in society, public hospitals operated under constraints different from those affecting other kinds of hospital. Public hospitals lagged behind voluntary ones in their provision of specialized services, their standard of nursing, and the extent to which they implemented the prevailing technological standards of the day. Still, they should not be pictured as places of total neglect and incompetence. Such was not the case. Public hospitals, with their enormous intake of patients, were rich situations for teaching, and for this reason they were able to attract medical schools and doctors who wanted exposure to a wide array of cases. Although many public hospitals had no teaching affiliation, some became rich training grounds for doctors (Ludmerer 1986).

The world of public hospitals, then, was one in which several major and discrete types of institutions were found—a relatively small number of teaching hospitals, a small number of massive general hospitals reserved generally for the indigent, a number of hospitals in urban areas with profiles not clearly distinguishable from voluntary hospitals in those settings, and a very large number of smaller, rurally based hospitals.

In other words, the public hospital sector during the twentieth century has been very heterogeneous. While most attention has historically focused on the large urban public hospitals, which have provided a disproportionate amount of care to the poor, most public hospitals have not been located in the nation's largest cities, have been relatively small, have tended not to provide a disproportionate amount of care to the poor, and have served no teaching function. And yet, the explanation for the existence of the public hospital sector is very different from that for hospitals in the private sector. In general, public hospitals tended to emerge in areas where there were more homogeneous demands for collective goods. Where there was considerable consensus in communities about the role of a hospital, it tended to emerge in the public sector. Where there were minorities or heterogeneously demanded public goods, voluntary hospitals tended to emerge. Or, on occasions when minorities wanted a hospital but had insufficient capital to finance one, the public sector, with its coercive power to raise revenue, responded by providing a public one. But as the above discussion has suggested, the source and level of funding for public hospitals tended to place limits on their ability to fulfill their goals.

As was suggested in the previous chapter, working-class power, as mobilized through the Labour party, was a force of some importance in the nationalization of the British hospital system and the emergence of the NHS. And in the United States also, the social structure very much influenced the types of hospital that emerged. In the United States, however, the society's ethnic and religious diversity may have prevented the working class from mobilizing its power through friendly societies, powerful trade unions, or a working-class political party. However, the very existence of ethnic and racial diversity did give rise to a large number of ethnic and religious hospitals in the private sector. And over the longer term, this meant that, in contrast to the more centralized system of the NHS, the United States would have a plethora of redundant institutions that the decentralized and fragmented political system could not organize away. Thus, while various ethnic groups may not have been able to organize sufficient power in order to develop a national health insurance system for financing medical care, as happened in most European countries, they were influential enough to help maintain in many parts of the country an excess supply of hospitals, the long-term result being a very decentralized and fragmented hospital system—one that would be inequitable in terms of access to service, overly expensive, and inefficiently organized.

MEDICAL EDUCATION AND RESEARCH

The United States was in many respects a country that needed doctors before it had a satisfactory way of training them (A. Flexner 1910: 14). As it was relatively easy in the nineteenth century to become a practitioner of medicine, U.S. medical education and training were poor by the best standards of the day. Even though there was much interesting research designed to classify diseases and to understand their causes in nineteenth-century Europe, research and educational institutions were relatively undeveloped in the United States. But it was the primitiveness and low level of institutionalization of U.S. medical education during most of the nineteenth century that differentiated it from that in England and permitted it to change with great speed in the early twentieth century. Had U.S. medical schools and research centers been less pluralistic in nature and enjoyed more legitimacy by 1900, the forces of tradition and inertia would no doubt have made it much more difficult for the practice and structure of medical education to adjust so quickly to scientific and technological innovations that occurred in Europe during the latter part of the nineteenth century.

The Early Years

Throughout most of the nineteenth century, the United States lagged far behind the best centers in Europe in standards for the training of physicians. Most American medical students became doctors after being an apprentice to a practicing physician, called a preceptor. The preceptor furnished books and whatever equipment was required, and at the end of the apprenticeship, he provided the student with a certificate of instruction. The student, in the meantime, would read medical books, accompany the doctor on house calls, and render whatever assistance was requested.

Many states during the nineteenth century certified in some perfunctory manner that the instruction provided medical apprentices was satisfactory training for one to practice. As the number of applicants for appenticeships increased, however, doctors realized that it was more economical to train several people at the same time, and numerous medical schools came into existence. As only a few faculty members were required, most medical schools were relatively inexpensive to operate. Most had few if any laboratories; they were rarely affiliated with hospitals or universities; and their capital outlays were generally quite small. Most states made the diploma from a medical school the functional equivalent of a license to practice, and over time, the tendency was for the proportion of apprenticeships to decline and the number of students attending medical schools to increase.

Once most states had abolished formal licensing requirements, the number of medical schools proliferated, causing the competition among them to increase and their standards to deteriorate. Of course, the more medical students who attended a school, the more profitable it was for the faculty, as student fees went into a fund from which medical teachers drew their income.

In short, the education of doctors became a business. As well as student fees, an additional incentive for practitioners to open a school was the anticipated consultation fees that the professor would gain from his former students. The financial success of the proprietary schools varied greatly from school to school. Of course, many failed. So easy was it to start a medical school that there were more than 400 of them in the country at various times in the nineteenth century (Fleming 1954; Waite 1945; Rothstein 1972; Kaufman 1976; Norwood 1944).

Of course, some schools were much better than others, but from the vantage of hindsight, one is struck by the inadequacy of the best medical schools in the United States in comparison with the better centers for training in Britain. Among the best in the country in the late nineteenth century were those at the University of Pennsylvania, the Jefferson Medical College in Philadelphia, Harvard, Yale, the University of Michigan, and Columbia. And yet the training at each of these schools fell far short of the medical advances of the time (Shryock 1967: 43; Flexner and Flexner 1941; Fleming 1954; Kaufman 1976: 130; Eliot 1923: 28, 35; Burrow 1963; Ludmerer 1981; 1986). During the 1870s and 1880s, some of the better medical schools did succeed in making modest reforms. For example, ten introduced a three-year, graded curriculum during the 1870s. But the overwhelming majority were unwilling to raise their standards because of the intense competition for students (Rothstein 1972: 286).

During most of the nineteenth century, medical schools in the United States were very practically oriented, being little concerned with training students to become scientific investigators. Indeed, most provided very little clinical training. And unlike the British medical schools, even the best ones in the United States provided clinical instruction in hospitals that were unaffiliated with a medical school. And when hospitals were used for clinical purposes, the hospital management tended to give medical education a low priority. Even at the better medical schools, most of the instruction consisted of didactic lectures and demonstrations. In an era with so many medical schools, it was indeed difficult for the public to know whether a doctor's diploma was granted by a reputable school (Fleming 1954; Walker 1891; Kaufman 1976: 131; Rothstein 1972: 289–90; Bordley and Harvey 1976: 96; Atwater 1983; Ludmerer 1981; 1983; 1986).

Because medicine was so commercially oriented in the United States, many young people could easily leave a trade and enter a medical school, most of which had no entrance requirements. And when medicine proved uninteresting, many students then left medical school, causing the drop out rate among medical students to be relatively high (Walker 1891).

The German Model

Throughout the nineteenth century, Europeans were making impressive discoveries—especially in the sciences that provided the basis for the practice of medicine. But most of the European advances in the medical sciences during the first three quarters of the nineteenth century were relatively unknown in the United States (Bonner 1963: 12).

In 1882, however, when Robert Koch announced that he had isolated the bacillus of tuberculosis, many in the U.S. medical profession took notice, for in numerous parts of the country, tuberculosis was the leading cause of death. Increasingly, a number of American medical men wanted to become better informed about the scientific transformations that were occurring in Europe, as there was no center for advanced medical education in the United States. As Germany became the center for scientific medicine in the late nineteenth century, more than 15,000 Americans went there between 1870 and 1914 to study one or more of the medical sciences. In the history of U.S. medicine, few things are of greater importance than the traveling of this generation of Americans to Germany, especially during the 1870s and 1880s. What they found they attempted to bring back, and it was this response to European institutions and ideas that ultimately revolutionized science and clinical medicine in the United States. Specifically, it was a modification of the German model for organizing scientific research that fundamentally transformed U.S. scientific investigation in the late nineteenth and early twentieth centuries. Unlike science and medicine in England, scientific traditions in the United States were still relatively primitive, with low levels of institutionalization and legitimacy, and for this reason, scientific and medical institutions had much greater potential to be transformed than those in England and Wales (Bonner 1963).

The key to German scientific advances was the way in which science was organized. And it was the difference in the method of organizing scientific investigation that explains why English and French scientists were not the ones who led in the scientific advances of the nineteenth century. The French, like the English, tended to separate the medical clinic from the research laboratory. Moreover, French research institutes tended to be outside the universities, which were highly centralized and uncompetitive institutions existing primarily for instructional purposes. The university teacher was free to do research, but his status was determined by his teaching abilities. In short, the organization of the French university system placed severe constraints on the development of original contributions to knowledge and creative, original medical thinkers (Ben-David 1971; Flexner 1912; 1925).

For similar reasons, the organizational structure of English medicine could not keep pace with German medical advances. As was suggested earlier, English medical instruction was generally separated from the university. Most medical schools tended to be located in teaching hospitals, while most serious research was located in the universities. The clinical type of medical school that existed in both England and France had essentially a single goal: the training of students to be practicing physicians, not medical scientists.

In contrast, German medical instruction was centered on the university, but the German university devoted as much emphasis to research as teaching. Just as the leading German scientists had their institutes for research and teaching in the basic sciences, similarly the outstanding clinician was also a university professor, but his training was in scientific investigation. More often than not, his early training was in anatomy, chemistry, physiology, or pathology, and only later did he move to the clinical side of medicine. But ultimately in his career, there was no clear distinction between practicing, teaching, and research.

By the late nineteenth century, virtually every German university had a major medical center. They had independent, well-organized and well-financed laboratories headed by distinguished researchers in anatomy, bacteriology, physiology, and pathology. In addition, there were clinics, each with its own laboratory, in such fields as medicine, surgery, pediatrics, obstetrics and gynecology, dermatology, otology, and ophthalmology. To the Germans, it was very important that medical training and research be tightly integrated with the rest of the university. The clinics were organized to carry out three purposes: to treat patients, to teach students, and to conduct research. Being in close proximity to institutes for pathology and biochemistry, the clinician and students had enormous support facilities and were very interdisciplinary in orientation (Flexner 1912; 1925; Great Britain, University Education 1912).

A major reason for the excellence of German scientific investigation was its decentralized, competitive character. In France, where control over research funds and the university were highly centralized in ministries, it was frequently difficult to bring about innovations without the active participation of people in high levels of government. In Germany, however, the universities were relatively autonomous, and while they were creatures of the state within a federal system, the central government exercised virtually no control over the universities. Enormous rivalry and competition developed among institutes at various universities, and as a result, the scientific output was enormous (Ben-David 1971).

For those Americans who had never entered a well-equipped laboratory in their own country, the ability to work in some of the best-equipped laboratories and with some of the most distinguished medical scientists in the world was an exhilarating experience. It was all the more exciting during the last three decades of the nineteenth century as new and major scientific breakthroughs were occurring almost every year. The importance of this foreign experience for the young Americans is difficult to exaggerate. An entire generation of them was educated by German scholars in the fields of anatomy, bacteriology, biochemistry, physiology, pathology, and pharmacology, as these were the disciplines that German scientists had transformed during the later half of the nineteenth century.

For the Americans who returned from Europe—particularly those in the medical sciences—their ideal was to transfer as much of the German model of a university to the United States as possible. Specifically, they wished to duplicate the great laboratories, the dedication to research, and the stimulating teaching they had experienced in Germany. For an entire generation of leading American medical men, their German experience left an indelible mark. No other factor was of greater importance in explaining the remarkable progress of medicine in the United States in the next quarter-century than the effort of this generation to duplicate the spirit of German scientific investigation (Bonner 1963: 136; Ludmerer 1986; Fleming 1954; Kaufman 1976). Ultimately, it was the relative success of that effort that helps to explain why the United States by the middle of the twentieth century had become the world's center of scientific investigation.

And even if medical science made much less spectacular progress in developing cures for diseases than it did in identifying causes of them, many citizens began to believe that, if medical men were properly supported and trained, they would eventually be able to eliminate diseases. In the short run, however, many who wanted the society to benefit from the fruits of scientific medicine believed that fundamental changes would have to occur in the way that medical research and practice were organized in U.S. society. First, the medical schools would have to be restructured in order to facilitate original scientific research and to train medical practitioners who would have familiarity not only with scientific methods but also with the latest research in the basic medical sciences such as pathology, physiology, bacteriology, biochemistry, and pharmacology. Very much related to this was the second imperative, and that was to make certain that only those who had been trained in medical schools steeped in scientific medicine could be practitioners.

Without a fundamental change in the education of physicians, it would not have been possible to move the medical profession in the United States toward the medical engineering and scientific model that educational reformers had in mind. As late as 1900, fewer than 10 percent of the practicing physicians were graduates of a genuine medical school, since most had received their training through apprenticeship or in a proprietary school (Stevens 1971: 60).

The Johns Hopkins Model

Perhaps the most important single set of events in changing the medical school structure was the establishment of The Johns Hopkins Hospital and Medical School in 1893. The John Hopkins experiment was a radical innovation within the context of the United States, a new institution unencumbered by the traditional way of doing things. Unlike most U.S. and English medical schools, Hopkins was to be thoroughly integrated with both a teaching hospital and a university. It was to have small classes, excellent laboratories in the basic sciences, and clinical teaching in a hospital setting. And unlike those in London, the heads of the clinical departments were to be university professors.

Hopkins represented a basic departure from the tradition of U.S. medical schools in that previously most had relied on student fees for their operating budget. With its large endowment, Hopkins planned to recruit the highest-quality faculty available, build an excellent hospital, and equip modern laboratories. It deliberately set out to have a small medical school with the highest entrance standards in the country, requiring a bachelor's degree and a reading knowledge of French and German for admission. While most London and U.S. medical schools relied on local practitioners for their teaching staff, Hopkins took the revolutionary course of recruiting faculty from all of North America. Significantly, almost every senior member of the teaching faculty was thoroughly familiar with the German model of medical school.

The faculty that Hopkins assembled was eventually to be not only the most distinguished that a U.S. medical school had ever appointed but also more distinguished than any previous school in England. As Donald Fleming has written, the group "included the best pathologist, the best surgeon, the best clinician, the best gynecologist, the best anatomist, and the best pharmacologist, the best hospital administrator, and the second or third best physiologist in America" (1954: 102).

At Hopkins, the ideal was to instill in the medical student the habits of scientific investigation. The goal of its medical school was not merely to train medical practitioners but to produce medical scientists. Indeed, the Hopkins goal was to exalt the scientist over the practitioner, to make the ideal of scientific medicine the pursuit of each physician and surgeon. The laboratory and the hospital wards were to be integral parts of medical teaching. By integrating the laboratory with medical teaching, the bacteriological revolution would be brought in line with medical education.

Johns Hopkins also pioneered in developing postgraduate medical training. While the internship had previously been sparingly used in the United States, Hopkins introduced specialty training, whereby a sizeable number of interns competed for residency positions. Residents would remain for a number of years, working as medical house officers while they gained skills as researchers and/or medical teachers (Stevens 1971: 121; Turner 1974: 232). And this model has become the standard one for training specialists in medicine and surgery throughout the nation.

Although it is very important that Hopkins in its early years reflected the German model and German ideals, it is even more important in the history of U.S. medical education that Hopkins diffused this spirit throughout the society (Turner 1974: 233). By 1900, Hopkins had already made a reputation for training the best undergraduate medical students in the world. Even though the creative and original scientific research at Hopkins was still inferior to that in Germany, its method probably provided better instruction in both laboratory and clinical methods than that found in any German medical school. And the graduates of the Hopkins school were soon in great demand as teachers in the better schools throughout the United States. Within two decades after it had opened, more than sixty U.S. universities had three or more people who held medical degrees from Hopkins and who held rank of professor. At some of the better medical schools, Hopkins graduates were the heads of all major departments. Hopkins teachers and graduates founded new medical journals, societies, and specialties (Bonner 1963: 62; Turner 1974: 130, 226). As Kenneth Ludmerer had argued, by 1900 "it was American medical graduates without any European educational experience who assumed the leadership of medical education" (1986: 83).

One may of course exaggerate the uniqueness of all aspects of The Johns Hopkins Medical School. Somewhat independent of Hopkins, several other schools actively uplifted medical education. By 1910, a small number of medical schools were clearly moving in the direction of achieving the type of excellence for which Hopkins stood. As early as 1871, Harvard had established a modest laboratory of physiology modeled after Ludwig's in Leipzig. And by 1900, it was progressing in basic science research. Before the Johns Hopkins school opened, those at Pennsylvania and Michigan had also carried out major reforms (Ludmerer 1986: 47–61). Moreover, the University of Michigan and the University of Pennsylvania built university hospitals during the late nineteenth century. While the establishment of The Johns Hopkins Medical School was the clearest example of the impact of German medicine on U.S. medical education, a substantial portion of the medical school faculties of Harvard, Pennsylvania, and Michigan had also spent some time studying at a German university (Bordley and Harvey 1976: 22).

In part, it was the very weakness of medical education in the United States—its low standards and competitive aspects—that made the influence of the Hopkins model possible. The Hopkins experience, with its emphasis on extended scientific training, was clearly associated with specialization. Its products were elite researchers and practitioners who used technology to move the medical delivery system away from its traditions of generalist services and caring and toward acute/intensive specialties. The Hopkins model, however firmly tied to basic research, was relatively little concerned with problems of access to medical services for the masses. Rather, it was created and propagated by elite consumers and providers.

A Professional and Philanthropic Alliance

If the model of The Johns Hopkins Medical School diffused relatively rapidly across the country, it was not because the administrators of other schools simply observed the desirability of Hopkins and decided to adopt it as their model. Indeed, there were many impediments to change, and it was only as a result of the stick wielded by the American Medical Association (AMA) and the carrot offered by the large philanthropic foundations that rapid structural change in medical education occurred.

Of course, a number of medical educators—a minority to be sure—had for some time attempted to reform medical schools. Because most schools were unwilling to adopt common entrance or curriculum changes, however, it was not possible for the medical professors to reform schools from within. Rather, educational reform could only occur as the result of some outside force, such as the AMA.

The issue of educational reform, by promising to reduce the number of people entering the profession, attracted the support of the AMA and elite medical deans. At the turn of the century, the United States had substantially more doctors per capita than any other Western country. For example, the United States had one doctor for every 580 people, while Germany had proportionately only one-fourth as many doctors, or approximately one for every 2,000 people, and in England and Wales, there was one doctor for every 1,450 people. The competition among U.S. doctors caused many to fear that their standard of living would decline unless something was done to check the situation (Stevens 1971: 42–61; Markowitz and Rosner 1973; Burrow 1963; 1977).

John Shaw Billings, the president of the AMA in 1903 and one of the most influential medical men in the United States, spoke for many of his colleagues by indicating that the way to elevate standards and to reduce competition simultaneously was to close down the poorer proprietary schools. Significantly, the more vigorously the AMA pushed the logic of this argument, the more members it attracted.

In 1904, the AMA established a new and permanent council, the Council on Medical Education, charged with investigating the quality of education in existing medical schools and with raising educational standards. Implicit as well as explicit in the AMA's discussions of medical reform was a fundamental restructuring of medical education. Since most schools could not finance a quality system of education, the number would have to be reduced. The decrease, accomplished partly through the consolidation of smaller schools, would result in bigger medical schools with the potential to manage large hospitals and outpatient clinics. The efforts to implement these proposals would mean that medicine would become increasingly bureaucratized. All of this, of course, would represent a frontal assault on the small proprietary medical schools (Stevens 1971: 65; Markowitz and Rosner 1973: 93; Burrow 1963).

When the Council on Medical Education inspected 160 schools in 1906–1907, it found that almost one-half had a quality below acceptability. As the campaign against the small proprietary schools heated up, the number of schools and students began to drop and continued to do so for several years. In 1904, there were 166 medical schools in the United States, and the number had declined to 136 in 1910 (Burrow 1977: 41; Kaufman 1976: 163).

Another major agent for educational reform was the Flexner Report, financed by the Carnegie Foundation. The foundation arranged for Abraham Flexner (brother of Simon Flexner), who was a graduate of The Johns Hopkins Medical School and director of the Rockefeller Institute for Medical Research, to conduct a survey of medical education in the United States and Canada. In 1910, after investigating 155 medical schools and postgraduate institutions in the United States, Flexner reported his findings. The report singled out the small proprietary schools for especially strong criticism, describing them as "wretched," "dirty," "disorderly," "inadequate," "filthy," "foul," "overcrowded," and "hopeless." Flexner was particularly critical of the commercial spirit that pervaded many of the proprietary schools. He accused some of spending more money on advertising than on laboratories, of publishing catalogs filled with "exaggeration, misstatement, and half-truths" (Flexner 1910: 188, 205, 216, 256, 292).

Throughout the report, The Johns Hopkins Medical School was the ideal with which all other schools were compared. For Flexner, the key to Hopkins's success was that it had ample funds to finance a high-quality faculty, well-equipped laboratories, and a hospital to be used for medical instruction. He strongly urged the integration of medical schools into the mainstream of the university structure, and he advocated the linking of medical teaching, laboratories, faculty, and hospital facilities with universities. And to achieve this goal, he proposed the reduction of the 155 existing schools to 31 (Flexner 1910: 154). Flexner was little concerned about routine schools that would produce family doctors. Indeed, he seemed to hold general practitioners in low esteem. All medical schools should be dedicated to producing scientific and sophisticated clinicians. Flexner did not reflect on the long-run consequences of training medical scientists. He was little concerned with issues involving the delivery of medical services, as there seemed to be an abiding faith that if cures and preventions could be discovered, they would automatically diffuse throughout the population (Chapman 1974).

While the Flexner Report is clearly one of the most important documents in U.S. medical history, one may overstate its importance, for medical reform was well under way before its publication. The AMA Council on Medical Education and the American Association of Medical Colleges had already prepared the way for the Flexner Report, and a number of schools had closed prior to its publication. Others had already made substantial reforms (Ludmerer 1986: 81). But the effect of the report was electrifying, and more than any other single event, its publication focused popular attention on the inadequacies of medical education in the United States. Many proprietary schools lost all semblance of legitimacy and closed, and some merged with others. Between 1904 and 1920, the number of medical schools declined from 166 to 85, and as the number declined, entrance requirements rose. Medical schools became more closely tied to universities and began to have better access to hospitals for teaching and research purposes.

Much of the thrust for change in medical education was financed by subsidies from philanthropic foundations. Had the Flexner Report been issued sixty years prior to the breakthroughs in European medical science or prior to the acquisition of great fortunes in the United States in the late nineteenth century, the change in the structure of U.S. medicine would probably have been less dramatic. But the timing of the breakthroughs in modern medicine, combined with the development of a number of great fortunes, produced a revolution in the structure of medicine. In short, technological change combined with a fundamental change in the social structure produced dramatic changes in the nation's medical delivery system.

To understand the changes in the structure of the delivery of medicine in the United States during these years, it is important to consider the thinking of the economic elite about medical technology. Scientific medicine captured the imagination of the nation's economic elite in the late nineteenth century. Throughout their history, Americans have been in search of a new and better world, and now scientific medicine held out the promise not only to prevent but also to cure disease. If scientific medicine could improve the health of the society's work force, perhaps it could also help to increase the nation's economic efficiency and productivity. In short, scientific medicine was viewed as the key to alleviating misery, improving welfare, and bringing about economic progress. Fredrick T. Gates, the manager of John D. Rockefeller's philanthropic enterprises, reflected the thinking of many of the nation's new elite when he wrote that "disease is the supreme ill of human life and it is the main source of almost all other human ills: poverty, crime, ignorance, vice, inefficiency." He went on to explain that these ills could not be cured by economic readjustments, as many socialists believed. Rather, society's problems were technical in nature and required technological solutions, which medical science could provide (Berliner 1977: 107; 1986). Thus scientific medicine cemented the political alliance between the elite of the medical scientific community and the corporate class in the United States.

For Rockefeller and Carnegie, as well as many of their associates, science and medicine acquired religious dimensions. For them, scientific medicine was an instrument for building a new and better world, for uplifting and civilizing one's fellow man. Research institutes and medical schools were to become the functional equivalent of temples for the new religion, while medical investigators were to become the religious priests who could reduce human misery and poverty.

While the advocates of medical science argued that The Johns Hopkins Medical School was the model that should be duplicated, it was expensive to provide well-equipped laboratories and to fund high-quality medical teachers. The type of capital required to finance a modern medical school with all of its supporting apparatus according to the Johns Hopkins model was beyond the means of local charities and the medical profession. And the pressures were not yet operating on the state—whether it be local, state, or national government—to construct and operate the new temples of medical science. A new national wealthy class of people had emerged in the late nineteenth century, and it was to this class that the new medical men looked for financing.

The philanthropic funding of medical science proceeded on several fronts, the two most important being the development of medical research institutes and the upgrading of selected medical schools. Though there had been a number of world famous medical research institutes in Europe in the late nineteenth century (e.g., the Pasteur Institute in Paris, Ludwig's physiological institute in Leipzig, Koch's institute in Berlin), there was nothing comparable in the United States. To fill this void, John D. Rockefeller established in 1901 a new type of research institute, the Rockefeller Institute for Medical Research. The institute became a famous example of what private philanthropy could do in the area of medical research. Whereas most European institutes had a rather narrow focus—usually concentrating on one academic discipline—the Rockefeller Institute from the outset was committed to fighting a broad range of diseases, seeking in the process an understanding of their causes and treatment. Another goal of the institute was to train hundreds of medical researchers. Whereas the European institutes were usually dominated by the research of a single individual, the Rockefeller Institute reflected the disinclination in the United States to build research around a single individual and the preference to support the research of hundreds of leading researchers. Moreover, the institute was primarily for research, with its staff to be free of teaching and private practice (Corner 1964; Kohler 1976). Rockefeller had hoped that the model of the Rockefeller Institute would catch on in the United States and that other philanthropists would also endow research on the medical sciences. Medical research, he hoped, would help the practitioners of medicine to realize the dignity and importance of their profession. Rockefeller was not disappointed, for across the country other wealthy families began to endow major medical research centers (Karl and Katz 1981; Ludmerer 1986: 197–98).

The Rockefeller philanthropic interests did not wish to support local hospitals and charities in the traditional sense. Their intent was to support medical research, which would eventually diffuse to all local centers. In Gates's mind, the more physicians engaged in private practice, the less rapid the advance on the scientific front (Berliner 1977: 192; Rockefeller Foundation, box 4, folder 79).

Increasingly, the wealthy, like all Americans, were fascinated by the potential wonders of scientific medicine. Whereas the economic notables of an earlier age had been captivated by religion and had built churches, cathedrals, and monasteries, notables in the United States endowed foundations that built hospitals, medical centers, and laboratories that functioned as modern religious temples. In the nineteenth century, a wealthy person often contributed money to a well-endowed church for a window in memory of a loved one, whereas in the twentieth century, wealthy Americans gave money to medical schools to memorialize a relative. Often a gift was directed to support research on a particular disease as a result of a family tragedy (Turner 1974: 95).

In 1890, the financial conditions of the nation's better medical schools had been dismally poor. Whereas the nation's better theological schools were moderately well endowed, all of its medical schools combined had a total endowment of only $500,000. After 1900, the establishment of separate foundations that generously contributed to selected schools changed the nature of medical education. Between 1900 and 1934, nine foundations alone granted approximately $150 million to various medical schools (Stevens 1971: 56). And it was the Rockefeller-sponsored foundations that led the way. For example, Rockefeller had secured the incorporation by Congress in 1903 of the General Education Board, which, by 1929, had appropriated more than $78 million for medical education (Brown 1979: 155; Shryock 1947b: 95).

It was the Johns Hopkins model of research-oriented clinicians, with the assistance of Rockefeller money, that diffused throughout many of the U.S. medical schools. As more and more distinguished clinical teachers in the nation's schools devoted all of their time to teaching and research, they instilled in their students the ideals of medical investigation and specialization. The ideology of scientific medicine was rapidly diffused throughout society. By the 1920s, state governments were spending large sums of money on the equipping of state medical schools. If the United States by 1970 had a higher percentage of its medical profession practicing in a medical specialty than any other country, part of the explanation must be traced to the fact that, as a result of the Hopkins model combined with Rockefeller money, medical students became increasingly socialized into a profession that was oriented to intense specialization, complemented by scientific investigation.

By 1920, medical education had been greatly reorganized. The AMA Council on Medical Education—which for some years had been grading the quality of medical schools—was able to grade most schools in class A by 1930. And by 1933, the number of medical schools had declined to sixty-six, one hundred fewer than there had been thirty years earlier (Shryock 1947b: 120–21). As medical schools adopted the scientific medical model, the variation in their quality narrowed considerably. The Hopkins ideal of the medical school as as integral part of a university was largely realized by 1930. Moreover, most medical schools had become integrated with a teaching hospital. Throughout the country—but particularly in urban areas— medical schools took over the management of local hospitals. Often this was facilitated by foundation money or funds provided by a local benefactor who was interested in uplifting both medical care and the quality of medical instruction (Markowitz and Rosner 1973: 103; Ludmerer 1986: 219–27; *Journal of the American Medical Association* 62 [Apr. 25, 1914]: 1335; [June 6, 1914]: 1816; [June 13, 1914]: 1898).

The reforms in medical education also had several other long-term consequences. For example, medical education in the United States adopted a distinctly class bias. Prior to 1900, the commercialized type medical schools were open to virtually all comers, meaning that blacks, the poor, and the working class were able to study medicine. But one of the goals of some of the education reforms was to give the medical profession a new image. In short, medical reformers wanted to create a profession that was high in social status and respectability. In an effort to upgrade standards, black schools were among the first to be closed. At the turn of the century, there were eight schools that trained predominantly black physicians, but by 1923 all but two (Howard University Medical School and Meharry

Medical College) were closed. By the end of World War II, it was rare for a black to attend any of the nation's better medical schools (Turner 1974: 509).

Discussing the class bias of U.S. medical schools, Rosemary Stevens has written, "The poor boy began to find it more difficult to enter medicine as costs rose, the curriculum lengthened, and the night schools disappeared" (Stevens 1971: 71). Moreover, the percentage of women graduates from medical schools also declined. But the "nonregular" schools were particularly hard hit. The number of homeopathic, eclectic, and physiomedical schools and students declined dramatically after 1900. And by 1920, most of the "nonregular" schools had simply been wiped out (Markowitz and Rosner 1973: 96–97).

Medicine in the United States, in less than one-third of a century, had undergone a revolution that demonstrated that, under the proper structural conditions medical knowledge would quickly diffuse across national boundaries. By 1930, some of the better U.S. schools were viewed by many medical leaders in Europe as equal to the best anywhere. And in some medical specialties, the U.S. centers were considered to be even superior.

Had the system been highly centralized, with the key decisions about such matters as standards and financing made in a government ministry in Washington, the revolution in medical education would probably not have occurred. The decentralized and fragmented system, with the availability of philanthropic money, permitted the Johns Hopkins model of excellence to emerge. And it was the decentralized, competitive nature of the system, backed by capital from some of the world's wealthiest families, that permitted the model to diffuse to many other centers of learning.

Even though the medical profession was committed to good medical care for the public, it was in the final analysis the profession's concern about financial security that made the reforms so attractive to medical practitioners and the AMA. Because of the widespread competition within the medical profession, it wanted to close down many medical schools and to raise academic standards as a means of reducing the number of practicing physicians—the net effect of which would raise the income of doctors.

By supporting a microcausal scientific approach to medicine, foundations in the United States failed to give much attention to important historical trends in European medicine, which emphasized the social context of medicine. The micro approach deemphasized the relationship between the individual and the environment and focused instead on the cause-effect relationship between germs and disease (Rosen 1972: 45). From a theoretical point of view, medicine was simplified without being sidetracked by social and environmental concerns.

And yet, during the latter part of the nineteenth century, there was a very active and legitimate European field of social medicine led by some of the

best scientific minds of the nineteenth century. For example, Rudolf Virchow, one of the leading medical scientists of modern times, was very much
in the forefront of social medicine, being especially concerned with the way
that nutrition, poverty, occupation, and housing influenced the level of
health. Partly for these reasons, medicine, for Virchow, was "a social
science, and politics nothing but medicine on a grand scale." Elaborating
his views in a series of articles, he and dozens of prominent nineteenth-
century scientists argued that disease was the result of oppressive power
relations in society, and in order to fight disease, it was necessary to alter the
existing social structure (Virchow 1849: 48; 1848: 21–22; Rosen 1972: 37).

   At the turn of the century, research and education in the United States
were weak in all fields of medicine. And firm financial support could have
established strong centers for education and research which emphasized
caring and curative approaches to medicine, or centers that emphasized
social and environmental medicine, or all three. To a considerable extent,
the decision was made by an alliance of wealthy laymen and medical educators, who stressed the strategy of curative medicine. By funding medical
schools and research that emphasized an individual or micro approach to
health, a group of economic elites were of critical importance in causing the
United States to deemphasize the social and environmental side of health
(Rosen 1965). As a result, the scientific revolution in medical education and
research tended to focus on the prevention of infectious disease and on
treatment for people who had already contracted disease. However, the
research strategies of the new medical science tended to mask the social and
occupational nature and origin of disease (Berliner 1977: 120; Brown 1979;
Navarro 1976a; 1976b; 1980). Because the nation's corporate elite were
greatly involved in a variety of activities dealing with the social and environmental impact on health, perhaps it is understandable that they and
their foundations chose not to provide substantial support for the advancement of social and environmental medicine.*

Medical Ethics

While changes in medical education were extremely important in limiting
the size of the U.S. medical profession, medical practitioners also pursued
other strategies that limited entrance into the profession and placed constraints on the conduct of physicians. Entry into the profession was very

---

* This discussion focuses on the reasons why a particular style of medical services emerged in
  the United States and does not imply that, when other countries adopted similar practices,
  they had identical social processes. However, the kinds of practice that did emerge in most
  Western countries were consistent with capitalist ideology and the interests of the capitalist
  class—both of which were dominant in North America and Western Europe.

effectively restricted by the passage of medical licensing legislation by all states between 1870 and 1920. During much of the nineteenth century, many states had been unwilling to place severe restrictions on the right of an individual to practice. But the scientific breakthroughs in modern medicine in the late nineteenth century caused the society to be willing to restrict the practice of medicine to those who could demonstrate that they had been properly trained. Some of the long-range consequences of these changes were to increase the cohesiveness and relative power of doctors.

Observing that the United States had more doctors per capita than any other Western nation, some medical practitioners demanded that drastic action be taken to restrict the number of doctors. Many practitioners were in even more serious financial trouble than the contract doctors in England and Wales prior to the introduction of NHI. Many doctors could only practice part-time and had to support themselves with other occupations. Many simply turned to other occupations within five years after leaving medical school. One New York medical journal observed in 1889 that "fully two-thirds of the physicians in New York City were living in a life of dignified starvation" (quoted in Shryock 1947a: 116). And many who remained in the profession were frequently unable to collect their fees (Markowitz and Rosner 1973: 89). In short, economic considerations provided the incentive among doctors to demand a smaller profession, and scientific breakthroughs in the late nineteenth century provided the opportunity to convince the public that the time had arrived to restrict the practice of medicine to those who were "properly trained."

In this climate, state legislatures, beginning in the 1870s, established medical licensing examination boards, and by 1898, all states had licensing boards dominated by state medical societies. Once the legitimacy of a medical license was established as a prerequisite for the practice of medicine, "regular" physicians began almost immediately to lobby for more stringent requirements, ones that would eliminate the "nonregular" physicians from practice. Between 1900 and 1907, 30 states responded by enacting new medical practice legislation, enabling regular physicians to establish eventual dominance over the nonregular physicians (primarily homeopaths and chiropractors). As a result, the regular medical profession was eventually able to bring about a substantial reduction in the number of nonregular practicing physicians and the decline of medical pluralism in America. Education reforms, combined with new strict licensing practice, were important in reducing the number of doctors in the country from 172 per 100,000 population in 1900 to 132 in 1930. In sum, the regular practitioners in the medical profession had succeeded by 1910 in establishing a monopoly over the practice of medicine. Whereas no more than 10 percent of practicing physicians were graduates of a medical school in 1900, by 1920, virtually all newly licensed physicians were graduates of a medical school (Berlant

1975: 55, 234–35; Kaufman 1976: 146; Rothstein 1972: 89–91; Brown 1979: 89–91).

The role of public authorities in shaping the provision of medical services was through limited state regulation and did not imply the emergence of a more centralized medical delivery system. Rather, it was an example of how private, prestigious networks were able to use the state in order to further their ends.

The desire to establish monopoly power over the practice of their profession was not unique to physicians. Indeed, there are certain sociological principles inherent in the monopolization of professional power—and these principles are very evident in the twentieth-century history of the medical profession in the United States. Most professionals, like American physicians, attempt to achieve professional homogenization and to drive out competitors by upgrading educational standards and setting high standards for licensing. Similarly, professions tend to turn to the state to drive competitors from the marketplace and to grant the profession preferential or monopolistic privileges (Larson 1977). If successful, the profession enhances its per capita income. And this is what happened with the medical profession. Whereas a sizable proportion of doctors had been unable to support themselves in 1900, the medical profession by 1930 received more income per practitioner than any other profession (Friedman and Kuznets 1945).

If the state grants a profession special monopolistic powers over services, the society tends to legitimate that type of monopoly power only if professional conduct is perceived as ethical and deserving of trust. For this reason, the medical profession in the United States, at the time when it was obtaining monopolistic power from the state, found it necessary to implement codes of ethics to which its practitioners were expected to adhere. In other words, medical ethics have been used to enhance restrictive and monopolistic practices by physicians (Larson 1977).

Medical ethics are necessary to subordinate the private interests of the individual practitioner to those of the entire medical profession, generate professional solidarity, and develop and maintain public trust in the profession. A system of medical ethics is, of course, not unique to the U.S. medical profession. Its ethics have a long history and were transmitted in revised form from the traditions of the medical profession in Europe and Britain, but medical ethics in the United States have been reshaped to conditions that are unique to the society (Berlant 1975: 66, 81–82, 126–27).

The medical profession in England and Wales has historically had sharp cleavages between general practitioners, who have generally been excluded from hospitals, on the one hand, and the hospital-based practitioner on the other. In that type of system, medical ethics have tended to reinforce the existing hierarchies within the profession. It has long been understood that the general practitioner should refer complicated cases to consultants, and medical ethics have elaborately defined the relationships between the two types of practitioner.

In the United States, the medical profession has long been much more egalitarian, and medical ethics have played an important role in governing the relationship among practitioners. Lacking the sharp divisions that exist in England, general practitioners in the United States have been permitted to treat complicated illnesses for which they have not necessarily been trained. Indeed, in the early 1970s almost one-half of the surgery performed in the United States was done by doctors who were not certified by one of the medical specialty boards. Since medical ethics constrain American practitioners from criticizing the work of a colleague, medical ethics have permitted a more frequent practice of poor-quality medicine than in the system in England and Wales. Because medical ethics in both systems constrain doctors from weeding out incompetent practitioners, the system with the more frequent complaints (i.e., the U.S. system) has turned to the legal system to regulate the practice of medicine, and this is one reason why there have been many more legal malpractice suits per capita in the United States than in England and Wales.

Because some of the main functions of a profession's ethical system are to inspire public trust in the profession and to legitimate its monopolistic domination of the marketplace, the profession must focus a great deal of delicate attention on the subject of professional fees. Even though a consequence of monopolistic power is to raise the income of practitioners (Friedman and Kuznets 1945), the U.S. medical profession in the twentieth century has attempted to avoid the appearance of being commercially oriented and greedy, thinking that this would create public distrust. To avoid the appearance of commercialism, the profession has attempted to exercise strict prohibitions against advertising and competitive price setting. Of course, the avoidance of competitive price setting is consistent with monopolistic behavior (Feinbaum 1970; Derbyshire 1969; Berlant 1975: 79).

Throughout the twentieth century, the U.S. medical profession has insisted that physicians have an obligation to charge an "honest price" for their services. The profession has developed rules for determining fair prices, and of course, the rules that have been adopted changed according to historical circumstances. The rules have tended to vary between one extreme, at which the fee is determined on a sliding scale (the patient is billed according to capacity to pay) and the other, at which the physician has a uniform fee for everyone (i.e., the prevailing rate). Whether the profession tends toward one or the other extreme of this dimension is influenced primarily by the state of the market. When the profession has operated in an oversupply market—similar to that at the turn of the century—it has tended to resort to a sliding-scale fee. This fee was designed to accommodate everyone. In such a market, it was more profitable for the physician to charge whatever a patient could afford to pay than to turn away those who could not pay a fixed fee (Berlant 1975: 74, 101). However, the physician was justified in treating charity cases without a fee, for the wealthy made this possible by the high fees they paid. It was with these general principles in mind that the great Johns Hopkins surgeon William Halsted in 1903 charged a wealthy patient $10,000 (1903 prices) for an appendectomy and that his colleague Howard Kelly, at about the same time, asked a $20,000 fee for a major operation (*Medical News* 83 [Oct. 3, 1903]: 661; Konold 1962: 58).

Many doctors believed that it was unethical to undercharge or to demand less than a patient could afford to pay. The profession in many communities established minimum fees for services, but where this occurred, the ethical code permitted a physician to charge a fee above the going rate. By this conduct, one risked pricing oneself out of the medical market, which was permissible conduct. But if one undercharged, one was engaging in unethical or unfair competition with one's colleagues (Berlant 1975: 101).

Many nineteenth-century physicians—especially those in large cities—donated much of their time in charity clinics. Nevertheless, many physicians, in the United States as well as in England and Wales, became very upset during the first two decades of the twentieth century when they believed that numerous patients who could afford to pay for medical service were presenting themselves at charity clinics for free care. In this context, leaders of the AMA and the BMA denounced indiscriminate charity treatment as being unethical (Berlant 1975: 62; Gould 1894: 547–48; Honigsbaum 1979).

Years later, when there was more of an undersupply of doctors than existed in 1900, the U.S. medical profession increasingly moved to the other end of the pay continuum: a uniform fee for all patients. Whereas the practitioners attempt to maximize the number of patients in an oversupply market by resorting to a sliding scale, the undersupply market is one in which there is an abundance of patients. Of course, there were still charity patients, but in this market, the profession advocated a strict means test in order to prevent those who could pay for services from receiving free care.

Both the sliding-scale and uniform fee were consistent with the monopolistic behavior tendencies of the profession in that each attempted to restrict price competition among practitioners. At later dates, the profession would confront a variety of institutional mechanisms that challenged the profession's monopolistic control over fees: among them prepaid medical care plans, commercial health insurance, and state regulation.

Medical ethics, especially as they involved fee setting, provided mechanisms uniting the profession additional to those derived from control of medical education and state-level licensing.

TRENDS TOWARD SPECIALIZATION

Specialization issues became even more salient as a result of the increased frequency of surgery in the early part of the twentieth century. The issues revolving around specialization were intricately tied up with the fragmented hospital system in the United States. The plethora of hospitals, the different patterns of ownership and clientele, and the open-staff tradition—whereby hospitals provided access to all doctors who believed themselves competent to perform surgery—necessitated some system for measuring physician qualifications. It is not surprising that the Americans adopted the solution of having a very high percentage of doctors as specialists. Of course, the method whereby specialists were to be trained reflected basic tendencies in medicine. Thus, first, specialists were trained in a great variety of institutional settings but without a highly standardized training program. Second, private bodies (i.e., specialty boards) held the ultimate authority for certification. Third, the specialty training process facilitated the commercial aspect of medicine, for the doctors providing the training did not have to limit their practice to hospitals as long as doctors in training were there to take care of patients. Senior doctors could spend most of their time seeing patients elsewhere and make hospital visits of only limited duration. Finally, without central government intervention, there was little planning or rationalization about specialization. The dynamics of specialization were simply let loose, subject only very generally to market and institutional constraints.

As surgery increasingly took place in the hospital, issues involving hospital privileges thrust specialization before the profession as a subject of considerable controversy (Stevens 1971: 145; M. Davis 1927: 5–9). The existence of an egalitarian spirit among American physicians and the lack of a national health insurance system tended to mean that most medical practitioners thought that no doctor should be excluded from hospital practice. Whereas in England and Wales, the general practitioner developed the practice of referring patients to specialists in the hospital, the American general practitioner—while occasionally referring a patient to a doctor with more specialized skills—tended to retain control of his patient both in and out of the hospital. To refer a patient to another doctor meant to most American practitioners an admission of incompetence. And while some U.S. hospitals (mostly teaching hospitals) developed a closed-staff system similar to that in England and Wales, a large percentage by 1920 were organized on an open-staff principle. The vast majority of American medical practitioners believed that hospitals with a closed-staff system were monopolistic and unfair. Since many hospitals did not have the closed-staff system, a continuing problem in the history of medicine in the United States has been how to develop institutional mechanisms so that the most competent practitioners could be identified (Stevens 1971: 83).

Because of the egalitarian tradition and rhetoric of the profession, dissension resulted when those with more specialized skills wanted special recognition and privileges. This issue became intense in the first part of the twentieth century as surgery seemed to be expanding in all directions. Specialties developed, for example, in neurosurgery, urological surgery, and orthopedic surgery. The general practitioner—long accustomed to doing surgery—remained free to operate. But as surgical subspecialties emerged, better-trained surgeons believed that there should be an organization that would make a distinction between those who were good surgeons and those who were not. The American College of Surgeons was established in 1912, in response to this line of thinking, and, by U.S. standards, it established rather strict prerequisites for membership, which included a one-year internship following a four-year medical school, three years' training as a surgical apprentice, fifty case abstracts, and visits to surgical clinics—though at the outset, several hundred of the nation's leading surgeons simply had membership conferred upon them. Significantly, no formal examination was required for membership. The founding of the American College of Surgeons represented an effort of one group of providers to convey information to consumers and hospitals about the product being consumed, while the rest of the providers had a vested interest in suppressing information about product quality. As Rosemary Stevens has reminded us, the American College of Surgeons, by trying to uplift the practice of surgery and eliminate the poor surgeons, was doing little more than the entire AMA had done several years earlier when it attempted to eliminate weak medical schools. Medical school reform had then appealed to most of the profession, for it restricted access to the profession and thus reduced competition (Stevens 1971: 93, 125).

While there was substance to the charge that the American College of Surgeons was elitist, it was fundamentally different from the type of elitism that characterized the British royal colleges of surgeons and physicians. The American College of Surgeons was basically a compromise with the egalitarian spirit that had historically pervaded the U.S. medical profession. Its purpose was not to exclude all but the very best but to raise minimum standards for surgical practice. The establishment of the American College of Surgeons was important in the history of medicine in the United States because it established the precedent that professional qualifications for medical specialization would be controlled in the private sector by the profession and not the state.

Shortly afterward, a group of internists, who considered themselves to be specialists, wanted a separate identity and thus adopted the model of the American College of Surgeons by establishing in 1915 the American College of Physicians. Like the former, the latter did not require examination for admittance. It was more of a specialist society in internal medicine than an organization that had quasi-licensing functions. Partly because pediatricians, neurologists, psychiatrists, and other nonsurgical specialists also had their professional associations, the American College of Physicians did not attract all types of nonsurgical specialists on the same scale as the Royal College of Physicians in Britain.

The two U.S. colleges emerged from the developing complexity of medical technology and represented the tendency of those who had specialized training to differentiate themselves from the rest of the profession. These colleges were created at the time when the medical establishment was facing the problems of where education after undergraduate medical training should take place and what group, by what procedure, should certify that a practitioner had been properly trained and had met specified standards of excellence.

Over time, the U.S. medical profession has tended to handle the problems of medical training in a sequential fashion, focusing first on undergraduate training, next on the internship, and finally on postgraduate specialist training. Basically, the internship was an extension of undergraduate education, but ironically the medical schools failed to supervise it. Numerous hospitals—both teaching and nonteaching—provided an internship program. The interns provided valuable service within the hospitals, administering anesthetics, conducting routine laboratory tests, and assisting the attending staff in numerous ways. Even though the AMA Council on Medical Education prepared lists of approved training hospitals, the quality of internships varied greatly from hospital to hospital. And the decentralized, understandardized type of internship program, relatively unregulated by any national organization, became very important in establishing a precedent for postgraduate *specialist* medical training (Stevens 1978). By the late 1920s, at least 95 percent of medical school graduates were taking an internship. But it was the medical profession and the hospitals, not the universities, that had taken control of the internship, and the precedent was to carry over to postgraduate training.

As medical technology became increasingly complex throughout the Western world, higher levels of specialization developed. But two critical questions that have confronted the medical profession in the United States throughout the twentieth century have been how specialist training should be organized and how the quality of training should be regulated or certified. In solving these problems, the society has had many options. Specialized training could take place in medical schools and universities or it might occur in hospitals independent of medical schools and universities, as did intern training. Or there might be no organized system for training specialists, and each practitioner would acquire specialty skills by attending short courses, studying independently, or working as an apprentice to an experienced specialist. In fact, all of these options were tried (Stevens 1971: 122; 1978: 6; U.S. Commissioner of Education 1915: 218).

Although they had reformed and to a large extent standardized undergraduate medical education, universities were reluctant to undertake responsibility for graduate-level specialist training. Some medical schools did provide short-term specialist training courses for practicing physicians, though most short-term courses were provided by various local medical societies (Stevens 1971: 122, 261).

During the period between the two world wars, hospitals became more complex institutions with a need for an in-house staff, a phenomenon that caused residency programs to spread to numerous hospitals that had no university affiliation. As the number and type of residencies proliferated, there was no standardization of residency training. Each hospital tended to develop its own training program. In some hospitals, there were no educational directors and no graded system of training and responsibility. Aside from the first years of the medical curriculum, the medical schools exercised no monopoly over medical education.

By 1920, U.S. medical specialization began to be caught up in a web of contradictions. The more specialists there were, the more doctors believed that they must specialize to keep up with advances in knowledge and compete with colleagues. Moreover, specialists tended to hospitalize patients more than general practitioners did, and this meant that, as the level of specialization increased, the demand for hospital beds increased, and the society greatly expanded the number of hospitals and hospital beds. But this expansion generated demand for hospital house staff (i.e., doctors training to become specialists) to assist with patient treatment. The more specialists there were, the higher the level of hospitalization, though the greater the hospitalization, the greater the number of residency training programs in medical specialties—which in turn generated more specialists, who hospitalized more patients, and so on.

By 1960, approximately 1,400 U.S. hospitals were offering residency programs. It had obviously become difficult to maintain control over their quality with so many hospitals providing training. Moreover, the larger the number of training programs in each specialty, the more competitive each specialty became. In the early part of the twentieth century, the medical profession had responded to increasing competition and low-quality training institutions with the Flexner Report, which was designed to reduce both competition among practitioners and the number of training institutions. Why did the medical profession not respond to the training of medical specialists in the same way? The basic explanation is that much of the medical profession greatly benefited from a decentralized, local system of specialist training that provided local hospitals with a house staff of "junior professional associates." A very large proportion of medical practitioners centered their basic practice outside the hospital, even though they spent a great deal of time tending to patients within hospitals. Office-based practice was possible for doctors when they knew that they could assign their patients to the care of a resident in the local hospital—particularly since the resident was a junior member of the hospital staff, an apprentice who was in training and was in no position to steal the attending physician's patients.

If the U.S. medical delivery system had not used specialty training as a means of filling hospital positions, perhaps almost 70 percent of the medical profession by 1970 would not have been engaged in specialty practice. In England and Wales, where most specialists conducted almost all of their practice in a hospital setting, it was not necessary to have a large training staff substituting for them. With hospital growth relatively uncoordinated in the United States and with no centralized system to plan and to control the distribution of medical specialists, the growth of hospital beds generated the demands for hospital house staff (i.e., doctors in training).

With a very decentralized and diverse medical training system, a major problem was how to certify the quality of the training. Although there were many options, the profession tended to adopt the practice that a group of ophthalmologists developed, by which each specialty developed its own procedures for certifying training and quality. Like their colleagues who established the American College of Surgeons, ophthalmologists were anxious to create standards of proficiency for themselves. Thinking that their status and income were somewhat threatened by the expansive activity of opticians, a group of elite ophthalmologists formed in the American Board for Ophthalmic Examinations in 1916. The basic function of the board was to establish standards of training in ophthalmology for those who wished to be certified, to conduct examinations in order to test qualifications, and to provide certificates for those who were judged qualified to practice.

The precedents established by the ophthalmologists were also important for what was left undone. Certified in ophthalmology was a voluntary action on the part of the individual practitioner. One was not required to be a certified specialist in order to practice a specialty in ophthalmology. University specialist training was not required. The board diploma was to certify that one had attained a minimum level of competence in the specialty, not a high level of skill. Many doctors continued to practice in ophthalmology even though they were not certified in the area (Stevens 1971: 112–14; Rosen 1944).

The course of action taken by the ophthalmologists was widely discussed but not widely emulated until the depression of the 1930s caused American specialists to become much more self-conscious. The average income of private, nonsalaried physicians dropped by more than 50 percent between 1929 and 1933, while industrial wages had declined by approximately 42 percent. Doctors increasingly realized that if they could clearly differentiate themselves by level of training, they could better compete in the medical marketplace. Moreover, hospitals became more concerned over the fact that they had few criteria for evaluating the competence of their staff. As a result, the 1930s were the decade when the established precedents were followed by numerous specialty groups. By the end of 1937, there were ten new specialty boards in existence; by 1940, there were fifteen, and by 1970 there were twenty (Lippard 1974: 91; Stevens 1971: 176, 201–2, 215).

There was little coordination among the different boards, and as a result, there was little standardization in training and quality across the various boards, and specialist training was decentralized in hundreds of hospital residencies throughout the country. In an effort to coordinate specialty training and to prevent unnecessary fragmentation, a number of medical organizations did form in 1934 the Advisory Board for Medical Specialties. The Advisory Board specified standards for each new board and outlined qualifications expected of board certified specialists. The Advisory Board was a reflection of the laissez-faire attitude that pervaded much of medicine in the United States, for its role in regard to the various specialties was only advisory (Stevens 1971: 215–16, 245).

With the publication in 1940 of the first *Directory of Medical Specialists*, those who were certified in a medical specialty were clearly differentiated from those who were not. Thereafter, board certification became an important requirement for the appointment to the staff of many hospitals—particularly to surgical services. Moreover, medical school faculties increasingly denied appointments to physicians who were not board certified (Lippard 1974: 95). However, certification has at no time been a requirement for specialist practice.

It was much easier for specialty boards to examine candidates than to specify and regulate training. With more than a thousand hospitals providing specialty training, effective regulation was virtually impossible. In an effort to standardize residency training, most specialty boards provided a syllabus for residency programs. However, each hospital continued to have its own training program, and there was virtually no standardization of training in any specialty. And each board was concerned only with the residents in its specialty area, and this meant that there was no organizational structure for regulating the education program of specialty training in the United States (Stevens 1971: 259).

In general, hospitals with residency training hardly conducted themselves as though they were engaged in training highly educated young people. Instead of resembling graduate education that existed in the universities, the training of specialists was more analogous to the apprenticeship type education that one observed in medical schools in the pre-Flexner days, with each institution setting its own standards. Residents finished their training upon completion not, as in university graduate education, of a prescribed course of training but simply of a specified time period. As one eminent educator observed, graduate medical education in the United States resembled that "of a vocational school rather than a graduate university discipline designed for mature students who have already completed eight years of higher education" (Millis 1967: 1103). There was no university type faculty in the non-university-affiliated teaching hospital to assume responsibility for the details and evolution of a curriculum. As a result, the resident was primarily an apprentice attached to a particular chief of service (Knowles 1968: 81–82).

During the 1960s, two national studies, the Millis Report and the Coggeshall Report, vigorously attacked the existing organizational structure of postgraduate medical education and advocated an integrated system in which undergraduate and postgraduate medical education would come under the control of the universities. As a result of these two reports, substantial changes did occur in postgraduate medical education. By the 1970s, the internship was being phased out, and medical school graduates proceeded immediately to a residency program. But a more important change was the centering of residency training in university-affiliated hospitals. In 1960, approximately one-half of the nation's residencies occurred in hospitals with at least minimum university affiliation. Thereafter, medical school faculties began to take increased responsibility for the training of residents. Even so, the responsibility for the training of medical residents remained diffused throughout the 1970s. Though most residencies were occurring in university-affiliated hospitals, most training of residents remained under control of the hospital, not the university. And though much of the supervision of residents was done by members of medical school faculties, they supervised not as such but as members of a hospital medical staff. In most institutions, residents were still regarded as house officers and not as university graduate students, and their certificate for the completion of their training was not a university degree but a certificate issued by the hospital. Because residency programs were accredited by more than twenty review committees—each being independent and autonomous—no organization had the responsibility for the complete education and training of physicians. As a result, the responsibility for medical training remained very fragmented and decentralized (Millis 1971: Coggeshall 1965; Stevens 1978). Residency programming thus reflected the basic trends in the United States toward decentralization and the privatization of decision making about the delivery system.

SOME CONSEQUENCES OF THE SYSTEM

Historically, Americans have relied on the marketplace to regulate the specialty areas that attracted young doctors. This has been very much in contrast to Britain's NHS, where the government had to approve the number of hospital doctors who were training in various specialties—a situation that gave the government a rather effective means of regulating the total intake of specialists, as well as the number of specialists in each field of medicine and surgery. In contrast, large numbers of graduates of U.S. medical schools went into those fields with the most prestige and financial rewards—the various surgical specialties (Beeson 1974: 44). However, no organized body had the authority to develop and implement plans for the distribution of medical and surgical specialties. Unlike the situation in Britain, specialists in the United States have been able to practice wherever they wish, without permission from any planning organization.

By international standards, it would appear that the unregulated intake of the U.S. specialty system produced a surplus of surgeons and an excess of operations. In 1967, there were in the United States 39 doctors per 100,000 population in the full-time practice of surgery or its specialties, as opposed to only 18 per 100,000 in Great Britain. In addition, 10,850 American general practitioners were engaged in part-time surgical practice (Great Britain, MOH 1967; 1968; Bunker 1970: 136). Not only were there twice as many surgeons in the United States per head of population as in Great Britain, but the American surgeons conducted approximately twice as much surgery. Whereas there was an operation rate of 3,770 per 100,000 population in England and Wales in 1966, the U.S. rate was 7,400 per 100,000. Especially significant is the fact that the Americans tended to perform almost twice the rate of elective surgeries (Bunker 1970: 135–37; 1985; Rutkow and Zuidema 1978).

In order to determine whether there has been a surplus of surgeons in the United States, it is not enough simply to compare the proportion of surgeons to the population with that of other countries with comparable levels of health. American surgeons differ somewhat philosophically from their colleagues in many countries. For example, the British surgeon has long been somewhat more modest in expectations than his American counterpart. The British doctor has generally been less supportive of surgical therapy and as a result may miss opportunities for a cure or treatment. In contrast, the American has been trained to be more aggressive, to have higher expectations of what surgery and other forms of active intervention can produce. Ever since the turn of the century, foreign observers have noted the quickness with which Americans have resorted to surgery. Some might observe that this is consistent with a basic trait of the American character to believe that technology can solve most any problem.

Some argue that even though Americans operate twice as often as the British, this does not necessarily mean that there is twice as much surgery as the public health justifies. Some contend that there have been many British patients in need of surgery, but long waiting lists act as deterrents to surgery. This argument is, of course, difficult to evaluate, for while waiting lists in Great Britain are a public statistic, there are no comparable data for the United States. Many Americans assume that there are no prolonged delays in the United States, but one study of two communities—one in Great Britain and one in the eastern part of the United States—demonstrated that the waiting time was very similar in the two communities (Bunker 1970; Simpson et al. 1978). Waiting time has been the British method of rationing medical care, while in the United States the price of medical service has been the basic instrument for rationing care. Those Americans who could afford medical care have tended to get service quickly, while those who have had no way of financing medical care have often had to do without.

In the final analysis, it is somewhat difficult to develop hard comparisons of the quality of medical care in the United States with that in Great Britain. Almost any measure of comparison is likely to be controversial. However, it is important to confront the problem of the consequences that follow from the training practices inherent in the U.S. medical delivery system. And it is the judgment of many American medical educators that the system has resulted in too many surgeons and an excess of surgery over an amount consistent with the public health (Bunker 1985). There have been a number of studies on the amount of unnecessary surgery in the United States, but one of the most conservative estimates is that in 1974, 2.4 million unnecessary operations were performed and that these led to 11,900 unnecessary deaths (U.S. Congress, House, Commerce 1976: 2). In Britain, almost all surgery is performed by consultant specialists or senior registrars who have had not less than four years of surgical training. And if the qualifications and training of a surgeon are used as an index to quality of care, the quality of surgical care would appear to be superior in Great Britain. Of the 68,000 American physicians listed in 1968 as engaged in full-time or part-time private practice of surgery, fewer than two-thirds were certified by a surgical board (Bunker 1970: 143). Studies prior to 1970 estimate that more than 50 percent of surgery in the United States was performed by general practitioners or osteopaths (Anderson and Feldman 1958: 2; American College of Surgeons 1975: 11). Moreover, U.S. recruitment methods to surgical practice were somewhat less rigorous than those of the British. In Britain, there have been for many years more than twice as many applicants for surgical specialties as positions available—thus there has been ample opportunity for quality control. In the United States, in contrast, the control over residency positions has been at the hospital level, and there have been many fewer applicants than positions. And while many hospitals have required board certification or equivalent learning as a prerequisite for staff privileges, a substantial percentage of hospitals have not, as the U.S. medical profession has traditionally resisted elitism under almost any guise (Stevens 1971: 163; Bunker 1970: 143).

Even when doctors are compensated in the same manner, there are regional variations in practice, whether in England and Wales or in the United States. Doctors in the same area tend to follow what is common practice in that community. Those who follow the practice of their colleagues tend to be safe from criticism and are able to avoid having to defend themselves before their colleagues (Bunker 1985: 8). At the same time, there seems to be little doubt that the fee-for-service form of pricing has contributed to the excess of both surgeons and surgery in the United States. A number of studies uniformly demonstrate that, when surgeons are paid on a salary basis, there is a substantially less elective surgery involving tonsillectomies, hysterectomies, and hemorrhoid operations. These same studies suggest that a health delivery system with surgeons paid on a capitation or salary basis requires fewer surgeons than one based on a fee-for-service mechanism (Huebscher 1970: 1106; Blackstone 1974: 343–44).

FINANCING AMERICAN MEDICAL CARE

The distribution of power among particular interest groups is the key to understanding how medical care is financed in various countries, for the power of various groups constrains the type of structure that emerges. In countries in which consumers were relatively well organized in relation to the providers of health care at the time that the financing of medical services became a salient issue, a national health insurance program emerged with the state playing a rather prominent role in its organization and regulation. On the other hand, in countries in which the providers were stronger and better organized than consumers at the time when medical care became a salient issue, the development of a national health insurance program has been retarded or nonexistent. Under the latter circumstances, the method of payment has been determined in the private sector, with the providers playing a more prominent role in the system. In the United States in contrast to England and Wales, differences in the distribution of power between consumers and providers in the early twentieth century help to explain why the two countries have had such different histories in the financing of medical care (Abel-Smith 1965).

In the United States, the organized strength of consumers was weak relative to their power in England and Wales. For example, less than 3 percent of the U.S. labor force was organized into labor unions in 1900, while the percentage was almost five times greater in England and Wales at that time. Relative to the level of economic development, trade union organization and working-class consciousness were retarded in the United States because of religious, racial, and ethnic cleavages. In Britain, however, by 1900 there were more than 5 million members of friendly societies, most of which had contractual relationships with doctors to provide medical services for their members. Thus the friendly societies dictated the conditions under which medical services would be provided, the terms under which a very large proportion of general practitioners worked. Under these contracts, remuneration for most general practitioners was by capitation. Later, the NHI scheme institutionalized and expanded the type of payment system already in existence. But without comparable strength among labor unions or friendly societies, American consumers of medical care were not in a strategic position to influence the method of financing.

There is a body of literature that contends that, in the early part of the twentieth century, the United States had several options as to how it could finance medical care. In addition, the literature suggests that during the second decade of the twentieth century, the United States came close to adopting a program of national health insurance. Actually, the adoption of such an option was extremely unlikely, for the United States did not have the structural conditions under which it was possible to enact a national health insurance system. This is not to suggest that American consumers at the turn of the twentieth century were completely uninvolved in organizing medical care. There were a few consumer groups that did dictate the conditions under which medical care was organized and financed, but relative to the size of the country, their activity was on a much smaller scale than in Great Britain (Schwartz 1965). Whereas in Britain contracts between doctors and the consuming public were dictated by consumers, the bulk of the contract practice in the United States was dominated by doctors and existed primarily in railroad, logging, and mining communities in which the workers were relatively isolated and a single doctor monopolized the medical practice.

Yet there were articulate Americans who believed that wage earners needed financial protection during times of illness, that existing institutional arrangements were insufficient to provide medical insurance and care for wage earners, and that some form of compulsory health insurance was necessary (Schwartz 1965). In the early part of the century, the American Association of Labor Legislation was the most important group dramatizing the nation's difficulties in the financing of medical care and making concrete proposals for solving the problems. Organized in 1906 and numbering 3,300 by 1913, members were mostly highly visible social scientists and lawyers. By 1915, the association drafted model bills for compulsory medical insurance, to provide not only for payment of medical service but also for sickness pay for a specific period. Many scholars view this campaign to enact this legislation as providing a critical option point in the financial history of U.S. medical care (Anderson 1950; 1951; Domhoff 1971; Numbers 1978).

During the American Association of Labor Legislation campaign, highly visible people throughout the country spoke out in support of national health insurance. George H. Simmons, the editor of the *Journal of the American Medical Association*, was very sympathetic to the national health insurance scheme that the British had recently adopted, as was Alexander Lambert, chairman of the AMA's prestigious Judicial Council, although both stopped just short of endorsing a similar system for the United States (Numbers 1978). Among the enthusiastic supporters of a national health insurance program were the president of the American Public Health Association, leaders from the U.S. Public Health Service, and some of the more prominent medical professors in the country. In New York, newspaper editors, labor leaders, the Consumers League, the Women's Suffrage party, and the Young Men's Christian Association supported compulsory medical insurance. Meantime, the governors of California, Massachusetts, New Hampshire, New Jersey, New York, and Wyoming supported national health insurance. Even the *Journal of the American Medical Association* published articles highly favorable toward it (*Journal of the American Medical Association* (63 [Jan. 30, 1915]: 386; [Dec. 11, 1915]: 2056–60; Anderson 1950: 386; Rayack 1967a: 10; Numbers 1978: 57–58).

As long as national health insurance was only being discussed and studied by prominent Americans, there was very little organized opposition to the program. But once the American Association of Labor Legislation settled upon a specific bill and had vigorously started a national publicity campaign on its behalf, the opposition surfaced and became very vocal (Numbers 1978: chap. 7).

Even though many leaders of the medical profession had spoken sympathetically for national insurance, the grass roots of the profession opposed it vehemently. For the majority, the source of payment for medical care was as important an issue as the method of payment, and they feared that if the source were to change, the method—fee for service—would be altered. Underlying much of the medical profession's opposition to compulsory health insurance was a negative reaction to their experience with workmen's compensation laws (Burrow 1977: 135–37, 202).

Had the working class been well organized and very much in support of national health insurance, the United States might have adopted the legislation. But labor was poorly organized and had a low level of class consciousness, and it was divided over the issue. A number of labor leaders did support the program, but the most influential labor leader in the country, Samuel Gompers, vigorously opposed it. And as a result of the division within the Executive Council of the American Federation of Labor, the council failed to take a public position on the issue of national health insurance.

National health insurance failed because its advocates, while highly visible and articulate, were not well organized. Moreover, the working class lacked cohesive views on the subject. On the other hand, those groups that were vigorously opposed to the program were well organized in state and national politics and were able to veto the idea. Because the leaders of the American Association of Labor Legislation were so optimistic early in their campaign, many historians have been persuaded that national health insurance was a distinct possibility. But given the structural distribution of power in U.S. society at the time—particularly the weakness of the consumer vis-à-vis the providers of services—national health insurance was not a viable option at the time. Because of the relative weakness of and the divisions within organized labor, the United States emphatically rejected compulsory health insurance at the time when it was becoming commonplace in other industrialized societies.

Historically, the battle over national health insurance was significant in that it helped to clarify, solidify, and institutionalize the position of the AMA with regard to national health insurance. By 1920, the AMA House of Delegates was vehemently and unequivocally on record as opposing all systems of compulsory health insurance. Thereafter, the association became highly politicized and in subsequent years devoted considerable energy to defining and clarifying what were to be legitimate types of state activity in regard to health care. For some years, the AMA became the dominant force in shaping the nation's health policies. Increasingly, its position was that government should be involved in the financing and providing of medical care only when there were diseases that could endanger the health of others and if individuals were truly indigent (Anderson 1968: 91; Burrow 1963). The AMA also opposed medical insurance in the private sector, contending that it would dictate the conditions under which the profession could practice, provide physicians with inadequate compensation, and eventually lead to a lowering of medical standards (*Journal of the American Medical Association* 80 [Dec. 3, 1932]: 1951; Rayack 1967a: 19; Anderson 1968: 100).

Technological change was taking place very rapidly, dictating for first one group and then another new forms of organizing and financing medical care, and eventually, the imperatives of the new technology brought about very slow incremental changes in the financing and organizing of medical delivery—particularly hospital care.

Hospital care was the health spending area in which new financing patterns first developed in the United States. There had long been a sizable percentage of patients who paid for their care, and as the technology in hospitals became more expensive, most people were expected to provide substantial payment for the hospital care that they received, and insurance appeared to be a logical means of financing the payments. The American experience was unlike the British in that British medical insurance first became widespread in nonhospital care, because most hospital care was free. European medical insurance plans were also different. They had come into existence at the turn of the century, when medical technology was relatively inexpensive, and as a result, most of the plans provided not only for medical insurance but more importantly for sickness pay also. By the 1930s, however, medical technology had become much more expensive. And when insurance developed on a large scale in the United States, the emphasis was on medical insurance, with relatively little concern with sick pay.

In serious financial difficulties throughout the depression, U.S. hospitals in large cities began to organize citywide group insurance plans. But the real boost for hospital insurance came from the American Hospital Association, which recommended a set of principles that hospitals should follow when establishing insurance plans and that authorized the use of the Blue Cross symbol by hospitals that adhered to the proposed principles. Some of the key provisions were the following:

1. Group hospital plans should provide payment only for hospital care and not for the professional services of physicians.
2. In the establishment of Blue Cross plans, organizers should seek the advice of physicians, hospital trustees, and other qualified individuals.
3. All subscribers should have free choice of hospital.
4. The prepaid plan should be nonprofit, with no group allowed any financial gain from it.

(Somers and Somers 1962: 258)

Spending much of their time in hospitals and being clearly dependent on their financial well-being, surgeons were very sympathetic to the Blue Cross plans. As a result, the American College of Surgeons endorsed the idea in 1934. Yet there was AMA opposition because of anticipated divisions between hospitals and physicians and diminished physician control over hospitals.

The Blue Cross plans began to grow rapidly and continued to grow without interruption through the 1970s. By 1978, there were 69 plans with over 83 million enrollments. The typical local Blue Cross plan was administered by a governing board, the majority of whom consisted of hospital representatives and physicians, but with the former in firm control. Significantly, the subscribers (i.e., the consumers) to the Blue Cross plans were essentially unrepresented on the governing boards (Anderson 1975).

As there were rapid increases in the number of middle-class Americans who purchased voluntary hospitalization insurance, the AMA, after some years of study, began to engage in incremental modifications of its earlier firm opposition to all forms of voluntary medical insurance. In 1938, it gave cautious endorsement to the principle of voluntary medical insurance. To astute observers, it was clear that the AMA would adopt as much flexibility on the subject of medical insurance as was necessary to prevent national compulsory medical insurance (Burrow 1963: 212, 228–51).

The California Medical Association responded in 1939 with a doctor-controlled insurance plan. In the same year, the Michigan State Medical Society organized a similar plan. And within a few years, comparable plans emerged all across the country. However, the growth rate of the Blue Shield plans was much lower than the hospital-sponsored Blue Cross programs, for most medical societies had little enthusiasm for medical insurance. By 1945, there were only 2.5 million members in 22 Blue Shield plans, in contrast to 15.7 million members enrolled in 75 Blue Cross plans (Somers and Somers 1962: 283–86). Like Blue Cross, the Blue Shield plans were non-profit programs. But in numerous states, the medical profession used its political power to enact legislation that prohibited the formation of any prepayment medical insurance plan unless it was controlled by the medical profession (ibid. 286). As a result, the medical profession in most states easily established a virtual monopoly in the prepayment medical care insurance industry (Rayack 1967a: 53).

Most Blue Shield plans provided for physician care, either in the doctor's office or in the hospital, and most plans incorporated a specified fee for certain types of physician service. When the fees for physicians' services were higher than those specified in the Blue Shield schedule—as they often were—the subscriber paid the excess charge.

It was not until World War II that there was substantial growth of voluntary medical insurance in the United States. In 1940, only 9 percent of the civilian population had any hospital benefits through private medical insurance, and only 4 percent had surgical benefits for doctor costs. By 1950, however, 51 percent had hospital insurance and 36 percent had surgical insurance. The growth rate of private insurance was so rapid that by the early 1950s, there was a widely shared view in American society that, as a result of extensive private insurance, universal national health insurance was not necessary and that at best, publicly financed medical care was needed only for those groups who could not afford to purchase medical care in the private sector. Very few Americans were prepared to argue that a revamping of the medical delivery system along the British lines was desirable (Stevens and Stevens 1974: 14–17, 20–21).

The federal government played an important role during World War II in stimulating the growth of private medical insurance. During the war the wages of most workers were frozen, but the federal government permitted fringe benefits to be negotiable, meaning that additional fringe benefits became the chief means whereby workers gained more compensation. As a result, employer contributions to voluntary health insurance plans became an important item in collective bargaining negotiations between labor and management during the war, and the number of people covered by voluntary medical insurance increased dramatically. Because the employers' contributions to health insurance were tax deductible as a business expense and the employee's coverage as a fringe benefit on the individual tax return was not taxable, the federal government was in effect subsidizing group medical insurance—but only for those groups who could negotiate this type of fringe benefit.

The success of voluntary hospitalization plans tended to obscure the shortcomings of medical insurance in the United States. Most middle-class families received only partial coverage of their medical needs, while most low-income and unemployed families were essentially uninsured. Meantime, many people who were treated in hospitals increasingly found that their policies had limited coverage and failed to provide benefits for their treatment. And many people who were employed found that, during a job change or a temporary period of unemployment, they lost their insurance coverage. The voluntary insurance industry by 1950 was primarily for middle-class Americans, who were relatively content with what they received. And over time, middle-income Americans had pressured their employers to purchase insurance with broad coverage and with low deductibles and low coinsurance provisions. As a result, there was not much incentive for well-organized groups to discuss the need to provide insurance for those who were not covered—essentially low-income Americans (Hirschfield 1970: 93–94).

Though increased specialization in the medical profession seemed to imply the need for greater coordination of the medical system in order to deal effectively with the multidimensional needs of patients, most American physicians continued throughout the period immediately following World War II to be resistant to new ways of organizing and financing medical care. While the U.S. medical profession on technical matters was one of the most innovative in the world, it was among the least innovative in regard to new ways of organizing and financing medical care. There were some efforts between 1940 and 1960 to develop alternative models for delivering and financing medical care, in particular prepaid group practice plans, but these were illegal in many parts of the country unless a majority of the boards of directors were doctors.

Even though most middle-class Americans had some type of voluntary medical insurance coverage by 1950, there were millions who had no coverage and who were unable to afford medical care. Many who could not afford to pay for medical care in time of need were able to seek charity from public and private agencies and from private practitioners (Stevens and Stevens 1974: 14). Government facilities of some type were usually available for those who had serious infectious diseases, and there were public mental facilities for those who needed to be institutionalized. It is true that, in some cities, there was between 1930 and 1960 an expansion of municipal hospital services for the indigent, but there were essentially two classes of medical care in most cities—relatively high-quality private facilities for those who could afford to pay or who had health insurance and somewhat lower-quality public facilities for the indigent.

By 1960, however, an increasing number of Americans had become dissatisfied with the nation's system of financing medical care. Much of the dissatisfaction was prompted by concern for the medical problems of the aged. Because of the decline of infectious diseases, a larger portion of the population was living beyond age 65, and many of them were not on public assistance programs. Without medical insurance, many of the elderly who became ill saw their lifetime savings vanish when they had to purchase complex and costly medical care. Because many had to rely on their children to pay medical bills, one of the major political issues of the late 1950s was how to provide adequate medical care for the elderly without subjecting them to the stigma of a means test. For most middle-income Americans, it was one thing to subject the poor to a means test, but they were not prepared to have their parents subjected to that demeaning stigma in order to have their medical needs financed. As a result, the political pressures increased for providing some type of medical assistance to the aged.

The federal government after 1948 played an important role in financing hospital construction with the Hill-Burton legislation, financed and promoted medical research, and played a major role in creating huge medical centers throughout the country. Implicit in these activities was the idea, strongly endorsed by the AMA and the American Hospital Association, that the federal government should help to advance medical knowledge and assist in the building of medical centers but should not be involved in directly organizing and financing medical care. This should be done in the private sector. In all of these activities, the federal government provided public funds as a result of pressure group politics, but in general, the government required very little evaluation of the social consequences of the funding.

Although by 1960, most Americans were still convinced that the private sector could provide for the health needs of most citizens, there was a debate over the extent to which the state should assist those who could not finance their own medical care—the elderly and millions of low-income Americans. Finally, in 1965, Congress responded to mounting pressures by passing two major pieces of legislation to confront these problems: Medicare, which provided medical care for the elderly and Medicaid which provided medical care for the indigent.

While these were the most important pieces of legislation relating to medical care in U.S. history, they had virtually no *direct* impact on restructuring medical delivery. Whereas Great Britain's major medical legislation in 1946 nationalized the country's hospitals and made most doctors employees of the state, Medicaid and Medicare nationalized no hospitals, and doctors continued to practice much as before. A key idea behind Medicare and Medicaid was that doctors, hospitals, and patients would all benefit financially through programs that incorporated basic principles well established in U.S. medical delivery: fee for service and professional control.

In an effort to guarantee that Medicare and Medicaid would not lead to government intervention in medical care delivery, the American Hospital Association and the AMA, as part of their acceptance of the legislation, persuaded Congress to mandate that the federal government would not become involved in the direct supervision or control over the way in which medicine was practiced. Congress agreed to finance medical care for a sizable portion of the U.S. population but decided not to be involved directly in regulating the nature of that care. To keep the federal government's control over the medical establishment to a minimum, Congress permitted hospitals and other medical facilities to name private organizations to act as fiscal intermediaries between the federal government and the providers of medical care. The fiscal intermediaries were to bill and receive payment from the Social Security Administration for all claims arising from the program.

As most hospitals and more than one-half of the nation's nursing homes named Blue Cross organizations as their fiscal intermediaries, one result of the legislation was to integrate Medicare firmly into the private health insurance industry. Because the Blue Cross organizations were essentially creatures of the hospital industry, most hospitals were to be regulated primarily by their own agency. A similar pattern was established under that part of the Medicare program that relates to physician care. Physician intermediaries were termed *carriers,* and the majority of the carriers were Blue Shield organizations—or the agent of the physicians (Law 1974: 46–47).

In some countries, France for example, the problem of how much doctors should be permitted to charge for each type of medical service has often been a very complicated and acrimonious one, with the government dictating the fee that doctors may charge for each service. In the United States, however, the state permitted hospitals and physicians to be reimbursed for services on the basis of fees that were "reasonable charges" in their particular geographical area. And a reasonable charge was the customary and prevailing one in the particular area. Because the Blue Shield and Blue Cross organizations had extensive experience with billing, they presumably were better informed than the government about the prevailing fees in their particular area. To those who drafted the Medicare legislation, it seemed very reasonable that private insurance organizations should have the responsibility for paying the providers. But in the final analysis, the basic setting and the paying of fees depended on the integrity of the medical profession and their captive fiscal intermediaries.

The Medicare legislation did provide physicians with an option for recovering their fees. They might bill the patient, who would then file a claim for reimbursement from the physicians' carrier—presumably the local Blue Shield organization. With this approach, physicians were free to establish their own fees without any obligation to be constrained by the prevailing rate in their area. Alternatively, physicians might bill the carrier directly for their fees, but with this type of reimbursement, they were obliged to accept fees that were the prevailing and customary ones in their area (Stevens 1971: 445–49).

As Rosemary Stevens remarked, "Medicare was thus seen as an extension of existing mechanisms rather than as a strange or alien system, or even at times as being a governmental system" (1971: 449). Even as the state began to finance a much larger portion of the nation's medical bill, medical delivery remained laissez-faire oriented, decentralized, and pluralistic in its basic structure, with individual physicians remaining free to treat and to charge patients as they pleased.

All licensed physicians were permitted to participate in the Medicare program. Moreover, general practitioners and other physicians who were not board certified were permitted to perform major surgery on the elderly and to be reimbursed with federal funds. Medicare provided financial relief to the elderly in the short term, but it was also very beneficial financially to the medical profession. No longer did the profession have to practice charity medicine, as physicians were now able to treat the elderly without having to worry about their ability to afford medical care. Indeed, by 1970, the average payment from Medicare funds was approximately $7,000 annually to each practicing physician.

Whereas Medicare was a medical insurance program for the elderly, Medicaid was a welfare program for people of low income. Though Medicare legislation was quite precise as to who was eligible for its benefits, the legislation language underlying Medicaid was vague. Medicare covered all the rich and poor elderly alike, while Medicaid was designed for the indigent. And whereas Medicare was a federal program, Medicaid was primarily a state program, with the federal government initially offering states a grant ranging from 50 to 83 percent of the state's total Medicaid expenditure—the amount determined by the welfare grant system used in grants-in-aid programs to the states (Marmor 1970; Stevens 1971: 441–51).

Even though there have been many political problems with Medicaid, it did provide medical assistance to millions of Americans—to more than 18 million in 1972—and it substantially increased the number of hospitals and physicians willing to provide care to the poor. In addition, a sizable portion of Medicaid's funds have been used to support long-term nursing care for the elderly.

All states participating in Medicaid programs were required to provide assistance for those covered by cash welfare assistance programs, and a number of states provided medical assistance for many who were not eligible for cash assistance. Because Medicaid is a state program, benefits have varied greatly from state to state. For example, the Medicaid payment was five times higher in Connecticut in 1970 than in Mississippi, even though the per capita income in Connecticut was nearly twice that of Mississippi (Holahan 1975: 13). There have been estimates that in some states fewer than 10 percent of the poor have been covered, while in others (e.g., California) most of the poor and many nonpoor citizens have received benefits (ibid.: 9–13).

Most hospitals were initially reimbursed under Medicare on a full cost reimbursement basis—that is, a reimbursement for all labor, materials, debts, depreciation, and interest charges. Physician charges were based on what was "reasonable" or "customary and usual" in their particular area. Of course, physicians quickly learned what the "reasonable" fees were and charged that level, as there was no incentive for them to charge a lesser fee. For this reason, the "customary and usual" charge was prone to be inflationary, as charges constantly escalated. A medical delivery system in which the government financed much of the medical care but delegated the regulation of prices and the quality of care to private providers was particularly conducive to escalating costs.

Once Medicaid and Medicare were implemented in 1966, the rate of increase in medical costs was more than twice what it had been prior to 1965. Hospital costs increased at a particularly rapid rate, rising 15.4 percent in 1968, 13.2 percent in 1969, and 12.4 percent in 1970, substantially above the overall cost of living (Weiss 1972: 638–39; Law 1974: 1). By 1970, the United States spent a higher percentage of its GNP on medical care than any other country in the world, yet there was very little evidence that the medical needs were met as satisfactorily as those of most other advanced industrial societies.

As organizations that administered much of the Medicare and Medicaid programs, the Blue Shield and Blue Cross programs were involved in a fundamental conflict of interest. As the private intermediaries between providers and federal government, they had responsibility for regulating the providers, but in fact, most of the Blue Cross and Blue Shield organizations were dominated by the providers. In short, the federal government in the 1960s had asked providers in the private sector to regulate themselves in what had become one of the largest sectors in the U.S. economy. On the other hand, the state had become the major financer of medical care in the United States, and as a result it would subsequently become a dominant actor in shaping medical policies, though the history of medical institutions and the distribution of power among corporate elites, the working class, and medical providers would set limits on the direction in which the state would assert its power.

CONCLUDING OBSERVATIONS

The dominant medical paradigm has been similar in both the United States and Britain during the twentieth century. What has differed has been the relative power and influence of groups, as well as the traditions from which they have emerged. It was these differences that led the two countries to develop such different types of medical delivery system during the twentieth century. In the early part of the century, the consumer was not a key actor in shaping the delivery of medical services in the United States, and for this reason, the system reflected the values and preferences of the economic elite and the medical profession more than was the case in England and Wales. As Navarro (1976a; 1980), Hollingsworth and Hanneman (1983), and others have demonstrated, the medical delivery systems of both societies have operated under the hegemony of the economic elite.

In no Western, highly industrial society is consumer power dominant in controlling the delivery of medical services. However, there is variation among societies in the relative power of consumers and providers. In Western capitalist societies, the variation is influenced in part by the size of the society and its ethnic, religious, and racial heterogeneity. In large democratic societies with very heterogeneous populations, the working class has had considerable difficulty in organizing and mobilizing sufficient power to influence medical policies. And where this occurs, the systems are located more in the private sector, are more decentralized, and are more provider dominated, as in the United States. On the other hand, smaller societies that are relatively homogeneous ethnically and religiously—as in Great Britain—have consumers who historically have been more successful in mobilizing power, and they have used that power via the state in order to shape medical policies. Thus the systems in which consumers have been more influential have tended to be more in the public sector, be more centralized, and have a higher degree of coordination of the various parts.

Thus size of country, heteorgeneity of population, the relative power of consumers and providers, and the degree of centralized coordination of the medical delivery systems explain, in part, some of the variation in the degree of specialization and type of financing in the U.S. and British systems.

Historically, the larger and more heterogeneous U.S. system has been located more in the private sector, has been dominated by providers, and has had little effective mechanism for constraining the level of specialization and for influencing the distribution of resources. Because the method of financing has been provider dominated, even when consumers have succeeded in having the government finance medical care for certain groups (i.e., the elderly and the indigent) via Medicare and Medicaid, the funding mechanisms have been shaped in such a fashion as to be very beneficial to the providers. Comparison of the British and U.S. systems suggests that the more powerful providers are at the time when the financing of medical technology first becomes a highly salient issue, the greater the likelihood that the system will emphasize specialized services, rely on private financing, and have less equality in access to care. In contrast, systems, such as that in Great Britain, in which consumers have been able to mobilize more influence, tend to place less emphasis on specialized services, have greater equality of access to care, and rely more on public funding. Thus variation in the power of consumers and providers has led to divergent types of decisions about specialization and the financing of medical services in the two societies. This is not to suggest that providers have not been a very powerful group in the British system. Rather, the argument is that providers have been less powerful in the British than in the U.S. system.

Of course, the state has also been an active participant in shaping the differences between the two systems. In capitalist countries, the role of the state in shaping medical policy varies, but irrespective of the country, the twentieth century has witnessed the expansion of the state in financing and regulating medical delivery systems.

Following the enactment of Hill-Burton legislation and the implementation of Medicare and Medicaid, the state became a major actor in the medical system in the United States. It became increasingly involved in addressing new organizational forms of health delivery, in improving access to medical care, and eventually in constraining medical costs. Because of the fragmented and decentralized structure of the U.S. political system, however, the state has been relatively ineffectual in developing optimal tradeoffs among such competing goals as improving quality, access, and cost control.

The lack of coordinated policies by the federal government has resulted, in part, from the fact that within it there have been three sets of actors. The first, Congress has been the most important, but its preferences have been shaped very much by the power of providers at the local level. The second actor, the federal bureaucracy, has developed a good grasp of the complexity of the medical system and the difficulty of formulating and implementing policies, but it has been less sensitive to the pressures of organized groups. And the third actor has been the presidency; but with the exception of Lyndon Johnson, presidents have rarely exerted leadership in the area of health policy.

Prior to the 1980s the federal government attempted to develop two broad types of policy. The first involved policies whose implementation depended primarily on groups within the private sector and hardly at all on the state bureaucracy—at either the national, state, or local level. Through the mid-1970s, these programs involved Medicare, professional standards review organizations, and health maintenance organizations. In implementing these programs, the federal government tended to take the position that if programs were to work, the cooperation of powerfully organized providers was necessary. Therefore, the federal government tended to treat regulations as guidelines, as instruments for educating providers about desirable goals. In such a process, however, powerfully organized interest groups eventually shaped regulations to suit themselves (L. Brown 1978: 54). The second type of policy involved programs implemented at the state level. Examples of these were Medicaid and the Hill-Burton program for hospital construction. At the state level, however, powerfully organized interest groups dominated the policy process. With both types of process, the key actors have been providers because of their organizational cohesion, status, wealth, and professional legitimacy.

In one sense, the federal government demonstrated a willingness to respond incrementally to the shortcomings of the U.S. medical system. In contrast to the British political system, which was much smaller, less complex, and more centralized, however, that in the United States had considerable difficulty in establishing the authority with which to govern. As a result, the U.S. medical system remained much more private and market oriented.

Because the system in the United States remained to a much greater degree in the private sector, it was more susceptible to market forces than the system in Britain. Like other private sector industries in which technology was highly complex and changes very rapid, the medical system remained relatively competitive instead of becoming oligopolistic or monopolistic in nature. Being highly competitive, the U.S. system—in constrast with the British—tended to be more adaptive to rapidly changing technology and more supportive of personalized services. Because consumers were less well organized in the United States, access to medical care remained a more serious problem for the low-income population than in Britain. In short, the two systems continued to differ in their levels of decentralization and competitiveness and in the degree to which they constrained costs, emphasized access to care, were receptive to highly complex technology, and gave high priority to personalized services.

Because the structure of the U.S. medical system facilitated cost escalation during the 1960s and 1970s, predictably the most powerful actors who paid the bills would, at some point, lead the move to control medical costs. Of course, the two most influential sets of actors paying the bills were large corporations and state and federal governments. Hence it should not be surprising that by 1980 the traditional alliance between big capital and the medical profession broke down. Instead, big capital and state increasingly joined hands in an effort to control costs.

In one sense, the medical system in the United States had come full circle. Early in the twentieth century, corporate capital and the medical profession joined in an alliance that eventually transformed the system from a cottage industry to a large-scale, corporate type system. But this system had built-in contradictions: its high costs would eventually tax its legitimacy and lead to efforts to contain escalating expenditures. This has resulted in a rupture of the traditional alliance between the medical profession and corporate capital. As corporate capital and the state attempt to change the nature of the system in the 1980s, however, the American consumer, still relatively unorganized, remains an actor with little influence. But for the first time in the twentieth century, the providers must now compete with the power of corporate capital and the state in order to shape the future of the U.S. medical system.

As providers (i.e., doctors and hospitals) and employers paying huge insurance premiums increasingly have fundamental conflicts of interest, the potential for the state to assert its autonomy has risen. And during the 1980s, the federal bureaucracy has made serious efforts to curb medical spending and to make the U.S. system more efficient. As the number of actors with contradictory interests has become greater, it has become possible for the state to assert its autonomy and become an independent actor. In this sense, despite all of the rhetoric about the increased competitiveness and market-oriented U.S. medical system, the U.S. state pays an increasingly higher percentage of the society's medical costs. And it is this fact that is slowly leading to a more state-oriented medical system in the United States.

This perspective is, of course, entirely consistent with a rich body of recent literature inspired by Theda Skocpol that demonstrates that social policy is slowly but incrementally shaped by state bureaucrats and reformist policy intellectuals who engage in political learning from their previous experience (Amenta et al. 1984; Evans et al. 1985; Heclo 1974; Orloff 1985;

Orloff and Skocpol 1984). And in the United States, as bureaucrats in the Department of Health and Human Services have acquired expertise in reimbursement procedures and costs of delivering medical services, they have become the most informed set of actors in the U.S. scene, and it is as a result of their political learning that they have become a dominant actor during the 1980s in shaping medical policies.

Part Two
System Performance

Introduction

Concentrating on the evolution of the medical delivery systems of Britain and of the United States, part I has demonstrated that variation in the relative power of consumers vis-à-vis providers at the turn of the century has substantially influenced variation in the subsequent institutional development between the two systems. The British system—with consumers better organized than in the United States—tended early to shift considerable responsibility for medical care to the public sector. And by definition, as this occurred, that system became more centralized. Consumers were much more fragmented ethnically in the United States and somewhat more weakly organized. Hence providers have been able to wield much more influence. Because the NHI system, which was established in 1911, placed constraints on the development of specialization in England and Wales, specialization developed to a much greater extent in the United States.

Part II deals with a different set of issues. What consequences follow from variation in the structure between the two systems? Rather than focusing primarily on particular policies, the next several chapters will be concerned with how differences in the distribution of power, the level of centralization, and the level of specialization have influenced the performance of the two medical delivery systems.*

Because the performance of the two systems has altered as changes have occurred in the distribution of power and in their structure, the following chapters will not be static in nature. Rather, the analysis will be process oriented, and it will focus on how differences in the distribution of power and in the levels of centralization and specialization have influenced performance. While there are several strategies for measuring performance (Hage and Hollingsworth 1977), the following chapters will focus primarily on three measures: innovativeness, equality, and costs. In other words, the analysis is concerned with the question of how differences in the distribution of power, levels of centralization, and levels of specialization have influenced differences in the diffusion rate of new technology, research styles, equality, and costs.

When analyzing the behavior of medical delivery systems, one must be sensitive to their costs. Most highly industrialized societies during the 1970s and 1980s became increasingly concerned with an impending fiscal crisis of the state (O'Connor 1973). And in response there began to be con-

---

* For a fuller elaboration of this perspective, see Hage and Hollingsworth 1977. In the development of this perspective, I am indebted to Jerry Hage, with whom I have had numerous conversations about system performance and structure during the past decade.

siderable concern with ways to contain public expenditures in one sector after another. Because medical expenditures were rising more rapidly than those in most other sectors, the task of controlling them gained high priority in most Western countries. For this reason alone, it is important to understand how differences in the organizational structure of medical delivery systems have influenced differences in the level of medical expenditures.

Why is innovativeness an important performance measure for evaluating a medical delivery system? Regardless of how one values innovations, a system that is highly innovative is one that is technologically more complex and differentiated. Since these are important measures by which medical delivery systems differ, it is important that we try to understand the conditions that lead to variation in levels of innovativeness. However, it is useful to draw a distinction between the act of discovery or invention and its diffusion. And my concern in this study is with the latter.

There are at least three ways of conceptualizing equality, and the analysis that follows is concerned with all three. First, there is equality of access to a particular good. When this type of equality exists, all groups have the same access to a service. Second, there is a regional dimension to equality: resources may be concentrated more in some regions than others. Of course, when this occurs, there usually is not equality of access to services by all social classes and income groups. And finally, there is equality in regard to some output. For example, do all social classes and income groups have equal life chances or levels of health? Does equalizing access to care and resources across regions lead to equal levels of health among social classes and income groups? And the analysis that follows confronts the problem of how variation among countries in the distribution of power and the levels of centralization and specialization influences these three types of equality.

There are trade-offs among these various performances, as no system is likely simultaneously to be highly innovative, very egalitarian, and highly successful in constraining medical costs. Systems that are highly innovative tend to have many specialized and individualized services and may be quite inegalitarian. Because it usually is not financially possible to provide the same highly specialized services to everyone, a highly innovative system tends to have resources distributed inequitably across regions and to be inaccessible to many citizens. Such systems also tend to have less effective cost controls. More complex technology leads to increased costs, in part because it provides more individualized services and is usually both labor and capital intensive. In other words, new technology tends not only to be more expensive but also to require more labor to operate it. Indeed, production functions operate rather differently in social services than they do in the manufacturing sector, where new technology often has a labor-saving function. Because cost constraints and innovativeness are somewhat in opposition, they often create a dialectic in policy debates. Some groups—usually providers—place greater emphasis on highly individualized and specialized services, while others—usually government administrators—stress cost containment. Some systems tend to place more emphasis on highly specialized services, while others give much higher priority to cost containment.

These three performances—innovativeness, equality, and cost containment—tend to be somewhat incompatible and difficult to achieve simultaneously. Perhaps performance will be impressive in two of these areas, but most likely not all three simultaneously. Therefore, the three recommend themselves as ideal utilities for this analysis. Invariably, systems make choices, and the concern in the next several chapters is with how the organizational structure of medical delivery systems and the distribution of power within them influence these choices. Significantly, these three performances have been implicit in many if not all major policy debates about twentieth-century medical care in both Britain and the United States. While providers and consumers want to maximize all three performances, they differ in the relative importance that they attach to each of them. And differences in the relative power of providers and consumers across the two countries are an important variable in explaining the different choices made with regard to these performances.

Finally, part II will also discuss the question of how the distribution of power, the amount of centralization, and choices about system performance influence the patterns of medical education and research. Intuitively, one might assume that a system—such as that in the United States—with consumer power weakly mobilized, centralization low and specialization high, weak cost controls, and a high commitment to innovativeness would be one that has placed considerable emphasis on the training of medical specialists, been very research oriented, and committed a high portion of its GNP to research. Conversely, one might intuitively expect the opposite pattern to have operated in Britain. Thus part II will also discuss the problem of how the distribution of power, the structural variables, and system performance are intermingled with the processes of medical education and research. In the final analysis, differences in styles of medical education and research influence differences in system performance.

3
Centralization,
Funding Patterns,
and Costs

The medical delivery systems in all Western countries have increasingly come under more centralized government control. However, the rising level of centralization in some systems has fueled expanding medical costs, while in others it has played an important role in containing them. Thus, this chapter poses, at a theoretical level, the question of what type of centralization leads to the containment of medical expenditures. The chapter will also focus on the different processes by which the British and U.S. systems have made decisions related to financing.

The problem of containing medical costs is, of course, one that has attracted widespread attention, as all industrialized countries struggle to satisfy increasing demands for medical services without intolerable costs. Indeed, this has become the most salient political problem involving medical care in all highly industrialized countries. This chapter argues that the specific type of centralization and coordination of the NHS has permitted it to perform more successfully in controlling costs than the more decentralized, competitive type system that exists in the United States. This discussion is especially appropriate at the present time, as there is in the United States a conflict between those who argue that the most effective means of controlling costs is to have a decentralized, highly competitive system—one with a variety of incentives to encourage consumers to purchase the most cost-efficient type of medical insurance (Olson 1981)—and those who argue that a centralized system of price controls is necessary—that is, a variant on the diagnostic-related group (DRG) program.

THEORETICAL PERSPECTIVES

From a theoretical perspective, all too little is known about the structural characteristics that tend to provide adequate medical services with a minimum level of expenditures. In the literature, one argument for quality medical care at minimum cost relies on the theory of the "invisible hand," which Adam Smith set forth more than two hundred years ago: that is, the most cost-effective medical delivery system is a highly decentralized, competitive one, in which large numbers of consumers transmit their tastes to numerous health providers, who respond by providing medical care at competitive prices. Or, to phrase it differently, high quality and low costs would be maximized if there were perfect markets. With medical care, however, this perspective is inadequate, for the marketplace works differently from that anticipated by Smith. For a decentralized medical marketplace to perform as he predicted, consumers must be able to evaluate the quality of the medical treatment that they wish to consume. There is a vast literature, however, that demonstrates that consumers have inadequate knowledge about the quality of services in the medical marketplace (Donabedian 1976; Monsma 1970; Marmor and Christianson 1982). Whereas consumers generate the demand for goods and services in many markets, this is less true in the medical sector. Medical providers exert a strong influence over not only the supply of but also the demand for medical care in terms of both quantity and pattern. As the patients' agent, the physician exerts considerable influence on their perceptions of their needs (Evans 1974; Feldstein 1967; Cooper 1975; Brearley 1978: 26–27). Thus medical care is an excellent example of how markets fail.

Certain doctors generate more demand and thus more expenditures than others. Thus cross-national variation in the level of specialization among doctors leads to variation in the level of medical expenditures (Hollingsworth et al., forthcoming). A critical problem in allocating national resources to medical care has been to determine the appropriate level of specialization to achieve the maximum health outcomes with the lowest cost. Policy makers have had difficulty in determining this level, for specialized knowledge has an inherent self-generating dynamic. Because knowledge grows exponentially, medical specialization begets new occupations, specialties, and capital equipment (Price 1963; Hage and Aiken 1970; Stevens 1971). And the more specialized the medical delivery system, the greater the number of diagnostic tests and treatments that can be performed on patients, a development that in turn leads to cost escalation (Donabedian 1976).

Of course, there are variables other than the level of specialization that influence variation in medical expenditures among countries. For example, the more countries can afford to spend on medical care, the more they spend. Thus an increase in GNP tends to bring about higher levels of medical expenditures. The same is true of the changing age structure of industrialized countries (Great Britain, NHS 1979: 61). In other words, the medical needs of a population increase as a function of age: as the proportion of the population that is elderly increases, the need for and utilization of medical care rises dramatically. This rise, combined with an increasingly complex technology, has contributed to a medical price spiral in all advanced industrial societies.

After one controls for the level of GNP and the age structure of the population, the basic structure of national medical delivery systems also influences the variation between countries in spending for medical services

(Hollingsworth et al. 1983). Specifically, the more centralized and more coordinated the medical delivery system, the less costly it is—a view contrary to the argument of neoclassical economists that a decentralized, highly competitive system would be more cost-efficient.

Conceptually, centralization refers to the level at which decisions are made. The most centralized system is one in which all key decisions are made by the central government. The most decentralized system is one in which all decisions are made in the private sector. Between these two extremes is a medical delivery system in which all decisions are made at the state and local government level.

More specifically, a highly centralized medical delivery system is one in which most of the revenue for medical services is raised by the central government and the regulation of medical services and prices is very much under its control (Stevens 1966; Lindsey 1962). This system is more effective in controlling costs because the central government is in a key position to ration the resources that flow to the medical delivery system, even though much of the demand for services may be shaped by providers (Cooper 1974; 1975).

On the other hand, when some decisions are highly centralized and others are decentralized, the net result may be escalating costs, and this is what has occurred in the United States for some years. Medical revenues have increasingly been raised by the central government and other third parties (i.e., private insurance companies, Medicaid, Medicare), a fact that has meant that there has been more and more money to pay for the rising demand for services. But prior to the DRG system, which was introduced in 1983, control over prices was held by the providers and was very decentralized (Stevens and Stevens 1974). Thus there were few barriers to the consumption of services in the U.S. system, and spiralling costs resulted as the demand for and consumption of services continue to rise. As David Mechanic reminds us, neither providers or consumers under this arrangement had an incentive to forgo medical services that offered even the most remote possibility of some health benefit (1977).

To understand medical expenditures, it is also necessary to consider the role of third-party payers in setting prices, for the greater the extent of third-party financing, the greater the potential for an increase in demand, prices, and expenditures. Hence the following generalization, which is based on the history of several Western medical delivery systems (Hollingsworth et al., forthcoming): "The greater the percentage of medical care financed through third-party intermediaries, the higher the level of medical expenditures unless there are effective controls by the central government over the price of the services."

Central governments have attempted to contain the expenditures resulting from third-party financing in a variety of ways. Some governments that have provided widespread funding for medical services have attempted to regulate prices and limit the demand and spending by rationing services with such devices as coinsurance and deductibles. For example, the French government during the 1970s not only set prices for medical services but also required the consumer to pay for 20 percent of the charges for ambulatory services (Glaser 1970). In theory, rationing through deductibles is supposed to encourage consumers to limit consumption, but if there are no effective controls over the development and distribution of medical technology, the effects of such rationing are limited, for providers continue to shape much of the demand (Hollingsworth et al., forthcoming).

Another form of government influence on prices has been what David Mechanic has called "implicit rationing" (1977). An example is the NHS in Great Britain, which has placed a limit on total resources available for hospital beds, specialties, and so on. Implicit rationing has forced medical administrators to limit the distribution of medical resources.

A system in which the government pays for many of the services but imposes few limits on consumption and distribution leads to expanding costs. Prior to the DRG system, the United States was moving in this direction, and there was considerable evidence that the system resulted in unnecessary surgical procedures, physicians performing services for which they were not qualified, and physicians migrating to areas where income maximization was greatest (American College of Surgeons 1975; Blackstone 1974; 1977; Bunker 1985; Glaser 1970).

The utilization and prices of medical services are very much influenced by the extent of third-party insurance and the degree to which third parties attempt to constrain prices. An examination of utilization and cost levels before and after the introduction of new financing arrangements provides valuable insights into the impact of the change. In the United States, the introduction of Medicare and Medicaid did make medical care more accessible to the aged, the black population, and other low-income groups. Because there were no provisions for effective cost controls, Medicare and Medicaid led to overinvestigation, unnecessary expansion of capital equipment, an excess of specialty skills, and escalating medical costs (Donabedian 1976; Law 1974; Blackstone 1977). In contrast to the U.S. system of high third-party financing without effective controls over spending, when Britain adopted the NHS there was a rather significant increase in the demand for services but only a modest rise in spending—because of government control over spending and prices (Abel-Smith and Titmuss 1956). In sum, substantial alteration in the financing of health care has usually had some major impact on utilization rates. However, the impact on medical costs of a major expansion in third-party payments varies with the effectiveness of third-party controls (especially control by the central government) over spending.

Thus far, some of the discussion has focused on the relationship between expenditures on medical care and several independent variables: consumer needs, specialization, and centralized controls over revenues and prices. The causal relationship among the different variables is portrayed in figure 2.

One might think of rising levels of specialization as a proxy for increasing levels of medical technology. Historically, the following process has occurred in most Western industrialized societies. As medical technology is believed to have become more efficacious, knowledge about it has been communicated to patients, who have increasingly consumed more medical care. As the levels of technological complexity and consumption have increased, the costs of medical care have risen, and there has been increased popular demand that the costs and risks be spread among larger populations. In response, central governments have become more involved in financing and regulating medical care. When increasing complexity and demand have led to more centralized sources of revenue without effective price controls, as in the United States, the effect has been escalating costs. Only where there have been both centralized sources of revenue and centralized control over prices has there been effective cost containment.

Of course, cross-national variation in the level of centralization exists for several reasons. First, systems have started from different levels of centralization. And second, there has been variability in the relative strength of providers and consumers. Previous chapters have demonstrated that the more powerful the consumer of health care vis-à-vis the provider, the higher the level of centralization. Historically, the provider has been less powerful in comparison with the consumer in Great Britain than in the United States, and for this reason, the British system has been more centralized. In both countries, however, as the state has become more centralized, it too has become more of an autonomous actor in shaping medical policy.*

---

* Although the social science literature is filled with discussions about the concept of centralization, there is no consensus about its meaning (Hollingsworth and Hanneman 1983). Scholars often treat it as though it were a one-dimensional concept. However, it is multidimensional, and if our understanding as to how centralization influences performance is to be advanced, it is necessary that this multidimensionality be captured in the operationalization of the concept.

Decisions, whether in delivery system or in complex organizations, are made at multiple levels. And in discussing centralization, one should identify the level at which various types of decisions are made. For purposes of the discussion of national medical delivery systems, there are two key dimensions along which one might identify these levels: the amount of revenue raised for medical care, and the prices to be set for it. Obviously, there are other dimensions that are important when one is discussing centralization: e.g., the levels of which standards are set and at which personnel are appointed. However, these other dimensions are highly correlated with those on which this discussion focuses (Hollingsworth and Hanneman 1983). In other words, the two dimensions of revenue and price capture most of the concept of centralization.

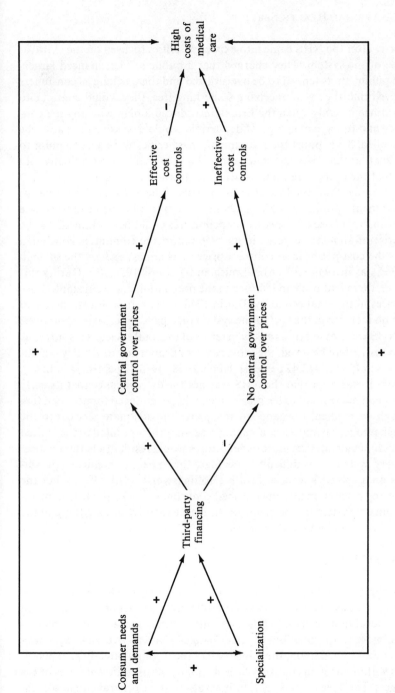

Fig. 2. Medical Delivery System Variables and Medical Expenditures

137

The National Health Service

Shortly after the NHS came into existence, critics focused on the extravagance of the system. They charged that a public service financed largely with public funds tended to be overutilized and that, as long as consumers believed that they were receiving something free, they would continue to overutilize it. Only when the British introduced a plan whereby the consumer had to pay some type of deductible would excessive utilization be controlled. To support their argument, these critics were able to point to the fact that the NHS cost much more than the public was originally told and that the costs were rapidly escalating from year to year.

Very much concerned with the rising costs of the NHS, the Conservative government appointed the Guilleband Committee in 1953 to investigate costs and to advise how medical expenditures could be contained. To the surprise of almost everyone, in its 1956 report the committee concluded that "the cost per head at constant prices was almost exactly the same in 1953–54 as in 1949–50" (Abel-Smith and Titmuss 1956: 46). During this period, there had been an increase in the population and a substantial rise in prices in the total economy. But in 1948–49 constant prices, there had been no increase in the cost of the system on a per capita basis. Moreover, the NHS was not nearly as costly in terms of the total society's resources as many critics had believed: the gross cost as a proportion of GNP was actually less in 1953–54 (3.42 percent) than in 1948–49 (3.57 percent) (ibid.: 60).

Once it was clear that the NHS was not the extravagance that its early critics had made it out to be, it was, ironically, denounced for not spending enough on medical care and for not providing adequate services to the British public. To make a convincing case, the critics pointed to the United States for evidence that more expenditures would result in a better medical delivery system. It is difficult to evaluate the impact of medical expenditures on a society's level of health (Hollingsworth et al. 1978a), but the following discussion attempts to shed some light on why the British medical delivery system has been one of the least expensive among those of the more advanced industrial societies.

Decision Making

Until the early 1970s, the Treasury and the Ministry of Health agreed that each year the expenditure levels of the different branches of the NHS would be at a level similar to that of the previous year. There was some incremental adjustment for inflationary price changes. Once an overall budget allocation was agreed upon, the ministry had the flexibility to adjust expenditures within line items but very little flexibility across different items of the budgets. The Treasury also carefully scrutinized the general budget allocations to the ministry as well as individual capital expenditures that exceed specific limits. In general, however, the Treasury allowed the Ministry of Health and its successor, the Department of Health and Social Security, to determine its own capital expenditure priorities, a situation that meant that there was a great deal of fierce infighting over the allocation of money for capital expenditures.

The National Health Service Act of 1946 stipulated certain procedures for the budgetary process, which varied, depending on whether budgets were for general practitioner services at the executive council level, for local health authorities, or for hospital services. For example, at the end of every fiscal year, each executive council was required to submit to the minister an estimate of its expenditures for the following year for all of its services. In practice, these estimates were very much tailored to those of the previous year. The amount allocated to the executive councils reflected estimates of the number of general practitioners, dentists, and pharmacists, and the size of the population by age and sex.

The budgetary process involving the local health authorities was somewhat more complex. Until 1959, the local health services were financed equally by funds from the central government and from local rates (Lindsey 1962: 105). Thereafter, the central government contribution was more in line with the general grant it made to local authorities for carrying out all functions of government. Each local health authority outlined its expenditures and revenue, and the minister then provided a grant of not less than three-eighths and not more than three-fourths of this amount. The central government exerted a control that was quite loose and indirect, leaving the local authorities a great deal of independence in allocating their funds.

As the government attempted to contain expenditures, the NHS focused close attention on hospital spending, and thus the budgetary process for hospital and specialist services became somewhat complex. The process was complicated because of the existence of multiple authorities: the boards of governors of the teaching hospitals, the RHBs, and under them the HMCs. Originally, each HMC would submit proposed expenditures for the coming year, based on those for the current year, to the RHB, which, in turn, would submit its proposed budget to the ministry. The costs were broken down into administrative costs and hospital operating costs such as salaries and wages, maintenance of buildings, food, and heating. The ministry then allocated a sum, based essentially on the previous year's level of expenditure, to boards of governors and RHBs, and the latter then distributed funds to the HMCs in their areas.

Soon, however, it became quite evident that this type of budgetary process was unsatisfactory, as the allocations were not very responsive to the real needs of an individual hospital authority, a particular region, or the country. This type of process tended to preserve inequities in the allocation of resources that had existed when the NHS began. Moreover, it was not suitable for determining the relative efficiency of individual hospitals. In its place, the Nuffield Provincial Hospital Trust and several other nonprofit organizations proposed a budgetary process based on departmental costing (Feldstein 1963: 173). After careful study, the government proposed that hospitals move as quickly as possible to the use of departmental costing. This meant that hereafter budgets were prepared according to the needs and expenditures for specific hospital departments (e.g., outpatient, radiotherapy, and medical services). This allowed the ministry and RHB more accurately to identify those hospitals and departments that diverged from national averages. It also permitted follow-up studies, so that officials could distinguish those factors that tended to promote higher costs. And finally, departmental costing raised the potential for both the ministry and the RHB to increase equity among regions in the allocation of resources. Although this method of budgeting had great potential for cost control and increased equity in the distribution of hospital resources, the ministry did not address some of the larger issues of the methods of achieving efficiency in hospital care. Neglected were the larger questions of the cost-effectiveness of one type of treatment versus another and of the choice of inpatient versus outpatient care for certain medical problems. In other words, the NHS was very much concerned with how to keep costs low and how much inequity there was among hospital regions. The government appeared relatively unconcerned with the more micro type problem of how much an extra unit of hospital resources would impact on an outcome (Feldstein 1963: 174).

To break with the pattern of an inherited budgetary program, the Department of Health and Social Security in later years resorted to planning, programming, and budgeting. As a result, the RHBs and the boards of governors were required to defend all of their budgetary requests by evaluating the effectiveness of each program and by considering alternative ways of achieving the same objectives. While much of this type of budgeting was less than ideal, it did help to place limits on hospital spending.

Meantime, it became increasingly obvious to the ministry and its critics that regional inequities persisted in the distribution of health resources. As a result, the government designed a new formula for equalizing resources over a ten-year period. Beginning in 1971, revenue was allocated to regions according to three basic variables: (1) the population, weighted for an age-sex distribution; (2) the daily total of occupied beds for each region by specialty (in order to calculate the allocation required to finance the existing bed stock at a national average cost); and (3) the type and number of cases (i.e., inpatients, outpatients, and day patients) treated. These three variables were then used to develop an allocation for each region. After a formula for allocation had been determined, a comparison was made with historical allocations to each region. When a discrepancy was determined in this respect, regions that had been receiving more would, over a ten-year period, receive less, and vice versa. Ideally, at the end of a ten-year period (1981), all regions were to be receiving more equitable allocations (English 1976: 164–70; West 1973: 153–66).

Compared with the medical delivery systems of other societies, the British NHS was relatively successful in controlling costs. On the other hand, its basic structure failed to maximize ideal cost-effectiveness. The division of the NHS into three basic services—hospital, local authority, and executive council—meant that there was no single process for allocating resources and for planning. Moreover, coordination was difficult because the boundaries of the hospital districts were not congruent with those of the executive councils and local health authorities (Feldstein 1963: 176). The British had a medical delivery system that was quite centralized in that, as compared to the system in most societies, a high proportion of the resources were allocated and regulated by the central government. And while the various parts of the system were well coordinated relatively to other national medical delivery systems, the fragmented nature of the British system meant that it was still somewhat deficient in coordination.

Expenditure Trends

From its inception, the hospital sector of the NHS, like that in all highly industrial societies, has been the most expensive. In the entire United Kingdom, the hospital sector was responsible for 55 percent of the total spending of the NHS in 1950, but this had increased to 66 percent by 1972. The use of the hospital as a site for treating patients has increased in Britain as in all other advanced industrial societies. The number treated as inpatients increased by almost 90 percent between 1949 and 1971, while the outpatient load increased by approximately 40 percent. Meantime, expenditures for general outpatient services declined from 12 percent to 8 percent during the same period. But as a percentage of gross domestic product (GDP) in Britain, expenditures of the NHS increased from 3.5 percent in 1950 to 4.6 percent in 1972 (see table 2), substantially less than medical expenditures in other advanced industrial societies (Cooper 1975: 29–30).

Some observers argue that the NHS throughout its history has had a serious shortage of hospital doctors, nurses, and beds and point to the long waiting lists for hospital treatment that have persisted throughout its history. For example, there were approximately 530,000 people on waiting lists in 1950, about the same number as 20 years later (see table 3). And the long waiting lists do receive a great deal of attention in the press, in Parliament, and abroad—particularly in the United States. Were the British spending more money on hospital beds and doctors, however, it is not at all

Table 2 Medical Expenditures as a Percentage of GNP, Great Britain and the United States, 1950–1980

	Great Britain	United States
1950	4.1	4.6
1960	3.8	5.2
1970	4.6	7.4
1980	5.9	9.4

Source: Great Britain, NHS 1979: 431; Hollingsworth et al., forthcoming; U.S., Comm., Census 1981: 99, table 149.

Table 3 Hospital Waiting Lists per 1,000 Population, England and Wales, 1949–1970

	Number on Waiting List	Number on Waiting List per 1,000 Population
1949	497,700	11.37
1950	530,500	12.11
1955	454,900	10.24
1960	465,539	10.17
1965	517,142	10.84
1970	555,883	11.35

Source: Cooper 1975: 23.

certain that the waiting lists would be any shorter. As was suggested earlier, Feldstein (1967) and others (Donabedian 1976; Cooper 1975: 22) have demonstrated with various studies that an increase in beds based on an assessment of need as defined by admissions and waiting lists has very little meaning. Need tends to increase as the supply of beds expands. Thus, in Britain, the size of waiting lists has proven to be insensitive to an increase in the supply of services, since doctors increase the demand for medical care as the potential for more services rises. Some argue that the long waiting lists, therefore, are not a valid indicator of inadequate responsiveness to demand on the part of the government. Rather, the British government has recognized that much of the demand for medical care is unlimited, and that only by rationing supply can there be a cost-effective national health service.

Obviously, the issue of waiting lists is complicated, and there are many dimensions to the problem. They are one mechanism for controlling access to care. In the United States, hospital entry is restricted by financial constraints on patients rather than by waiting lists. The NHS has a good record of providing rapid treatment of urgent cases. One extensive survey of waiting time found that 80 percent of all inpatients indicated that they were not caused any inconvenience or distress by waiting for admission to a hospital. It also found that 45 percent of all inpatient admissions took place within one month of placement on the waiting list, though 6 percent of patients had to wait longer than one year (Great Britain, NHS 1979: 125–27).

Moreover, waiting lists should be viewed in the context of certain changes in the NHS. In England, the number of patients receiving inpatient care almost doubled between 1949 and 1976, increasing from 2.8 million to over 5.2 million, while the number on waiting lists rose from 497,700 to 607,000. When the waiting lists are viewed as a percentage of the total number admitted to hospitals, the proportion falls from 17.8 to 11.7 percent, a consideration that is rarely noted (Jones and McCarthy 1978: 34–36).

It is in the allocation of capital expenditures that the decision to ration medical resources has been most apparent under the NHS, and it is also in this area that the consequences of rationing have been most controversial. Most of the capital expenditures have been for hospitals. In the years following World War II, however, the restrictions on all capital expenditures, including those for hospitals, were considerable. Money and building materials in postwar Britain were simply in short supply, and priority was given to the construction of houses and schools. Of course, capital investment could not be permanently postponed if a high-quality medical service was to be maintained. The desirable level of capital investment in a national health delivery system depends on many considerations—principally the quality of the existing equipment, the speed with which technology is changing, and the ability of the existing system to accommodate the demand for care. Whatever the criteria for judging the adequacy of capital investment, however, it would appear that the NHS, in its early years, spent too little on this. By almost every account, the hospital stock was in poor condition before the NHS came into existence. For example, the hospital survey for the northwestern area of England reported in 1945 that "the existing hospitals, considered as buildings, fall far short of a satisfactory standard. Indeed, considering the high place which England takes in the medical world, perhaps the most striking thing about them is how bad they are" (Great Britain, MOH 1945: 9). The survey for South Wales made a similar point: "A number of hospitals visited are so old or badly designed that they cannot be regarded as worth retaining. . . . Roughly one-half of the hospital accommodation, expressed in terms of hospital beds, is structurally ill-adapted for the purpose for which it is used." Furthermore, "many hospitals erected in comparatively recent years are poorly designed, and do not conform to modern principles of hospital construction" (ibid.: 11). In 1948, approximately 45 percent of all the existing hospitals had been constructed before 1891, and at least 21 percent were erected before 1861. The oldest were those for the mentally ill, 40 percent of them having been constructed before 1861 (Abel-Smith and Titmuss 1956: 54).

As was suggested above, there were multiple reasons for the run-down condition of the hospital stock. Private philanthropy in the pre–World War II period was not sufficient to maintain the nation's hospitals in excellent condition, and local governments were either incapable or unwilling to raise the necessary capital for expanding and upgrading the municipal hospitals consistently with the nation's needs. Of course, the central government did improve many hospitals during World War II, but many hospitals delayed making capital improvements during and immediately after the war in anticipation of the changes that a national medical system was expected to introduce (Hollingsworth and Hollingsworth 1985).

During the first six years of the NHS, less than 1 percent of all national investment was allocated to capital investment in the medical sector. The allotment to each region was so modest that prewar regional inequities persisted in the allocation of hospital beds and other capital equipment. Of the total NHS budget for England and Wales during these years, approximately 3.5 percent was for capital expenditures, mostly for hospitals. For example, in 1948–49, 75 percent of all NHS capital expenditures for England and Wales was for hospitals, and in 1953–54 84 percent. Nevertheless, only 10 percent of those expenditures was for new hospital construction or major extensions. Most went into improving laundries, kitchens, and heating plants, as much of this type of equipment was outdated and had deteriorated. However, the newer equipment was much more efficient to operate, providing savings of approximately 25 percent per annum (Abel-Smith and Titmuss 1956: 133–36).

It is, of course, impossible to estimate the level of capital expenditure that would have been invested in hospital construction had there been no NHS. Certainly the government had substantially increased the number of beds during the war under the Emergency Medical Service, thus reducing somewhat the pressure for hospital expansion that had existed in 1938. Because the costs of the NHS were somewhat higher than it had anticipated, however, the government decided after 1948 that capital investments were the type of expenditure that could be postponed without incurring political costs. It is noteworthy, however, that the ratio of capital expenditures on hospitals to all expenditures on hospitals showed the NHS spending considerably less than the hospital authorities before World War II had done, or than the United States was spending in 1951. For example, capital expenditures represented 19.6 percent of all NHS expenditures in 1938–39 in England and Wales but only 4.1 percent in 1952–1953, while the comparable U.S. figure for 1951 was 23.4 percent.

Most observers agree that during the early years of the NHS, the British investment in hospital construction was less than one-half of what was necessary to maintain a satisfactory supply of hospitals. During the first thirteen years, the construction of only one new hospital was completed in England and Wales (Cooper 1975: 40). After 1955, however, capital became available for the construction of new hospitals, and by 1975, almost 12 percent of the NHS budget for Britain was for capital expenditures. Even so, by that date, only 18 percent of all hospital beds were in new or replacement buildings that the NHS had provided, and over one-third of the hospital stock, in terms of floor area, had been built before the turn of the century, the average age of English hospitals in 1971 being over 61 years (Great Britain, NHS 1979: 141). But by 1970, the NHS was beginning to allocate capital expenditures across hospital regions in a manner that had some effect in reducing inequities of medical resources.

Because of variability in hospital design and usage, there are no reliable studies that recommend an optimum useful life for a hospital. In general, hospital stocks in twentieth-century Western Europe and North America have had a life of only twenty-five to forty years. And if the same rate of replacement existed in the United Kingdom, well over one-half of the NHS hospitals would have been replaced by 1975. It should not be assumed, however, that a building is unsatisfactory simply because it is old. While the Americans have had a tendency to replace hospitals, the British, being less wealthy and more concerned with costs, have been more involved in adapting, upgrading, and extending them. Whereas the Americans have attempted to introduce elements of cheerfulness, the British have been more tolerant of hospitals that to an American would appear gloomy and depressing. In a U.S. hospital with an overcrowded and old structure, staff morale is likely to be very low, but there is substantial evidence that British medical professionals are more tolerant and have greater capacity to do efficient and excellent work under such circumstances.

Private Medical Expenditures

Virtually all citizens of Great Britain have relied on the NHS for medical care throughout its history. Much of the private care has been provided by consultants employed by the service, with treatment performed in either NHS hospitals or private facilities. Unfortunately, there is no complete data on the extent of private expenditures for medical care. However, in 1973, approximately 1 million people subscribed to various provident insurance companies for medical coverage for 2.1 million people, with many middle- and higher-grade staff of business firms and their families receiving this type of coverage. In 1973, the various provident schemes in Great Britain cost about £29 million, and approximately £24 million were paid out in benefits—or less than 1 percent of total NHS expenditures, and less than 2 percent of the NHS expenditures on hospital and specialist service. About one-half of these fees were for hospital costs, and the remainder were for consultants' and specialists' fees. Excluding drugs, in 1973, an additional £15 to £25 million were spent on private medical care. Much of the additional expenditures were for care in nursing homes, which were exempted from nationalization in 1948 (Cartwright 1967).

Private care has frequently been purchased by foreign visitors in Great Britain who have been ineligible for treatment under the NHS. In addition, it has increasingly been bought by those who wanted to be assured of treatment by a consultant of their choice, the privacy of a hospital pay bed, and immediate hospitalization if necessary. In short, private care has been considered more convenient. In recent years, as labor unions have attempted to expand the benefits of their members, many have demanded and received private medical insurance. At the same time, approximately 90 percent of those interviewed throughout the history of the NHS have expressed strong satisfaction with the NHS. Moreover, well over 80 percent of those who have been hospitalized thought that the care they received was good or very good (Great Britain, Central Office of Information 1974; Brearley 1978; Cartwright 1967; Gregory 1978; Klein 1983a: 206; 1983b: 153–59).

Obviously, there is some dissatisfaction with the NHS, or there would not be a private sector. However, the NHS has been relatively successful in responding to most people with life-threatening illnesses and the degenerative chronic illnesses of old age. It would appear, however, that it has been less successful in giving sufficient attention to the working population who have minor problems and want them addressed at a time of their choosing. Nevertheless, by 1980, spending on medical care in the private sector was less than 5 percent of the NHS total budget, another indicator that the population has been relatively satisfied with the service. Then why is there a widely held view in the United States that the NHS provides inadequate care, and why among some groups in Great Britain is there the perception that it spends too little on medical care and that the quality of that care leaves a great deal to be desired? The answer is to be found in the process with which labor-management relations in the NHS have been conducted.

Labor-Management Relations

Throughout its history, the NHS has had a highly centralized industrial relations system, but this has exacerbated relations between the NHS staff and management (the government). Labor management relations have been extremely complicated as a result of a highly centralized system with a strong commitment to cost containment and high quality care. Had the former not been such a high priority of the British government over the years, perhaps there would have been more money available for wages and less conflict between employees of the NHS and the government.

Because of the virtual monopoly that the NHS exercises over the delivery of medical care, most medical practitioners have had no alternative employment opportunities. Thus, when they have wanted to improve their take-home pay and work conditions, they have had a strong incentive to emphasize the inadequacies and shortcomings of the NHS. As Rudolph Klein (1983a: 202) has suggested, employees of the NHS have tried to improve conditions for themselves by dramatizing how awful conditions are for patients. Like teachers' unions in the United States and Great Britain, the BMA, the royal colleges, and various employee unions from time to time issue warnings about the dire consequences that will follow if the NHS does not receive more money.

Quite apart from stresses resulting from issues of pay and work, there were strains within the NHS because of the changing roles of medical professionals. For example, the morale of some consultants was adversely affected by the increased influence of nurses and other hospital staff and the development of a multidisciplinary approach to patient care. Although these trends have occurred on both sides of the Atlantic because of changes in medical technology, their effect probably had more negative consequences on the morale of hospital-based doctors in Britain because the more centralized system did not have the capacity to make compensating adjustments and symbolic responses to those who have felt aggrieved.

If the British had had a pluralistic and decentralized health delivery system like the U.S. one, disputes involving pay and morale would have been diffused among multiple centers of power. Because the system is so highly centralized, however, discontent has often focused on the central government, and this has brought bad publicity to the NHS. Disagreements over pay disputes and morale problems have tended to be featured on television and in the newspapers, and this has had over the years a cumulative effect of undermining staff morale.

Although hospital workers have consistently felt considerable social responsibility for patients, over the years they have observed workers in other industries benefiting from strike action. As a result, since 1960, there has been an expansion of trade union membership among NHS professional workers. By 1976, every grade of hospital staff had engaged in some type of strike action over a multiplicity of disputes involving work conditions, pay, and disciplinary matters. Even so, the number of days lost through strike action by NHS staff was very small in comparison to the British workforce as a whole (see table 4), though the labor problems in the NHS did become very severe in 1973. There have been many types of industrial action other

Table 4 Days Lost through Strike Action, National Health Service
and Total British Work Force, 1966–1977

	Number of NHS Stoppages	Number of Staff Involved	Average Number of Days Lost per 1,000 NHS Staff	Average Number of Days Lost per 1,000 Employees in Great Britain
1966	2	500	.69	100
1970	5	1,300	8.46	499.2
1973	18	59,000	353.50	324.4
1975	19	6,000	21.88	270.6
1977	21	2,970	8.44	448.0

Source: Great Britain, NHS 1979: 163.

than strikes, however—for example, working to rule, going slow, and refusing to cooperate with management on specific issues.

The various unions representing NHS staff have met nationally to negotiate work conditions in bodies known as Whitley Councils. Doctors and
dentists, however, negotiate directly with the government and are subject
to the periodic recommendations of the Doctors and Dentists Review
Body. The Whitley Councils have provided standardized, centrally nego-
tiated terms of work and have promoted the unity of the NHS, but they
have tended to ignore the complexities of many local issues, thereby causing low morale at the local level. In addition, the negotiators on management's side usually have had little or no control over the amount of money
available, as the NHS was mostly Treasury financed. As a result, unions
have often been frustrated when management negotiators have been over-
ruled by other parts of the government, and this has caused labor to be
distrustful of the negotiating process (Great Britain, NHS 1979: 165).

Over the years, some of the less influential NHS staff strongly believed
that the service had not dealt fairly with them. For example, the hospital
ancillary workers were clearly underpaid and underappreciated during the
first two decades of the NHS. And as late as 1972, a substantial number of
these workers were paid salaries below the government's official poverty
line and would have been better off financially had they stopped working
and received unemployment and social security benefits (Widgery 1976:
304).

Another group long dissatisfied with their work conditions were the
hospital-based junior doctors. The Junior Hospital Doctors Association
emerged during the 1960s "to dramatize the conditions of house officers
doing their compulsory preregistration jobs in a sort of medieval apprenticeship" (ibid.: 303).

As the result of taking vigorous industrial action against the NHS, and
after much confrontation, the ancillary workers and junior doctors were

able to improve their pay as well as work conditions. This, of course, encouraged other groups to believe that, in order to bargain effectively with an employer as highly centralized and powerful as the NHS, it was necessary for them also to use vigorous countervailing power and the threat of strikes. And it was the frequent threat of strike action by first one group and then another within NHS that caused the politics of health care to become a national topic of daily discussion by the 1970s.

The problem of industrial relations has posed one of the most serious challenges to the NHS. Its highly centralized structure has encouraged employees to develop their own organizations: highly centralized government power has generated countervailing power among workers. Because labor organizations tend to be protective of their members, resistance and opposition to change and innovations can easily develop. The character of medical care is constantly changing—often very rapidly—and an efficient medical delivery system thus requires enough flexibility for tasks and functions to be easily redistributed among professionals. To meet the challenge of change and innovations, staffing structures need to be flexible, so that professionals whose skills become obsolete may either acquire further training or be retrained. Duties often have to be redefined. But as professional and labor organizations acquire more power to protect their members, so the potential for serious tension between the need for a flexible delivery system and the desire of staff to protect their positions increases. It remains to be seen whether a system as centralized as the NHS, containing many well-organized blocs of power, can continue to maintain, as it has so far, the necessary flexibility to adjust to the changes dictated by new medical technology.

Even if the highly centralized NHS was relatively successful in controlling costs and tended to produce more equality in the distribution of resources across regions than a decentralized system, it did encounter costs with its personnel. A highly centralized system is more impersonal, and it is difficult for its employees to develop a strong positive identity with the system. In a decentralized or smaller system, there is a likelihood that staff members will have greater loyalty to the system and that their morale will be higher. The NHS system has tended to generate countervailing power that is highly mobilized among its constituent parts, and this power in turn has led to protracted and intense negotiations between management and labor. Employee loyalties to nationwide labor unions and professional associations have become stronger, while loyalties to particular hospitals or the NHS have become weaker. There has been very limited ability to contain labor-management disputes at the local level, as cleavages and disputes have tended to become nationwide in scope.

In contrast, the decentralized U.S. medical delivery system has had much less strife between its constituent parts. Of course, even in the United States, there was increased unionization during the 1960s and 1970s among hospital workers, nurses, and doctors, but negotiations between the unions and management were usually confined to the level of an individual hospital and were not nationwide. Moreover, a high percentage of American physicians either were self-employed or worked in private clinics. It was the decentralized structure of the system that enhanced its ability to contain labor disputes at the local level or within a single hospital, a situation that in turn did much to prevent labor-management disputes from undermining the legitimacy of the entire system. On the other hand, it has been a fee-for-service method of financing the system in the United States that has posed threats to its legitimacy. Of course, that method of financing has meant that providers of care have been better compensated in the United States than in Great Britain. However, the decentralized U.S. medical system has not had sufficient power concentrated in one place in order to control the inflationary tendencies inherent in the medical care sector.

The U.S. System

In contrast to the centralized British system of controlling medical revenues and prices, the United States has had a third-party retrospective system of reimbursing medical expenditures, which has substantially eliminated all fiscal constraints on providers and consumers. By 1970, the elderly and the indigent were covered by Medicare and Medicaid, and 90 percent of other Americans had some form of medical insurance, so that most patients, physicians, and hospitals had little incentive to take the cost of care into account when making decisions about consumption.

Third-Party Retrospective Reimbursement

The incentives in the fee-for-service system rewarded more rather than less costly types of care. Though physicians were the gatekeepers to medical care, most of them during the 1970s had little knowledge about the costs and had incentives not to be concerned (Enthoven 1980: xvii, 212). As Walter McNerney observed, the structure of the nation's medical delivery system encouraged the use of medical technology all along the line, and "quality is the doctor's wild card and the provider's defense against proposals for change" (1980). In contrast to earlier periods in the twentieth century, the well-trained physician was increasingly able to practice his profession without having to worry about the ability of patients to pay their medical bills. And in the eyes of many observers, this resulted in a great deal of clinically unnecessary care.

Similarly, hospitals had few incentives to take costs into account or to make consumption and production choices. They competed with one another in terms not of cost but of scope and intensity of services. For example, when one hospital acquired a computed tomography (CT) scanner, neighboring hospitals attempted to do so also, even if the area needed, in terms of economies of scale, only one.

The retrospective system of payment provided an increasing percentage of GNP for medical care, a system that rewarded behavior that increased costs and punished behavior that attempted to contain them. U.S. hospitals have been reimbursed on the basis of either costs or charges based on costs, and more costs have meant more revenue for the hospitals, for most costs were passed on to third-party payers. Obviously, such a system was somewhat inflationary and wasteful (Enthoven 1978b: 1229; 1980: xvii). A study commissioned by the President's Council on Wage and Price Stability concluded in 1977 that there were few incentives in the medical provider system to "control costs; to encourage, or to weigh the *costs* of a proposed action—the purchase of new equipment, the expansion of a hospital, or the selection of a course of treatment—against its benefits" (Feldstein and Taylor 1977: ii).

For several years following its inception, federal funding for Medicare and Medicaid was relatively open ended. The range of services was broad, with Medicare covering most of the elderly and Medicaid a sizable portion of the needy. But the cost-based reimbursement system encouraged providers to dispense unnecessary services and raise their fees, while the existence of public funding—like other third-party payment schemes—encouraged patients to receive more services than would have been the case without it. In short, an open-ended funding system threatened to produce open-ended spending on medical care. And by 1978, the United States was spending 9.1 percent of its GNP on health care, and many Americans were talking about the levels increasing to 11 percent (Mead 1977a: 40–41; Enthoven 1980).

Though medical costs have dramatically increased since Medicare and Medicaid came into existence, it is, of course, not only these programs but the structure of the entire system that has led to the inflation of medical costs. One factor that observers often overlook when trying to understand the costs of the U.S. medical system is the nation's tax laws. Since the 1940s, the tax system has provided a major subsidy for the purchase of health insurance: employees' health insurance costs have been tax deductible business expenses but benefits have not been taxable income to employees and have not been included in the base on which social security taxes have been computed. Medical benefit packages became a by-product of the collective bargaining process in the United States although such arrangements were not necessarily the most efficient way of using medical dollars. Feldstein and Friedman estimated that on the margin, the tax subsidy during the 1970s represented approximately 35 percent of the cost of health insurance (1974). The tax laws have encouraged employers and employees to buy insurance with low deductibles, so that most bills may be paid with untaxed rather than after-tax dollars. Feldstein estimated that most wage earners were able to purchase nearly 50 percent more medical care for the same money in this fashion (1977). As a result of the nation's tax laws relating to medical benefits, state and federal governments received $14 billion less in tax revenues in 1979 than they would have otherwise (Enthoven 1980: 19). Because of the nature of third-party payers, most consumers have had little incentive to question the value of service or to seek out a less costly provider or style of care (Enthoven 1980).

Over time, the medical profession justified its opposition to consumer and government cost control efforts by invoking the doctor-patient relationship and by arguing that it was improper for groups other than the organized profession to monitor professional decisions. While physicians have been sincere in wishing to protect the doctor-patient relationship, those who pay the nation's medical bills have had a vested interest in controlling costs. Though medical ethics represent noble aspirations on the part of the medical profession, they have not been useful as a guide for containing costs or for shaping social policy. Physicians are certainly motivated to cure the sick and to provide excellence in medical care, but at the same time, the profession has profited greatly by dominating the nation's medical delivery system. There is no one correct way to organize and administer medical care, but the power of the American medical providers has severely limited the options for organizing the delivery system.

The Politics of National Health Insurance

For several years after the enactment of Medicare and Medicaid, their were serious discussions about the desirability of some form of national health insurance, but by the end of the 1970s, movement in this direction had effectively stalled. While there was considerable national support for broadening the extent of coverage and assuring beneficiaries of financial protection against medical costs, there was substantial divergence of opinion over the appropriate way to respond to these pressures. Powerful and well-financed interest groups supported a particular type of plan, but if their particular scheme were not enacted, they preferred no plan. As a result, the political compromise was to do nothing. There was general agreement that a national health insurance plan had to be fiscally and politically feasible, but there was no consensus over how to finance it (private versus public, payroll tax versus general revenue financing) or control its costs, quality, and economic effects. And while a high percentage of the American people were disturbed by the high cost of medical care, less than 10 percent were dissatisfied with their individual medical care. Since approximately 90 percent had some type of medical insurance coverage, there was no intense pressure to enact a national health insurance plan. Whereas the debate about national health insurance earlier in the century had focused on the need to broaden coverage for low-income citizens, the debate in the 1970s had shifted to how best to control the soaring costs of medical care. As a result, a national health insurance plan seemed less likely in 1980 than in 1970. Indeed, many observers tended to view national health insurance as a "giant step sideways," arguing that resources should be invested in preventive care—environmental reform, antismoking campaigns, nutritional education—rather than in traditional and costly curative care (Marmor 1977; Fox 1977; Carlson 1975).

Strategies for Containing Costs

Conceptually, there are several strategies for containing medical expenditures. They are (1) government regulation of a private medical delivery system, (2) market incentives to consumers and providers, and (3) nationalization of the medical delivery system, a strategy the British have adopted. Obviously, the structure of a given system influences the strategies it chooses to pursue and the success it achieves.

Government Regulation

Americans who emphasize government regulation as a means of containing medical costs believe the problem lies with excess capacity (i.e., too many hospitals, too much costly technology, etc.), which is exacerbated by the fact that, in the medical area, supply generates much of its own demand. They argue that government regulation is necessary because third-party payers have diminished the concern of consumers over medical costs, while most physicians and hospitals have little incentive to hold them down but instead do have incentives to overprovide services. Hence without regulation, it has been argued, there will be wasteful duplication of facilities, fragmentation of services, and excessive consumption of care.

During the 1970s, government regulation received considerable public support, for it was widely believed that medical care was different from many other sectors of the economy, in that consumers, because of their ignorance, had little choice but to delegate decision making to non-cost-conscious providers—that is, doctors and hospital administrators (Havighurst 1973; 1977; Mayer 1980; McNerney 1980). The most vocal participants in demanding state regulation were officials of the central, state, and local governments. Because governments during the 1970s paid approximately 50 percent of the nation's hospital expenditures, they thought they had little choice but to contain these costs or cut back on other programs at a time when tax increases were becoming increasingly difficult to achieve.

Moreover, the central government was under pressure to reform the Medicaid program in order to bring states with limited coverage up to the standards of those with broader coverage. Threatened with fiscal crisis, governments turned to regulation of costs as a means of achieving high-quality services while spending less money (Joskow 1980: chap. 3).

After the introduction of Medicare and Medicaid, most regulatory activity focused on hospital costs and concentrated on three fronts: limitation on the expansion of hospital capital, facilities, and services; regulation of hospital rates and revenues; and controls on utilization (Steinwald and Sloan 1980).

The regulation of hospital expansion found its rationale in Roemer's Law, which asserts that the supply of hospital beds creates its own demand (Roemer and Shain 1959; Roemer 1961; Sloan and Steinwald 1980; Steinwald and Sloan 1980). Much of the thinking about hospital regulation of the 1970s emerged from local, state, and federal efforts at comprehensive planning for the provision of hospital facilities. Local efforts at health planning had originated in the United States as early as the 1930s, while the Hill-Burton Act of 1946 had mandated a state hospital planning program. Perhaps the most important federal efforts to develop hospital planning was the National Health Planning and Resource Development Act of 1974, which created a national network of health systems agencies, which were required to collect and analyze data related to health planning. An important provision of the legislation required states to establish certificate of need programs.

The idea behind certificate of need programs was relatively simple. Hospitals were prohibited from increasing the supply of beds or making certain other capital investments without the permission of a health planning agency. And if hospitals added beds or certain types of capital equipment without permission, they were to be penalized by forgoing federal funds. Eventually, some Blue Cross plans adopted a similar approach, requiring, as a prerequisite for the reimbursement for hospitals services, approval of capital expansion from state health planning agencies. By the end of the 1970s, approximately one-half of the nation's seventy-two Blue Cross plans had hospital contracts that required agency approval, while all but one state had adopted certificate of need legislation (Joskow 1980: chap. 7; Frech 1980; Steinwald and Sloan 1980).

However, evaluation research has failed to demonstrate that certificate of need programs were effective in controlling expenditures for hospital care. After reviewing numerous studies, economist Paul Joskow concluded that he could find "no evidence that CON [certificate of need] regulation alone has any significant effect on expenditures" (1980: chap. 8). Several studies have concluded that certificate of need regulation had the effect of reducing the growth rate in beds but increasing that of assets per bed. Other studies demonstrated that large, powerful, and more complex hospitals succeeded more frequently in obtaining capital equipment under the programs than smaller and less prestigious ones (Bicknell and Van Wyck 1979; Salkever and Bice 1976; Zeckhauser and Zook 1980). Moreover, certificate of need programs tended to shift capital from hospitals to unregulated physician offices and private clinics.

While the federal government was not very involved in setting rates for hospitals until 1983, several states had earlier established agencies to do so. Within the health industry, it was difficult to establish a consensus for the establishment of rate-setting regulatory machinery, for hospitals varied in the types of patient they served, the level and types of service they provided, and the degree to which they had costly teaching responsibilities. And while there have been numerous strategies in various states to regulate hospital costs, increases have continued. Several studies have focused on state mandatory rate-setting programs and have concluded that hospital rate regulation has helped to curb expenses per day but that these programs have had the effect of increasing the length of stay and, in some instances, the level of admissions. Thus the total effect has been little influence in controlling the inflation in hospital costs (Worthington and Piro 1982; Sloan 1983).

One of the most significant developments in hospital rate revenue control has been the introduction of prospective reimbursement systems, as distinct from retrospective cost-based and charge-based systems, which have generally been characteristic in the United States. At the state level, the most ambitious and comprehensive prospective reimbursement control system occurred in New Jersey. Classifying illnesses into more than 400 DRGs, the New Jersey plan was designed to give hospitals an incentive to provide medical care efficiently. Hospitals were no longer to be reimbursed for what they spent on a particular patient. Instead, the state—as regulator—determined in advance how much a hospital would be reimbursed for a particular type of care. If a hospital spent more than a specified rate to treat a patient, it would absorb the loss; if it spent less, it would keep the savings. Applying this concept to all third-party payers, New Jersey officials hoped that such a flat rate would discourage unnecessary diagnostic testing and overly long hospital stays. The rates, which were tailored to each hospital, included an allowance for hospital overhead and the costs for treating uninsured patients who could not pay their bills.

After several years, New Jersey found that this type of regulation failed to curb hospital costs. Indeed, in each of three years after the DRG program was implemented, hospital costs continued to rise. While careful evaluations of the program are yet to be made and the reasons for continued escalation in hospital costs in New Jersey are complex, tentative evidence suggests that while DRG programs have reduced the length of hospital stay, they have led to more admissions. And since the most expensive days in an hospital are the early ones, the New Jersey DRG program simply cut back on length of stay, but there were more patients with an early and more expensive period (Morone and Dunham 1983; 1985; *New York Times*, Mar. 12, 1983).

Meantime, Congress in 1983 adopted a modified version of the New Jersey DRG plan. Pertaining only to Medicare patients, the federal plan established for each of 467 DRGs a payment rate based on its national average cost. Except for adjustments for factors such as area wage differences and teaching costs, the federal plan established a single payment rate by DRG for all Medicare patients. As long as the DRG scheme applies only to Medicare patients, hospitals are expected to raise the costs of non-Medicare patients. But even if there were a uniform DRG rate for all third-party payers, many scholars believe that the effect throughout the nation would very likely be similar to the experience in New Jersey: the length of stay would be reduced but the number of admissions would increase—with very little effect on the spending by hospitals. At this writing, it is too early to assess the effectiveness of DRGs to control costs and to enhance the quality of care.

The DRG program is somewhat different from most hospital regulatory policies and does represent some structural change in the governance of U.S. hospitals. For example, in the treatment of Medicare patients, it represents a transfer of power from physicians and hospital providers to the federal bureaucracy. To implement its program at the local level, the Health Care Financing Administration (HCFA)—the federal bureaucracy responsible for the DRG program—has a contracting relationship with local or state peer review or organizations that are (1) to review the "reasonableness, necessity, and appropriateness" of hospital admissions, (2) to review the quality of care provided, and (3) to validate the diagnoses that determine reimbursement. As a result of this process, the federal government is no longer totally dependent on organized medicine for expertise in order to carry out its policies. After many years of paying Medicare bills, HCFA has established national norms and standards against which to measure medical practices and to monitor each local physician's practice. In this sense, the state appears to have the potential to become a much more important actor in the governance of the U.S. medical system. Even so, the DRGs at the present time relate only to hospitalized Medicare patients, and doctors who want to avoid DRG regulations can simply shift many of their patients from a regulated hospital setting to an unregulated outpatient setting.*

---

* For the discussion of the DRG program, I am very indebted to the manuscript of James W. Bjorkman (forthcoming 1986).

Meantime, governments have not directed all of their regulatory activities at hospitals. Because medical costs soared after the introduction of Medicare and Medicaid, Congress concluded that physicians, as the key decision makers in the medical delivery system, also should be regulated. Several congressional committees reported that a significant proportion of the health services provided under Medicare and Medicaid were not medically necessary (U.S. Congress, House, Commerce 1976). Accordingly, Congress in 1972 mandated that utilization review be vested in physician peer review bodies, known as professional standards review organizations. These were independent, nonprofit associations of physicians, broadly representative of the practicing physicians in each local area, which had the responsibility for monitoring the decisions of individual physicians involving the use of medical resources funded by a federal medical program. The organizations were to compile profiles on individual physicians in order to identify those who overutilized certain procedures, overprescribed certain drugs, or failed to meet other stipulated guidelines. While the information was not to be released to the public, it was released to individual doctors. Medical care that was judged by a review organization to be medically unnecessary would be denied federal funding. The federal professional standards review organization guidelines were designed to achieve cost containment by reducing unnecessary utilization, but with "proper quality of care" as the primary objective. As utilization reduction and quality enhancement were potentially conflicting goals, these objectives did not receive equal consideration from the physicians who participated in the organizations. Rather, they tended to emphasize quality considerations and give cost concerns very low priority. As a result, the review organizations had little or no effect in containing medical costs, though there is slight evidence that they helped to reduce the average length of stay in nonfederal, short-term hospitals (Ginsburg and Koretz 1979; Campbell 1978: 133–34; Joskow 1980). The medical profession operated at a micro level, providing care to individuals, while the problem of containing medical costs has been nationwide or a macro type problem. In the two years after the establishment of the review program, national medical expenditures increased by 30 percent, while Medicare and Medicaid spending increased by more than 50 percent (Mead 1977a: 42). By the end of the 1970s, the United States had been divided into 195 professional standards review areas, but none had yet fully implemented all the requirements of the law—a fact that demonstrates the difficulty of implementing federal medical programs unless they are quite consistent with the interests of the medical profession.

Significantly, clinical autonomy has been much more sacrosanct in the nationalized British system than in the market-oriented U.S. system. Unlike the situation in the United States, the NHS has made no effort to control or investigate the decisions of clinicians. In contrast to the professional standards review and DRG programs, the Ministry of Health in London would not think of telling surgeons how long their patients should be in the hospital. On the other hand, the British government does emphasize the desirability of getting better data about effective treatment into the hands of doctors. In other words, persuasion and education are used to maximize appropriate medical practice in Britain, where physicians are paid on a salary basis, but in the United States, where fee for service is much more widespread, government regulation is used.

As one evaluation study after another concluded that government regulation had been relatively ineffectual in curbing the costs of medical care, the enthusiasm of public officials began to wane during the early 1980s—despite the DRG program. Moreover, economists and medical providers began to attack the regulation of the medical delivery system as being inflationary, inefficient, and crippled by red tape. And indeed, there was considerable evidence to demonstrate that the particular type of regulation that had emerged in the United States did tend to beget special privilege and to benefit those inside the system more than it did the public (Havighurst 1973; Olson 1981; McNerney 1980). However, it must be emphasized that this type of regulation resulted from the distribution of power of highly organized groups and should not be taken as evidence that regulation would be worthless were power organized differently.

Certainly, the medical care industry was more difficult than some others to regulate effectively. In general, public regulation is more effective in those industries in which there are monopolistic practices or few providers; there is a single product; and there is very good information on the efficaciousness of the technology. But none of these criteria applies to the field of medicine. Instead of there being few providers, there are more than 6,000 hospitals and several hundred thousand physicians, a large proportion of whom are in private practice. And instead of there being a single or a simple product, medicine has numerous products, and even among practitioners there is often serious disagreement over which treatment strategy to pursue in regard to a particular disease. Industries in which there are trade-offs among competing values are especially difficult to regulate. For example, decisions about the choice of kidney dialysis or a transplant for a patient with renal failure are difficult to make on the basis of statistics.

While regulation is more effective in some industries than others, Americans are generally prepared to view most regulatory devices as ineffective before they find out why or before the regulatory process has time to work. Regulatory processes, to be effective, require time, for new procedures must be established, new personnel must be hired, and the regulated industry must have time to respond to the regulatory process (Vladeck 1980: 256).

Despite the potential of the DRG program, many American health economists and some public officials have become convinced that existing efforts at government regulation are not effective in containing expenditures and have begun to focus more attention on market incentives as a means of influencing utilization, personal habits, and clinical decisions (Zeckhauser and Zook 1980). In particular, serious efforts have emerged to develop incentives to purchase less medical insurance as a strategy for containing medical costs.

Market Incentives

Believing that the U.S. system of fee for service, retrospective cost reimbursement for hospital care, and third-party intermediaries for the consumer tend to reward cost-increasing behavior, medical economists in the late 1970s began searching for a rational health plan in the private sector that would reward cost-reducing behavior. The type of plan that attracted much attention was the prepaid group practice. While there are many types of prepaid practice, they have in common the following principles: a group of physicians, working together, provides comprehensive care to a defined population for a fixed prospective per capita payment. Some prepaid practices have been organized and sponsored by physicians, some by consumer cooperatives, insurance companies, hospitals, universities, and others. The physicians are generally paid on a capitation basis or salary and may or may not receive a share of the organization's net income; the group may or may not have its own hospital; it may emphasize primary care and refer more complicated cases to appropriate specialists or it may include a broad range of specialists. One of the best examples of a type of prepaid group practice in the United States is the HMO. Although HMOs in the United States have long been severely hampered by opposition from the medical profession, restrictive legislation by state and federal governments, and constraints on their marketing activities, they have demonstrated a capacity to provide quality medical care at prices below other forms of third-party coverage. Because of their prospective budgeting, HMOs have strong incentives to place considerable emphasis on patient education and preventive measures, to eliminate redundant diagnostic tests, to substitute nonphysician for physician manpower, and nonhospital or outpatient for inpatient treatment whenever possible. There are a number of studies that have demonstrated that HMOs reduce total per capita costs of medical care from 10 to 40 percent compared with the costs and quality for similar people who are insured by fee-for-service plans. By 1980, HMO plans covered millions of Americans, and there was some evidence that with HMOs it was possible to contain costs without reducing the quality of care (Enthoven 1978a; 1978b; 1980; Havighurst and Blumstein 1976; Luft 1978; Anderson et al. 1985).

The research on HMOs demonstrates that they have attained their cost savings not from a more efficient production of a given set of services but from differences in practice patterns—that is, the number and mix of services. For example, many of the basic savings of HMOs over fee-for-service systems resulted from lower rates of hospitalization as opposed to shorter stays. Minneapolis, which had a relatively high percentage of its population in HMOs, had a hospitalization rate of 500 days per 1,000 HMO members annually, compared with 850 days for similar people in the same community who were covered by fee-for-service type insurance. There is some evidence that where HMOs were widespread, other providers responded competitively by also resorting to lower levels of hospitals utilization (Luft 1978; Enthoven 1978a; 1978b; 1980; Mayer 1980; Christianson and McClure 1979; Anderson et al. 1985).

Research about HMOs has remained very modest, however. It is still unclear whether their performance is shaped by the incentives inherent in their structure or the type of providers and consumers who self-select into HMO plans.

For many policy makers who were impressed with the cost-saving potential of HMOs, the critical problem was how to move the society to rely even more extensively on them. To achieve this, serious efforts began in order to remove other constraints that make it difficult to obtain efficient contractual relationships among consumers, insurers, and providers. Specifically, there were mounting pressures to alter the tax laws so that there would be a ceiling on the amount of medical insurance that an employer may deduct as a business expense; to offer physicians incentives to join cost-saving prepaid health plans; and to deny tax deductions and copayment schemes.

As the nation encountered serious economic problems simultaneously with mounting medical costs, many leaders of monopoly capital began to attack the cost-inefficiencies of the petit-bourgeois mode of medical services in the United States (structured around solo fee-for-service medical practice and cost reimbursement for hospital care). For example, General Motors' expenses for health insurance increased sevenfold between 1965 and 1977, from $170 million to $1.2 billion. Realizing that some of this money could have been used for more pay or different types of fringe benefits, many large employers became supportive of HMOs as organizations for realizing substantial savings. As a result, many members of Congress and a number of banks, insurance companies, and other corporations advocated the widespread establishment of large HMOs as a means of moving medical delivery from the control predominantly of petit-bourgeois practitioners to that of the corporate sector. Some of the nation's largest insurance companies by 1980 were developing alternative delivery systems and positioning themselves for a market of medical plan competition (Enthoven 1980: 155; Sullivan 1984).

While tax revision and consumer incentives have some potential for increasing competition and placing some limits on increases in medical expenditures, the prospects by the mid 1980s appeared mixed that the United States would substantially deregulate the medical delivery system and move primarily to a market system with incentives designed to shape behavior among consumers and providers. The Reagan administration, while rhetorically committed to deregulation, had endorsed the DRG program for regulating Medicare—one of the most extensive regulatory programs in the medical area ever developed by the federal government. Given the unique character of the market, competition has marked limits in shaping prices in the medical marketplace. As the pros and cons of regulation versus incentives derived from competition are debated, the distribution of power among competing groups in society suggests that Americans will not rely exclusively on either a regulatory or a competitive model but will instead attempt to strike a balance between the two.

Centralized Control of Cost Containment

The Americans spend a substantially higher portion of their GNP on medical care than do the British, primarily because of their different ways of organizing cost controls. In the United States, most decisions about medical care are first made by patients and providers, and reimbursement is made retrospectively. In other words, the spending decisions over time have been made, for the most part, in a decentralized system, with the central government and other third-party payers obligated to pay out what the providers and consumers demand. In contrast, the centralized British system has been much more successful in controlling costs, for the providers under the NHS have had to make do with the more limited resources that have been allocated to them. Unlike the situation in the United States, provider decisions in Britain have been made after spending decisions. As a result, British hospitals have been older, and there have been less duplication of equipment and fewer redundant diagnostic tests. But it would be difficult to demonstrate that as a result of these differences the British people have been in worse health than the Americans.

One cross-national and cross-temporal study has demonstrated that the more a medical delivery system departs from a market type system and becomes coordinated by the state, the lower the level of medical expenditures. In that study, there were two variables that measured the degree of departure from a market type system. They are, firstly, the degree of control by the state over the source of revenue for medical care and secondly, the degree of state control over prices of medical services and the appointment of personnel. Controlling for level of GNP, as well exogenous variables and medical delivery system characteristics, the study demonstrated that the greater the percentage of all expenditures the state provides for medical care, the higher the level of medical expenditures. This finding is not surprising and is consistent with the widely acknowledged view that once the U.S. government began to fund Medicare and Medicaid, the level of expenditures increased substantially. On the other hand, the study demonstrated that those systems had lower levels of medical expenditures in which the state exercised substantial control over the price of medical goods and services and the appointment of personnel. Moreover, the study demonstrated that the British NHS was the most successful system in controlling medical expenditures in Western Europe and North America (Hollingsworth et al., forthcoming).

Western medical delivery systems reflect the broader social structure and the historical background out of which they have emerged. Faced with a fragmented and decentralized state system and living in a multicultural society, Americans have historically attempted to solve medical problems in the private sector and with a minimum of state power. As a result, the idea of containing costs by nationalizing the delivery system has attracted very little attention. Nor is it likely to attract much support in the future. Rather, Americans have tended to focus on state regulation and economic incentives in the private sector as means of control.

Significantly, one area in which the American state is succeeding in curbing costs is in the provision of medical care for the poor. Throughout much of the country by the end of the 1970s and early 1980s, efforts were made either to stabilize or to reduce funds for Medicaid, while eligibility requirements became more rigorous. In other words, the poor—the one group with very little power and influence—were once again having serious problems in getting access to care. Meantime, many of the large urban public hospitals that have served the poor were experiencing serious financial stress (Sulvetta 1985; Feder et al. 1984). Ironically, by the end of the 1970s, the United States—in contrast to Britain—was once again moving toward a two-tier medical system: one for the poor and one for the non-poor. However, the cutbacks in Medicaid had little effect in curbing the rate of increase in medical spending. Given the rate with which medical expenditures were rising in the 1970s and given the small size of Medicaid as a percentage of the total, even had all Medicaid expenditures been eliminated in the 1970s, there would have been only a modest overall reduction in medical expenditures in the United States (Hollingsworth and Hollingsworth, forthcoming).

CONCLUDING OBSERVATIONS

The explanation for rising medical expenditures in Western industrialized countries is complex. Certainly, increases in GNP and general inflationary forces have contributed to substantially higher levels of spending. In a number of cross-national studies, it has been shown that much of the variation in medical expenditures is explained by variation in GNP. But across countries, some of the variation is due to differences in the basic structure of medical delivery systems. And in contrast with the British system, the structure of the U.S. system is not conducive to effective cost controls.

In both countries, the medical delivery systems are quite paternalistic: it is the doctors who make the major decisions about the type and level of treatment that patients receive, for it is widely assumed that consumers do not have adequate information to make intelligent choices about medical care. In Britain, however, bureaucrats and politicians make the decisions about the amount of money that will be spent. Because of its monopoly status, the NHS can effectively control costs: it can negotiate vigorously in determining wages, and it can effectively constrain capital expenditure. British doctors have agreed to work within budgetary limits, but in turn, they have insisted that the government not interfere with their clinical autonomy. Nevertheless, the government has influenced clinical decisions by publishing data on cost-effective treatment methods and limiting resources. And for all of these reasons, the NHS has been very effective in limiting demand.

In contrast to the monopolistic and highly centralized system in Britain, that in the United States is competitive, decentralized, and somewhat market oriented. In an effort to control costs, the system has in recent years resorted to strategies emphasizing regulation and competition. Thus far, however, regulating physician fees and hospital costs has had limited effect in controlling rising medical costs. Meantime, the idea of increased competition as a means of containing costs resonates well with such American values as free enterprise and entrepreneurship. In response to policies designed to generate greater competitiveness, the U.S. system is rapidly changing. Some hospitals are closing, while many others are engaged in horizontal mergers. The federal government has reduced the amount that it will pay hospitals rendering care to Medicare and Medicaid patients. As a result, some hospitals, as prior to 1965, are again attempting to avoid certain types of patients. Meantime, some segments of the hospital industry are becoming vertically integrated. Many physicians are developing alternative sites for the delivery of medical services. For example, hospitals no longer have a virtual monopoly on diagnostic work-ups, as an increasing proportion of surgical procedures are being done in doctors' offices. As the emergency rooms of hospitals close, proprietary free-standing medical centers are emerging. Almost 40 percent of all surgery in the United States by 1983 occurred outside hospitals—much of it in doctors' offices (Goldsmith 1981; Hollingsworth and Hollingsworth, forthcoming).

This type of transformation in delivery is not likely to reduce the outlays for medical care, however. While the cost per surgical case is lower in a doctor's office than in a hospital, the shift is likely to result in much more and probably lower-quality surgery. As a result of the greater competitiveness of the U.S. system, it is becoming much more differentiated than the British. But it is also likely to continue being a much more expensive system.

In both countries, there is still very little knowledge about the clinical effectiveness or cost-effectiveness of alternative treatment strategies (Bunker 1985). Neither society has a good understanding of how to assess medical need; instead, need is very much determined in line with resource restraints, as providers tend to shape services according to available resources. Whether the American people are better off because their medical system spends substantially more than the British one is impossible to determine. In both countries, medical resources have improved the quality of life: they have minimized suffering and have maximized the ability of people with chronic diseases to lead active lives. More resources are not necessarily a good thing, however, as was indicated by a recent study at a U.S. university hospital. It demonstrated that 9 percent of the patients receiving medical services suffered an iatrogenic illness so severe that either it was life threatening or it produced considerable disability. Thus, even if the NHS received higher levels of funding, there is certainly no guarantee that the funds would be used in a cost-effective way to minimize suffering and improve health (Aaron and Schwartz 1984).

The policies and performance of medical delivery systems tend to reflect the way in which power is distributed in the system. For the United States, containing medical expenditures will require fundamental structural change and a redistribution of power in the society and not simply either the adoption of technical changes to be managed by a group of bureaucrats or the development of a more competitive system. Thus far, most U.S. policy makers have failed to understand that the basic structure of the medical delivery system places fundamental constraints on the success of particular policies in controlling spending on services. Without changing the basic structure of the medical delivery system, the formulation and implementation of specific policies to curb expenditures are unlikely to be successful.

4
Centralization and the Diffusion of Innovations

This chapter addresses the question of how differences in the structure of the British and U.S. medical delivery systems have influenced the speed with which new medical technology has diffused in the two countries. In all Western countries, increases in the per capita GNP and in the level of modernization have stimulated advances in medical technology and have accelerated the pace with which it diffuses. Even so, the basic structure of medical delivery systems places limits on the speed with which innovations diffuse across countries.

Specifically, the following are a few of the questions which the chapter confronts. Has variation in centralization influenced the speed of the diffusion of medical innovations? Because publicly financed and centralized systems are somewhat more subject to the pressures of the ballot box than those that are decentralized and predominantly in the private sector, are centralized systems likely to be quicker to adopt those innovations that are homogeneously demanded by the population but slower to adopt those that are demanded by small and specialized constituencies? There are both theoretical and empirical reasons for believing that the more any particular level of government pays for medical care, the more it will eventually attempt to place limits on increases in prices and expenditures (Marmor and Christianson 1982: 70). Therefore, since the NHS has been much more concerned with controlling medical costs than the key actors in the U.S. system have been, will we find that the NHS has slowed down the diffusion of expensive medical technology? On the other hand, do centralized and decentralized systems differ in the speed with which they adopt innovations that are inexpensive, highly efficacious, and in demand by almost everyone?

This chapter assumes that a host of variables influences the diffusion rate of innovations. It is specifically concerned with the way in which the following influence the rate of diffusion: the centralization of the delivery system, the heterogeneity of demand, the cost of the innovation, the perception of its efficaciousness, the type of funding, and the power of providers.

In analyzing the diffusion rate, the chapter draws a distinction between the lag time and the total diffusion time. The lag time is the period between a discovery or an invention and the time when it is first introduced into a country. The total diffusion time is the period between a discovery or an invention and the time when it diffuses throughout the system.

This chapter will conduct three types of analysis:

1. The effect of centralization on the total diffusion time of inexpensive, highly efficacious, and homogeneously demanded technologies.
2. The effect of centralization on the lag time of inexpensive, highly efficacious, and heterogeneously demanded technologies.
3. The effect of centralization on the total diffusion time of expensive and heterogeneously demanded technologies.

When efficaciousness is not highly demonstrable, other variables such as the type of funding and the power of providers come into play.

Obviously, there are many technologies that one might analyze in order to answer these questions, and the analyst must be somewhat selective. Even so, the following discussion does shed considerable light on how the structure of medical delivery systems influences the diffusion of innovations.

TOTAL DIFFUSION TIME OF INEXPENSIVE, HIGHLY EFFICACIOUS, HOMOGENEOUSLY DEMANDED TECHNOLOGIES

There is a substantial literature that suggests that the speed of the diffusion process is influenced by the costs, efficaciousness, and risks of technologies (Hollingsworth et al., forthcoming). Technologies that are inexpensive, highly efficacious, and low risk tend to diffuse rapidly, but one would like to have precise data on their diffusion rate. Such a data set across countries would permit one to control for these characteristics and thus gain some insight as to the influence of the underlying structure, which varies across systems, on the speed with which technologies diffuse. Because there is not comparable data in both countries on technologies of this type, the choice here is the next best strategy, that is, to focus on technologies that are so efficacious that one can clearly measure their diffusion rate by observing their effect on the health of a population as the technology diffuses. And vaccines provide such a technology. For example, the impact of vaccinations leaves a clear line in declining morbidity and mortality rates and makes possible a retrospective analysis of the speed with which the vaccine diffused. Certain vaccines are not only highly efficacious but also relatively inexpensive and demanded by most of the population.

As previous chapters have demonstrated, the British, throughout most of the twentieth century, have had a medical delivery system that has been both more egalitarian and more centralized than that in the United States. Because the more centralized British system has long had a stronger commitment to providing egalitarian access to general services for its population than the U.S. system, one might expect vaccines to have diffused more rapidly in Britain than in the United States. And with data on England and Wales in table 5 one may gain some insight as to whether this expectation is correct. The table lists for each country the date at which the technology

Table 5 Total Diffusion Times for Vaccines, the United States and England and Wales, 1922–1972

	U.S.	England and Wales
Diphtheria	1922–54	1923–52
	32 years	29 years
Tetanus	1927–64	1927–54
	37 years	27 years
Whooping Cough	1926–59	1927–59
	33 years	32 years
Tuberculosis[a]	1947–66	1947–66
	19 years	19 years
Polio	1953–64	1953–64
	11 years	11 years
Measles	1964–68	1965–72
	4 years	7 years

Sources: Official statistics in each country; United Nations (various years); U.S., Comm., Census 1979a; *Mortality Statistics* (numerous reports); Great Britain, Registrar General, *Statistical Review* (annual).

[a] Tuberculosis represents a special case. The French developed a vaccine against it during the 1920s, but it was not very efficacious and was hardly used outside France (Parish 1968). During the 1940s, however, a chemotherapy for tuberculosis was developed that was so efficacious that most authorities agreed that no one receiving the treatment should die from the disease (Johnson and Wildrick 1974). Thus the analysis is of the chemotherapy, not the vaccine.

first became available and the date at which the disease was essentially erradicated. Because the complete elimination of a disease is rarely achieved, the tactic here is to define its end point as the approach of some asymptote. But how does one define the correct asymptotic point? For this reason, it seems appropriate to speak of a steady state as a means of measuring the end of the diffusion process. Thus the end of diffusion is defined as that point at which only 5 deaths per 1 million population were attributed to a particular disease.

Table 5 suggests that technologies diffused slowly throughout both the United States and England and Wales early in the twentieth century and much more rapidly in recent years. In the early part of the twentieth century, the diphtheria antitoxin and tetanus vaccine diffused more rapidly in England and Wales than in the United States. On the other hand, even though the two systems were organized in very different ways, the diffusion time was identical for technologies pertaining to whooping cough, tuberculosis, and polio. Surprisingly, it required a longer period of time to reduce deaths from measles in England and Wales than in the United States, despite the fact that the NHS provided free vaccinations and had a more systematically developed system of preventive health care. Thus the data presented here suggest that medical technologies that were highly efficacious, low cost, and in considerable demand by a large percentage of the population did not systematically diffuse more rapidly in the more centralized and egalitarian system of which England and Wales form a large part. Among the six technologies, two diffused more rapidly in England and Wales, one more rapidly in the United States, and three at essentially the same rate.

LAG TIME OF INEXPENSIVE, HIGHLY EFFICACIOUS, HETEROGENEOUSLY DEMANDED TECHNOLOGIES

The preceding discussion focused on innovations demanded by almost everyone. But how does the structure of delivery systems influence the diffusion time with technologies that are relatively inexpensive but in demand by a much smaller percentage of the population? Are more centralized systems slower to adopt this type of innovation than decentralized systems? There is a vast body of theoretical literature that suggests this is the case (Hollingsworth et al. 1983). To answer these questions empirically, the analysis focuses on data involving the speed with which the British and Americans adopted new drugs after 1962.

As a result of the adverse public reaction to the medication Thalidomide, which was responsible for the birth of thousands of deformed babies, the United States in 1962 passed amendments to the 1938 Food, Drug, and Cosmetic Act. The 1962 legislation required the federal government, through the Food and Drug Administration (FDA), both to gain more control over the premarket testing of new drugs, and to change the criteria for the marketing of them. Because of the legislation, the new FDA regulations had the effect of imposing a gestation period of some years before many new drugs were approved as being both safe and efficacious. And over time, the period of time required for the testing and approval of new chemical entities has increased to slightly more than eight years (*Patent-Term Extension and the Pharmaceutical Industry*, 1981: 34).

While the U.S. medical delivery system, measured in the aggregate, is relatively decentralized, the process for the approval of new drugs since 1962 has ironically been somewhat centralized. Because of these centralized and bureaucratized procedures, the regulation of the marketing of new drugs became as stringent as in any country in the world.

It is somewhat paradoxical that in the highly centralized system of Great Britain, where physicians practice what many Americans label "socialized medicine" and where almost all of the hospitals have been nationalized since 1948, there was less regulation of the marketing of new drugs during the 1960s and 1970s than in the United States. Ironically, British physicians were more free to exercise their professional judgment in prescribing drugs than doctors in the United States, where the medical delivery system was decentralized and in the private sector to a greater extent than in any other highly industraized society. The process of approving drugs demonstrates that a system that in the aggregate is highly centralized may be engaged in some activity that is quite decentralized, and vice versa.

The ultimate power to approve a drug for public use in the United States lies with the full-time civil servants in the FDA, whose careers have depended on not approving a dangerous or ineffective drug and whose judgment is constantly subject to considerable examination by committees of Congress. In Great Britain, however, the approval of drugs during the 1960s lay with the nonstatutory Committee on the Safety of Drugs, which began operating in 1964. A voluntary body, the committee was a small body of unpaid experts (e.g., physicians, pharmacists, and scientists) who had the responsibility for evaluating the safety of drugs but were not charged with evaluating their comparative efficacy. Pharmaceutical companies voluntarily agreed to submit data on new medicines both before they were put into clinical trials with humans and again before they were marketed. Moreover, companies agreed not to market new medicines without or against the advice of the committee.

For a while, this procedure seemed to be quite acceptable in Britain, for many of the leading pharmacists, physicians, veterinarians, and pharmaceutical industrialists knew one another and were on friendly terms, whereas in the much larger United States this was not possible. As Sir Derick Dunlop, chairman of the Committee on the Safety of Drugs has written, "much of the Committee's contact with applicants—the requests for clarification and amplification—took place in robust but usually good-humored encounters over the telephone or in informal meetings rather than in official communications duplicated for the record" (Dunlop 1973: 232). The U.S. system, however, with its complex set of rules, had more of a centralized political and bureaucratic character to it. In contrast to that system, with its bias in the direction of caution and delay, the one in Britain, with its less centralized control, had shorter review times (Wardell and Lasagna 1975: 98−99, 105−7; Grabowski 1976: 31−34; Dunlop 1973: 230−42). And as the following discussion demonstrates, the difference in the level of centralized regulation in the approval of new drugs in the two countries meant a shorter lag time in the adoption of new drugs in Britain than in the United States.

Prior to the U.S. legislation in 1962, the rate of drug innovation in the United States exceeded that in Great Britain, but between 1962 and 1971, the pattern was substantially reversed (U.S. Congress, Senate, Judiciary 1974: 9804; Wardell 1973a). Indeed, shortly after the 1962 legislation, the Americans still had a slight lead. For example, between 1962 and 1965, 24 new drugs were introduced in *both* the British and U.S. markets. While 2 were introduced into both markets in the same year, 10 were introduced into Britain earlier than the United States by an average of 1.2 years. On the other hand, 12 were introduced into the United States earlier than Britain by an average of 2.1 years. But between 1966 and 1971 there was a pronounced change. During this period, 58 new drugs were introduced into both countries, 14 in the same year. But in 33 cases, Britain introduced the drug earlier than the United States by an average of 6.6 years. Thus, when one compares the periods 1962–1965 and 1966–1971, there was a distinct turnaround, the British having a shorter lag time with new drugs in the later period (U.S. Congress, Senate, Judiciary 1974: 9840; Wardell 1973a).

But when one looks across the board at all new chemical entities introduced into the two countries, the British lead became even more pronounced. More than twice as many new drugs were introduced in Great Britain than in the United States during the years between 1966 and 1970. For example, 123 new chemical entities were introduced first in Great Britain, but by 1971 only 40 percent of them were available in the United States. Meantime, 77 were first introduced into the United States during the same period, and by 1971, 79 percent had been introduced into Great Britain (U.S. Congress, Senate, Judiciary 1974: 9427).

In some areas, the British lead was even greater. During the period between 1962 and 1971, there were in nine major therapeutic areas 98 drugs exclusively available in either Great Britain or the United States. For example, 77 new drugs were available solely in Great Britain, where their introduction occurred an average of 3.3 years earlier than in the United States. There, 21 drugs were exclusively available an average of 3.2 years ahead of their introduction into Britain. In terms of drug years of availability on an exclusive basis, the figures were 68 for the United States and 256 for Great Britain. Thus expressed in terms of both number of drugs and drug years of exclusive availability, the data show that the British had a lead of approximately four times that of the Americans (Wardell 1973a; 1973b; 1975).

In the important area of hypertension, not one new chemical entity was approved for the U.S. market during the decade after 1963, even though many antihypertension drugs were introduced into Great Britain (Wardell and Lasagna 1975). One study of American physicians demonstrated that in 1971 the therapies of choice presented by British experts in several important disease areas were not even available to American physicians. The study revealed that most American physicians were not aware of a number of new drugs even when they were the ones of choice in Britain. This trend was especially pronounced in therapeutic areas involving angina, hypertension, asthma, pyclone phritis, and gastric ulcer (Wardell 1973a; 1975: 166).

When an FDA advisory committee was still debating the approval of propranolol for the treatment of angina in patients prior to or instead of coronary surgery, it was so commonly used in Great Britain that failure to prescribe it would have been regarded there as suboptimal medical practice. The drug was introduced seven years earlier in Great Britain than in the United States (U.S. Comptroller General 1982: 8). And when it was finally approved in the United States, it was first approved for only minor use, but not for the treatment of angina.

Nine of the 12 most frequently used drugs that were introduced into the United States during the 1970s were available earlier by an average of two years to patients in Great Britain. Six of these 12 were actually developed in the United States. And by industry calculations, only 2 of the 63 new chemical entities launched worldwide in 1981 were first introduced in the United States (*Economist*, Aug. 7, 1982: 69). The comptroller general of the United States chose 14 of the most important new drugs during a three-year period between 1975 and 1978, and found that once they were submitted to the FDA, that body required an average of twenty-three months to approve the drug, whereas the British government required only an average of five months (U.S. Comptroller General 1982: 7).*

Some scholars have argued that on a worldwide scale there was a decline in the rate of innovativeness even before 1962 due to the lack of advance in basic knowledge; therefore, the argument goes, much of the decline in the United States after 1962 could not have been due to the more rigorous regulation of drugs. And while there indeed was a decline in innovativeness on a worldwide scale that predated 1962, the interesting point is that there was variation in the innovativeness across countries, and that was due to variation in the regulation of new drugs. The rate of decline was far more pronounced in the United States than in Great Britain and other countries where the regulatory process was less stringent. In countries, such as Sweden and Canada, that had essentially the same centralized, regulatory standards of safety and effectiveness as the United States, the timing of the introduction of new drugs was quite similar (U.S. Congress, Senate, Judiciary 1974: 9386). While there are economic considerations that influence the rate at which drug firms introduce new drugs into various countries, the sheer size of the U.S. market was a strong incentive for companies around the world to introduce new products there. And because of the size of the

---

* Hence, even when one takes into consideration the quality of new chemical entities, most of the important ones were first introduced in at least one foreign country before they were available in the United States. Of course, several new drugs that were first introduced in a foreign country were later withdrawn because of toxicity problems. Nevertheless, these benefits were small relative to the forgone benefits of having advances for the treatment of many patients. For example, no beta blockers were available in the United States for the treatment of patients surviving heart attacks until 1980. And the effect of not having them sooner was the loss of several thousand lives a year.

U.S. system alone, more companies would probably have marketed new drugs there after 1962 had it not been for the restrictive policies of the FDA.

The original voluntary arrangement for the Committee on the Safety of drugs in Britain was terminated in 1968. The British then adopted a more centralized and somewhat more stringent method of evaluating new drugs. The government established a Statutory Medicines Commission, which came into existence in 1971. Even so, the new system was still less centralized than that in the United States, and the British still introduced new drugs more frequently than the Americans (U.S. Congress, Senate, Judiciary 1974: 9381–9481, 9802–61; Temin 1980: 148–51; Wardell and Lasagna 1975: 165–81; Cuthbert 1976; Graham-Smith 1981; Whittet 1970).

The differential in the lag time of new drugs between Great Britain and the United States sheds interesting light on the theoretical formulation of this study. During the 1960s and 1970s the United States had more physicians per 100,000 people, more specialists per 100 physicians, and a higher index of social development (e.g., literacy and per capita income) than Great Britain. These are variables that expedite the diffusion of medical innovations across countries. Were these variables decisive, however, the United States would have had a faster rate of adopting new innovations than Great Britain. But the more centralized and cautious procedure for approving new drugs was of greater importance in shaping the lag time than the social development, professionalization, and specialization variables.

Despite the high level of medical specialization in the United States relative to Great Britain, several studies have demonstrated that, during the 1960s and 1970s, U.S. textbooks on pharmacology and therapeutics were substantially out of date in comparison with those published in Great Britain, primarily because of the slowness with which new medications were introduced into the U.S. system. William Wardell, a leading authority on the subject, has written that "while all textbooks are out of date, American textbooks are so hopelessly out of date when used abroad as to be often irrelevant" (Wardell 1975: 165). In this respect, communications about new drugs were severely hampered by the centralized character of drug regulation. And it was this centralized and cautious process of decision making that led many experts to conclude that the lag time in introducing new drugs into the United States during the 1960s tended to develop a set of conservative therapeutic practices, some of which led to adverse medical consequences for the U.S. population (Wardell 1975: 165; 1973a; 1973b; U.S. Congress, Senate, Judiciary 1974: 9802–13).

One reason why the British have been willing to have a more decentralized and less rigorous testing program for new drugs than the Americans is that they have a more effective postmarketing surveillance system. Countries that have highly developed national health delivery systems with government controls have effective follow-up procedures for adverse drug reaction reports. This type of system tends to have more lax and less centralized regulatory procedures for premarket testing of drugs than the system—such as that in the United States—that attempts to eliminate drugs with undesirable side effects prior to marketing (U.S. Comptroller General 1980; Steward and Wibberley 1980).

Total Diffusion Time of Expensive, Heterogeneously Demanded Technologies

Earlier discussion indicated that centralized systems are somewhat slower to adopt innovations that are inexpensive and demanded by a relatively small percentage of the population. The analysis now addresses a different question. Because highly centralized systems tend to be more cost conscious than decentralized ones, are they more reluctant to adopt highly expensive innovations than decentralized systems, which are less constrained by financial concerns? Since centralized systems are more successful in controlling costs, do their systems have a trade-off between being cost conscious and being innovative with high-cost technology? Are decentralized systems—which are not very cost efficient—more willing to adopt new and expensive technologies?

While the British approach to drug regulation during the 1960s and 1970s was quite decentralized and hence highly innovative, when one views the British medical system in the aggregate, it has of course been highly centralized. And while the NHS has often adopted many costly innovations shortly after their development, it has used its power to slow down the diffusion throughout the society of a number of costly innovations. The differences between centralized and decentralized systems in their adoption of costly innovations on a wide scale is demonstrated by the way that the United States and Great Britain responded to kidney dialysis machines and the CT scanner.

Kidney Dialysis Machines

When dialysis technology was perfected in the late 1960s, it was Great Britain, with its centralized financing, that quickly became a pacesetter in the development of facilities for long-term dialysis. Using funding from the central government, the centralized NHS early made a decision to adopt and provide its citizens with the dialysis technology. Before long, however, it realized that the technology was extraordinarily expensive, and because of limited resources, providers used medically grounded criteria to restrict the number of people who had access to dialysis.

Because the NHS chose to curb its expenditures on kidney dialysis, a number of other countries soon had many more patients per 1 million population using dialysis machines than did the British. For example, West Germany, France, and Italy averaged 37 new patients (under 60 and having no serious coexisting disease) per 1 million population in the early 1970s, but at the same time Britain had only 15.1 new patients per 1 million. In the United States, however, there were approximately 60 new patients per 1 million population (Office of Health Economics 1978; 1980).

Of course, kidney dialysis is an expensive technology, and one of the major limitation on the extent to which it diffused throughout a society was the availability of money. Among eighteen European countries in 1978, the zero order correlation coefficient between the number of patients receiving kidney dialysis per 1 million population and GDP per capita was .18. Though this relationship was not statistically significant, countries such as Sweden, Denmark, Switzerland, and the United States, which had higher per capita incomes than Great Britain, had many more patients per 1 million population using the machines. In 1978, Great Britain had 53 patients per 1 million using dialysis machines, Sweden 65, and France 133. But the United States, which had one of the most inegalitarian medical delivery systems among highly industrial nations, led the world, with approximately 172 patients per 1 million on dialysis machines (Prottas et al. 1983).

Why was it that the United States led the world with this particular technology? Predicting from the per capita income of the United States and from the greater inequality in access to care relative to most European countries, one would expect many fewer Americans to be using the machines.* In 1972, however, Congress voted to extend Medicare coverage to virtually every American who suffered from chronic renal failure. The key to an understanding of this policy was the very decentralized structure and the retrospective system of reimbursement, combined with the enormous power of providers to shape public policy. And of course, it was not inci-

---

* There is some suggestion that the United States has a higher dialysis rate because blacks have a higher incidence of renal disease and European countries have relatively few blacks. It is true that the proportion of the U.S. population that is black explains 49 percent of the difference between the U.S. dialysis rate and the highest rate in Europe—that of France (Prottas et al. 1983: 95). The most plausible explanation for this difference is that the stresses blacks in the United States face are associated with increased rates of hypertension, a prime precursor of end-stage renal disease. If blacks had better access to preventive care and better socioeconomic conditions, they probably would have lower rates of hypertension and less end-stage renal disease. American providers have found it more consistent with their class interests to advocate the expensive dialysis care for those who need it than the redistributive policies associated with changing the basic socioeconomic status of blacks in American society.

Table 6 New Dialysis Patients per 1 Million Population, Great Britain, West Germany, and France, 1978

Age Group	Great Britain	West Germany	France
35–44	33.1	41.2	34.2
45–54	43.5	58.8	59.8
55–64	22.7	71.3	69.5
65–74	3.5	49.9	56.6
75+	0	8.6	17.6
All ages	19.2	30.9	30.4

Sources: Proceedings of the European Dialysis and Transplant Association (1978); Office of Health Economics, 1980: 3; Cameron 1981: 161.

dental that kidney dialysis in medical treatment centers is a very lucrative source of income for physicians and hospitals. Thus, when American hospital administrators and renal specialists became passionate advocates of denying no one access to dialysis machines, Congress responded accordingly. Clearly, patients with end-stage renal failure benefited by this policy, but had the financial rewards not been so substantial for providers, it is doubtful that the pressures would have been generated for Congress to make the treatment so accessible (Relman and Rennie 1980: 996–98).

In contrast to the U.S. policy of universal coverage for dialysis, the British policy has been to provide it only for otherwise healthy people under age 45; due to resource constraints, British policy deliberately discriminates against older individuals who need dialysis treatment (Office of Economics 1978: 52; Golding and Tosey 1980: 195–97).

Table 6, which contains data on the age-specific rates of intake of new patients in 1978 in the United Kingdom, West Germany, France, and Italy, demonstrates that the rates for Britain were comparable to those for other countries up to age 44. For the age group 45–54, however, the rate in Britain was considerably lower. And it became substantially lower with increasing age thereafter—especially for those in the age group 65–74. And the NHS accepted no new patients for dialysis in the age group 75 and over. In other words, the British have permitted several thousand patients to die whose lives could have been prolonged had there been a different policy.

As was suggested above, delivery systems with high levels of centralization tend to give high priority to constraining costs. Hence cross-national variation in the type of technology to cope with chronic renal failure has been very much influenced by cross national variation in the commitment of governments to controlling medical expenditures. For example, home dialysis in Great Britain and the United States after the first year is approximately one-half as expensive as dialysis in the hospital, and the British, consistently with their cost consciousness, have led the way with home dialysis.

In Great Britain, there have been extensive efforts to install dialysis equipment in the homes of younger patients with chronic renal failure and to train patients to dialyse themselves (Office of Health Economics 1978: 36). By 1976 approximately two-thirds of the British dialysis patients were on home dialysis (by far the highest percentage in the world), compared to only one-fifth in Europe as a whole. Many analysts believe that, irrespective of costs, home dialysis is preferred over dialysis in medical centers. Aside from the advantage of economy, home dialysis, by isolating patients from one another, has substantially limited the transmission of viral hepatitis. Moreover, those who receive dialysis at home are more easily able to receive three treatments weekly rather than two, as is the norm in medical centers. And the more frequent blood cleansing results in reduced transfusion requirements (Bluemle 1971: 355). Moreover, home dialysis is the most practical means of rehabilitation to the lifestyle a patient had prior to the onset of kidney failure. On the other hand, many individuals are better treated in a medical center if they live in poverty, have inadequate living quarters, either live alone or have very large families, or are emotionally immature.

Meanwhile, a U.S. trend toward home dialysis was sharply reversed by 1972 federal legislation that discouraged it. For example, approximately 40 percent of American dialysis patients were on home dialysis in 1972, whereas in 1979, the figure had dropped to less than 10 percent (Office of Health Economics 1978: 38; Cameron 1981: 166). This occurred for several reasons. First, the level of federal reimbursement for physicians and other providers was much higher for in-center treatment than for home dialysis during much of the 1970s. Second, the method of reimbursement for home dialysis was much more cumbersome and slow than for that received in medical centers. And finally, the level of patient reimbursement for home dialysis was substantially lower than that provided by Medicare for in-center dialysis (Fox and Swazey 1974: 345–75). In other words, the more decentralized, retrospective method of provider remuneration influenced the type of technology that diffused most widely in the United States.

Despite Britain's poor level of intake of new dialysis patients, the British do compare favorably with other nations in rates of kidney transplants. Significantly, transplantation—when the proper donor kidney is available—is preferred over dialysis as a method of treatment for certain age groups. And while the British tend to do substantially less surgery per 1,000 persons than the Americans (Bunker 1970), in the mid 1970s, they were doing more kidney transplants per 1,000 persons than the Americans (Cameron 1981: 182). Because of the numerous complications that result from long-term dependence on kidney dialysis, many physicians increasingly advise a transplant when possible instead. Moreover, a functioning transplant is substantially cheaper per year of life than dialysis, and this is a major reason why the NHS has provided services and resources to increase kidney transplants. There is some evidence that, because dialysis is far more lucrative than transplantation, the structure of the U.S. system has been less receptive to the idea of transplantation (Bunker 1970; Office of Health Economics 1980). Table 7 provides information concerning the relative costs in the United Kingdom for home dialysis, center dialysis, and successful transplants—all in 1980 prices. The price differentials are similar in Great Britain and the United States. There is no substantial difference in the costs of the three approaches in the first year of treatment, but in subsequent years, the center dialysis treatment is more than twice as expensive as home dialysis. But center dialysis is ten times more expensive in subsequent years than the successful transplant.

Of course, the success of transplants varies with the age of the recipient and with the donor (relative or cadaver). But in some centers, with the introduction of effective immune suppressive drugs, there is not much difference in mortality between dialysis and transplantation when the donor is a relative. For example, in a sample of 110 patients who received transplants in the Oxford region of England, there was a 95 percent survival rate at the end of one year, with most of the grafts being from cadavers, though the failure rate with cadaver grafts is generally higher in most centers (Office of Health Economics 1980: 4; Oliver and Morris 1978).

As the above discussion suggests, the centralized NHS, with its strong commitment to and reputation for equality of care, has been in the position of providing less than egalitarian access to treatment for patients over 45 years of age suffering from end-stage of renal failure. And in contrast, the U.S. system, which has a long history as one of the most inegalitarian medical delivery systems, has provided almost universal access to kidney dialysis machines. This particular technology suggests that as centralized delivery systems opt for cost-effectiveness, they may place constraints not only on the rate of diffusion of expensive technologies but also on access to them. And while a decentralized system with retrospective reimbursement schemes may tend to limit access to care, it is very receptive to the diffusion of expensive technologies that are financially beneficial to providers.

Table 7 Comparative Costs of Treatments for End-stage Renal Failure, Great Britain, 1980 Prices

	First Year (Pounds)	Subsequent Years (Pounds per Year)
Home dialysis	13,500	6,000
Center dialysis	12,500	12,500
Successful transplant	12,000	1,200

Sources: Cameron 1981: 163; Blagg and Scribner v. 2, 1976: 1733; U.S. Congress, House, Committee on Ways and Means 1978: 115–16.

The Computed Tomography Scanner

Comparing the reaction of the British and U.S. medical delivery systems to the CT scanner, one notes some of the same types of trade-off as with the kidney dialysis technology. The CT scanner is another technology in which variation in the structure of the two delivery systems helps to explain variation in the rate of diffusion.

At the time of its invention, CT scanning represented the most important advance in diagnostic radiology since the development of image amplification. In evaluating problems involving the brain, it provided more information with less risk than invasive techniques that involved the injection of dye into blood vessels or air into the spinal column (Baker 1979: 155). There are basically two types of CT scanners: those that scan the entire body and those that scan only the head. By 1979, the overwhelming majority of scanners in operation in Britain and the United States were full body scanners.

Even though the CT scanner was developed primarily in Great Britain, it has been much more widely adopted in the more decentralized and less cost-conscious U.S. system. The English company EMI, Ltd., developed the first scanner and during the first four years installed all scanners that became operational. Costing in the mid-1970s approximately $500,000 per unit, the CT scanner was at the time, one of the most expensive medical machines ever manufactured, and its annual cost of operation ranged from $259,000 to $379,000. Not only were the machines costly, but they were so profitable that within a few years at least 19 companies were manufacturing them (Banta 1980: 253).

While Britain's prospective system of hospital budgeting has been tightly regulated by the central government and regional authorities, the U.S. system, with its retrospective funding and decentralized structure, has facilitated the diffusion of this expensive type of technology. Whereas in Britain, funding and technological complexity of hospitals have been tightly controlled at centralized levels, in the United States, the hospital administrators' quest for status has played an important role in constantly increasing the level of technological complexity of hospitals. The status of hospitals— and of hospital administrators—is assumed to vary with the range of services and personnel provided by them. The more expensive and highly specialized the equipment and personnel relative to other hospitals, the greater the hospital's status. For this reason, whenever one U.S. hospital has acquired expensive new equipment, other hospital officials have believed that they have fallen behind and must catch up. Moreover, hospitals administrators, especially in large cities, have believed that they must acquire expensive and sophisticated equipment in order to attract and retain high-quality physicians on their staffs (Abt Associates 1975; K. Davis 1972a;

1972b; Lee 1971; Jacobs 1974: 86). On the other hand, physicians place demands on administrators to increase the supply of hospital equipment, for an expansion of new equipment has not only added to their status, but it has also meant shorter waiting times for their patients and easier accessibility to equipment. And as one hospital in an area has acquired expensive new equipment, others have quickly attempted to follow suit. By the middle 1970s, it was not at all unusual for several hospitals in a U.S. metropolitan area to have CT scanners when one would have met the documented need. As late as 1978, there were 52 in Great Britain, while in the United States in 1979 there were 1,254 in use—over one-half of which had been produced in Britain. In the Los Angeles Health Service Area alone, there were 76 scanners in use in 1978, or 46 percent more than existed in all the United Kingdom. Indeed, there were more CT scanners in California than in all of Europe (Baker 1979: 157). Per 1 million population, the United States had more than five times as many as Great Britain. In fact, normed per 1 million population the United States had more CT scanners than any other country in the world—more than three times as many as any European country.

Whereas Congress had made kidney dialysis available to virtually all citizens, the CT scanner was less available. In New York City, for example, there were 33 scanners in the late 1970s, but only one of the public hospitals—Bronx Memorial—had one. Such large New York public hospitals as Bellevue and Kings County Hospital, whose patients were largely low-income, were without scanners, as were Cook County Hospital in Chicago, Cleveland Metropolitan Hospital, and the Charity Hospital in New Orleans (Banta 1980: 261).

Of course, health systems agencies had the responsibility for trying to regulate the diffusion of expensive technology in hospitals, and, partly because of their efforts to reduce the diffusion rate of CT scanners, many were purchased by private physicians and installed in their offices. In 1977, at least 10 percent of scanners in the United States were owned or leased by physicians but located in hospitals—something that would be unthinkable in the NHS. Of course, the scanners were very profitable not only to the manufacturers but to the American providers as well—and this is part of the reason why the United States has more scanners per 1 million people than any other country. For example, the U.S. Office of Technology Assessment has estimated that physicians and hospitals have earned profits on their scanners ranging between 39 and 229 percent annually (U.S. Congress, Office of Technology Assessment 1978).

Because Americans were so quick to purchase the CT technology, which was changing very rapidly, a number of hospitals bought equipment that they quickly considered to be obsolete. Within one decade, improvements in technology occurred so rapidly that four successive generations of scanners were available—each generation providing significant improvement in image quality over earlier ones. As a result, some hospitals bought additional units in order to compensate for their loss in technological advantage (Baker 1979: 155, 159).

Despite the rapid rate of diffusion of scanners and their high cost, there was prior to 1978 no systematic effort to evaluate the usefulness and efficacy of the technology. While hardly anyone will doubt that CT scanning has an important role in modern medicine, there was by 1980 little knowledge concerning the impact of scanners on patient outcomes. For example, scanners are widely used to evaluate the condition of patients who have suffered strokes, but one 1978 study demonstrated that they had little influence on either the course of treatment or the outcome for stroke patients. Indeed, strokes can generally be well diagnosed clinically, and there was virtually no therapy that a scanner would dictate (Larson et al. 1978; Banta 1980: 263–64).

Slowly cost-benefit analysis of CT scanning is emerging, and there is some literature suggesting that it is less expensive than many critics earlier thought to be the case. For example, CT scanning has reduced the incidence of nuclear medicine scans, plain radiographs, air studies, and angiograms. Moreover, there is some evidence that it has led to reductions in surgical procedures, length of hospital stays, and other medical costs. Even so, most of the information concerning cost-benefit analysis was quite crude and unsophisticated as late as 1980 (U.S. Congress, Office of Technology Assessment 1978; Evens 1980; Gempel et al. 1977; Abrams and McNeil 1978).

At a time when the United States had adopted several times more CT machines than any other Western country, Abrams and McNeil of the Harvard Medical School wrote the following in a careful report of the literature on CT scanning: "Acceptable evidence of the efficacy of CT and in particular of its marginal contribution to diagnosis, its effect on the cost of medical care, on short-term health outcomes and on long term health outcomes is not available" (1978: 317).

Thus, when one faces the question of why there was such gross variation in the diffusion of scanners in the United States and Great Britain, one is forced to point to the different ways in which the systems were structured and financed. The highly centralized British system, with its prospective method of funding, had effective mechanisms for limiting expenditures on costly new technology. The U.S. system was structured in such a way that physicians and hospitals benefited financially by costly new technologies, and since they had considerable influence to shape decisions about the acquisition of new technologies, it is not surprising that the United States had more scanners than any other country in the world at a time when there was little systematic information about the efficaciousness of the technology.

* * * *

Where technology has become extraordinarily complex, it can be difficult for policy makers to measure the need for it with any accuracy. Hence,
where the money is available, there is a tendency to err on the side of consuming more rather than less technology. And the differences in structure
between the British and U.S. medical delivery systems and the differences in
their funding mechanisms suggest that the British will continue to be more
parsimonious in rationing costly new medical technologies than the
Americans.

CONCLUDING OBSERVATIONS

Many things influence the relative speed with which technology diffuses in
different societies. Specifically, increases in the level of wealth, communications, and specialized knowledge in the twentieth century have led to faster
rates of diffusion of medical technology. But irrespective of the level of
wealth, the nature of the communication system, and the level of medical
specialization, the underlying structure of medical delivery systems has influenced the speed with which certain types of medical technology have
diffused.

The data on vaccines show that, when the technology is inexpensive,
highly efficacious, and desired by a high percentage of the population, differences in the structure of the medical delivery system have little impact on
the speed with which innovations diffuse throughout a country (i.e., the
total diffusion time).

The discussion on the drug industry suggests that, where there are relatively inexpensive technologies that are demanded by only a small percentage of the population, the structure of the system places real constraints on
the lag time (i.e., the speed with which an innovation is first introduced into
a country). Thus the highly centralized regulatory procedures for the testing and marketing of drugs in the United States led to a much slower rate of
adoption of new drugs than in Britain, where there were less centralized
regulatory procedures.

Even though the NHS vis-à-vis the medical delivery systems of other
countries has been very egalitarian in terms of access to care, it has been
inegalitarian in regard to very expensive technology such as kidney dialysis. Given the option between making a very costly technology available to
everyone in need and controlling costs, the NHS has opted for the cost-
saving strategy. Similarly, it chose to limit the diffusion of the CT scanner.
The key actors in the much more decentralized U.S. system, with its retrospective funding system, have used their influence to bring about the diffusion of costly medical technologies. While centralized systems generally
tend to have a greater commitment to equality than more decentralized

systems, the greater cost-consciousness of the former leads them to restrict access to certain types of expensive technologies. Centralized systems tend to facilitate equality of access and cost controls, but the data above suggest that, if the two are in conflict, centralized systems opt for cost controls. On the other hand, decentralized systems tend to be more innovative and more costly.

Of course, any system is subject to political pressures, and because of these pressures, there is little difference in the diffusion of certain high-cost technologies in Britain and the United States. In both countries, there is the expectation that illnesses of children and young adults will be treated aggressively—even if the costs are high—but in Britain there is much more rationing of high-cost technology in regard to the elderly. Not only do the elderly in Britain have less access to kidney dialysis machines, but also, coronary artery surgery—another high-cost technology for older populations—is used at least nine times more frequently in the United States per 1 million population. Moreover, the British are less aggressive in treating older patients who are terminally ill with cancer than are the Americans. On the other hand, such high-cost technologies as bone marrow transplants and the treatment of hemophilia are used with about the same frequency in both countries. Significantly, these are technologies that are needed mostly by children and young adults. In general, the higher the quality of life after a successful treatment, the smaller the differential between the two countries in the rate with which a given technology is used.

The British medical profession has defined standards of care in such a way that they can avoid the recognition that financial limits compel them to do less than their best and tends to argue that nothing of medical significance is denied to any patient. As Aaron and Schwartz suggest, British doctors have a medical rationale for what is fiscally necessary. With limited resources in a highly centralized system, the British doctors have preserved their professional autonomy and a belief that they practice high-quality medicine. Meantime, on most crude indicators of health status (e.g., life expectancy at birth and infant mortality rates) the British perform better than the Americans. These measures, of course, do not demonstrate that the British medical delivery system is better or worse than that in the United States, but they do suggest that the differences in medical technology and expenditures in the two countries are not associated with substantial differences in life chances of different age groups (Aaron and Schwartz 1984: 12–13, 28, 101–2, 110, 129).

5
Equality

This chapter is concerned with how the structure of a society's medical delivery system influences (1) the degree of equality of health across social classes and groups, (2) the spatial distribution of medical resources, and (3) the level of health of the society. The previous chapters, as well as much existing scholarly literature, make certain assumptions about these matters. This chapter attempts to make these views more explicit. Specifically, the chapter assesses the adequacy of the following generalizations about medical technology, the structure of delivery systems, and levels of health in the United States and England and Wales:

1. As medical technology either becomes more efficacious or is so perceived by the society, and as its costs mount, there will be rising public demand for increased government provision of medical services, and consequently the delivery system will become more centralized.

   There is, over time, an increasing effort to have the state finance the development and distribution of medical technology, for otherwise many citizens would find it prohibitively expensive. And once the financial responsibility for the provision of medical services is shifted toward the public sector, the medical delivery system, by definition, becomes more centralized.

   Centralization is the level at which strategic decisions are made about personnel, budgets, programs, and standards. As suggested above, a delivery system in which all of these decisions are made in the private sector is more decentralized than one in which the decisions are made in the public sector. And in the public sector, a delivery system in which all decisions are made at the national level is more centralized than one in which all decisions are made by local or regional authorities.

2. As medical delivery systems become more centralized, services will become more accessible to all social classes and groups.

3. As medical delivery systems become more centralized, the allocation of medical resources will become more equitable across regions of the country.

   Increases in the level of centralization impact substantially on the performance of delivery systems. The major advantage of a more centralized system is that it allows for greater coordination in the delivery of services. Moreover, it can more easily provide the same services to all and at a lower cost per person. Centralized systems also provide more standardization of programs and services across regions, social classes, and groups than do decentralized systems. The familiar joke about the French educational system—that the same book was being read at the same hour throughout the country by all children of the same age—nevertheless contains one of the principles of centralized decision making: the same decision is made for all. In short, increases in the level of centralization tend to bring about increases in equality of access to services and distribution of resources, both across regions and across social classes and groups.

4. As medical delivery systems become more centralized, as access is improved, and as resources are more equitably distributed across regions, there will be a convergence in levels of health (measured by mortality) across regions and across social classes.

The literature is contradictory about the way changes in the level of technology in influence levels of health. One body of literature tends to assume that greater equality of access and distribution of resources over a long period will promote greater equality of results (see the discussion in various essays in Haveman 1977). Other scholars, however, suggest that equality in health outcomes are influenced substantially not by the structure of the delivery system but primarily by the total structure of the society. Even if a single system is egalitarian in access and in the distribution of resources, outcomes will not be equal as long as there is fundamental inequality in the society's basic reward structure (income, occupational attainment, status, etc.).

(Bowles and Gintis 1976; Jencks et al. 1972)

These four generalizations are summarized in figure 3.

In an attempt to assess the adequacy of these generalizations, the discussion will now focus on changes in technology and the structure of the medical delivery systems of the United States and in England and Wales during the twentieth century and on changes in levels of health (measured by mortality rates) across social classes and regions during the same time span.

EVALUATION OF THE MODEL

Almost everyone would agree that medical technology has become more complex since the late nineteenth century. At the turn of the century, much of medical knowledge could be applied with the contents of a little black bag, but over time, as medical care has become more complex, it has increasingly centered in hospitals and large clinics with the capacity to carry out extensive and increasingly more expensive diagnostic procedures. Even those scholars who have tended to minimize the efficaciousness of twentieth-century medical technology acknowledge that much of it has been

Delivery System Changes

Rising levels of complexity, and costs of technology → + Increased demands for equal rights → + Public funding → + Centralization → + Equitable resources → + Equitable access → ? More equitable outcomes for individuals

Fig. 3. Theoretical Framework for Consumption Policy

complex and somewhat effective (Powles 1973; L. Thomas 1977; Knowles 1977). For purposes of the discussion here, it is important to note that the consuming public since the late nineteenth century has increasingly believed that medical technology has become more efficacious, complex, and expensive. And this has led to increasing demands for health services (Stevens 1966, 1971; Rothstein 1972; Eckstein 1958; Titmuss 1950; Hollingsworth and Hanneman 1983).

Technology is a difficult concept to measure, but there are several useful indicators that demonstrate that its level of complexity has been increasing over time and that the public's belief in its efficacy has increased. For example, the proportion of medical practitioners who are specialists is a good indicator of the increasing complexity of medical knowledge. And the proportion of a society's population that is hospitalized annually is an indicator both of the change in technological complexity and the increasing demand for medical technology. The society's level of expenditures on medical care reveals the extent to which the increasing complexity and the rising demand for medical services have led to increasing costs.

From table 8 we observe that, during the first two decades of the twentieth century, England and Wales had a higher proportion of doctors who were specialists than did the United States, and moreover a larger percentage of its population received hospital care. Subsequently, however, the United States surpassed England and Wales in both of these indicators. And while medical costs have increased both absolutely and as a proportion of GNP throughout the twentieth century in both countries, they have been consistently higher in the United States.

If one views the entire period since 1900, it is clear that both the British and U.S. medical delivery systems have become more centralized, but the British system became centralized first, for as technology became more complex, as the demand for it increased and became more expensive, British low-income consumers were better organized than their American counterparts to demand that government become more involved in making medical resources more accessible and in distributing them more equitably across regions. In the United States, where low-income consumers were fragmented by ethnic, racial, and religion cleavages, the medical profession was more highly organized than consumers, as it did not have the deep cleavages between general practitioners and the more specialized doctors that existed in Great Britain. Moreover, upper-income consumers in the United States were politically quite powerful and tended to favor specialized services delivered by private markets. Acting in combination with the medical profession, they were able to resist for a longer period the trend toward greater centralization, even though the U.S. medical delivery system also had a technology that was becoming more complex, had increasing demands placed on it, and was becoming increasingly expensive. His-

Table 8 Technological Complexity, Demand, and Costs of Medical Care, England and Wales and the United States, 1890–1970

	Specialists per 100 Doctors		Hospital Admissions per 1,000 Population		Medical Care Expenditures			
					Per Capita in 1938 Constant Dollars		As a Percentage of GNP	
	England and Wales	United States	England and Wales	United States	England and Wales	United States	England and Wales	United States
1890	N.A.	1.0	21.9	11.7	N.A.	8.41	N.A.	1.9
1900	3.1	2.5	28.3	17.0	8.37	10.76	1.6	2.3
1910	5.2	3.6	33.5	37.2	8.39	14.31	2.0	2.9
1920	7.0	9.6	39.2	56.9	6.71	15.55	1.5	2.4
1930	7.8	17.0	56.4	58.1	9.63	25.21	1.9	3.6
1940	8.2	23.5	67.6	76.5	20.37	29.55	N.A.	4.1
1950	24.2	36.8	73.9	112.6	28.24	43.37	4.1	4.6
1960	27.2	57.3	94.8	139.1	36.23	61.21	3.8	5.2
1970	34.1	77.0	115.4	155.8	56.87	119.45	4.6	7.4

Sources: Stevens 1966, 1971; Hollingsworth et al., forthcoming; *Journal of the American Medical Association*, annual issues; Great Britain, Department of Health and Social Security, *Health and Personal Social Service Statistics*, annual issues; Pinker 1966; Hollingsworth and Hanneman 1983; U.S., Comm., Census 1979a.

torically, it was differences in the relative power of groups in the two countries that led to differences in the demand for public services, which eventually produced medical delivery systems with different levels of centralization (Hollingsworth and Hanneman 1983).

As was suggested earlier, centralization is a multidimensional concept, and there are any number of indicators with which to measure its extent in the British and U.S. medical delivery systems. Because previous research indicates that the various dimensions are highly correlated (Hollingsworth and Hanneman 1983), this chapter will use the type of funding (i.e., central government, state and local government, or private sector) as a proxy for measuring the general level of centralization. With this strategy, we observe from table 9 that over time the systems in the United States and in England and Wales have become more centralized. In England and Wales, there was a modest shift toward a more centralized system after the introduction of the NHI system in 1911, but the more dramatic shift occurred with the implementation of the NHS in 1948. In the United States, the sharpest shift occurred with the introduction of Medicare and Medicaid in the 1960s. The system in England and Wales has been somewhat more centralized than the U.S. one since 1911, but especially so since the introduction of the NHS in 1948.

EQUALITY OF ACCESS

But has centralization led to greater equality of access to medical care? The data on access by social class between 1890 and 1970 are unfortunately most imperfect, but there is sufficient information to conclude that for both countries the answer is yes.*

England and Wales

In Great Britain, even before the introduction of the NHS in 1948, the development of a number of state programs (which meant an increase in centralization) led to greater access to and equalization of medical resources. First, the medical inspection of schoolchildren (introduced in

---

* There are alternative strategies for measuring equity in the use of medical facilities. The National Center for Health Statistics has collected data for an use-disability index that summarizes the ratio of mean physician visits to mean disability days for the respective age and income groups. This index is a physician-use indicator adjusted for acute illness, as the majority of the disability days are associated with acute conditions. Moreover, the center has collected data for the proportion of chronic illness among the poor and nonpoor by age and frequency of consultation with physicians. For further discussions of data of this type, see Aday et al. 1980.

Table 9 Centralization in Medical Delivery Systems, the United States and England and Wales, 1890–1970 (percentage of revenue by source)

	United States				England and Wales			
	Private Individuals	Local and State Government	Central Government	Weighted Index of Centralization	Private Individuals	Local Government	Central Government	Weighted Index of Centralization
1890	98.6	1.3	0.2	.009	N.A.	N.A.	N.A.	N.A.
1900	83.8	15.4	0.8	.085	88.1	11.9	0	.06
1910	87.6	11.8	0.5	.064	77.6	22.4	0	.112
1920	83.6	12.0	4.4	.104	66.3	33.7	0	.169
1930	86.1	9.7	4.2	.091	67.4	32.6	0	.163
1940	79.5	15.4	5.1	.128	N.A.	N.A.	N.A.	N.A.
1950	75.0	13.0	12.0	.185	15.4	5.7	78.9	.818
1960	75.3	14.2	10.5	.176	18.7	6.3	75.	.782
1970	62.0	13.3	24.7	.314	11.4	5.9	82.7	.857

Source: Hollingsworth and Hanneman, 1978.

Note: To observe the trend toward centralization, one may wish to study only the portion of medical revenues derived from the central or state and local governments, or the private sector. However, this table also presents a weighted index of centralization constructed in the following manner: The percentage of revenue derived from the central government was given a weight of 5, that from state and local government a weight of 3, and that from the private sector a weight of 1. The weighted sum of each of these levels was then transformed to vary between 0 and 1 in the following manner: (weighted sum − 1)/₄ = Index.

1907) had become sufficiently institutionalized by 1920 for every school-child to be assured of at least three medical inspections before age 15. And when parents were unable to pay for the child's medical care, most of the local authorities assumed the cost (McCleary 1933; Political and Economic Planning 1937).

Second, Parliament in 1918 urged the local authorities to provide maternity clinics and infant welfare programs, with the result that by 1938, more than one-half of Britain's expectant mothers received free prenatal care, and a sizable portion of mothers and infants received home visiting and post-natal care (Political and Economic Planning 1937).

Third, the introduction of the NHI system in 1911 provided nonhospital medical care for 10 million low-income working people who previously had not been covered by any form of medical insurance. Data on the extent of care are inexact, but the introduction of the system substantially increased access to care for those who were insured; by the 1930s, this included throughout Britain 77 percent of all men aged 14–64 (Titmuss 1958; Levy 1944).

Fourth, the indigent and the elderly also received medical care from the state, though the quality of care varied from place to place and over time. After the passage of the Old Age Pension Act in 1908, those people who were eligible for old age pensions were also eligible for the services of the Poor Law medical officer. As a result, many of the elderly received Poor Law outdoor medical assistance. After the abolition of various Poor Law facilities, the quality of public medical facilities and access to care improved for the indigent and elderly (Gilbert 1966).

Even though access improved over time as the state provided first one type of medical service and then another, the services prior to 1948 were a patchwork with considerable variation from group to group in terms of what the state provided. Once the highly centralized NHS was introduced in 1948, however, everyone was entitled to the same services without regard to income or other restrictions (Stevens 1966; Titmuss 1958; Eckstein 1958).

Table 10 provides information on the annual number of consultations in England and Wales for individuals by income level before and after the introduction of the NHS. As the lowest income group generally has more medical needs than the highest (Le Grand 1978; Morris 1979), it is not surprising that in 1947, the year before the introduction of the NHS, the lowest income group of males had 1.7 times as many consultations as the highest income group. Even so, one year after the introduction of the service, when medical care was available to everyone without a fee, the ratio of lowest to highest income group for both males and females increased substantially.

There are no data on the consumption of medical care in England and Wales by income after 1952, but the British have collected medical data by five occupational groupings, and with these it is possible to observe changes in consumption of care by different classes for other periods. Social class I (or occupational class I) consists of higher professional and administrative occupations; class II of employers in industry and retail trades, as well as the lesser professions; class III the skilled occupations; class IV, partly skilled occupations; and class V the unskilled occupations.

These data reveal, for the period between 1955 and 1975, the same pattern as the data on medical consumption by income distribution: people from lower occupational groups consulted doctors more often.

While the historical record during the twentieth century is one of greater equality of access to medical care in England and Wales, the trend is somewhat less egalitarian when one takes into consideration the frequency of consultation in relation to need. Though there are difficulties in developing valid indicators of need, a number of studies demonstrate that, in proportion to reported sickness and absence from work due to sickness, those in semiskilled and unskilled occupations make less use of general practitioner services than do other groups. Moreover, the semiskilled and unskilled have received less consulting time than other groups (Cartwright 1964; Cartwright and O'Brien 1976; Townsend and Davidson 1982: 78–79; Walters 1980: 129–40). But even if class inequalities in access to care still exist in England and Wales, they are substantially less than in the United States or at earlier times.

The United States

While the long-term trend has also been for the U.S. medical delivery system to become more centralized, it has been a slower, less dramatic, and less systematic trend than in Great Britain. And because the level of centralization of the medical delivery system has been much lower, the U.S. system at each point in time has been much less coordinated than the British. Because of the lack of coordination—exacerbated by a federal governmental system—the U.S. system has consistently had more serious gaps in medical services, more inefficient uses of manpower, and greater duplication of facilities. For these reasons, increasing centralization has had less dramatic effect in providing greater access to lower-income groups in the United States than in England and Wales.

Most of the efforts of the federal government in providing more access to medical facilities have been of two types: (1) categorical grant-in-aid programs to the states and (2) programs for specifically designated groups.

Table 10 Average Annual Physician Consultations in England and Wales, Selected Years (in Pounds Sterling.)

Weekly Earnings

	>10	7-10	5-7	3-5	<3
Aged 16 and older [a,b]					
1947 Males	4.7[c]	4.1		4.6	8.2
	(1.0)	(0.9)		(1.0)	(1.7)
Females	5.9	5.0		4.6	6.6
	(1.0)	(0.8)		(0.8)	(1.1)
1949 Males	4.3	4.1		5.4	10.7
	(1.0)	(1.0)		(1.3)	(2.5)
Females	5.6	5.3		5.9	7.6
	(1.0)	(0.9)		(1.1)	(1.4)
Aged 21 and older [b,d]					
1951 Males	4.1	4.3	4.9	7.1	9.2
	(1.0)	(1.0)	(1.2)	(1.7)	(2.2)
Females	4.7	5.3	5.6	6.7	7.4
	(1.0)	(1.1)	(1.2)	(1.4)	(1.6)
1952 All	3.1	4.1	4.5	5.8	7.4
	(1.0)	(1.3)	(1.4)	(1.9)	(2.4)

Social Class

	I	II	III		IV	V
Aged 15-64						
1955–56 Males	2.2	2.5	3.1[e]		3.4	3.7
	(1.0)	(1.1)	(1.4)		(1.5)	(1.7)
Aged 16 and older						
1964 All	3.5	3.5	4.4	4.6	4.9	6.0
	(1.0)	(1.0)	(1.3)	(1.3)	(1.4)	(1.7)
Aged 15-64 [f]						
1970–71 Males		2.7	2.6	2.9	3.5	
		(1.0)	(1.0)	(1.1)	(1.3)	
Aged 15 and older [f]						
1970–71 Males	3.1	3.0	3.3			3.9
	(1.0)	(1.0)	(1.1)			(1.3)

Sources: Logan and Brooke 1957: 57; Rein 1969: 46; Great Britain, Office of Population Censuses and Surveys 1973: 319, 342.
Note: Ratio of rate for each group or social class to rate for highest income group or social class I is in parentheses.
[a]Data for 1947 and 1949 refer to groups classified according to the weekly income of the family's "chief wage earner."
[b]For 1947, 1949, and 1951, the annual average consultation rates are estimates calculated from published data referring to average monthly consultation rates per 100 persons.
[c]Average annual consultation rate per person.
[d]Data for 1951 and 1952 refer to groups classified according to the weekly income of the head of the household.
[e]For 1964 and 1970–71, the two categories of social class III data refer to nonmanual skilled and manual skilled occupations, respectively. For 1955–56, these data were collapsed in the source.
[f]Data referring to social classes I and II, and classes IV and V, were collapsed in the source. Data for the age groups 15–64 and 15 and older were calculated from published data referring to the age groups 15–44, 45–64, and 65 and older, using sample populations as weights.

Grant-in-aid Programs to the States

Federal grant-in-aid programs for medical care date back to the Sheppard-Towner Act, which Congress passed in 1922. Under it, a federal agency, the U.S. Children's Bureau, administered grants to the states for the improvement of the health of mothers and children. Though this program was discontinued in 1929, the federal government renewed medical grant-in-aid programs in June 1933 by expanding the Federal Emergency Relief Administration and by providing medical care for those who were receiving unemployment relief. The program came to an end, however, with the passage of the Social Security Act in 1935, which authorized a permanent public assistance program. On the other hand, the Social Security Act authorized another grant-in-aid program that related to child health and maternal programs (Serbein 1953: 262). While the Children's Bureau of the federal Social Security Administration had administrative control over these programs, they were implemented by state and local officials. These programs established prenatal clinics, public nursing clinics, immunization campaigns, clinics for healthy and ill children, and a range of services for crippled children. By 1950, approximately 2.9 million people were receiving public health nursing services and 2.2 million received direct medical services under these programs (ibid.: 263–64). By 1970, 491,000 children were receiving medical services under the program, though the various programs providing services for children never reached more than a small proportion of the nation's poor (Dunham and Marmor 1978: 274).

During World War II, the Emergency Maternity and Infant Care Program emerged and was administered by the Children's Bureau through state departments of health. The program provided the following services for the wives of armed forces servicemen in the lowest-paid ranks: antepartum, obstetrical, and postpartum medical care by physicians and hospitals of the patient's choice. By the time the program was abolished in 1947, it had provided care for 1.2 million maternity cases. A similar program was established in 1956 by the Servicemen's Dependents Act, which provided medical services for wives and dependents of men in the armed services either at military facilities or, if these were not adequate, with civilian resources (Anderson 1968: 116).

One of the more important federal programs was the Hill-Burton Act of 1946, which over time provided more than $4.5 billion for the construction and modernization of hospitals. Federal subsidies for construction, normally limited to one-third of the cost, were administered through state Hill-Burton agencies, which were usually the state health departments. By the early 1970s, the program had helped to finance almost 11,000 construction projects, involving approximately 350,000 hospital beds and 60 percent of the nation's hospitals. The program contributed to equalizing the supply of beds across the states and increasing the number of hospitals in rural areas and small towns. And by increasing the number of hospitals and beds in those areas, it provided an incentive for doctors to locate there (Dunham and Marmor 1978: 280).

Programs for Specifically Designated Groups

Over time, the federal government has assumed complete responsibility for providing medical care to members of the armed services, eligible veterans, members of the merchant marine, native Americans, and certain categories of people disabled in government service. In addition, it has increasingly made funds available for medical services to the elderly and low-income groups through Medicare, Medicaid, and other programs.

Originally, the federal government provided direct medical services only to those veterans who had an illness or accident as a result of active military service, though since 1952 those with non-service-connected disabilities have been provided with medical care if the veteran has been unable to pay for private care. In theory, eligibility has been extended to approximately 29 million veterans.

For years, the federal government has provided direct medical care for approximately half a million native Americans. While for some years, the cost of this program exceeded the national per capita expenditure on medical care, the health status of native Americans has nevertheless remained below that of the rest of the population (U.S. Dept. of Health, Education, and Welfare 1957).

Measured by expenditure level, the two most important federal health programs have been Medicare and Medicaid, which by 1970 accounted for approximately 60 percent of all public spending in the health sector (Dunham and Marmor 1978: 266). Medicare is a federal health insurance program for the elderly and has no income restrictions, and while it has not covered all the medical needs of the elderly, it was designed to reduce their most costly medical services.

Unlike Medicare, Medicaid is a state-operated program, and the eligibility, depth, and extent of coverage are matters that have been determined at the state and local levels. In expenditures and number of people covered, it is the largest government health program for the poor and provides a wide range of medical services for the poor as well as those who are medically needy and would be on welfare if their incomes were any lower (Davis and Schoen 1978: 49).

One of the more innovative federal programs was that establishing neighborhood health centers. Recognizing that access to care by low-income individuals was severely limited by a scarcity of physicians and inadequate facilities in low-income areas, the federal government instituted this program in 1965 in an attempt to provide comprehensive medical services in low-income neighborhoods. Ideally, the neighborhood health centers were to be located in rural or urban areas, serve from 10,000 to 30,000 people, and provide an array of services: diagnostic care, treatment of illness, preventive health services, family planning, mental health services, rehabilitative services, and in-home care of the chronically ill. By 1973, however, there were only 1.3 million persons registered in approximately 100 centers, and their expenditure levels were quite low as compared to Medicare and Medical programs (Davis and Schoen 1978: 161–202).

After 1963, the federal government also began to increase its share of financial responsibility for many maternal and child health programs. Although little information is available on the comprehensiveness of federal maternity services in clinics, it is known that, in 1972, approximately 335,000 women, representing approximately 9 percent of all live-births, were receiving services under the program. Under another federal program, nurses visited the homes of newborn infants and provided nursing services to 624,000 women in 1972. Most of these services were to women who lived in urban areas with high mortality rates, low per capita income, overcrowded public health facilities, and an inadequate number of physicians in private practice (Davis and Schoen 1978: 120–60; K. Davis 1976b).

As a result of federal legislation in 1967, 1970, and 1972, the federal government also subsidized family planning services for low-income women. This program was designed to reduce infant mortality by lowering the incidence of unwanted births, many of which are high risk. The subsidies have gone to family planning clinics, state and local health departments, and many other public agencies, and the number of women receiving services increased from 900,000 in 1968 to 3.4 million in 1974 (Grossman and Jacobowitz 1981).

These centralizing tendencies in medical delivery in the United States have resulted from a patchwork of legislation, with pockets of federal activity scattered among more than 220 different agencies and departments (Stevens 1971: 502). In contrast to Britain, there has been much less national commitment to comprehensive health planning at the community, state, regional, or interregional level in the United States. Moreover, the fragmented nature of the U.S. medical delivery system, involving thousands of government units, has been exacerbated by the decentralized, federal structure of the political system and by the fact that the medical system has been dominated by providers who have been able to determine the type of care available to the society, the system of paying for it, and its overall price.

Even so, the increasing centralization of the U.S. medical delivery system has tended to promote greater access to care (see tables 11 and 12).

In 1928–31, the first period for which there is a systematic survey of the consumption of medical services in the United States, less than one-half of all Americans consulted a physician. And in 1963–64, before the enactment of Medicare and Medicaid, the American families in the lowest third of the income scale but with the highest medical needs were consulting physicians less frequently than those with higher incomes (see table 12).

Table 11   Percentage Consulting Physicians during Survey Year by Family Income, the United States, 1928–1976

	Income Group[a]		
	High	Medium	Low
1928–31	53	47	44
(Whites only)	(1.0)	(.89)	(.83)
1963–64	72	64	56
	(1.0)	(.90)	(.79)
1970	71	67	65
	(1.0)	(.94)	(.92)
1976	79	75	73
	(1.0)	(.94)	(.92)

Sources: Falk et al. 1933: 101; Andersen et al. 1976: 44; Aday et al. 1980.
Note: Ratio of consultation rate of each income group to consultation rate of high income group is in parentheses.
[a]For each time point, approximately one-third of the families surveyed were in each of the three income groups.

Table 12 Mean Number of Physician Consultations per Person per Year by Family Income, the United States, 1928–1976

	Income Group[a]		
	High	Medium	Low
1928–31	3.1	2.2	2.0
(Whites only)	(1.0)	(.71)	(.65)
1963–64	4.6	4.3	4.4
	(1.0)	(.93)	(.96)
1970	3.6	3.9	4.9
	(1.0)	(1.08)	(1.36)
1976	3.8	4.0	4.6
	(1.0)	(1.05)	(1.21)

Sources: Falk et al. 1933: 110; Andersen et al. 1976: 48; Aday et al. 1980.
Note: Ratio of mean number of physician visits in each income group to mean number of physician visits in high income group is in parentheses.
[a]For each time point, approximately one-third of the families surveyed were in each of the three income groups.

Table 12 reveals even more strikingly the changes that have occurred in access to medical care across income groups. In 1928–31, individuals from the lowest income group visited physicians substantially less frequently than those with higher incomes, while in 1963–64, the mean number of physician visits across the various income groups was almost the same. After the introduction of Medicare and Medicaid, however, individuals in the lowest groups, being in greater need of medical care, visited physicians more frequently than those with higher incomes. The increase in access to medical facilities was especially marked among poor children, one-third of whom had not seen a physician for two years or more in 1964. By 1975, however, children from low-income families visited physicians as frequently as those in high income families. And whereas only 58 percent of low-income women saw a physician early in pregnancy in 1963, that figure had changed to 71 percent in 1970 (Davis and Schoen 1978: 41–43).

And yet serious inequities remain in the U.S. system. For example, Medicare was designed to provide uniform benefits to all elderly persons covered by the social security retirement program. But after more than a decade, there were substantial differences between income and racial groups in the use of services and in the receipt of Medicare payments. Elderly persons with high incomes have received twice as much in Medicare payments as individuals with low incomes. The average reimbursement for each physician visit has been 50 percent more for higher-income than for low-income individuals, higher-income persons have visited physicians almost 60 percent more frequently than lower-income persons with similar health problems; and higher-income people have received 45 percent more days of hospital care than lower-income people with similar health conditions (Davis and Schoen 1978: 92–119; K. Davis 1975a). Part of this differential in Medicare benefits has resulted from the fact that upper-income individuals were more likely to seek out physicians who were specialists, whose practices were in high-income areas, and who were staff members in high-image hospitals, while low-income individuals have tended to gravitate more frequently to general practitioners, whose practices were in low-income neighborhoods. And the low-income person was more likely than an upper-income person to visit an emergency clinic or to be hospitalized in a large, crowded public general hospital.

While Medicare guidelines were scrupulous in specifying that services available to the elderly were to be on a nondiscriminatory basis, black Americans have tended to receive fewer services than white Americans under the Medicare program, even though the former have tended to have more serious health problems. For example, whites in the late 1960s received 60 percent higher benefits for physician services under Medicare and more than 100 percent higher benefits for skilled nursing home services than blacks. In general, blacks have tended to receive more of their Medicare services from less specialized physicians and from hospital outpatient departments, care that has been more fragmented and impersonal than that received by whites, who have had greater access to private physicians (K. Davis 1975a).

The greatest problem in achieving equity in the Medicaid program is that people in equal circumstances have not been treated equally across the country. States have varied substantially in determining eligibility requirements. By 1975, at least 8 million poor people were excluded from Medicaid coverage, and, if one adjusts for the large number of people moving in and out of Medicaid over time, some studies suggest that as many as 40 percent of the poor population was not covered at any given time. In 1969, Medicaid payments were 75 percent higher for white than for black recipients. Part of this differential resulted from the fact that more blacks were concentrated in the south, where Medicaid programs were very limited, but even in the northeastern states, whites received almost 50 percent more in Medicaid benefits than blacks. Clearly, Medicaid did not achieve the goals of providing poor people with the best medical practice the country was capable of dispensing. Many physicians were discouraged from participating in Medicaid not only because of its lower rates of reimbursement than those of private insurance companies but also because of the cumbersome bureaucracy, delays in receiving payment, and the restrictions on covered services (K. Davis 1976b).

Despite government programs for low-income groups, the poor and the nonpoor in America in 1980 were still receiving very different types of medical care. The poor still tended to receive much of theirs in crowded, even dirty clinics with long waits and few amenities. Their care was usually fragmented, impersonal, and episodic. A small proportion of poor children received care from pediatricians, and higher-income women were twice as likely to be cared for by a specialist as poor women. The poor tended to spend 50 percent more time than the nonpoor traveling and waiting in order to see a physician. Moreover, persons with low incomes spent essentially the same fraction of their income on medical care as in 1963—before Medicaid and Medicare came into existence (K. Davis 1976a; 1976b; Davis and Schoen 1978; Robert Wood Johnson Foundation 1983).

While the poor and the nonpoor have received different types of medical care, the poor have made substantial gains in access to care in comparison to the nonpoor in respect to needs. According to Aday et al., the poor in 1963 tended to see a doctor 28 percent less often than physicians thought was necessary, whereas the nonpoor failed to consult doctors 12 percent less often than physicians thought appropriate. By 1976, however, the poor and nonpoor were seeing a physician with approximately the same frequency in relation to need; each seeing a doctor approximately 5 percent less often than physicians thought desirable (Aday et al. 1980).

REGIONAL EQUALITY

England and Wales

Even though the state provision of medical services has brought about more equal entitlements and use of medical services, increasing centralization has not eliminated inequities in their spatial distribution, although it has reduced them.

Table 13 shows the distribution of medical doctors and nurses in the regions of England and Wales between 1891 and 1971. Significantly, much of the variation among regions was reduced before the introduction of the NHS. For example, the index of regional variation for doctors had declined from 23.5 in 1891 to 12.4 in 1941, while the variation among nurses declined from 44.2 to 13.8 in the same period. On the other hand, there has been considerable reduction in the regional variation among doctors since 1951, and the NHS is partly responsible for the more equitable distribution. In an effort to rationalize the distribution of doctors across Britain, the NHS instituted a system of "negative direction" by closing adequately served areas to newcomers. As a result, the percentage of the population living in areas officially designated as "underdoctored" fell from 52 percent in 1952 to less than 18 percent in 1961 (Cooper 1975).

The NHI system provided medical care only from general practitioners; thus it did not affect the distribution of specialists and hospital beds, in

Table 13 Regional Distribution of Medical Personnel per 100,000 Population in the United States and England and Wales, Selected Years

	England and Wales								
	1891	1901	1911	1921	1931	1941	1951	1961	1971
Regional index: doctors	23.5	21.06	20.3	23.8	21.97	12.42	15.2	11.15	8.18
Regional index: nurses	44.23	39.18	32.12	34.12	22.81	13.76	21.29	11.4	4.7

	The United States								
	1890	1900	1910	1920	1930	1940	1950	1960	1970
Regional index: doctors	10.08	12.49	11.1	9.46	12.72	18.84	18.45	17.3	16.35
Regional index: nurses	47.21	35.60	38.17	34.82	31.63	28.84	24.47	15.3	14.5

Source: For England and Wales, county-level data arranged by 1921 census regions. Great Britain, Decennial Census, 1891–1971. For the United States, state-level data arranged by census regions. U.S. Census, 1890–1970.
Note: Regional Index (mean absolute deviation/mean) x 100.

which there were considerable inequities during the interwar years. The decentralized system of distributing specialists meant that their location was determined more by the opportunities for doctors to earn a high income than by the medical needs of an area. Before 1940, many counties had no gynecologists, thoracic surgeons, dermatologists, pediatricians, or psychiatrists (Titmuss 1950). Not only were there gross inequities in the distribution of hospital beds, but also the hospitals in many regions had grossly inadequate x-ray and pathology equipment.

The NHS, however, changed the situation. True, spatial inequities still exist. Several studies have demonstrated that there is a negative correlation between the proportion of the population in unskilled and semiskilled occupations and community health expenditures as well as hospital expenditures (Townsend and Davidson 1982: 82). For example, middle-class areas had general practitioners with smaller lists. Moreover, such areas had higher proportion of doctors with further qualifications, more with degrees from Oxford and Cambridge, and more with hospital appointments than working-class districts (Walters 1980: 129–55).

Although the NHS has not dictated where specialists may practice, it has specified where they may not do so, and this type of negative allocation of manpower has over time brought about a more equitable distribution in England and Wales. And while the inequities that existed before 1948 were difficult to rectify, the centralized allocation of resources has made the distribution of hospital beds more equitable over time. Moreover, the regional variations in the allocation of per capita expenditures for care and in the distribution of resources have diminished. Since 1970, there has been a much more determined effort to equalize regional resources, especially to shift more from London and the Southeast to other areas. The centralized structure of allocating resources has clearly narrowed spatial inequalities. In this respect, it is important to observe regional inequities over time, and when one does this, it becomes obvious that the British centralized system has reduced regional inequities far more rapidly than has been the case in those countries with relatively decentralized systems (Cooper 1975; Lindsey 1962; Stevens 1966; Eckstein 1958; Forsyth 1966; Culyer et al. 1980).

The United States

A discussion of the impact of centralization on the spatial distribution of medical resources must confront an alternative explanation for the fact that resources have become more uniform geographically. The competing explanation is that a tendency toward a more even distribution of per capita income and wealth over regions will bring about a similar tendency in the distribution of medical resources. In both the United States and Great Britain, there has been a trend toward a leveling of per capita income across regions. However, the experience of the two countries has been very different in the reduction of regional inequalities of those medical resources for which we have comparable data across regions. As there has been a stronger trend toward uniformity in the regional distribution of medical resources in England and Wales, it appears most likely that it is due to the greater centralization in the British system rather than to the convergence in per capita income across regions (see table 13). It is particularly significant that the regional variation in the distribution of physicians and nurses in England and Wales has declined somewhat dramatically since the introduction of the NHS. In the United States, however, the variation in numerous medical resources hardly changed between 1940 and 1970. Not only is this true for doctors, but the regional variation remained almost the same for the number of beds, the average number of hospital patients, and the number of hospital admissions per 100,000 population (see table 14). There was even an increase in the regional inequality in the number of hospital personnel per daily average patient and in the hospital expenditure per daily average patient between 1950 and 1970 (see table 14).

The data for the United States suggest that there has been little reduction in regional inequality in medical resources, despite regional income convergence and some increase in centralization. The British system, with more centralization, did have greater regional equalization. Thus, the experience of these two countries suggests that it is not convergence in income

Table 14 Interregional Variation* in Hospital Indicators, England and Wales and the United States

Variation in Revenue Allocation per Capita for Regional Hospital Boards, England and Wales, 1950–1972

Year	Index of Variation
1950–51	20.93
1960–61	13.75
1971–72	8.16

Hospital Resources, United States, 1950–1970

	Beds per 100,000 Population	Average Daily Patients per 100,000 Population	Admissions per 100,000 Population	Personnel per Daily Average Patient	Expenditures per Daily Average Patient
		Index of Variation*			
1950	13.87	16.28	8.66	5.95	8.83
1960	20.89	17.25	5.07	6.35	10.16
1970	12.54	14.54	6.69	10.03	12.75

Sources: For England and Wales, Great Britain, DHSS, 1972: 20,71; Cooper 1975: 65. For the United States, see U.S., Comm., Census 1979a; Hollingsworth et al., forthcoming.
Note: *(Mean absolute deviation/mean) x 100.

distribution but increases in the level of centralization that reduce inequality in the regional distribution of medical resources.

This regional variation in distribution is reflected in the regional inequality in the availability and utilization of federal medical programs for different groups of individuals. Even though Medicare was designed to be a uniform program throughout the country, elderly persons residing in the Northeast and the West have received substantially higher benefits than those in the South and the North Central regions. The elderly residing in the South in 1968 received 32 percent less in payments for inpatient hospital care and 43 percent less in physician benefits than those residing in the West. Moreover, the elderly in the West received two-and-one-half times in payments for extended care facility services of those in the South. Because the South has fewer physicians and fewer extended care facilities, utilization of these services has been lower there. So long as there has been geographical variation in the availability of resources and costs of care there have continued to be variations in the use of medical services across regions (K. Davis 1975a).

But there is much greater variation in Medicaid services across regions, for the program is quite decentralized, with each state setting its own eligibility requirements. In many states, poor families have not qualified for Medicaid because both parents live in the household and do not qualify for benefits under the federal program of aid to families with dependent children (AFDC). In 1976, twenty-five states restricted eligibility for Medicaid to AFDC families with only a mother present. In most southern states, only about one-tenth of all poor children were covered by the program in 1970, while in the Northeast almost all the poor and many of the near-poor were covered. And while almost 50 percent of the nation's poor lived in the South in 1970, only 17 percent of Medicaid payments were in southern states (K. Davis 1975b). Poor families in rural states have fared much worse in Medicaid benefits than those in more urban states, for a much higher proportion of poor rural families have both parents living together. On the other hand, transportation difficulties and the limited availability of medical personnel have also led to regional divergences in the utilization of Medicaid services.

EQUALITY OF RESULTS

Though the centralization of the medical delivery system has, over time, narrowed the legal inequality in entitlements to medical care and, to a lesser extent, the variation in regional distribution of medical resources (especially in England and Wales), the story is much more mixed when one analyzes inequality in levels of health over time. There is no direct measure for this, but there are reliable mortality data across time, by region, and by social class. And while mortality is far from a perfect indicator of levels of health, death statistics do provide some of the most reliable data on health that are comparable over time and across countries.

For some years, scholars have attempted to develop an index of health status, and work in survey research has encouraged this type of activity. Thus far, however, such indices have highly subjective components, and it appears unlikely that there will be in the foreseeable future a health status index that is comparable to the GNP index for measuring economic activity (Sullivan 1966; Katz et al. 1973). For cross-national and cross-temporal analysis, mortality data remain the most reliable indicator of health status available. Among such data, infant mortality is probably the most accurate and objective indicator for measuring the health status of populations over time and across societies.

Regional Mortality

The data for England and Wales in table 15 are somewhat consistent with the hypothesis that equality in the distribution of health resources leads to equality of results. A more centralized medical delivery system, with resources more equitably distributed across regions, appears to be associated with less variation in health across regions. For almost every age category,

Table 15 Index of Regional Variation in Mortality Rates, England and Wales and the United States, 1890–1970

	1890	1900	1910	1920	1930	1940	1950	1960	1970
All Persons, Age 0–1									
England and Wales	8.1	9.6	9.6	13.9	14.7	N.A.	13.9	7.1	6.9
United States									
White	26.9	12.9	19.4	13.2	9.6	13.9	11.8	6.6	5.5
Nonwhite	39.3	30.9	33.3	21.6	18.6	10.6	19.3	11.2	9.0
Total	26.6	25.0	21.7	12.2	10.8	17.8	15.8	12.2	9.7
All Persons, Ages 25–44									
England and Wales	11.6	8.0	9.2	9.5	12.4	N.A.	12.6	11.1	7.8
United States									
White	6.2	10.7	10.1	7.3	8.5	8.6	8.0	6.9	8.0
Nonwhite	8.9	10.4	18.8	7.0	10.4	11.5	12.1	11.8	14.0
Total	5.7	15.0	12.4	13.3	18.8	17.1	15.3	12.1	11.9
All Persons, Ages 45–64									
England and Wales	11.0	9.1	9.1	8.5	8.5	N.A.	10.2	8.0	6.9
United States									
White	12.0	13.9	11.1	7.9	7.8	7.3	7.4	5.1	4.0
Nonwhite	14.5	10.6	20.2	10.8	13.0	13.0	15.0	13.4	13.7
Total	11.9	17.2	12.2	8.2	9.1	8.4	7.7	6.2	7.3
All Persons, Age-Sex Standardized Population[a]									
England and Wales	9.3	8.4	7.9	8.1	8.9	N.A.	8.2	6.4	5.4
United States									
White	9.1	8.8	10.4	5.9	5.2	3.2	3.3	3.1	2.6
Nonwhite	17.7	13.6	27.3	8.8	8.1	7.1	8.8	7.4	10.7
Total	10.8	14.1	12.0	5.7	7.0	5.3	4.8	4.2	4.3

Sources: Great Britain, Office of Population Censuses and Surveys 1891–1971; Great Britain, Registrar General 1891–1971; U.S., Comm., Census, *Vital Statistics* (annual reports).

Note: Index = $\dfrac{\text{mean absolute deviation}}{\text{mean}}$ x 100

[a]Standardized on the population of England and Wales, 1931.

there was a substantial reduction in the regional variation in mortality following the introduction of the NHS. Indeed, although regional variation in infant mortality had increased in England and Wales between 1891 and 1931, it declined substantially between 1931 and 1971. This same pattern occurred with the age group 25–44, whereas with the group aged 45–64, most of the decline in regional variation occurred after the introduction of the NHS, even though some decline had occurred prior to 1948. Similarly, the age-sex-standardized death rates across regions showed their most dramatic decline between 1951 and 1971, with modest decline occurring during the sixty years prior to 1951.

However, the data will not permit one to conclude that increased equality in the distribution of medical resources across regions led to increased equality in levels of health across regions. The relationship may well be a spurious one. Since the late nineteenth century, there has been a decrease in the variation in per capita income and in the standard of living across regions. Quite possibly, it is the decreasing income variation that has most efficiently contributed to the reduction in differences in death rates across regions. Fortunately, data on the United States provide some insight into this process. The United States has a decentralized medical delivery system in which variation in the distribution of medical resources across regions has diminished very little, but regional variations in mortality have diminished, in association with declining variation in regional per capita income. Most likely, it is the narrowing in the standard of living across regions in the United States that has led to a narrowing of the variation in regional mortality rates.

Mortality by Social Class

England and Wales

Mortality data for England and Wales have been collected by the same five occupational classes for which physician consultation rates have already been presented. The rates range from social class I (i.e., the higher professional and administrative occupations) to social class V (i.e., the unskilled occupations). And with this data, it is possible to determine if increasing the equality of access to medical services has increased the equality in levels of health across social classes.

Infants.   The infant mortality data for England and Wales analyzed below are presented by occupation of the father. The social class data for infants are somewhat more meaningful than the data that analyze the mortality of adults by occupation. Most children are born when their fathers are between ages 20 and 50 and engaged in their main occupation. Thus the environment of the infant is likely to be a real reflection of the father's social and economic status. The occupation of an adult at time of death is slightly more problematic, for as an adult male gets older, suffers from ill health, or becomes physically disabled, he may hold an occupation that differs from the one he held throughout most of his adult life. Though utilizing occupational groups of adults has some modest disadvantages, it is useful for comparing mortality rates among people in the social structure. The population was categorized into five broad social classes in order to denote an economic grading from high to low income.

Table 16 Neonatal and Postneonatal Mortality per 1,000 Births by Social Class, England and Wales, Selected Years

	Neonatal					Postneonatal				
	I	II	III	IV	V	I	II	III	IV	V
1911	30.26 (1.0)	36.5 (1.2)	36.8 (1.2)	38.6 (1.3)	42.5 (1.4)	46.2 (1.0)	69.9 (1.5)	75.9 (1.6)	82.9 (1.8)	110 (2.4)
1921	23.4 (1.0)	28.3 (1.2)	33.7 (1.4)	36.7 (1.6)	36.9 (1.6)	15.0 (1.0)	27.2 (1.8)	43.1 (2.8)	52.7 (3.5)	60.1 (4.0)
1930–32	21.7 (1.0)	27.2 (1.3)	29.4 (1.4)	31.9 (1.5)	32.5 (1.5)	11.0 (1.0)	17.8 (1.6)	28.2 (2.6)	34.9 (3.2)	44.6 (4.1)
1939	18.9 (1.0)	23.4 (1.2)	25.4 (1.3)	27.7 (1.5)	30.1 (1.6)	7.9 (1.0)	11.0 (1.4)	19.0 (2.4)	23.7 (3.0)	30.0 (3.8)
1950	12.9 (1.0)	16.2 (1.3)	17.6 (1.4)	19.8 (1.5)	21.9 (1.7)	4.9 (1.0)	6.0 (1.2)	10.5 (2.1)	13.9 (2.8)	18.8 (3.8)
1964–65[a]	9.2 (1.0)		11.8 (1.3)		13.2 (1.4)	3.5 (1.0)		5.4 (1.5)		7.6 (2.2)
1970–72[b]										
Males	8.9 (1.0)	9.7 (1.1)	10.7 (1.2) 11.0 (1.2)	12.7 (1.4)	17.0 (1.9)	3.5 (1.0)	4.1 (1.2)	4.6 (1.3) 6.2 (1.8)	7.3 (2.1)	14.6 (4.2)
Females	6.3 (1.0)	7.4 (1.2)	7.6 (1.2) 8.2 (1.3)	9.1 (1.4)	12.6 (2.0)	2.3 (1.0)	3.2 (1.4)	3.1 (1.3) 5.0 (2.2)	6.0 (2.6)	11.6 (5.1)

Sources: Titmuss 1943: 37; Great Britain, Registrar General 1938: 24; Spicer and Lipworth 1966: 21, 26; Great Britain, Office of Population Censuses and Surveys 1978: 157.

Note: Ratio of mortality rate in each social class to mortality rate of social class I is in parentheses.

[a] For 1964–65, data references to social classes I and II, and classes IV and V, were collapsed in the source.

[b] For 1970–72, the two categories of social class III data refer to nonmanual skilled and manual skilled occupations respectively, and postneonatal mortality refers to infants aged 1–11 months rather than 1–12 months.

Table 16 presents data for neonatal (the first 28 days of life) and post-neonatal (months 1–12 of life) mortality rates for England and Wales between 1911 and 1970–1972. A high proportion of neonatal deaths results from congenital defects and complications in childbirth, although these have declined markedly as improvements have occurred in prenatal care as well as in the delivery of medical services during childbirth. The number of postneonatal deaths is more susceptible to improvements both in the socio-economic environment of children and in the delivery of medical services, and these have generated a remarkable decline in postneonatal rates. Whereas in 1905, one-third of infant deaths were in the neonatal and two-thirds in the postneonatal category, by the early 1930s, more than one-half of the infant deaths were neonatal. And by 1970, the trend was a complete reversal of that which existed at the turn of the century: two-thirds of the infant deaths were in the neonatal and one-third in the postneonatal category.

Even though every occupational grouping benefited by a substantial decline in the neonatal and postneonatal mortality rates over time, there has not been much equalization of mortality for this age group across the various classes. The ratio between class V and class I in neonatal mortality rates was 1.4 in 1911, whereas it was 1.7 in 1950 and approximately 2 in 1970–72. But the postneonatal rates over time are even more interesting. In 1911, the ratio between class V and class I was 2.4, while in 1950, it was 3.8, and in 1970–72, it was between 4 and 5. In other words, the data suggest that there had been no narrowing of neonatal and postneonatal mortality rates but, rather, a distinct increase in inequality between these two classes.

Over time, however, the size of the population in class V has declined while that in classes II, III, and IV has increased somewhat, and for these reasons it is especially useful to observe the trends in these middle classes. The trend is less distinct in the neonatal rates, but in the postneonatal rates, there does seem to be some narrowing of inequality during the period since 1921. For example, the ratio for the postneonatal rates between class IV and class I changed from 3.5 in 1921 to 2.8 in 1950 and to approximately 2.4 in 1970–72. This type of narrowing also occurred for classes II and III, suggesting that improvement in the access to medical care may have had some modest impact on equality of health for middle-class infants, though greater inequality resulted for those at the bottom of the social state.

The infant mortality rates for England and Wales, of course, as presented in table 17, reveal a similar pattern, as rates for infants are the sum of the neonatal and the postneonatal rates. The data for 1899 are only for York, but in that city, the ratio between class V and class I was 2.6. For 1911, however, the data are for all of England and Wales, and the ratio was 2. Across time, there was no significant improvement in the ratios between these two classes. Rather, there was some decline in the level of health of

Table 17 Infant Mortality per 1,000 Live Legitimate Births by Social Class, England and Wales, Selected Years

	I	II	III		IV	V
1899[a]	94[b]	—	173		184	247
	(1.0)	—	(1.8)		(2.0)	(2.6)
1911	76	106	113		122	153
	(1.0)	(1.4)	(1.5)		(1.6)	(2.0)
1921–23	38	55	77		89	97
	(1.0)	(1.4)	(2.0)		(2.3)	(2.6)
1930–32	33	45	58		67	77
	(1.0)	(1.4)	(1.8)		(2.0)	(2.3)
1939	27	34	44		51	60
	(1.0)	(1.3)	(1.6)		(1.9)	(2.2)
1949–53	19	22	29		34	41
	(1.0)	(1.2)	(1.5)		(1.8)	(2.2)
1964–65[b]	12.7		17.2		20.8	
	(1.0)		(1.4)		(1.6)	
1970–72[c]	12	14	15	17		
	(1.0)	(1.2)	(1.3)	(1.4)	(1.7)	(2.6)

Sources: Great Britain, Office of Population Censuses and Surveys 1978: 182; Great Britain, Registrar General 1923, 1927, 1938; United Nations, various years; Parker et al. 1972; Rowntree 1908: 198–208.

Note: Ratio of mortality rate of each class to mortality rate of class I is in parenthesis.

[a] The 1899 data were provided by a source and computed by a method different from the data between 1911 and 1970. However, it is useful to compare the 1899 data with the other years for which we have available data. For 1899, data refer to the servant-keeping class of York and to selected districts in York coded by Rowntree (1908) according to the proportion of families living in primary and secondary poverty as determined by a comparison of family income and minimum budgets. Rowntree defined primary poverty as a state in which family income was insufficient to purchase the physical necessities of life. Families in secondary poverty could potentially afford necessities, though in fact a portion of their income was absorbed by "useful or wasteful" expenditures. The population of Rowntree's area A consisted of 6,803 people (1,642 families) of whom 70% lived in primary or secondary poverty. Thirty-seven percent of the 9,945 inhabitants of area B lived in primary or secondary poverty. None of the 5,336 people in area C lived in primary or secondary poverty. In this table, area A data is coded as class V, area B data as class IV, area C data as class III, and the servant-keeping class as class I.
[b] For 1964–65, data referring to social classes I and II, and classes IV and V, are collapsed.
[c] For 1970–72, the two categories of social class III data refer to nonmanual skilled and manual skilled occupations respectively.

class V relative to class I. When one compares classes II, III, and IV with class I in both 1920–1923 and 1970–1972, one observes that there was some shift toward equality in levels of health for those groups.

Women. There are no reliable data on the mortality of women for the entire period between 1890 and 1970, nor are there time-series data on the occupational mortality of women other than that coded by the husband's occupation. Between 1930 and 1950, there was some movement toward equality across the various classes. The NHS had been in existence for only two years in 1950, and one must conclude that it would have had little effect in narrowing the inequality that one observes between these two dates. Between 1950 and 1970, the trend was somewhat mixed, but in general there was an increase in inequality, greater with some groups than with others.

Among women who died in childbirth, there was between 1930 and 1950 a marked trend toward equality for each class—indeed, maternal mortality was even lower for classes II, III, and IV than for class I (Hollingsworth 1981). It is impossible to determine how much of this trend was due to the improvement in antenatal care and childbirth services before the introduction of the NHS. Between 1950 and 1970, however, the trend was reversed toward greater inequality among classes III, IV, and V.

Men.   The occupational mortality data for adult males reveal no distinct movement toward equality over time. At best, the inequality between classes V and I was stable throughout the entire period between 1890 and 1970. But if one uses 1930 as the point of comparison, the data suggest a distinct increase in inequality. And since the introduction of the NHS, it would appear that instead of a narrowing, there has been a distinct widening in the ratios between classes III, IV, V and class I (Hollingsworth 1981).

Data on hypertensive diseases, cancer, diabetes, bronchitis, tuberculosis, and suicide reveal the same pattern: a general trend toward inequality in levels of health—indeed, in the cases of diabetes and tuberculosis, a very sharp increase. When the NHS was introduced, the death rate from diabetes in class I was greater than in any other class, but in recent years, the pattern has been reversed.

The United States

The British data are very intriguing in their implications. For a longer period of time, the British medical delivery system has been more egalitarian in terms of access to services than any in North America or Western Europe, but its history suggests that equalizing access to care does not necessarily lead to equalizing performance in levels of health (when measured by mortality data) across social classes. The U.S. system over time has had much less equality in access to care than the British system. Have levels of health across income groups and occupations therefore been even more inegalitarian than in England and Wales? Or, if access is not highly efficacious in influencing levels of health, might the same type of trend in levels of health across income and occupations be present in the United States as in England and Wales, even though the structure of the health delivery systems is substantially different?

Unfortunately, exactly comparable data over time do not exist for the two countries. Highly industrialized countries tend to collect vast quantities of data on those services that are most egalitarian and popular. The British, with their very egalitarian health delivery system, have excellent data on the relationship between social class on the one hand, and utilization rates and mortality on the other. In contrast to their egalitarian education system, on which there is excellent data on access and performance, the Americans have somewhat less satisfactory data over time on health care and levels of health (Hollingsworth and Hanneman 1983). Even so, the U.S. data do permit some insight into how inequality in levels of health has changed over time.

Infants. Other than data for individual cities, there is systematic data on American infant mortality by income of parents (not occupation of father) for only two periods: 1911–1916 and 1964–1966. This information is presented in table 18. The 1911–1916 data are for only seven U.S. cities and therefore are not a national sample. The data for 1964–66, however, are a national sample. Insofar as it is appropriate to compare the data for the two time periods, it would appear that the neonatal mortality ratios across income groups have been relatively stable over time, with some modest widening of inequality between income groups I and V. The differentials between these two groups in 1964–66 are somewhat similar to the occupational groupings for England and Wales at approximately the same time. The ratios between income groups I and V for U.S. postneonatal mortality rates appear to have remained relatively stable. But when one compares the postneonatal ratios between income groups I and V in 1964–66 with the highest and lowest occupational group in England and Wales at approximately the same time, one observes that there is considerable similarity. The data on mortality for all infants suggest some increase in equality across time. Moreover, the U.S. infant mortality data for 1964–1966 is quite reliable, and a comparison of the ratios with the data for England and Wales at that time point suggests that there was less inequality between class I and V in the United States than in Great Britain (see tables 17 and 18).

Because much inequality in American society has resulted from its multiracial character, it is appropriate to analyze infant mortality of whites and nonwhites across time. Table 19 shows a substantial decline in mortality rates between 1925 and 1975 for both groups. However, the gap in infant, neonatal, and postneonatal rates widened between whites and nonwhites between 1925 and 1964. Black infant mortality rates were 1.62 times higher in 1925 and 1.92 higher in 1964 than those of whites. Black neonatal rates were 1.35 times higher in 1925 and 1.65 times higher in 1964 than those of whites, while the black ratios for postneonatal rates increased from 1.95 to 2.70 in the same period. Throughout this time, the rate of decline in infant, neonatal, and postneonatal mortality rates were somewhat greater for

Table 18 Neonatal, Postneonatal, and Infant Mortality by Income Level, the United States, 1911–1966

	I	II	III	IV	V
	Neonatal				
1911–16[c]	36.6[a]	41.3	46.0	44.6	54.2
	1.00[b]	1.13	1.26	1.22	1.48
1964–66[d]	18.5[a]	17.1	16.8	22.4	30.2
	1.00[b]	.93	.91	1.21	1.63
	Postneonatal				
1911–16[c]	27.5[a]	50.2	62.9	76.7	107.8
	1.00[b]	1.83	2.29	2.78	3.92
1964–66[d]	3.9[a]	4.9	5.1	8.5	15.1
	1.00[b]	1.25	1.30	2.14	3.83
	Infant				
1911–16[c]	64.0[a]	91.5	108.7	120.8	162.0
	1.00[b]	1.43	1.70	1.89	2.53
1964–66[d]	22.4[a]	22.0	21.9	30.0	45.3
	1.00[b]	.98	.98	1.38	2.02

Sources: Woodbury 1925: 148–51; National Center for Health Statistics, Computer Tape of the National Infant Mortality and National Natality Survey (for discussion, see U.S. Dept. of Health, Education, and Welfare, NCHS 1972).
[a] Deaths per 1,000 live births.
[b] Ratio of death rates for each income level to death rate for income level I.
[c] The data for 1911–16 refer to all births and postneonatal deaths in seven cities, each surveyed for twelve consecutive months between 1911 and 1916. The cities were Baltimore, Md., New Bedford, Mass., Brockton, Mass., Waterbury, Conn., Manchester, N.H., Akron, Ohio, and Saginaw, Mich. The data have been reanalyzed for purposes of this table.
[d] The data for 1964–66 are based on a national probability sample of legitimate and illegitimate births.

white than for black infants. After 1964, however, when Medicaid was introduced and the Maternal and Child Health Program focused on the reduction of infant mortality in low-income families, the rate of decline in infant deaths was greater for blacks than for whites, that is, the ratios between black and white infant, neonatal, and postneonatal deaths began to converge. It is of course difficult to identify and measure all of the factors that caused infant mortality to decline more rapidly for one group than another, but the different types of access to medical facilities probably has some impact on the differential. Of course, black-white income differentials narrowed somewhat between 1964 and 1975, and that was probably of some importance in narrowing infant mortality rates between the two groups. But the improvement in prenatal and postnatal care after 1964 for blacks was undoubtedly also important. One study demonstrated that

Table 19 White and Nonwhite Neonatal, Postneonatal, and Infant Mortality per 1,000 Births, the United States, 1925–1975

	Neonatal			Postneonatal			Infant		
	White	Nonwhite	Ratio of Nonwhite to White	White	Nonwhite	Ratio of Nonwhite to White	White	Nonwhite	Ratio of Nonwhite to White
1925	36.8	49.5	1.35	31.5	61.3	1.95	68.3	110.8	1.62
1950	19.4	27.5	1.41	7.4	17.0	2.30	26.8	44.5	1.66
1960	17.2	26.9	1.56	5.7	16.3	2.86	22.9	43.2	1.88
1964	16.2	26.5	1.65	5.4	14.6	2.70	21.5	41.4	1.92
1975	10.7	15.8	1.47	3.7	7.1	1.92	14.4	22.9	1.59

Source: Grove and Hetzel 1968.

maternal and infant care projects caused a 23 percent reduction in neonatal death rates among low-income black infants (K. Davis 1976b: 226–27).

One gains some insight into the efficacy of medical delivery in bringing about the decline in infant mortality rates by comparing the rates of decline in the United States with those in England and Wales between 1925 and 1975. Between 1925 and 1947, there was a great deal of inequality in access to prenatal and postnatal medical care in both the United States and in England and Wales, but in the United States, there was a somewhat higher standard of living, (measured by per capita income) and the rate of change in per capita income was substantially higher. And the rate of decline in infant, neonatal, and postneonatal mortality rates was much greater in the United States than in England and Wales. Between 1948 and 1965, however, the per capita income remained substantially higher in the United States, though the rate of decline in infant, neonatal, and postneonatal mortality rates was much greater in England and Wales. And it was un-doubtedly the introduction of the NHS in 1948, with its greater equitable access to medical care for expectant mothers and infants, that contributed to higher levels of health. In the United States, during the 1950s and 1960s, there was a widespread belief that U.S. infant mortality rates had reached a plateau below which they were not likely to fall. After the introduction of Medicaid and other Great Society programs for the care of pregnant women and infants, however, the rates began to fall much more rapidly in the United States than in England and Wales (see table 20). For example, between 1966 and 1975, the U.S. rate of decline in infant, neonatal, and postneonatal rates was almost twice as rapid as in England and Wales. In short, the date at which medical care became more accessible for mothers and infants appears to have influenced the rate at which infant mortality rates declined.

After controlling for a variety of factors that impact on neonatal and postneonatal mortality rates (e.g., education of parents, age of mother, birth order of child, family income, mother's previous pregnancy expe-

Table 20 Percentage Decline in Neonatal, Postneonatal, and Infant Mortality, the United States and England and Wales, 1925–1975

	Neonatal		Postneonatal		Infant	
	United States	England and Wales	United States	England and Wales	United States	England and Wales
1925–47	41	30	72	56	55	44
1948–65	20	34	29	58	23	44
1966–75	32	17	32	18	32	17

Sources: U.S., Comm., Census 1979a; *Vital Statistics* (annual reports); *Statistical Abstract of the United Kingdom.*

rience), recent studies demonstrate that prenatal care does act to reduce neonatal deaths (Gortmaker 1977; 1979a; 1979b; Kessner et al. 1973). But the lack of comprehensive prenatal care has continued to be a serious problem in the United States, with 13 percent of all mothers and 24 percent of black mothers receiving either late (third trimester) or no prenatal care in 1969. As of 1 July 1974, twenty states did not provide prenatal care under Medicaid to first-pregnancy mothers.

There are several reasons why Sweden has the lowest infant, neonatal, and postneonatal rates in the world: prenatal care is provided to all pregnant women at neighborhood clinics; more than 99 percent of all deliveries take place in hospitals; and postpartum physician checkups occur throughout the first year of the infant's life. And all of these services are free to the recipient. It is these differentials in service that contribute to the differential ranking of the United States and Sweden in infant mortality rates, the United States being fifteenth in the world in 1970 (Falkner 1969; Geijarstam 1969).

Women. Data do not exist to make possible a longitudinal comparison of adult female mortality rates across occupations or income groupings within the United States. When one compares age-adjusted death rates for all white and nonwhite females between 1920 and 1970, however, nonwhites had rates 1.60 higher than whites in 1920 and 1.54 higher in 1970—a considerable stability over time. When one compares mortality rates for a few specific age groups among females across time, however, one observes some convergence. For example, the nonwhite death rate was 2.74 times higher than that for whites for the age group 45–54 in 1930 but had declined to 1.90 times higher in 1970. For the age group 55–64, the corresponding ratios for the same dates were 2.08 and 1.74 (Grove and Hetzel 1968: 330–31). For these age groups, obviously, many variables caused the convergence, narrowing income and educational differentials being among the more important ones.

But maternal mortality rates are more revealing about the relationship between access to medical care and levels of health than other mortality rates for women. While maternal mortality rates have declined substantially for both whites and nonwhites since 1920, the ratios between the two groups have widened over time. In 1920, nonwhites had maternal mortality rates 1.68 higher than whites; in 1960, 3.76 times higher; and in 1970, 4 times higher.

Men. Data for adult American males comparable to those compiled by the registrar-general in England and Wales do not exist for all years, but there are enough data to observe that the United States has had the same trends in adult male mortality as in England and Wales (see tables 12 and 17). If one looks simply at the data for adult white males in the United States between 1950 and 1960, it is apparent that there was a widening of inequality, just as there was in England and Wales during the same period. On the other hand, when one compares nonwhite occupational groups I and V with whites in 1950 and 1960, it appears that the gap between whites and nonwhites was narrowing. In 1900, the mortality ratio between groups V and I was wider in England and Wales than in the United States, but by 1950, the gap had closed more in England and Wales than in the United States. In 1960, the gap was about the same in England and Wales as for white American males, though, if one considers both nonwhites and whites in 1960, there was greater inequality in health in the United States than in England and Wales (U.S., Comm., Census 1896: 64, 67; 1902: cclx, cclxi; Guralnick 1963: 107–12; Kitagawa and Hauser 1973).

CONCLUDING OBSERVATIONS

The data reported here do not permit any definitive conclusions about the relationships between changes in the organization and technology of medical services and changes in health across social classes and regions, but they are suggestive. The history of centralizing medical delivery systems is clearly one of increasing equality in both the access to medical resources and their spatial distribution. Moreover, there is evidence from England and Wales and from the United States that over time, lower-income groups have tended to increase their utilization of medical services and eventually to use them more than upper-income groups (see tables 3 and 5). It should be noted, however, that the needs of the former are greater than those of the latter. On the other hand, upper-income groups in both countries, occasionally though not always, consume more medical care resources for each episode of illness than do lower-income groups—though lower-income groups have more frequent illnesses (Le Grand 1978; Collins and Klein 1980; Morris 1979). Even so, the evidence is very clear that one of the most egalitarian medical system in the Western industrialized world, the NHS, has not brought about a marked convergence in the levels of mortality across occupations, though there is some convergence over time on a regional basis.

Why has an increase in the equality of access to medical resources across social classes not narrowed the variation of deaths across occupations? The answer must be somewhat speculative in nature. Of course, levels of health have improved over time for every social group, but they have improved less rapidly for the lower occupational grouping. This raises some interesting problems about the efficacy of medical technology: equalizing access to medical care and medical resources over a period of several generations has had limited success in equalizing results.

Social and environmental factors are of great importance in explaining levels of health across social classes. Income is still very inequitably distributed in England and Wales, although there has been some narrowing among social classes. This inequitable distribution is strongly reflected in gross variations in life styles across social classes, and that variation is important in understanding class differences in mortality. Education, too, is still very inequitably distributed in England and Wales. This has probably contributed to the continuing inequality in health across social classes. Indeed, there are studies that indicate that level of education is more important than level of income in explaining health (Lefcowitz 1973). There are also studies that indicate that the more education individuals have, the more frequently they see a physician, the more medical services they consume, and the more they adopt a life style consistent with good health. Moreover, better-educated citizens make more use of preventive health services than those with less education and lower income (Alderson 1970; Cartwright 1967; Townsend and Davidson 1982; Cartwright and O'Brien 1976; Walters 1980; Le Grand 1978). These studies, when considered in conjunction with the data presented above, suggest that even though the British NHS is one of the most egalitarian one in the Western world, gross inequalities in levels of health are likely to persist across social classes as long as gross inequities in the distribution of income and education persist.

In Britain and the United States, the dominant medical model has been a curative and caring one, and it has had the effect of diverting attention from detrimental effects of occupational hazards, environmental pollution, poor diet, poverty, inadequate housing, job insecurity, and alienating work situations. Medical research in both countries has tended to minimize the link between these social characteristics and good health. By emphasizing a curative and caring approach to health, Britain and the United States have failed to appreciate the fact that equalizing levels of health requires essentially a political and social approach to health. By providing greater equality in access to medical technology, the government in both societies has legitimated the medical profession's definition of health, but in the process it has obscured the understanding of the determinants of health and has placed limits on the development of effective policies that might equalize levels of health (Walters 1980).

6
Styles of Medical Research

This chapter focuses on the extent to which there is variation in the structure and process with which medical research is conducted between the two countries. Specifically, the concern is with the following questions: Have the two countries differed in the way that biomedical research has been organized? Have they differed in the methods and levels of funding scientific research, and if so, with what consequences?

BRITAIN

In contrast to the U.S. system of medical research, the British one has been much smaller, more centralized, and better coordinated. The British system has had fewer sources of funding, with the result that there have been fewer overlapping and duplicating research projects and internally, the system has been less competitive than that in the United States.

During the twentieth century, most serious medical research in Britain and the United States has been conducted within universities, but the research activity has been much more centralized in Britain because of the centralized sources of funding from the University Grants Committee (UGC) and the Medical Research Council (MRC). When the British universities found themselves in serious financial difficulties at the end of World War I, the government established in 1919 the UGC to provide an intermediary organization through which Parliament could pass large sums of money to the universities without political interference. In one sense, the academic community has been much more involved in shaping university funding decisions in Britain than in the United States, for a sizable number of academics and former academics have sat on the UGC. And over time it has been the committee that has made the major decisions concerning the distribution of resources to universities. Most of the UGC money has been allocated for five years at a time, as every five years the universities have submitted detailed estimates of their needs for the forthcoming quinquennium. Most of the funds allocated to the universities for research by the UGC have generally been for buildings, basic equipment, and salaries. These funds have been supplemented by other organizations for research programs of a specific nature and for relatively short periods of time.

Of course UGC funds have been used to support specific research projects. But after receiving reports from individual universities about their research programs, the committee has provided a lump sum to each university, which has then decided how to allocate the funds internally. Thus the funds provided by the UGC have tended to keep researchers somewhat dependent on their university for research funds. At the same time, individual researchers within the university structure have also become dependent on external sources of funds.

For more than sixty years, the MRC has been the most important source of funding for specific university medical projects. The council has for some years been financed by the government through the Department of Education and Science—but, like the decisions of the UGC, those of the MRC have been immune to political influence. This has been facilitated by the fact that, from its beginning, the council has maintained an independent permanent staff of extremely high quality (Thomson 1973; 1975).

Between the two world wars the UGC did not have the funds with which to provide capital grants for medical research, and the charter of the MRC prevented it from making charter grants. The Rockefeller Foundation, however, formulated a policy for medical education and research that called for dividing the world into different regions, and London was chosen as a major center for medical education and research for the fulfillment of its policies in the British Empire. Primarily as a result of the foundation's activities, the London School of Hygiene and Tropical Medicine was established, and University College and its hospital and medical school were converted into a major medical center. And while research on the scale of the leading U.S. centers did not occur, the Rockefeller Foundation's grants for medical research did encourage other medical schools and universities to increase the importance of medical research as an integral part of their activities. Increasingly, the MRC provided supplemental support to those departments or schools that received grants from the Rockefeller Foundation. By the end of the 1920s the foundation was also assisting in the establishment of full-time professorships in clinical research in the University College Hospital Medical School. Altogether, the foundation provided approximately £2.5 million for medical teaching and research in British universities between the wars. Overall, the development of a serious medical research agenda in London during this period was a result of a partnership between the MRC and the Rockefeller Foundation. In 1936, however, Lord Nuffield provided £2 million to endow the Medical School Trust at Oxford University. This now permitted the initiative for medical research in England to pass from the Rockefeller Foundation (Fisher 1977, 1978; Thomson 1973, 1975; Kohler 1976, 1978).

In the United States between the wars, university medical researchers worked closely with chemical and pharmaceutical firms, often creating a strong network among universities, medical schools, and industrial firms. In Britain, however, professors were much more reluctant to become involved with industry, for fear that their professional impartiality would be called into question. As a result, the MRC assumed the lead in coordinating medical research in the country. Whereas the Americans early in the century institutionalized a pattern of multiple sources of funding for medical research, the British became accustomed to funds from relatively few sources. As Robert Kohler has written the MRC was trying to do for medical research "what had been done in Germany by state ministries and in the United States by the joint action of professional societies and the large foundations" (Kohler 1978: 450; Liebenau 1981).

The early directors of the MRC analyzed the behavior of medical schools in the United States and attempted to establish comparable models by setting up demonstration projects at Cambridge and Oxford and in the clinical departments of London University. By the 1930s it had created research units in several carefully chosen institutions and was supplementing the salaries of individual clinical professors, for all practical purposes permitting them to become full-time teacher-researchers. Eventually, the NHS stipulated that research was to be an integral part of the duties of NHS clinicians and thus achieved by legislation what the MRC had attempted for several decades by persuasion but with meager funding. Thus, by the late 1940s, the MRC had greatly expanded budgets (Kohler 1978; Thomson 1975).

Between the wars, the MRC had very much modeled itself after the Rockefeller Foundation, in that both organizations attempted to operate in a flexible manner by supporting specific research projects and by designating specific institutions to become centers of excellence. Because of the close communication between the Rockefeller Foundation officials and the directors of the MRC, it is not surprising that medical researchers and educators shared similar approaches to illness and disease during much of the twentieth century (Fisher 1978; Thomson 1975).

By 1970, the MRC had two research centers of its own: the National Institute for Medical Research, in Mill Hill, London, for research in the basic sciences and the Clinical Research Centre in Harrow, Middlesex, about six miles from the Mill Hill institute. Each of these centers has maintained exemplary standards of excellence, supported the research of senior scholars, and launched the careers of many young investigators. In addition, the MRC has supported considerable basic and clinical research within universities. In the late 1960s, for example, it supported more than seventy medical research units, and in addition, it provided research funds to individuals, most of whom were attached to a university or a hospital. Moreover, it made block grants to several research institutes, and there the grants were administered by the director and the governing body of the institute (Thomson 1973; 1975).

Meantime, the Department of Health and Social Security, besides administering the NHS, has provided modest funding for medical research, mostly in hospitals and in local communities. Unlike the MRC, which has been very much concerned with basic research, the NHS has been more concerned with promoting applied research designed to improve patient care.

Whereas the early thrust for medical research in the United States came from private foundations, the British impetus for most medical research was provided primarily by the UGC and MRC. Since the 1930s, however, several private foundations based on large industrial fortunes have followed the American pattern of supporting medical research. The most important ones have been the Wellcome Trust (pharmaceuticals), the Nuffield Foundation (automobiles), and the Leverhulme Trust (soaps and detergents). While the private foundations have attempted to support research that government funding agencies could not support, their efforts, relative to the public sector activities, have been modest (Symposium on Medical Research Systems in Europe 1973).

The British have had much less duplication of research effort than the Americans for several reasons. While there are several sources of government funding for medical research in Britain, there are nevertheless fewer sources than in the United States, and thus organizations in Britain have more effectively been able to exchange information and to monitor one another's activities and procedures in order to discourage multiple submission of funding requests. In addition to these structural limitations, there are also cultural ones on the duplication of scientific research in Britain. That is, British researchers have been somewhat disinclined to compete with one another. The Nobel laureate James Watson commented on this tendency in his book *The Double Helix*. "The English sense of fair play would not allow Francis [Crick] to move in on Maurice's [Wilkins] problem. In France, where fair play obviously did not exist, these problems could not have arisen. The States also would not expect someone at Berkeley to ignore a first-rate problem merely because someone at Cal Tech had started first. In England, however, it simply would not look right" (1969: 19). Thus the combination of the British sense of fair play and their centralized funding system have tended to prevent serious duplication of effort in the research community.

When British universities have submitted to the UGC requests for faculty positions in the biomedical sciences, it has usually been necessary also to submit a request to or at least to consult with the MRC concerning research funds. Each agency would then consult with the other, so that planning would be orderly and well coordinated. In contrast, it has been common practice for an elite university in the United States to appoint a faculty member and to support his research from local funds until outside research grants could be obtained. Furthermore, it has not been unusual for a university to attempt to lure a faculty member away from another university with all of his research funding. But in Britain, this kind of decentralized "raiding" has been relatively uncommon, not only because it would have been in poor taste but also because funds for specific research were to a considerable extent controlled from London (Gaston 1978: 53–54).

Medical researchers in the United States have long been entrepreneurs who "wheel and deal" for themselves to a greater extent than their counterparts in Britain (Ludmerer 1986: 203–6). This has come about, in part, because there have been many more research centers in the United States, the system of funding scientific research has been much more pluralistic and decentralized, and research centers have been relatively decentralized. The heads of U.S. departments have been more like administrators than distinguished scientists who direct research. In Britain, however, university departments and research units have been much more hierarchical in nature, often under the leadership of a distinguished scientist, on whom the individual researcher has been much more dependent for research direction and funding. In the decentralized U.S. structure, however, each researcher has had to be a bit of an entrepreneur, always seeking funds for research projects.

The difference in the structure of research in the two countries has led to some differences in research styles. Because research units have been much more hierarchical in Britain, biomedical researchers have been less inclined and have had fewer opportunities to do interdisciplinary work or to move into another discipline. Where there are many sources of funding, it is somewhat easier to obtain funding in order to change research areas or even disciplines. As a result, it has been much more difficult in Britain than in the United States for scientists to cross the boundaries separating the clinical and basic medical sciences.

The segmented nature of the London special hospitals and their affiliated institutes has also had a constraining effect on interdisciplinary research. Historically, the development of specialized hospitals helped to advance medical knowledge. By 1938, the staffs of the London special hospitals were "the quintessence of their specialty." Each offered the medical world high distinction in the accumulation of knowledge, experience, and skill involving a select group of diseases. Proximity and specialized knowledge meant that a researcher could easily visit the laboratory of a colleague or walk a short distance and consult the literature in a specialized library.

In the period since World War II, however, a sizable portion of the discoveries in medical knowledge have come from the basic sciences. As a result, many advances in the medical specialties did not come from the special hospitals and their institutes, partly because they have been too cut off from basic science. By the early 1960s, most of the London special hospitals were deficient in laboratory staff and equipment; were relatively isolated from the research of the basic sciences; had too little contact with general medicine and surgery; had inadequate funding for expensive and elaborate equipment (e.g., electron microscopes, high-speed centrifuges); and had limited library facilities in the preclinical sciences. Significantly, it was the Royal Marsden Hospital and its associated Institute for Cancer Research that suffered least among the specialized centers, for the research on the treatment of cancer cut across so many disciplines that this particular center was relatively well integrated into the research that was taking place in other medical sciences. The other special hospitals and institutes were so isolated from the currents in the basic sciences that the quality of research was seriously hampered (Great Britain, MOH 1962).

Throughout the twentieth century, there has been much more basic science research in U.S. medical schools than in those of England. In England, the tradition that basic science would occur in other parts of the university is still very strong. Before the NHS, the basic sciences were relatively weak in the English medical schools, and thus clinicians tended to set the intellectual tone and standards within the schools. Since the NHS came into existence, the importance of the basic sciences in the medical schools has increased, but because many of them have been geographically distant from the universities, clinical research and the clinicians have still tended to set the intellectual standards more than is the case in the United States. In contrast, basic scientists have done much to establish standards of excellence in U.S. medical schools since the 1920s. Some of the best basic science conducted in these schools would have occurred outside the medical school in England, in other parts of the university. Numerically, the basic scientists have been in the minority in U.S. medical schools, but they have set high standards of research that have influenced clinicians and students and caused the entire medical school environment to be more research oriented than the English medical school.

THE UNITED STATES

After the Flexner Report, the scientifically oriented medical education establishment and the private practice–oriented leaders of the AMA diverged in their emphases. It was the AMA and the private practitioners who dominated the basic organizational structure of the U.S. health delivery system in 1910. After 1920, it was advances in medical education and medical science, funded first by private foundations and later by the federal government, that were the driving force behind the technological changes. Had the model of scientific medicine not been so actively pursued in the United States, it is doubtful that specialization and specialty training would have accelerated so rapidly. And even if the private foundations, the federal government, and medical schools have not directly dominated the organizational structure of American medicine, they have indirectly changed it by the heavy emphasis on specialized medical research. Medical research has led to technological change, and change in technology has been the key to organizational change. As Kenneth Ludmerer has argued, the emphasis on research has dominated the course and direction of American medical schools for many years (1986: 218).

Unlike the situation in Britain, most U.S. medical research funds before World War II came from the private sector: from foundations, industry, and endowments (Coggeshall 1965: 10; Stevens 1971: 358; Berliner and Kennedy 1970: 666). By 1930, the faculty of the best medical schools were engaged in research as well as teaching. The best schools received a few large foundation grants for special research, but most medical school departments prior to World War II were small and made no basic distinction between teaching and research functions. At that time, the research budgets of most medical schools were very modest. Total expenditures for medical research in the United States were only $45 million in 1940, with only $3 million coming from the federal government.

Since World War II, however, there has been a fundamental change in the source of funding for medical research and in the relative importance of research in the medical schools. Federal legislation in 1930 had changed the name of the National Hygienic Laboratory to the National Institute of Health, but in 1931 Congress had appropriated only $43,000 for its support. During the depression, however, the federal government began to be much more concerned with the welfare of the American people. As a result, Congress passed in 1937 the National Cancer Act. This created the National Cancer Institute, which provided federal funds for medical research and for the advanced training of medical scientists. This legislation established various precedents for future activities of the federal government. It singled out a major disease area for concerted action; authorized federal support of project grants in nonfederal institutions; established federally funded fellowships for training; and provided for nonfederal researchers to dispense research funds. All of these ideas were later implemented in the National Institutes of Health (NIH) (Murtaugh 1973: 161).

But it was not until World War II that the federal government became heavily involved in medical research, when it began to be very much impressed with medical research that related to military problems. For this reason, it began to finance a great deal of research that was conducted in medical schools throughout the country. At the end of the war, wartime medical research contracts from the Office of Scientific Research and Development were transferred to the NIH and the Office of Naval Research. And when Congress in 1950 created the National Science Foundation, the decision was made to assign major responsibility for research in the physical and social sciences to that agency, while major responsibility for the biological sciences was to be with the NIH. In the same year, the Public

Health Service Omnibus Act granted the surgeon general authority to establish separate institutes of health to deal with major diseases. From these rather modest beginnings, the NIH eventually grew into fourteen major research institutes and major research divisions (Shannon 1967: 97–108; Lippard 1974: 74; Stevens 1971: 358). In addition to supporting the NIH, Congress provided funds to the Atomic Energy Commission for research on cancer, and the Veterans Administration also became very much involved in supporting clinical research (Bordley and Harvey 1976: 419). As much of the federal research money flowed to universities, this was a reversal of congressional policy of the prewar period, when the federal government had viewed it as improper—if not unconstitutional—to make federal research grants to private universities. Even the National Academy of Sciences in the 1930s had objected to permitting private universities to accept government research funds, for it had been part of the American belief system that such an arrangement would lead to government control of universities (Price 1978: 76).

It was the wartime experience of the United States that persuaded Congress and American society that basic research, generously funded, was necessary for technological progress. The wartime payoff from the physical sciences—particularly in regard to the development of radar and the atomic bomb—had given basic scientific research respectability throughout American society (Drew 1967: 75). For all practical purposes, the federal government nationalized medical research in the country by subsidizing medical school research with grants from the NIH. While the National Institutes of Health employed several thousand researchers, the U.S. model was essentially to grant money to individual scientists to conduct their own work within universities. This model had been established earlier in the century by the Rockefeller and Carnegie foundations, which made project grants to individual researchers. The purpose of the project grant was to assure that funds were used by specific researchers for particular research projects and not by university administrations for general purposes. To the scientific community, the project grant was appealing, for it provided scientists with independence not only from their own university administration but also from the bureaucrats in granting agencies.

But one of the most distinctive features of the structure of scientific research in the postwar United States resulted from the fact that senior scientists in the scientific community were given the authority to dispense federal funds. For example, a great deal of authority was vested by law in the advisory councils of the NIH. Within the NIH, grant proposals were reviewed by professional peers of grant applicants in order to determine their scientific merit and technical feasibility. Recommendations were then made to the advisory councils of each institute for final review, and it was

this type of process that tended to keep political considerations from influencing grant decisions.

Meantime, American scientists, like their counterparts in Britain, have
vigorously resisted efforts on the part of government administration to
make judgments concerning the disbursement of the nation's funds for research (Brooks 1973: 122–23). In Britain, the UGC has provided block
grants to universities, thus giving university administrators somewhat
greater influence over the use of research funds within the university. Because block grants from the federal government have been much less common in the United States, university administrators there have exercised
less control over the research process.

For the scientific community in the United States, the arrangement with
the NIH was ideal, for scientists wanted the society to support its work but
not to govern it. Moreover, the scientific community wished to exist as a
loosely organized entity, to have much more meritocratic anarchy than the
bureaucratic university structures were likely to permit. By permitting individual scientists to receive individual research grants from the NIH, the
federal government made it possible for them to develop their own research
projects without operating through their university's organizational chain
of command. To a greater extent than in any other highly industrial society, American scientists were free to decide what they wished to investigate, and, once the merit of their subject and their qualifications had been
certified by their peers, they were at liberty to pursue their work. In this
respect, U.S. postwar medical science was relatively free from any type
of authoritarian superstructure. And for most of the years following
World War II, it was very affluent, highly productive, and relatively sover-
eign over its own affairs. Of course, all highly industrial countries increased
their support of medical research in the postwar period, but in no other
country did individual researchers receive such a large share of the central
government's total research budget as did American scientists (Price 1978:
77–78; Greenberg 1967: 5, 161, 268).

To understand the rapid increase in federal support for scientific medicine, one must keep in mind that, during the post–World War II period, the
American people were extremely optimistic about the potential for scientific and technological progress (see table 21). There was a widespread belief that science and technology could solve almost any problem. And as
Americans focused on polio, cancer, cardiovascular disease, mental illness,
and other diseases, it seemed consistent with the American belief system
that more money would accelerate the discovery of cures for these and
other diseases. Of course, there was an effective medical lobby, often centering on Mrs. Mary Lasker, a wealthy public-spirited woman from New
York who was on first-name terms with well over half of the members of the

U.S. Senate, as well as some of the better-known physicians from the nation's great medical centers. Partly as a result, the NIH budget increased from $2.5 million in 1945 to well over $1.7 billion by 1974, while the federal government provided $2.7 billion for all biomedical research, or approximately 60 percent of all of the nation's biomedical research. Because much of the NIH budget flowed to medical schools, most members of Congress were anxious that those in their constituency share in the bonanza. As a result, Congress for a number of years allocated more research money for the NIH than the president requested. For example, when President Eisenhower requested $126 million for the NIH in 1957, Congress provided $183 million. And when he requested $190 million in the following year, Congress responded by appropriating $211 million. This tendency continued through both the Kennedy and Johnson administrations. As a result, total support for biomedical research increased almost 25 percent annually between 1955 and 1965. The type of research activity that had once been unique to the Rockefeller Institute for Medical Research had become common in most of the nation's major medical centers (Rogers and Blendon 1978).

By 1960, the NIH were supporting more than 10,000 different medical research projects in hundreds of universities and medical schools. And by 1970, the number had increased dramatically. The NIH were then supporting more than 67,000 senior research investigators and in addition was providing funding for the training in the basic sciences and various clinical specialties for more than 35,000 individuals (Bordley and Harvey 1976: 426, 429).

As a result of its approach to scientific research, the United States, by the 1960s, had clearly become the world's leading research country in the biomedical sciences. This occurred because of the massive scale with which the research was supported by the federal government, the large number of researchers, and the decentralized and very competitive structure of scientific research (Ben-David 1971). And the role of the NIH had been critical in bringing about U.S. preeminence in the biomedical science. They had provided substantial support for forty-one Americans who won Nobel prizes between 1945 and 1975. And several Nobel Prize winners did their major research at its research center in Bethesda, Maryland. Indeed, by 1970, the NIH had the world's largest and most diversified concentration of biomedical investigators, employing more than 13,000 full-time people (Bordley and Harvey 1976: 429; Strickland 1972: 236).

As long as there was an abundance of funding for biomedical research, the scientific community gave little attention to priorities. To have raised questions about priorities would have required scientists to apply criteria external to scientific logic. Of course, some of the lobbyists on behalf of scientific medicine pressured NIH to support work in specific diseases

Table 21 Central Government Support for Medical Research

United States, 1940–1974 (in Millions of Dollars)

Fiscal Year	Total Expenditures	Nonfederal Support	Federal Support	Percentage from Federal Government	Appropriations for NIH
1940	45	42	3	6.6	N.A.
1950	161	88	73	45.3	25.0
1955	261	122	139	53.3	60.8
1960	845	397	448	53.0	343.4
1965	1,837	663	1,174	63.9	831.1
1970	2,660	1,008	1,652	62.1	1,143.4
1974	4,452	1,698	2,754	61.8	1,790.4

Great Britain, 1960–1973 (in Millions of Pounds Sterling)

Fiscal Year	Total Expenditures	Nongovernment Support	Central Government Support	Percentage from Central Government
1960	26	11	15	58
1965	43	16	27	63
1970	80	30	50	63
1973	108	42	66	61

Sources: Office of Health Economics 1974; Berliner and Kennedy 1970; U.S., Comm., Census 1979a.

rather than basic research. But as long as there was a surplus of funding relative to the demand, priorities were not necessary, and the NIH funded applied and basic research. But ultimately, there was a limit to the continued increase in the NIH budgets. Eventually, politicians insisted that priorities be set within the scientific community that were consistent with principles of democratic accountability and larger American concerns. Congress by 1970 was beginning to ask for evaluations of the progress that its massive funding had made possible. And throughout the 1970s it began to cut back on some of its biomedical research support and insist that the scientific community engage in more self-governance and internal agenda setting. In turn, the scientific community began to recognize that political and public input were inevitable in the establishment of the general directions and goals of scientific research (Brooks 1978: 172–78).

The Effect on Medical Schools

As a result of the massive infusion of federal money for medical research, the basic structure of medical education in the United States was transformed after 1945. Between the two world wars, there was relative stability within medical schools of Britain and the United States, with departmental chairmen wielding considerable influence. In many respects, this tradition has continued in Britain. In contrast, almost no one was in control of the major U.S. medical schools during the period between 1950 and 1970, as university medical centers expanded and medicine became fragmented into many different disciplines. During this period, at least 50 percent, and in some schools as much as 75 percent of medical school expenditures were derived from the federal government. Whereas the mission of the medical schools in both countries early in the century had been primarily to train undergraduate medical students, the goals of U.S. medical schools in the postwar period became much more diverse and confused than in Britain. British and U.S. schools became complex scientific and research organizations, but because of the vast infusion of federal funds for individual researchers, the hierarchical structure of the U.S. schools became increasingly decentralized and pluralistic, more and more independent of the universities of which they were a part (L. Thomas 1983).

In Britain, the central government after 1948 was explicitly involved in funding medical school instruction. In contrast, the AMA, favoring specialized knowledge and scientific innovations, had supported federal aid for research purposes but had vigorously opposed it for teaching purposes. The AMA was fearful that if the federal government became involved in the funding of medical education, it would attempt to regulate the educational process. Whereas in British medical schools, research and education were viewed as highly integrated functions, the AMA, the medical schools, and the federal government made a sharp distinction between teaching and research. Teaching was considered a local and institutional concern, while research and research training were federal concerns, related to national needs and goals. Nevertheless, as research budgets rapidly expanded, most U.S. medical schools began to hide the financing of their expanding teaching faculty in research budgets. During the 1950s and 1960s, many medical schools paid their faculty from research and training grants, a fact that caused Robert H. Ebert, professor of medicine at Harvard, to state in 1973 that "bootlegging the support of education from research dollars has been one of the most destructive by-products of N.I.H. policy" (Bordley and Harvey 1976: 431). Increasingly, a high percentage of faculty were not involved in teaching medical students but were engaged in research. By 1970, approximately one-half of all medical school salaries were derived from federal research grants. As medical teachers were encouraged to seek out research funds, research slowly gained far more prominence than teaching in the schools' priorities (Stevens 1971: 359).

For some years, everyone seemed pleased by this arrangement, for the more research that was conducted, the more knowledge was advanced and, presumably, the greater the enhancement of medical excellence. But in the process, the entire mission of many of the nation's better medical schools was rapidly being transformed. Whereas British medical schools were primarily engaged in providing general undergraduate medical education, those in the United States began to emphasize the production of physicians who would become high-powered scientific specialists or research scientists.

By 1970, U.S. medical schools were turning out large numbers of research scientists, graduate physicians, and many others. Almost one-third of the Ph.D. degrees awarded in the biological sciences were received by scientists whose training was in a medical school graduate program. And across the country, there were a number of students who were simultaneously pursuing an M.D. and a Ph.D. degree, as a result of NIH funding. At the Yale Medical School in the 1970s, almost one-third of the entering class of first-year medical students had already received a Ph.D. degree (Anlyan 1973: 97–99).

Meantime, the change in the makeup of U.S. medical faculties was almost as dramatic. The most significant change was that the number of salaried medical teachers increased far out of proportion to the numbers of students, medical schools, or faculty in other parts of higher education. As each faculty member became successful in obtaining research grants, someone else had to be hired to fulfill the researcher's other obligations. By 1974, there were 2.9 salaried faculty members for every medical school graduate. Approximately 9 percent of all the nation's doctors were salaried members of a medical school faculty—many times that in British hospitals. Between 1962 and 1976, the number of full-time medical school faculty increased by more than 300 percent, from 13,681 to 39,300 (Rogers and Blendon 1978). While it is somewhat difficult to compare the size of medical school faculties in different countries because their functions are not entirely the same, a comparison of the size of several U.S. medical schools with that at Oxford University demonstrates substantial differences in the two systems. While the scale of research is much larger in the U.S. medical school, Paul Beeson, who had been a senior professor of medicine at Yale, several other distinguished U.S. medical schools, and Oxford, believed that the teaching at Oxford was equal to that in the best U.S. medical school and that patient care was superior at Oxford. Because of the intense specialization in U.S. medical centers, there was poor communication among specialists, which Beeson and others believed to be detrimental to good patient care and teaching (Beeson 1974; 1975).

The size of the British medical school faculty was somewhat arbitrarily constrained by government policy, while the size of the U.S. medical school was shaped more by the existing state of knowledge and the availability of money. Many medical schools in the United States attempted to have a professor who was an authority in every area of knowledge, though with the continued knowledge explosion, this approach to a determination of faculty size led to a rapid expansion of faculty (L. Thomas 1983).

As faculty members successfully acquired research grants that flowed to them as individual researchers, the structure of the U.S. medical school became increasingly large, decentralized, and complex (see table 22). Instead of the more centralized structures that powerful deans had controlled between the wars, schools after 1945 were structured around powerful "barons" who were able to control specific research projects. Departmental interests became defined less and less by the needs of undergraduate medical instruction and patient care in university hospitals and more in terms of well-supported research programs. Medical school administrators, in order to enhance the prestige of their schools, bestowed their blessing on those departments that were successful in obtaining large research grants.

Well-supported research programs led to larger faculties, with substantial research funds, that were producing a knowledge explosion. As more specialized discoveries were made, pressures mounted for medical schools to appoint more specialized researchers and practitioners, pressures that led to a restructuring of clinical departments not only in medical schools but in large general hospitals throughout the country.

In the period since 1950, the explosion in knowledge, combined with the abundance of money, brought about a proliferation of departments in U.S. medical schools. British schools, which were much smaller, were also less fragmented—despite the knowledge explosion (see table 23). In U.S. schools, however, surgery was subdivided into departments of urology, ophthalmology, orthopedics, and so on. Similarly, medicine was subdivided into departments of cardiology, allergy, rheumatology, gastroenterology, and the like. The splitting of departments into divisions had numerous advantages. It helped to generate more specialized knowledge and facilitated the training of advanced residents and fellows. In other words, the high level of funding of medical education and research led to greater differentiation in academic disciplines and more specialization in knowledge. On the other hand, the increasing fragmentation of knowledge and academic disciplines interfered with communication across specialities and often made the training of undergraduate medical students more difficult. As the level of specialization became more intense in the United States than in Britain, the problems of communication among medical specialists became especially severe among Americans.

In each of the subspecialties, the problems and techniques of research, diagnosis, and therapy often became so complicated and specialized that people in the same department seldom understood what their colleagues were doing. In both countries, departmental chairmen no longer had the opportunity to make long-term plans for their departments, for knowledge was expanding too rapidly—but the problem was more serious in the

Table 22   Medical Education, the United States, 1949–1974

	Medical Schools	Medical School Graduates	Teachers in Basic Sciences	Teachers on the Clinical Faculty
1949	78	6,000	2,400	2,200
1974	112	11,500	9,500	24,500

Source: Beeson 1975: 69.

Table 23   Medical School Faculties, Great Britain and the United States, 1974

	Full-time	Part-time
Oxford	69	114
Harvard	840	1,129
Ohio State	400	1,006
University of Washington	520	1,000

Source: Beeson 1974: 46.

United States. Nor were the present-day departmental heads in large medical schools able to keep abreast of teaching, research, and patient care, for most of their time was taken up with appointing new faculty and obtaining research funds for their staff and for the building of laboratories. As one can assume responsibility for such diverse tasks only for a relatively short period of time, the tenure of departmental chairmen became considerably shortened (Beeson 1975; Petersdorf 1980; L. Thomas 1983).

As the staffs of new departments grew and research and office space expanded in U.S. medical schools, heads of departments and other senior faculty began to spend much more time with research fellows and postgraduate trainees than with undergraduate students or with residents, whose work they were in theory supposed to be supervising. As a result, the resident in the prestigious teaching hospital probably had more autonomy over patient care than was the case thirty years earlier. One distinguished clinician expressed his concern in the following terms:

> This can lead to a system in which patients are at risk of what may be termed diagnostic overkill. The resident in charge of a ward may begin to play upon the resources of a large hospital as if he were at the console of a pipe-organ, inasmuch as he has only to touch a certain key to set in motion a series of events that culminates in a large effect—say a kidney biopsy or an aortic angiogram. When we add to that the effect of potent drugs now in use, we must admit that the hazards of hospitalization are real . . . the rapid progress made in the last 30 years has brought its own kind of medical pollution. (Quoted in Beeson, 1975: 74)

In a British teaching hospital, the junior staff (i.e., interns and residents) tended to clear all important decisions with the consultant in charge of the patient, but the American house officer had much more autonomy. As a shocked British physician observed about one of the best medical centers in the United States, "the house staff take the attitude that every conceivable differential diagnosis has to be excluded, including all possible tests, before a diagnosis can be reached. The patients . . . are subjected to many unnecessary tests. It is not hard to see why medical costs are accelerating so much" (quoted in Beeson 1974: 46).

American undergraduate medical students had access to more teachers in a medical school complex with specialized knowledge than had ever been the case. With knowledge so fragmented and with the medical school structure so differentiated into large numbers of departments, however, most American medical students during the 1960s, in contrast to their British counterparts, had little opportunity for prolonged interaction with their teachers. Some experienced clinicians argued that the changed structure of medical education had produced by 1970 a medical training that was inferior to that which existed twenty-five years earlier or to that which existed in Great Britain (Beeson 1975: 77).

CONCLUDING OBSERVATIONS

When one compares research in Britain and the United States, several distinct differences emerge. First, the latter has invested a much higher percentage of its GNP in biomedical research than has the former. For example, between 1961 and 1974, the United States spent between 1.7 and 1.9 times more of its GNP on medical research than did Britain (see table 24). And as a percentage of the labor force, the United States during the same period had twice as many scientists and engineers engaged in research and development in all fields as did Britain (*Science Indicators*, 1978: 8).

The Americans were more generous—if not wasteful—with research money. The NIH often funded numerous laboratories to conduct the same research, whereas in Britain the tendency was to have fewer research centers competing with one another. Because of the size of the American system, research funds were dispersed among more institutions in the United States than in any other country. Moreover, American medical researchers were able to seek funding from many more sources than is the case in any other country: from hundreds of private foundations, the NIH, the Department of Defense, the Department of Agriculture, the Atomic Energy Commission, the National Academy of Sciences, and many other government agencies. In Britain, however, research funding was much more centralized. Whereas in the United States there were numerous private univer-

Table 24   Spending on Medical Research as a Percentage of GNP,
the United States and Great Britain, 1961–1974

	Ratio of U.S. to British
1961	1.8
1965	2.4
1970	1.9
1974	1.9

Sources: Berliner and Kennedy 1970; *Health Care Financing Review* (Summer 1979); U.S.,
Comm., Census 1979a; Office of Health Economics 1978.
Note: The British base is 1.0.

sities and 50 state systems of universities, Britain had only one national
system. Nor did it have private universities equivalent to Harvard, Yale,
Chicago, the Massachusetts Institute of Technology, Stanford, and California Institute of Technology. And most of the British government funding for medical research was centralized through the UGC and the MRC.
As most research funds originated from the Department of Education and
Science, there was a tight network among members of that department, the
UGC, and the MRC. Because representatives from the various organizations sat on one another's committees, multiple sources of funding were
much less common than in the United States. In short, the British were
more successful in coordinating the distribution of research money (Gaston 1978: 36–54; Symposium on Medical Research Systems in Europe,
1973: 27–39; OECD 1967; Mulkay 1977: 224–55).

Second, the United States since World War II has produced more of the
world's literature in the areas of clinical medicine and biomedicine than any
other country. For example, in 1973, 39 percent of all clinical medicine
articles and 43 percent of all biomedicine articles were written by American
authors (*Science Indicators,* 1978: 15).

Because American and British researchers were responsible for a high
proportion of the world's biomedical literature, it is to be expected that the
literature from the two countries would be widely cited, and that was indeed the case. But the U.S. literature was cited more frequently than the
British, even when one controls for the number of articles by country of
origin. On a worldwide scale, U.S. and British literature were cited more
frequently than their numbers warranted, though the former—especially in
medical journals—was cited much more frequently than the latter. On the
other hand, British authors cited British authors a bit more frequently than
American authors cited American authors once one controls for the
number of publications by country of origin. But as table 25 indicates,
non-British authors cited the British medical authors less frequently than
the number of British articles would warrant.

Table 25 Citation of Biomedical and Medical Articles, 1975

	World Articles Citing U.S. Authors	World Articles Citing British Authors	U.S. Articles Citing U.S. Authors	British Articles Citing British Authors	Non-U.S. Articles Citing U.S. Authors	Non-British Articles Citing British Authors
Biomedical	1.53	1.31	1.53	1.67	1.30	1.16
Clinical medicine	1.61	1.03	1.61	2.08	1.13	.93

Source: Narain 1976: 35–38.

Note: A citation ratio of 1.00 reflects no over- or underciting of the scientific literature of a particular country, whereas a higher ratio indicates a greater citation frequency than would have been the case from the number of publications from that particular country in a specific scientific field.

Third, the style of funding research has varied somewhat between the two countries. For example, the MRC tended to provide more research funds to particular research laboratories for specific types of research, whereas the NIH tended to support project grants to individual researchers throughout the United States. As a result, American scientists have been able to work somewhat autonomously, while the institutional nature of much of British research funds has meant that a large portion of British scientists have been much more dependent on the support of an institute director.

Fourth, the British system of medical research has been more elitist than the U.S. one. In Britain, it has been very difficult to gain access to the system, for it has been extremely competitive, especially early in one's career. But once having attained a prominent position, one enjoyed considerable influence for the rest of one's career. In the United States, access to a scientific career has been much more open, but forced exit has tended to occur with greater frequency than in Britain. Even so, throughout the American's career, there has tended to be much greater mobility and career change than in the career of the British scientist.

And fifth, the overall quality of scientific medical work has been somewhat higher in Britain, primarily because fewer people with marginal ability have been able to engage in medical research (Brooks 1978). While the United States received more Nobel and other international awards in the biomedical sciences during the period since 1945, the British actually received more awards per 1,000 scientific researchers (Ben-David 1971: 186–99; Moulin 1955: 246–63). Moreover, British scientists have generally been more productive than American scientists. In both countries, there has been a continuous grading off of talent. As more money has been invested in research, the talent that has been tapped has been increasingly marginal. In both countries, research productivity has been highly skewed, with the most significant research being done by a small minority of scientists. But in the United States, there has probably been a higher portion of research that was marginal in quality, simply because there has been a larger portion of the entire medical community engaged in scientific research (Gaston 1978: 75–78; Brooks 1978: 175).

Even though there appear to be different styles of funding research in the two countries, there is variation within the United States. The Rockefeller Foundation, for example, has long been somewhat more flexible, informal, elitist, and international in its funding of medical programs than have most other large U.S. funding agencies, and its record was indeed impressive. For example, of sixty-seven Nobel prize winners in medicine and physiology between 1914 and 1962, 46 percent of them had already received research support from the Rockefeller Foundation—in some cases thirty years in advance of the award. And while scientists get financial aid from multiple sources, the record of the Rockefeller Foundation in supporting outstanding medical research is without parallel with any other private organization. In six years (1945, 1946, 1951, 1954, 1959, and 1962), the foundation had "grand slams" when the winners in medicine and physiology, physics, and chemistry were scientists who had previously received Rockefeller support (Rockefeller Foundation Archives).

In general, however, U.S. funding in the medical sciences in the postwar period has been influenced by the style of crash programs to develop the atomic bomb and to send humans to the moon. In contrast to the British, Americans have tended to take the view that it was desirable that there be a critical mass of people working on a problem and that, with many leads being explored simultaneously, a quick solution to problems was more likely. The British attitude—perhaps shaped by their long tradition in scientific endeavors—has been that most creative work in science is best performed by solo operators who have the time to think and reflect on the significance of scientific findings. For the British, not only is a critical mass of people a wasteful use of manpower but also, the resulting vast accumulation of publication introduces a great deal of confusion into the scientific community (Beeson 1975: 78; Mellanby 1974: 67).

The Americans have also tended to subscribe to the view that most scientists, even though they work on minor and relatively unimportant problems, make minor contributions, without which the breakthroughs of the truly creative and inspired scientists are not possible. In contrast, the British are less willing to acknowledge that the mass of the work is helpful for scientific progress (Cole and Cole 1972: 368–87). In contrasting the two communities, however, it is important to observe that each is part of a larger world system of science and that the British have benefited enormously by much of the less important and duplicative work that occurs in the United States. Moreover, one should be cautious about concluding that a substantial amount of the work in the U.S. scientific community is of a trivial nature. Retrospective evaluation of grants supported by the NIH in the mid 1960s concluded that not more than 5 percent of a sample of grants were judged unworthy of support, a very small percentage indeed in fields in which there are multiple paradigms (Brooks 1973: 125).

By 1980, the accomplishments of biomedical research in both countries were impressive. Medical science had made considerable progress in the management of many chronic diseases and had developed a number of vaccines for the prevention of a number of others. However, more money had been invested in cancer research and treatment than any other single disease, but the survival rates for most common types of cancer were relatively unchanged from those of twenty-five years earlier—though for the types comprising the remaining 20 percent of all cancers, some improvement had occurred. On the other hand, a number of medical scientists were somewhat optimistic that the world scientific community was on the verge of a breakthrough about how the disease develops—though most were quick to point out that such a breakthrough would not necessarily lead immediately to new breakthroughs in treatment (L. Thomas 1983: 195–207; *Science and Government Report*, Dec. 1, 1974; *New York Times*, Feb. 20, 1983).

Unfortunately, the decision to invest vast resources in cancer research is often poorly understood in its larger context. What would be the impact of a cure for cancer on the British and U.S. survival rates? One of the world's leading demographers, Nathan Keyfitz, has made what should be an obvious observation: that if all cancers were eliminated, populations would die from other causes. Using mortality rates of U.S. males in 1964 he estimated that the elimination of cancer would at best add approximately two years to male life expectancy (1977).

Then why have the British and Americans invested so much money in an effort to eliminate cancer? Obviously, the vested interests of medical researchers do much to explain this. But Nobel laureate Professor Baruch S. Blumberg has a more perceptive and charitable interpretation. He points out that, from a public point of view, our two societies are committed to making it possible for our populations to die in dignity, and that cancer is generally a most unfortunate way to die. And by investing vast resources to eliminate it, the two societies are committed to permitting their populations to have more preferred causes of death (personal conversation with Professor Blumberg, May 1982).

Despite the impressive progress of biomedical research, the medical research policies in both countries prior to 1970 were somewhat distorted. They represented a continuation of the emphasis on the curative model that John D. Rockefeller and Frederick T. Gates had done so much to develop early in the century. And while that model contributed substantially to providing insights into underlying processes of certain diseases, the level of funding and the contributions of research to environmental and social medicine as well as to epidemiology have been relatively unimpressive. For example, the link between unemployment and ill-health and early mortality has been poorly investigated. Moreover, there has been poor investment in the study of the relationship between dietary habits and disease patterns.

In sum, the biomedical research agenda of the two national governments and private foundations have had a relatively narrow focus. The agenda has been consistent with the powerful corporate financial interests in the two countries, many of which have long been anxious to improve their nation's health through investments in curative medicine. This limited perspective on medical research has been dominant in British and U.S. medicine since the turn of the century. It is this perspective that has provided funds to support medical schools, with their caring and curative-oriented curriculum and research, which in turn have produced several generations of highly proficient but narrowly trained American and British physicians. And because of the high priority given to a curative approach, health education for the entire society remains poorly developed in both countries.

In both countries, biomedical research has tended to take a microcausal approach to disease rather than a macrocausal one. The microcausal approach assumes that disease results from microorganisms (e.g., bacteria, viruses, and parasites), while a macrocausal one assumes that the way in which power is distributed in society helps to determine the nature and definition of disease and influence which groups tend to be afflicted with it. In other words, a macrocausal approach to disease focuses on how the social and economic environment gives rise to specific diseases and shapes the distribution of many diseases across social classes and income groups. Of course, this type of approach is not appropriate for understanding and eradicating all diseases. But the distribution of many diseases across social classes and income groups is clearly determined by the way in which the social and economic environment is structured, and one way to alter the frequency and distribution of these diseases is to modify the society's basic economic and social structure.

There is a tendency in both Britain and the United States to assume that a microcausal research strategy for eradicating disease is scientific and apolitical whereas a macrocausal one is unscientific and political. In fact, the research institutions and research strategies of a society very much reflect its class structure. Moreover, the dominant ideology of a society reproduces itself in the way in which scientists will deny that their work is value loaded and will argue that science is the epitome of objectivity. This is simply not the case. In almost every society, the scientific knowledge that emerges tends to be produced by scientists who are subjected to the society's class hegemony and share most of the assumptions of the dominant class. Of course, science is somewhat independent of a society's dominant ideology in that it has an internal logic of its own. On the other hand, every branch of science operates under the dominance of class ideology (Navarro 1976a; 1980).

Curative medicine, with its microcausal approach to disease, does not challenge the underlying social structure. As the British and Americans are both committed to this type of approach to medicine, their scientific establishments share common assumptions. Their basic differences are in style of research.

Part Three
The Relationship between Structure and Performance

7
Theoretical Perspective

This study has been a sociological history of the medical delivery systems of Great Britain and of the United States. Like most histories, it has touched on a variety of topics, though the central concern has been to advance our understanding of why there has been variation in the evolution of the structure between the two systems and to shed light on the kinds of performance that have followed from their different structures.

The bulk of the study has been concerned with how the two medical systems have evolved during almost a century. In 1890, the beginning date for this study, hospitals were shunned by those who could afford home care. Medical technology was not very complex, and most of the tools for medical care were portable. The training of doctors was not very complex, and professional associations were not very active. By 1970, the delivery of medical services had changed markedly in both countries. The British had institutionalized a national health delivery system, with visits to doctors and hospitals "free" to all and with state coordination important in the development and utilization of research and hospital systems. In contrast, the United States had a medical delivery system with much less state coordination. Rather, it was a system that was much more market oriented than that in Britain. Why the two countries have diverged so much since 1890 in the organization and performance of medical services has been the principal concern of the study.

A secondary concern is to develop a theoretical perspective for understanding the relationship between the structure and performance of a medical delivery system. This perspective is developed in this chapter. It is based on materials presented in the previous chapters and on existing historical literature.

The hope is that the theoretical framework has some potential for advancing understanding of the relationship between the structure and performance of other human service delivery systems (e.g., education and housing). Unfortunately, researchers in health policy rarely communicate with those who work in other policy areas, primarily because there is no common theoretical framework that extends across different policy sectors. And even within broad policy areas, research is so highly specialized that there is very little systematic building of general knowledge. However, the purpose of this chapter is not to dwell on this lament, about which most of us can agree. Rather, one purpose is to provide a theoretical framework for analyzing social policy. And while the framework is not a theory, it does develop a number of generalizations so that the potential for theory construction is enhanced.

In an effort to analyze the differences in organizational structure, social processes, and performance between the two medical delivery systems, the study has relied on two basic theoretical paradigms: (1) an interest group or group conflict paradigm,* and (2) a social structural paradigm. Interest group scholarship has long suffered from a dearth of generalizations concerning the values that are likely to be pursued by various social or political groups. This chapter speaks to this problem in order to move the study of interest groups to a more theoretical level of analysis. In doing so, it demonstrates how the power of interest groups influences the performance of a delivery system. It develops the argument that particular groups, both over time and across countries, have specific preferences for particular types of system performance and that the type of performance that gets maximized depends on the relative power of specific groups. In addition, the chapter attempts to specify the way in which the structure of a delivery system influences its performance. It is concerned with the following types of system performance: quality and costs of services, level of innovativeness, equality of access, and standardization across space.†

GROUP CONFLICT

The materials presented in the previous chapters suggest that, over time and across societies, groups differ in their policy preferences as to the types of performance desired from various delivery systems. Previously, most research on interest groups has been somewhat idiosyncratic, focusing on specific issues within a single country rather than looking for common themes across time within and across countries. To overcome this perspective, this chapter, drawing on materials presented earlier, presents a general scheme of interest groups and policy outcomes that applies to most indus-

---

* Some scholars might pursue an explicitly class analysis in attempting to explain the same differences in the two systems. However, I believe that class analysis is not sufficiently precise to capture the distinctions among professionals, government and party officials, and diverse consumer groups. On the other hand, Ivan Szelenyi, Erik O. Wright, and other colleagues of mine who do class analysis and have read parts or all of this manuscript have had little difficulty in fitting my analysis within their frame of reference. It is my hope that my analysis is sufficiently encompassing to be meaningful to those who are neo-Marxists or neo-Weberians. I have benefited enormously by the scholarship in both the Marxist and Weberian traditions.

† For a fuller elaboration of the theoretical position developed herein, see Hage and Hollingsworth 1977; Hollingsworth et al. 1978; Hollingsworth and Hanneman 1983.

trialized countries in Western Europe and North America. To make the discussion of interst groups more meaningful, most of the focus is on three major ones that are always relevant: consumers, providers (e.g., physicians and hospital administrators), and government officials. Consumers are subdivided into groups, essentially lower-income and upper-income, as their interests are frequently divergent.

Obviously, each of these interest groups is internally heterogeneous. And if one's concern were merely to explain the actions of various individuals and groups with respect to a particular piece of legislation or administrative decision, the lumping together of diverse groups and individuals into a single structural interest group would represent an oversimplification. But for the purposes of explaining investment decisions in medical care, the major decisions concerning access and the allocation and location of resources, and the readiness of systems to adopt various types of change, this strategy does identify the major groups. An analysis of internal group differences is often desirable in order to understand tactical behavior and short-term phenomena, but unless internal group differences are permanent and deep-seated, they are relatively unimportant for explaining variation in systems across societies and across long periods of time (Hage and Hollingsworth 1977; Alford 1975).

Certainly, there are many other groups involved in the delivery of medical care. Nurses and paraprofessionals are two that immediately come to mind. But when one is concerned with decisions about the level and nature of collective investments in medical care, access to it, or the key decisions involving its production (e.g., the location and the number per capita of doctors, clinics, and hospital beds), nurses and paraprofessionals have historically been relatively unimportant.

Some of the major findings of this study are sketched in figure 3, which diagrams the preferences of major interest groups. Lower-income consumers have tended to be interested in equalizing access to care and benefits via public spending and in promoting general services rather than highly specialized ones. Upper-income groups have generated pressures for highly individualized and differentiated services. Thus lower-income consumers have tended to be less concerned with innovations than higher-income consumers, who have been more concerned with promoting medical research and specialized personal services. Upper-income groups have tended to prefer goods provided by private markets, for the marketplace has permitted more prosperous individuals to exert influence over the form, quality, and utilization of consumption goods.

For the purposes of this study, providers influencing system performance are divided into two major types: professional providers (e.g., physicians and hospital administrators) and manufacturers. Professional providers have historically attempted to maximize programmatic and technological innovations, since these have called for more development of their special skills and have tended to enhance their incomes and/or prestige. For the same reason, both types of professional provider have tended to promote the development of specialized services, which in turn have stimulated technical innovations. Because professional providers have tended to prefer the type of organization into which they have been socialized, they have in both countries been much less inclined to be supportive of organizational innovations—even though the technical innovations they supported have often led to new types of organizations. In both countries, manufacturers were not a major actor when the level of technological complexity was relatively low, but over time, as technology has become more complex, they have become more influential in bringing about technological innovations, specialized services, and more spending for medical services, and these changes have in turn led to programmatic changes in medical services and organization. Hence manufacturers since World War II have become key actors in promoting change in the two systems.

Whereas professional providers have often opposed organizational and technological standardization for fear that they would exercise less control over services, government administrators in both countries have tended to favor standardized services as a means of reducing costs and maintaining control over public programs. For the same reasons, they have been less supportive of technical innovations. Of course, government officials have played an important role in legitimating the entire system in both countries, and as part of this effort, they have attempted to coordinate the interests of the other groups. But as the size of the public system has grown, government officials have acquired more autonomy and have had more of an opportunity for their values to shape the system.

Thus there are potentially several natural coalitions here. Lower-income groups and government bureaucrats have had some tendency to prefer the same benefits, whereas providers and higher-income groups have tended to agree on other preferences. Specification of the exact lines of disagreement or coalitions among and between interest groups has varied somewhat from case to case, according to the power of each group at specific times. But the basic distinctions between the two countries have been among lower- and upper-income consumers, providers, and government administrators, and each of the groups has tended to prefer the types of performance described in figure 4.

The power of interest groups to shape decisions about investments in medical care and the process of producing medical services has been considerable, and these decisions in turn have shaped the types of performance that have been maximized in the two systems. The power of groups has not rigidly determined in a mechanistic fashion which performances became

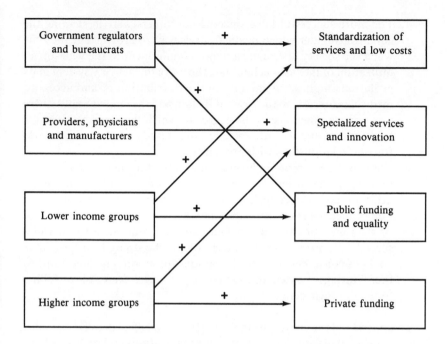

Fig. 4. Preferences of Interest Groups

maximized, but it has established probabilities that certain tendencies would occur.

Historically, the distribution of power among various groups has tended to give rise to a certain set of institutional arrangements that have shaped the performance of delivery systems, and these arrangements have had a tendency to persist for a considerable period. For this reason, it is important to understand the distribution of power among the key groups of actors at the time when the society first made a major commitment to the widespread distribution of medical technology and the development of a medical delivery system. Hence the power of groups is a critical variable for understanding cross-national variation in the structure of medical delivery systems over time. As the previous chapters have suggested, one needs to be very sensitive to the relative distribution of power among groups in the late nineteenth century in order to understand the institutional development of the different medical delivery systems in the two countries.

Historical generalizations relevant to the relationship between group power and the institutionalization of medical delivery systems are as follows:

1. The more successful lower-income consumers were in shaping the conditions under which medical services were provided at the time when the society first made a major commitment to the widespread utilization of medical technology, the more the delivery system in its evolution emphasized equality in the distribution of and access to medical resources. In the cases of Britain and the United States, there was a sharp difference in the degree to which the working class, via trade unions and friendly societies, organized and entered into contractual relationships with providers.

2. Conversely, the more influential and powerful the providers at the time when the society first made a commitment to the widespread utilization of medical technology, the more inequitable the distribution of medical resources subsequently.

3. At the time when the society first made a commitment to the widespread utilization of medical technology, the strengths of providers vis-à-vis consumers shaped the options for modifying later policies, thus limiting the extent to which the two societies were able or willing to modify their delivery systems.

To understand the cross-national variation in medical delivery systems, a historical explanation is necessary, for organizations and practices have tended to persist once they have been institutionalized and attained legitimacy. People have become socialized into different ways of doing things: relationships between clients and providers have become institutionalized, providers have become accustomed to certain forms of payment, and client responses to forms of organization have become routinized. Of course, organizations and practices of financing medical care that subsequently were unresponsive to popular demands and were based on a technology that clearly became obsolete have suffered losses in legitimacy, and when that has occurred, organizations and practices within delivery systems have become substantially modified.

Historically, one of the most important outcomes determined by group power was the way of paying providers, for differences in the method of payment between countries have been a key factor in determining whether the system would eventually become predominantly public or private, whether costs were subject to tight government control, whether it was highly egalitarian with an emphasis on standardized services, whether it was highly innovative, and whether it tended to place high or low emphasis on very specialized services.

By knowing which interest groups had the most power early in a system's history, one can make predictions about which funding outcomes were most likely to evolve in a national medical delivery system. The greater the power of professional providers vis-à-vis consumers, the greater the likelihood that payments would eventually become indirect (government or insurance company paying the consumer, who, in turn, would pay the providers), thus removing the provider from the control of the government or other insurer. The greater the power of the consumer vis-à-vis the professional provider, the greater the likelihood that payments would become direct (government or insurance company paying the provider), thus subjecting the provider to greater controls on the part of the paying authority. And historically, the more control the government or other insurers have exercised over the provider, the less costly and less innovative the system (Abel-Smith 1965; Hogarth 1963).

The method of funding for services has been highly useful for exploring inequality in access to medical resources. For example, the more extensive the public funding, the more equitable the access to delivery systems; conversely, when payments have been privately financed, there has been greater inequality in access to care. With private sector financing, access to services has been increasingly equitable when payments have been made in the following ascending order: (1) the consumer had paid the provider; (2) an insurance company has paid the provider indirectly; (3) the insurance company has paid the provider directly. With public financing there has been (4) even more equality of access to services when governments have paid providers indirectly; and (5) the greatest equality when governments have paid providers directly (Abel-Smith 1965; Hogarth 1963; Glaser 1970).

Thus the group conflict perspective developed in this study has argued that groups systematically have different preferences and that the distribution of power among groups in England and Wales and in the United States during the late nineteenth and early twentieth centuries influenced the medical payment mechanism. And the choices about payment mechanisms carried significant consequences for system performance in such respects as equality of access, costs, innovativeness, and standardization in spatial terms.

THE PROBLEM OF STATE CENTRALIZATION

The power of groups is only one type of variable that has shaped the history and the performance of the two delivery systems. Another key variable has been state centralization. This is an important variable that has too long been ignored in the social science literature, for it has a significant impact on the performance of national delivery systems. Irrespective of which group has dominated the system, the degree of state centralization has placed constraints on system performance. For example, increasing the level of state centralization has led to more public spending and generalized services, greater equality among social classes and groups, and more cost controls and standardization. Decentralization has led to specialized services, diversity of services among different groups, and technical innovations (Hollingsworth and Hanneman 1983; Hage and Hollingsworth 1977).

By centralization is meant the level at which strategic decisions are made about personnel, budgets, programs, and standards. A delivery system in which all of these decisions have been made in the private sector has been more decentralized than one in which the decisions have been made in the public sector. And in the public sector, a delivery system in which all decisions have been made by local authorities has been less centralized than one in which the decisions have been made at the national level. In reality, however, all strategic decisions have rarely been made at one level. In the United States, for example, there has been much private as well as public decision making about medical care at all levels of the society (i.e., local, state, and federal).

Too often, scholars have referred to a society as being highly centralized when in fact within the same society it has been possible for the medical delivery system to be decentralized. Moreover, the level of centralization is constantly changing in all systems, and it is desirable that scholars be mindful of this fact and that they attempt to understand how performance has changed in response to those changes in the level of centralization.

A major finding of this study has been that the organization of a medical delivery system has influenced the policies and aspects of performance that elites have tended to maximize. Much of the persisting concern about the pros and cons of centralization has revolved around greater control versus flexibility. Centralized systems have tended to opt for standardized programs and services for different groups and in different parts of a country, and thus, under certain conditions, centralized systems have had greater potential for cutting costs. Historically, the major advantage of a more centralized system has been that it has allowed for a considerable rationalization of service delivery. It has been able to provide essentially the same service to all and at lower costs. Thus, increases in the level of centralization have tended to bring about more standardization across regions, more effective cost controls, and greater equality of services among social classes and groups. Thus there have been certain trade-offs among the different aspects of performance. Systems that have been very egalitarian have had fewer specialized and individualized services. Those that have engaged in effective cost controls have tended to be somewhat reluctant to adopt costly innovations. (See fig. 5.)

Across countries, centralized systems have been less costly in financial terms, but they have tended to be less innovative, especially technical innovations, which are very costly. There has been much literature that indicates that centralization has stifled the adoption of new ideas and slowed down the process of communication (Hollingsworth et al. 1978a; Ben-

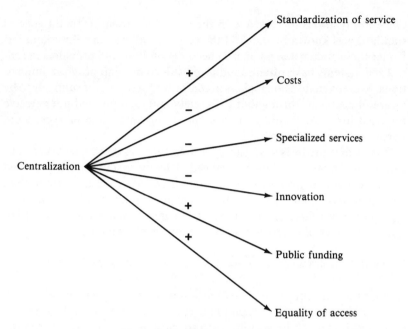

Fig. 5. Centralization and Performance

David 1960; 1971; Hage 1980; Aiken and Hage 1971). The previous chapters on the processes of policy formation in centralized systems provide a number of insights as to why: the exclusion of particular interest groups from the decision-making process, the reliance on public funding, and the avoidance of specialized services have made certain types of innovation appear costly and unnecessary. Decentralized systems—particularly those dominated by providers—have been much more willing to accept costly innovations.

Even though centralization has placed limits on the costs and the innovativeness of medical delivery systems, it is important to note that historically the costs and the level of innovativeness have increased within each country as its medical delivery system has become more centralized. As societies have acquired more wealth per capita in the process of economic development, they have spent more, and by spending more, they have become more innovative. The argument here is that, after one controls for wealth and other variables that influence costs and innovativeness, centralized systems have been less innovative and have spent less money than decentralized systems.

The role of standardization across regions is important in this regard as well. In highly centralized systems, the costs of changing standards and eligibility requirements become considerable. And over time, the reluctance to do so has increased with the cost. One reason is that a general standard was known by much of the country and was therefore familiar. Under these circumstances, inertia becomes built in, and providers in centralized systems have often found it difficult to develop program innovations. Moreover, decision makers in centralized systems were unlikely to be aware of problems throughout the society and therefore did not perceive the need for change until there was mounting unrest and pressure from particular interest groups.

What was sometimes less clear in the literature was the impact of centralization on equality. Publicly financed delivery systems have provided greater equality of access to services among social classes and groups than have privately financed ones. Moreover, publicly financed systems have been more centralized. Thus it appears that greater centralization has led to greater equality of access to services among classes and groups.

INTERACTION BETWEEN CENTRALIZATION AND INTEREST GROUPS

It is one thing to comprehend how variation in group power and in the level of centralization has influenced the performance of medical delivery systems, but it is much more difficult to specify the interaction between the two. In this connection, it is important to point out that, irrespective of what group has dominated a delivery system, the level of centralization has had predictable consequences on the system's performance. For example, providers have been more powerful than consumers in both systems, but levels of innovativeness have varied because of variation in levels of centralization.

Given an initial level of centralization, because subsequent levels are determined largely by group conflict, it is important to understand its influence. The group that has been dominant in the decision-making process at any moment has generally wanted to keep decision making at that particular level of centralization. At any one time, centralization limited the ability of particular groups to influence policy and on the choices available to policy makers. But over long periods, the power of groups and group conflict have changed the levels of centralization in both systems. Historically, those who have believed that they are unable to change policies in the decision-making process have often wanted to increase the level of centralization as a means of increasing their power, even though a higher level of centralization has often placed constraints on the types of utility that they have preferred. In an effort to standardize resources in spatial terms and equalize access to services, lower-income groups have usually attempted to shift decision making to a more centralized level. On the other hand, providers, on a few occasions, have preferred decision making at a national level, particularly when they have believed that they could mobilize power and operate effectively at that level. This was the case in 1948 when the British consultants preferred that they be employed by the national rather than the local government because they correctly believed they would have more influence at that level (Klein 1983).

As medical technology has been perceived as being efficacious, complex, and expensive, low-income consumers have turned to the government for assistance in providing medical care. As a result, most medical delivery systems have become more centralized over time, as lower-income groups have mobilized their power and demanded services.

In an effort to shape decisions, however, professional providers have usually had an advantage over lower-income consumers in mobilizing power at the central level. The degree to which a group has been able to organize effectively at the national level has depended on its total resources. These have consisted of the size of the group as well as such per capita resources as money, education, and status. Because physicians have had high per capita resources, over time they have generally had more success than consumer organizations in mobilizing political power at the national level, even though consumers may have initially been responsible for the system's becoming centralized. Moreover, relative to most consumer organizations, providers have long had an advantage in maximizing political power in that they have usually belonged to a single-issue organization and have been able to focus all of their energies on the one policy area with which they were concerned; most consumer organizations (e.g., labor unions), on the other hand, have been multi-issue organizations with their energies diffused among many policy areas. And relative to providers, consumers on a per capita basis have usually had lower status, less money, and less education, factors that have restricted their ability to mobilize power at the central level.

The emergence of a centralized decision-making process has required that groups maintain a high degree of internal coherence and organization if they are to be effectively represented via the indirect participating mechanisms inherent in decision making at higher levels of society. As higher levels of decision making have occurred, new, highly specialized interest groups have commonly emerged in medical delivery systems (e.g., organizations for medical specialists, medical insurance associations, and professional associations for hospital administrators). Because of their high level of information about the system and their ready access to the decision-making process, these groups, while often small and highly specialized, have had enormous advantages in terms of effective participation when compared to larger but less specialized groups, such as political parties and trade unions. Thus the shift of decision making to higher levels of society has acted both to limit the effective participation of consumer groups and simultaneously to assist in the creation of new but highly specialized and influential interest groups.

Thus there is a certain irony in the historical relationship between the participation of interest groups and increasing centralization. It has been the weakness of consumer groups vis-à-vis providers that has led them to demand higher levels of decision making. And they have usually been the catalyst in this respect. Consumers have generally believed that higher levels of decision making would enhance their interests. As centralization increased, however, the balance of power to influence decisions has tended to remain decidedly in favor of providers.

Groups that historically have been relatively ineffective in participating at the local level and/or in private systems have had few resources at their command except votes. The capacity of consumers to create decision-making authorities at higher levels of society by the mobilization of votes has tended to be far greater than the capacity to control such units once they have been created. This has been the case because the representation of groups in the decision-making process at higher levels of society has been limited and indirect and because, as the result of the institution of new authorities, new interest groups have generally been created that have been able to function quite effectively at the level at which they were organized.

The relationship between centralization and the degree of participation has been a complex one. At the most simple level, the shift of decision making to higher levels of society has generally been a direct consequence of increased participation by previously excluded groups. In turn, higher levels of decision making have usually accomplished the intended purpose of broadening participation, at least initially. However, the shift has altered the manner in which groups have been represented, created new and powerful interest groups and often led to a decline in the level of direct participation by those groups that were responsible for the change.

On the other hand, consumers have had one potential advantage over providers, and that has been their numerical superiority. Across countries, when consumers have been able to develop an encompassing organization (i.e., one that encompasses a substantial percentage of the society's total population), they have been able to exercise considerable influence over the decision-making process at the national level. But the ability of consumers to get organized at a national level in this fashion has depended on several variables. They have had greater potential to develop encompassing organizations, the smaller the country, the more homogeneous ethnically and linguistically the society, and the less complex and diverse the economy. Hence consumers in countries such as Norway and Sweden have had considerable capacity for encompassing group formation. Because the United States historically has been a large, multicultural society with a complex economy, consumers there have had low capacity for developing encompassing organizations and mobilizing consumer power at the local or national level. Thus providers have not had too much difficulty in dominating the decision-making process. England and Wales historically have fallen mid-way between the Scandinavian and U.S. cases in this respect (Hollingsworth 1982). Of course, professional providers have been powerful in the medical delivery systems of all highly industrialized societies. What is variable has been their power vis-à-vis consumers.

The influence of interest groups on centralization—both in establishing some initial level of centralization and in accounting for incremental changes over time—has not been just a one-way process. Centralization, or its absence, has tended to provide resources to certain interest groups, which in turn have influenced changes in centralization. For example, the decision in the United States by the federal government to provide funding for medical care for the elderly and needy without dictating prices benefited provider groups, in that doctors gained financially and became even more articulate about their preferences for medical delivery.

Over time, medical delivery systems have had multiple levels of authority in highly industrialized societies. In both countries, there has been an incremental shift toward multiple levels of authority, and there has been a persistence of decision-making authorities at lower levels of delivery systems—a persistence that is not difficult to understand from the interest group perspective. Each new level of authority has developed a set of officials and constituencies to participate in the decision-making process. Thus interest groups have been organized to participate at each level of decision making.

Meantime, public officials and administrators in both countries have been loath to see the decision-making process at lower levels eliminated, for these have shielded officials and administrators at higher levels from the pressures of various groups. Moreover, specialized interest groups have been reluctant to have the decision-making process eliminated at the level at which they have been able to participate most effectively. Thus, over time, there has developed proliferation of levels of authority, each permitting the participation of various interest groups. Partly as a result, the administrative machinery of both delivery systems has become increasingly complex. And while over time, consumer groups have played an important role in promoting a more centralized decision-making process, it has been providers as well as public officials and administrators who have become the most dominant actors in the decision-making process. While multilevel systems appear to be effective in broadening the scope of group participation, groups with high levels of organizational capacities and specialized knowledge have become more successful in influencing decision making in centralized delivery systems. Thus the proliferation of decision-making authorities has generally been the result of pressures for broader participation by consumer groups, but this has not resulted in their more effective participation.

DETERMINANTS OF GROUP POWER AND CENTRALIZATION

There are many things that have influenced the power of groups and the level of centralization of the two delivery systems, but there are four variables that consistently across the two societies and over time have placed limits on the power of groups and the level of centralization: (1) size, (2) social heterogeneity, (3) technology, and (4) wealth.

Size

When comparing social service delivery systems in democratic societies, one finds that those in large societies have been somewhat more decentralized than those in smaller societies (Hollingsworth and Hanneman, 1983). Of course, size does not limit centralization in some mechanistic fashion. But larger societies have more levels of hierarchy and more parts to be coordinated, and the number of these places constraints on how centralized a system may become. Hence, all other things being equal, one would expect a democratic country the size of the United States to have a medical delivery system somewhat more decentralized than that in Great Britain. And that is what has occurred.

Even though size of country in a cross-national perspective has been inversely correlated with level of centralization in the two systems, the relationship has been just the opposite when viewed historically within the two systems. Throughout the twentieth century, both medical delivery systems have increased in size as a result of the expansion in the number of physicians, nurses, paraprofessionals, hospital beds, and so forth. At the same time, both systems have become more centralized, as low-income groups have demanded that governments play a larger role in providing medical services. Hence, within the two countries, increases in the size of delivery systems and centralization have trended in the same direction, though this trend is not causally related. But even if the power of low-income consumers has been an important reason for centralization over time, medical delivery systems in larger "democratic" societies, at any one time, have tended to be somewhat more decentralized than those in smaller societies, for the larger the country, the more difficult it has been for low-income consumers to mobilize and organize sufficient power to change the structure of the delivery system. For the same reason, providers in a large society have been somewhat more influential relative to low-income consumers in shaping policy.

Social Heterogeneity

As was suggested above, because American society has been more heterogeneous ethnically, racially, and religiously, the lines of cleavage among
consumer groups have been very sharp, and for this reason, it has been
difficult for low-income consumers to develop organizations powerful
enough to dominate the medical delivery system. And because of the fragmented power of consumer groups in the United States, they have historically not been very successful in mounting the power necessary to bring
about a highly centralized delivery system. Conversely, because American
society has had greater social heterogeneity than British society, professional providers have exercised greater power vis-à-vis consumers in shaping the performance of the U.S. system.

Technology

The technology of all medical delivery systems has become more differentiated and complex during the twentieth century. And as the technology
has become more complex, professional providers and others with expertise have become more influential vis-à-vis consumers in shaping decisions
about the nature of medical investments and the production of medical
services—irrespectively of the level of centralization. Hence providers in
the U.S. as well as the British medical delivery systems have become increasingly influential during the twentieth century. However, the historical
record demonstrates that those systems that are decentralized and dominated by professional providers have tended to be somewhat more receptive to new and expensive technology than those that have been relatively
decentralized and dominated by low-income consumers.
   Systems that historically have been dominated by providers and quite
decentralized have tended to be very receptive to highly complex technology and to become increasingly antonomous as a result of high levels of
technological complexity. As medical technology has become more complex and specialized, it has become more difficult for any group to dominate and manage the system. Moreover, no group in either country has
been able to assess the technological needs of the society. As a result, technology has tended to develop a logic of its own, with specialization beget-
ting higher and higher levels of specialization. Therefore, there has been a
tendency in both countries to err on the side of expanding the system,
spending more money, and developing alternative but even more complex
technologies. In both countries, the systems have dictated much of their
own demand, and they have shaped the thinking of the entire society about
the type of technology needed in order to achieve good health. As the technology has become highly specialized, the policy debates about system

characteristics have become more and more restricted. Knowledge of the activities and behavior of the whole system has become increasingly irrelevant for policy decisions. Policy makers have tended to consider only those decisions whose known consequences have differed only marginally from the status quo. In both countries, it has become increasingly difficult for anyone to understand fully the entire medical delivery system because of its high degree of complexity. And since decisions have been made primarily about specialized parts but not the whole system, the system in each country has threatened to take on a life of its own as it has become increasingly immune to conscious interference from groups in its environment. Devoid of any clear vision of their purpose, the two systems have increasingly been shaped by an unfolding of the logic of technological imperatives. Because the British system has historically been more centralized and subject to more state control, it has tended to be more resistant to the absorption of new and more complex technology than the U.S. system. Moreover, the British system has remained somewhat less autonomous. But at high levels of technology, all systems have tended to become somewhat more autonomous.

As long as highly specialized systems have produced relatively satisfactory results, they have posed no serious problems. But highly complex medical systems tend to become increasingly costly and cause the society eventually to face a crisis over the costs of medical care, and this has been the case in the United States. Because the very structure of the system has been largely responsible for the crisis, American society appears to have had little capacity to cope with the crisis. On the other hand, the centralized British system, which historically has been more subject to state control and has been less permeable by high technology, has been more able to cope with the crisis of rising medical costs.

Wealth

The effect of wealth, like that of the previous variables, on the level of centralization and the power of groups in the two systems has been most indirect. Its effects have been mediated by its impact on the state and its revenue system. As the GNP has risen in Britain and the United States, they have tended to change their revenue system, with an increasing share of the revenue being raised by an income tax. Most income taxes have been raised primarily at the central level of government, and governments have had a tendency to formulate and implement policy at the level at which revenues have been collected. Hence, as more and more revenues have been collected at the central level, more functions (e.g., medical services) have been shifted to the central level. Meantime, technology has become more complex with the expansion of a society's wealth, and as low-income consumers have demanded that government make the technology available to them, the central government has responded by making medical resources available with funding at the central level.

At some point in the economic development of both societies, the state sector began to expand more rapidly than the economy. And in both societies, it was the state sector at the central rather than the local level that grew most rapidly—and thus medical delivery systems tended to become more centralized as the GNP expanded. Because those with specialized knowledge tended to operate more efficiently than low-income consumers at centralized levels, this type of process has tended to enhance the power of specialized providers and state officials in shaping decisions about the production of medical care.

LINKAGES BETWEEN NATIONAL AND SUBNATIONAL SYSTEMS

Thus far, the discussion has focused on the influence of group conflict and structural characteristics on the performance of national medical delivery systems of the two countries. However, it is also necessary to understand the linkage between the organizational structure of national delivery systems and organizations at the subnational level (e.g., hospitals) and the reasons why those organizations have performed as they have. To advance comprehension in this direction, it is useful to be aware that there have been three types of organizations in the two countries: those in the public, nonprofit, and for-profit sectors. And in order to comprehend how subnational organizations perform in each of these sectors, it is desirable to rely on the same group conflict and structural perspective employed in discussing the performance of national delivery systems.

Over time, the behavior of hospitals has been very much influenced by the preferences of the groups already discussed: professional providers, upper- and lower-income consumers, and government administrators. The preferences of these groups have shaped the performance of hospitals, since these groups have played an important role in providing hospital funding. In other words, the source of funding of hospital and other complex organizations has been a critical variable in shaping their behavior. Historically, when organizations have relied on a particular group for funding, they have attempted to be responsive to the tastes and preferences of that group. And the variation in the preferences of various groups does much to explain the variation in the behavior of organizations in the public, nonprofit, and for-profit sectors.

For example, voluntary or nonprofit organizations have tended to be dependent on charitable contributions for their survival and have tended to be very much influenced by the values of upper-income consumers and professional providers, who have provided much of the charity. (See fig. 3

for a description of the preferences of various groups.) For this reason, non-profit hospitals in both Britain and the United States, in contrast to public sector hospitals, have tended to be more innovative and provide more highly specialized and high-quality services. On the other hand, they have tended to be somewhat more expensive to operate per patient day and somewhat more inegalitarian in terms of access to services.

Meantime, organizations in each of these sectors, like national medical delivery systems, have been somewhat constrained by the variable centralization. (See fig. 4 for the relationship between centralization and performance characteristics.) Because voluntary organizations have been in the private sector, they have been less subject to the control of centralized authorities than those in the public sector. As voluntary organizations have been in a somewhat decentralized interorganizational network, they have tended to maximize the performance associated with decentralization, which has already been discussed: high innovativeness, inequality in access to services, and high operating costs. This pattern has been the case with U.S. hospitals throughout the twentieth century and with those in England and Wales prior to 1948, at which date virtually all hospitals were nationalized (Hollingsworth and Hollingsworth 1985; forthcoming).

In contrast to voluntary hospitals, public ones have tended to operate more in response to the values of low-income consumers and government administrators. As a result, public sector organizations have tended to be more egalitarian, less innovative, and less costly on a per capita basis. At the same time, they have tended to have fewer staff, more overcrowded facilities, and fewer individualized services. Because public organizations have been more under the control of centralized authorities than have voluntary organizations, public sector organizations have tended to maximize the types of performance associated with centralization (see fig. 4).

As for-profit organizations have tended to operate under the influence of upper-income consumers and professional providers, their behavior has tended to conform somewhat to the preferences of these groups: that is, they have tended to emphasize selective specialized services rather than a wide array of services and tended to be inegalitarian in access. Because these organizations have been in the private sector, they, like voluntary sector organizations, have been less subject to the rigorous control of state authorities, and thus they have performed more consistently with the behavior of decentralized systems, which have already been discussed.

The two countries have varied in the extent to which there have been hospitals and other organizations in these three sectors. The size of the three sectors has been quite large in the United States throughout the twentieth century. However, only the public sector has been of much consequence in Great Britain since 1948; all three existed before that date, but only the size of the public and nonprofit sectors was substantial.

The historical reasons why these two societies have decided to provide services in the public, for-profit, or nonprofit sector is a subject of considerable importance but one that is little discussed in the social science or historical literature. The following generalizations derived from the history of these and several other Western countries are designed to advance our understanding of why societies have opted to provide more services in one sector than in another. Societies that have been homogeneous ethnically, linguistically, and religiously have had more of their medical services provided by public sector organizations. For example, Sweden, which has been relatively homogeneous, has had most of its hospitals in the public sector. This is the type of society that historically has had encompassing group structures, and this type of power arrangement has facilitated the development of public sector activity. On the other hand, more heterogeneous societies have relied more on private nonprofit organizations to provide human services. Thus in the United States, where there have traditionally been many narrowly based interest groups—especially many religious denominations—there have been in the private sector Catholic, Jewish, Presbyterian, Methodist, and Baptist hospitals. In socially fragmented societies, groups have had different values and have attempted to establish organizations responsive to those who share the same values.*

Because class divisions were much sharper in Britain in the early part of the twentieth century than later, class structure was quite rigid and the society more heterogeneous. And significantly, England and Wales at that time had numerous hospitals in the voluntary sector. As the rigidity of the class structure later diminished and the society became slightly more homogeneous—especially during World War II—almost all hospitals became located in the public sector.

In most societies, there has historically been a widely shared view that hospitals in the for-profit sector have been somewhat less trustworthy than those in the public or nonprofit sectors. Hence the for-profit sector has been relatively small in most Western societies. However, when upper-income groups have not perceived the public and voluntary sectors to be responsive to their demands for specialized services, they have turned to the for-profit sector. For-profit hospitals have often been of short duration and lasted until the public or voluntary sectors developed sufficient resources to provide the services that the for-profit sectors were dispensing. In general, the for-profit sector has provided somewhat different types of goods from the type provided by the voluntary and public sectors. For example, the public

---

* For a discussion of the reasons why societies vary in the degree to which there are encompassing organizations, see Hollingsworth 1982 and Olson 1982. Weisbrod 1977 and Bendick 1975 discuss differences in the behavior of nonprofit, public sector, and for-profit organizations.

and voluntary sectors have tended to provide homogeneously demanded collective goods, while the for-profit sector has tended to provide heterogeneously demanded private goods. Thus patients in for-profit hospitals in both countries have tended to receive more personal and privatized services than those that are available in nonprofit and public sector hospitals.*

COMPARATIVE PERFORMANCE: BRITAIN AND THE United STATES

Because the British and U.S. systems have differed so much in their distribution of power and levels of centralization, they have performed very differently in terms of equality of access, costs, innovativeness, and quality of care.

Equality of Access

Both systems have become more egalitarian in access to medical care over time, but with respect to most medical technology the British system has remained much more egalitarian. In both countries, low-income consumers now visit physicians more frequently than do those with higher incomes. But in both countries, the physician spends more time per visit with upper-income consumers and is more knowledgeable about their problems. Moreover, there is evidence that upper-income groups receive a somewhat higher quality of care in both countries (Goodman 1980; Cartwright and O'Brien 1976; Le Grand 1978). Why this occurs is not entirely clear, but in both countries, upper-income groups ask doctors more questions and provide more information.

But a critical difference between the two countries is that approximately 28 million Americans are still not covered by private medical insurance, Medicaid, or Medicare (Robert Wood Johnson Foundation 1983: 8). And approximately 70 percent of these uninsured people are low-income indi-

---

* Even though for-profit hospitals have had a short life, this has been changing in the United States since the early 1970s, the end date for this study. In response partly to regulations imposed by state and federal governments in order to curb spending on medical care and partly to the excess capacity in the hospital industry, many for-profit and voluntary hospitals merged or consolidated in order to achieve economies of scale. The greater economies of scale have permitted hospitals to borrow from financial markets throughout the country and to continue purchasing expensive technology. Not only have horizontal mergers occurred (the linking together of hospitals) but there has also been considerable vertical integration (the linking of enterprises at different stages of production) in the U.S. hospital industry. Hospitals have merged with nursing homes, pharmacies, doctors offices, and even insurance companies. As a result of horizontal and vertical integration, the for-profit hospitals will probably have a much longer life span in the future than has been the case prior to 1970 (Hollingsworth and Hollingsworth, forthcoming).

viduals who are effectively priced out of the medical care market. In the more market-oriented U.S. system, prices limit the quantity of goods and services that are available for millions of Americans and thus act as a deterrent to the consumption of medical services. On the other hand, even though money prices have been abolished in the NHS, waiting lists act as a deterrent to the consumption of services; but these do not have a systematic bias against low-income consumers. Even so, upper-income consumers may "jump the queue" by purchasing care in the private market.

In both countries, there is still an inadequate relationship between the need for medical services and the distribution of medical resources: resources are least adequate in the areas that need it most. And British scholars have made much of the fact that there is still considerable inequality in the regional distribution of medical resources. Those regions that were well endowed with resources at the start of the NHS have tended to retain their advantages. However, regional variation has narrowed much more rapidly in England and Wales and most medical resources have been more equitably distributed across regions there than in the United States.

Costs

For some years, in Britain about one-half as much per person was spent on medical care as in the United States (table 8). Moreover, the British have spent a much smaller percentage of their GNP on medical care than have the Americans.

It is true that, as per capita income rises in a country, the percentage of the GNP that it spends on medical care rises, and that, because Britain's per capita income is lower than that of the United States, it would be expected to spend a smaller share of its GNP on medical care. But the organization of the delivery system is a key variable in controlling medical expenditures, and this is very evident when one compares those in Britain with those in the United States. The U.S. method of payment on a fee-for-service basis combined with a retrospective reimbursement scheme has encouraged a delivery system that has had little incentive for economy. Indeed, the U.S. system has rewarded providers of care for cost-increasing behavior.

In Britain, the government has effectively used its monopsony power to keep medical costs low. For example, the British have paid less for drugs than have the citizens of any other country in Western Europe and North America (Cooper and Cooper 1972; Goodman 1980a). And by U.S. and European standards, the salaries of British doctors have been quite low for more than a quarter-century. While one has heard more complaints among young doctors in training in Britain than in the United States, surveys of the British medical profession have consistently reported that the morale of the medical profession is quite high (Culyer et al. 1980; Klein 1983b; Great Britain, NHS 1979).

Doctors in the United States, in order to differentiate themselves from their peers and appear to be practicing high-quality medicine, have insisted on and generally received the best and most expensive medical technology available. In Britain, however, physicians have been less influential, and the system has tended to demonstrate a preference for routine and less expensive treatment strategies.

There appears to be some basis for concluding that the fee-for-service system operating in the United States has encouraged doctors to carry out more medical procedures than their counterparts in the NHS. On the other hand, some analysts have argued that the NHS system of paying practitioners on a capitation basis has encouraged them to prefer the trivial to the nontrivial case and to overrefer patients to hospital-based doctors (Glaser 1970; Goodman 1980a: 63). While there is some justification for this perspective, the British general practitioner has had an incentive to convince patients that the doctor is looking after their best interests, for otherwise they would gravitate to another general practitioner.

Innovativeness

This study has demonstrated that, while centralized systems tend to restrict the level of expenditures on medical care, centralization has placed constraints on the adoption of new ideas and slowed down the diffusion of complex and expansive technologies. Centralization has slowed down the diffusion process, for certain groups that have preferred innovativeness have had limited influence in the decision-making process. Moreover, centralization has meant that there has been greater reliance on funding from the state. And in centralized systems, government bureaucrats have been more involved in the decision-making process, and they, more than private entrepreneurs, have tended to perceive types of innovations as costly and unnecessary.

Throughout the twentieth century, the British system has been relatively inventive. However, the evidence concerning the diffusion of innovations is somewhat mixed. In the period following 1962, when the regulation of new drugs was more centralized and rigorous than in Britain, new drugs tended to diffuse more slowly in the United States. But over time, there has been convergence in the diffusion rates of new drugs in the two countries as the British regulatory system has adopted most of the U.S. guidelines for testing safety and efficacy.

On the other hand, the centralized and cost-conscious NHS has been much slower to adopt expensive new technologies. For example, Britain, consistent with its inventiveness, was the country where much of the technology for the full body scanner was developed. But as late as 1976, there were fewer than 25 brain scanners and only 4 full body scanners in use in all of Great Britain. In the United States at the same time, however, there were more than 1,000 scanners of both types in use—over half of which were produced in Great Britain (Goodman 1980a).

Again, the British were pioneers in the development of renal dialysis technology. But in 1976, the NHS accepted only one-half as many new patients per 1,000,000 population as most West European countries. At the same time as the British were treating 7.1 patients per 100,000 population with dialysis, the United States was treating 12 per 100,000. Meantime, the British have also made much less frequent use of open heart surgery and other expensive technologies—whose efficaciousness has often been open to question. In sum, the British have placed much less emphasis on nonroutine and expensive technology than have the Americans, who by the middle 1970s had what many medical economists considered to be an excess of hospital capacity in every metropolitan area and such a surplus of surgeons that most carried substantially less than a full workload (Fuchs, 1979; Aaron and Schwartz 1984).

Equality of Results

While almost every student of medical care is interested in assessing the quality of patient care, most scholars have little choice but to acknowledge the difficulty of operationalizing the concept. By definition, quality is concerned with the effect of care on the health of individuals. Though numerous researchers have attempted to develop an index of the quality of hospital care, thus far very little attention has been devoted to assessing the quality of national medical delivery systems. While at a high level of abstraction it is possible to compare almost anything, it is very difficult (though important) to compare the overall quality of care in Britain with that in the United States, for the systems have attempted to do quite different things. American practitioners during the twentieth century have been more concerned with diagnosing and treating sickness, while their counterparts in Britain have been more concerned with helping individuals to cope with their everyday work situations. Using a wide variety of laboratory tests, American physicians have tended to examine their patients more frequently and thoroughly for physical disease, while British doctors have tended to be more concerned with helping patients to deal with a variety of anxiety states and to cope with the stresses of everyday life. As Rosemary Stevens suggests, modern technology has "been incorporated into the systems of each country in different ways, reflecting pre-existing patterns of professional development and social attitudes toward the provision of care" (Stevens 1976: 28).

The most frequent complaint heard in and out of Britain about the quality of care provided by the NHS has focused on the long waiting lists for hospital care. Certainly, this is a complex subject. As a percentage of patients receiving hospital care, waiting lists have not over time increased in Britain. Moreover, they usually contain the names of some patients who have already been cured, have moved, or have died. However, econometric studies have demonstrated that increasing the supply of physicians and hospital beds has had little effect in reducing the size of waiting lists but, rather, has encouraged general practitioners to refer more patients to hospitals and hospital-based doctors to assign patients to waiting lists (Feldstein 1967; Culyer 1976; Klein 1983a). In short, waiting lists constitute a poor indicator of the quality of care provided by the NHS.

The Americans have excelled in the development of centers containing modern and expensive technology for the diagnosis and treatment of disease. And for upper-income groups, there may be no better diagnostic and treatment centers in the world. On the other hand, for low-income patients, the services provided by the NHS are probably better than those provided by the U.S. system.

* * * * *

Those who can afford the best in Britain have often complained about the inadequacies of the system, while low-income citizens have been very appreciative of the types of service that have been available (Culyer et al. 1980). In the United States, there has been a much greater difference between the poor and the nonpoor in the type of care received than in Britain. Moreover, many Americans (especially the poor) have had inadequate access to quality medical care, a phenomenon that disappeared in Britain with the adoption of the NHS.

CONCLUDING OBSERVATIONS

The record suggests that there have been trade-offs among certain performances. For example, there appears to have been a trade-off between a widespread commitment to equality of access to care and the rapid diffusion of new, expensive, medical technology. Moreover, this type of trade-off has occasionally compromised the principle of equality. Britain has had a much stronger commitment to equality than the United States, and to achieve this goal, the British have developed a highly centralized system in which government officials have been very cost conscious. But in the process, they have encountered fundamental tensions in performance between low costs and equality of access to expensive new technology.

The history of these two systems suggests that the system that opts to have very expensive and highly specialized services is likely to have many centers that dispense very high-quality services but are affordable only to upper-income groups. On the other hand, the system that has attempted to meet the minimum needs of all of its citizens—as the British have done— has tended to emphasize routine and less expensive treatment strategies and less specialized services.

Epilogue

As a result of differences in group power and variation in structure, the medical delivery systems of Britain and the United States have performed quite differently in terms of equality of access to care, costs, innovativeness, and quality of care. However, have variations in the organization of systems influenced variation in levels of health between the two countries? What has been the relative impact of medical technology on levels of health? While these are extremely difficult questions to answer, the evidence that has been accumulating in recent years causes one to be very cautious about attributing much of the decline in mortality during the twentieth century to improvements in medical technology.

This study has demonstrated that equalizing access to medical care does not equalize levels of health (measured by mortality) across social classes and income groups. These findings, when considered alongside those of many other studies, have obvious implications concerning the efficacy of medical technology as a determinant of the level of health.

While mortality rates continue to fluctuate for selected sex and age categories, there has been a marked decline in overall mortality in the United States and in England and Wales since 1900. Ironically, more than 90 percent of that decline occurred before 1950, at which time the precipitate and almost unrestrained rise in medical expenditures began. In both countries, the death rates of middle-aged males have even had a modest rise since 1950. By 1975, the life expectancy of males at age 65 had increased less than two years since 1900, while that of those at age 75 had not increased by even one year (McKeown 1975: 396; Powles 1973: 3; Fuchs 1974a: 15; 1974b; McKinlay and McKinlay 1977: 412–14).

Since 1950, investments in medical care and research have mushroomed in both countries. For example, the United States devoted 4.1 percent of the GNP to health services in 1940, but by 1983 the figure was 10.8 percent. Expenditures for medical research and development increased from $160 million in 1950 to more than $4.7 billion in 1975. And in the same period, the number of doctoral scientists conducting biomedical research increased sixfold to 90,000 (Powles 1973: 2; Fredrickson 1977: 160–62). Indeed, in all Western countries, the growth rate of the health sector has been more rapid than that of the GNP during the past quarter-century. During the two decades following the introduction of the NHS, the work force in England and Wales expanded by 10 percent, but the number of hospital workers increased by more than 70 percent.

Despite the increase in expenditures and research effort, there has been no major breakthrough in the management of disease since 1950. Indeed, the most significant advances in this respect occurred prior to 1950 with the development of medicines to deal with infectious diseases: the sulfon-amides, penicillin, and streptomycin. Age-adjusted death rates from cancer among the elderly even increased between 1965 and 1980. Of course, there have been advances in the management of specific diseases, particularly in regard to coronary heart disease and cerebrovascular disease. While mortality rates for ischemic heart disease increased dramatically between 1950 and 1968, there was a marked decline between 1968 and 1976. However, Britain and the United States are left basically with the same list of major diseases that existed in 1950. On the other hand, diagnostic laboratories have become more complex and clinical diagnoses much more precise. With the exception of substantial and impressive declines in infant and maternal mortality rates and some sharp decline in death rates ascribed to coronary heart disease since 1968, *there is not much evidence that this vast investment in resources has led to a population that is significantly in better health in either country* (Thomas 1977: 37–38; Rogers and Blendon 1977: 1710–14; Vogt 1981: 31–70; Fuchs 1986; Russell 1986; H. Levy 1981: 49–70).*

While immunization and antibiotics are efficacious in dealing with a wide array of diseases, it is important to put that capacity into a proper perspective. Most of the reduction in mortality over the past three centuries occurred before 1900 and was relatively unaffected by medical technology but was due primarily to improved nutrition, reduced exposure to air- and water-borne infections, safe water, and efficient disposal of sewage. In the twentieth century, much of the total reduction in mortality in both the United States and Great Britain occurred before 1931—before the introduction of complex medical technologies—and medical technology was certainly not the only and probably not the most important reason for further decline since 1931 (McKeown 1976; McKinlay and McKinlay 1977).

Meantime, there have been rigorous studies designed to assess the relationship between medical resources devoted to health care and the outcome of those services on levels of health. The studies generally are regressions of mortality on medical care resources across regions (most frequently regions of the United States). Usually, the authors have found no statistically significant relationship between medical resources and mortality and have therefore concluded that additional medical resources are likely to have

---

* Cardiovascular epidemiologists attribute most of the decline in cardiovascular mortality to changes in risk factor and life style factors (e.g., cholesterol intake, smoking habits, and exercise), while little credit is attributed to improvement in coronary surgery and medical treatment. See the discussion and bibliography in R. Levy 1981, especially pp. 66–67.

little effect on mortality (Auster et al. 1969; Letourmy 1975; Fuchs 1974a; 1986). In a very different type of study, Hollingsworth et al. (forthcoming) found in a cross-temporal study of France, Great Britain, Sweden, and the United States that variation in medical delivery systems had no independent effect on variations in mortality, though the impact of the standard of living (levels of income, education) on mortality was mediated through the medical delivery systems.

Of course, mortality is a crude index of level of health, and for this reason, the results of these studies are frequently viewed with scepticism. One study attempted to assess the impact of the availability of medical resources on a variety of measures of individual health status (elevated cholesterol level, high blood pressure, abnormal electrocardiogram, abnormal chest x-ray, varicose veins, and periodontal disease). The study (Newhouse and Friedlander 1977) revealed that variations in medical resources across thirty-nine metropolitan centers in the United States had no systematic effect on these various measures of health. Thus, one study after another has concluded that increases in medical resources, given a reasonable quantity at the base, have had very little effect on levels of health in advanced industrial societies. These findings have been quite consistent, irrespective of the country in which the data were collected and the measure of level of health.

Despite a great deal of evidence to the contrary, most doctors and patients have believed that improvements in health that have occurred during the past one hundred years were caused by the technology resulting from "scientific medicine." Clearly, enthusiasm for modern medicine has far outpaced its specific achievements. On both sides of the Atlantic—but especially in the United States—there has been increasing belief that the right doctor can treat almost any disease effectively. Increasingly, on both sides of the Atlantic, personal discontents and maladjustments (e.g., unhappiness, divorce) are viewed as medical problems. The physician in the United States today has increasingly assumed the role that the priest played in a different era.

In the United States, where television commercials and advertisements in popular magazines and newspapers have attempted to raise money for research on cancer and heart and kidney diseases, the public has developed unreal expectations from medical science and progress. As Lewis Thomas observed some years ago, "this attitude is in part the outcome of overstated claims on the part of medicine itself in recent decades, plus medicine's passive acquiescence while even more exaggerated claims were made by the media" (L. Thomas 1977: 45; also see Powles 1973: 14).

In both Britain and the United States during the twentieth century, there has been much investment in a curative approach, based on a medical engineering model, to medicine. In both countries, those who have exercised the most influence in the medical decision-making process have viewed human health in very mechanistic terms: like any machine whose structure and function are fully understood, the human body may be taken apart, repaired, and reassembled. Just as a mechanic repairs a machine, so the physician in the twentieth century has intervened with drugs or surgery in an attempt to restore a malfunctioning body to normality.

There is not much technology for a definitive cure of most disease, however. And when medical science has developed a definitive technology for a prevention or a cure, the technology has been substantially cheaper than that which was devised before the breakthrough. For example, before the discovery of streptomycin and isoniazid for the treatment of tuberculosis, the British and Americans constructed and operated very expensive tuberculosis hospitals. Similarly, before the development of the relatively inexpensive polio vaccine, the medical world relied on such expensive treatment as iron lungs, intensive medical care, and orthopedic shoes and braces. And today, medical practitioners use costly renal dialysis for the treatment of kidney disease and open heart surgery for heart disease, but these are at best "half-way technologies," as they provide no decisive means of turning off, reversing, or curing disease (President's Science Advisory Committee 1972: 10–11).

Even though there is increasing skepticism that differences in the organization of medical delivery have much impact on levels of health in highly industrialized societies, differences in the structure and financing of delivery systems have caused them to perform differently, as this study has demonstrated. But it would now appear appropriate that there should be serious public assessment on both sides of the Atlantic concerning the determinants of health.

Partly because twentieth-century medical educators in Britain and the United States have emphasized the potency of clinical intervention as a means of improving health, there has been relatively little medical research on an ecological approach to health. In recent years, however, the scientific literature has increasingly documented the tendency of a rising proportion of twentieth-century illnesses to result from man's difficulty in adapting to an environment of his own making. In short, there is a rapidly expanding literature that demonstrates that many of the more common and serious illnesses in the United States and Britain result from the environment in advanced industrial societies. For example, there is substantial scholarship that demonstrates that after one controls for age, there is a marked tendency for ischemic heart disease to rise with increasing economic development. Moreover, there appears to be a marked degeneration of arterial walls and a rise in blood pressure with age as the level of economic development increases. In other words, epidemiological studies demonstrate that these diseases are less prevalent for each age group in countries with low levels of economic development (Rose 1972; Jones 1970; Epstein 1965; Boyden 1970: 207–9; R. Levy 1981). While heart disease is associated with genetic predisposition, sex, inactivity, smoking, hypertension, and stress (Harper 1978), many epidemiological studies have found a link between a high incidence of heart diseases and high annual consumption of calories, protein, saturated fat, cholesterol, and sugar.

Numerous studies of mortality in advanced industrial societies have demonstrated that more than 20 percent of the total loss in life has resulted from cancer. And in adult males, 40 percent of that loss was due to cancer of the lung, most of which resulted from tobacco smoking (Royal College of Physicians 1971; Powles 1973: 8–10; Stamler et al. 1967). The second most common type of cancer among adult males has been cancer of the colon and rectum, whose incidence tends to increase with economic development. After studying the epidemiology of the subject, Dennis P. Burkitt argues that this results from the removal of dietary fiber and the high intake of refined carbohydrates that are common in most highly industrialized societies (Burkitt 1971). Another epidemiologist, after studying the geographical distribution of cancer, takes the view that "the marked differences in cancer incidence in different countries and the changes that have been noted in the experience of migrant groups when they move from one country to another are among the many pieces of evidence suggesting that most cancers are due to environmental factors. It follows that most cancers are, in principle, preventable" (Doll 1969: 8). Diabetes and other diseases also appear to be associated with diets rich in refined carbohydrates (West and Kalbfleisch 1971). Meantime, the cumulation of many years of exposure to various atmospheric pollutants has resulted in widespread chronic bronchitis and other forms of irreversible respiratory disease (Dubos 1968: 86).

As one epidemiologist has written, these diseases are the result of degenerative processes that result from man's inability to adapt to the environment he has created. They arise "because our earlier evolution has left us genetically unsuited for life in an industrialized society" (Rose 1972: 288).

Highly industrialized societies owe most of their advances in health to a set of ecological relationships that have reduced their vulnerability to infectious diseases, but the new patterns of life have produced their own disease burden, diseases of maladaptation. Even though there has been an increase in these, modern medical research has not taken much notice of evolutionary theory, historical demography, and medical ecology. Much of modern medicine has concentrated on trying to treat and cure disease but has remained relatively ignorant of the etiology of disease. However, curative medicine has to date made relatively little advance in reducing the cause of death from diseases of maladaptation. It has made some but very modest progress against heart disease, but the overall mortality burden resulting from cancer remains substantial. The curative model would appear to require even larger outlays of expenditures but with diminishing returns to health. Until medical science broadens its scientific base and supports careful, imaginative, and well-designed but comprehensive epidemiological studies that emphasize the prevention of disease, further improvement of health in Britain and the United States is likely to be marginal (U.S. Dept. of Health, Education, and Welfare, *Healthy People* 1979; Fuchs 1986; Russell 1986).*

It is wrong, however, to think of medicine only in curative and preventive terms. Irrespective of how medical research funds have been invested, it is important to recognize that much medical technology is useful only for caring for patients with chronic diseases. Physicians may not be able to cure most diseases of modern society, but they can alleviate symptoms and reduce pain. Indeed, most physicians do little more than "to palliate manifestations of the end-stages of long-established diseases" (Beeson 1977: 369).

To argue that the principal function of modern medicine is supportive rather than curative is not to downplay its importance. Even if cardiac by-pass surgery does not cure heart disease or have an intrinsic effect on length of life (Ross 1975), it has improved the quality of life for many patients by reducing pain from angina. The replacing of a diseased hip joint often improves the quality of life for an individual. Moreover, there have been substantial advances in the development of medications to control high blood pressure, to relieve asthma and pain, and to manage chronic diseases such as gout and diabetes. Indeed, more than three-fourths of the modern physicians's care is not curative but supportive.

When one recognizes that the function of most effective medical technology is supportive rather than curative, one tends to conclude that the U.S. and British medical delivery systems need to be redesigned to reflect this strength. It is true that the Americans have developed a network of excellent inpatient hospital teaching centers for coping with acute illness and a system for training science-based physicians that is not matched elsewhere. But since most patients need supportive care for long-term chronic illness, the U.S. and British systems—especially the former—have been less successful in providing health professionals to cope with patients' day-to-day health problems of a noncatastrophic nature (Rogers 1975).

Especially in the United States, an increasing percentage of resources and energy have been invested in the high technology of short-stay hospitals. But if one assumes that most health needs are chronic and incurable

---

* For further discussion of the problems of maladaptation, see the excellent essays in S. V. Boyden 1970, the perceptive arguments in René Dubos 1968, and the remarkable synthesis in John Powles 1973. For the complexity of studying the relationship between dietary habits and disease, see A. E. Harper 1978, 1980 and the numerous studies cited therein.

and require long-term support, one is led to question the wisdom of allocating an increasing percentage of medical resources in this type of institution.

The decision to allocate vast resources to acute care emerged from an institutional context established at an earlier time with quite different problems. By the beginning of the twentieth century, the large English and U.S. voluntary hospital made a concerted effort to limit their activities to short-term cases that were of greatest interest to their physician staff. They tended to exclude patients with infectious diseases, the destitute, the mentally ill, and geriatric cases. Over time, medical schools became attached to these hospitals, and the clinical teaching curriculum tended to conform to the established traditions of the hospital. As new teaching hospitals came into existence, they tended to conform to the existing educational practice. In this way, medical education was intricately tied to institutions that devoted little attention to the aged, the mentally ill, or those with long-term chronic illness. And over time, medical students in Britain and the United States received too little training in geriatrics, mental and other chronic illness, and preventive medicine.

The effects of medical education on medical delivery have been profound. Medical students have long been socialized by the example of their teachers, who have prepared young doctors to engage in the type of treatment that they themselves learned during their training. As a result, medical schools that have been relatively isolated from the aged, the mentally, and the rural ill have not produced physicians who are prepared to cope with the problems of these patients. Each generation of medical researchers has reproduced another that viewed preventive health and long-term care as unpromising areas of research or treatment. As a result, Britain and America have developed separate institutions to handle the chronic disease of the elderly. Nursing homes in the United States and the chronic hospitals for the elderly in Britain are the linear descendants of poorhouses, which historically were second-class institutions. With the development of the NHS, age and debility became substitutes for income as determinants for admission to these somewhat inferior institutions. With this trend, homes for the elderly became part of a long tradition of relative neglect of diseases of the aging (McKeown 1975: 86–98; Green 1977).

Despite rhetoric about comprehensive care, the British and U.S. medical delivery systems remain fragmented. In both countries, teaching about mental illness and diseases of the aged is still very much isolated from the mainstream of medical education. In addition, epidemiology and environmental and social medicine are still relatively neglected in both countries. Indeed, the British decision in 1948 to assign responsibility for treatment to the NHS and to delegate public health services to local governing authorities has helped to guarantee that environmental medicine will have a low priority in the education of physicians.

Once the public and physicians recognize that most medical services need to give greater emphasis to supportive rather than curative care, perhaps both societies will question whether there is a good logical reason for treating chronic, acute, and mental patients in separate institutions. If they develop balanced hospital communities in one site, it will be possible for the elderly and mental patients to have access to the best medical care when they need it. A balanced hospital community would help to guarantee that researchers, teachers, and students would have contact with a much broader range of illnesses and not just those that are viewed by researchers as interesting. Once there is a comprehensive community hospital with a full range of illnesses prevalent in advanced industrial societies, there will probably be greater interest in the study of the epidemiology of disease, which in turn is likely to lead to greater interest in environmental and social medicine. It is important that there be sufficient restructuring of medical training centers for medical personnel to be sensitive to the full range of problems impacting on health. Only then will society rise above the institutions of the past, which have obstructed a comprehensive approach to health problems. If that day arrives, there will be increasing realization that medical education requires more of a partnership between the medical profession and other professions (e.g., engineers, architects, city planners, politicians, and lawyers) in an effort to prevent disease.

This study has argued that the present performance of the medical delivery systems in England and Wales and in the United States is the product of their history and the distribution of power among various interest groups. If this is so, what reason is there for believing that there is potential for altering the approach to health care that has become so strongly ingrained in each country? Actually, the prospects for change in the structure and performance of the American medical system in the future are increasing, for the relative power of groups is changing.

There are several currents that are undermining the legitimacy of the present system's misplaced allocation of resources. First, there is increasing recognition that an important determinant of good health is an individual's habits in regard to nutrition, exercise, alcohol consumption, tobacco, rest, and the like. Meantime, recent scholarship demonstrates that, regardless of how health is measured, the level of an individual's education is one of the most powerful determinants. Just how education produces good health is not entirely clear, but most likely, individuals with better education choose better diets, are more aware of health risks, avoid unhealthy occupations, and select medical care with greater prudence (Grossman 1976; Fuchs 1979; 1986).

Second, some of the most powerful groups in American society are becoming disenchanted with the nation's basic approach to health care. For example, some of the nation's largest employers have become very much concerned with high rates of absenteeism related to alcoholism and drug abuse. Moreover, employers pay more than one quarter of the nation's rapidly increasing medical costs. To contain alarming increases in self-inflicted illness and the skyrocketing medical costs, some of the largest corporations in the United States not only are searching for alternative methods of organizing and financing medical care but are also becoming interested in ways of providing better health education for the entire society. Meantime, as medical benefits take an ever larger share of funds that might otherwise be available for wage increases, labor unions are also increasingly concerned with alternative means of promoting better health (Sullivan 1984).

As the Business Roundtable, the U.S. Chamber of Commerce, and labor unions increasingly urge the nation to adopt more of a preventive approach to care and begin to pressure the federal government to undertake more research on preventive health, the potential increases that American society will become more conscious of the relationship between styles of living and better health.

For the first time in the twentieth century, there is a fundamental cleavage within the capitalist class in regard to medical technology. While many corporations reap handsome profits from the explosion in medical technology, others are threatened by its high costs. With such fundamental divisions over its escalating cost, medical delivery systems in all advanced capitalist societies are in a crisis. As a result, there is a serious reassessment of the nature of disease and the appropriate ways of preventing and treating it. Crises generate the potential for new attitudes and alternative institutions. And in this context, there is potential for reorienting the systems of medical care in American and British society. The process of educating the citizenry about better health is already underway. And in both countries, this educational process promises to acquire increasing political momentum. However, the way in which medical problems are defined and the strategies for solving them will probably respond to the needs of the society as perceived and defined by upper-income groups, as well as by state bureaucrats and policy-oriented intellectuals. In this sense, the medical profession's influence on the future of the medical delivery systems of Britain and the United States is likely to be somewhat diminished.

Bibliography

ABBREVIATIONS

GPO	Government Printing Office
Great Britain, Metropolitan Hospitals	Great Britain, Parliamentary Papers (Lords), *Report of the Committee on Metropolitan Hospitals*
Great Britain, MOH	Great Britain, Ministry of Health
Great Britain, NHS	Great Britain, Royal Commission on the National Health Service
Great Britain, Poor Laws	Great Britain, Parliamentary Papers (Commons), *Report of the Royal Commission on the Poor Laws*
Great Britain, University Education	Great Britain, Royal Commission on University Education in London
HMSO	Her/His Majesty's Stationery Office
U.S. Comm., Census	United States Department of Commerce, Bureau of the Census
U.S. Congress, House, Commerce	United States Congress, House, Committee on Interstate and Foreign Commerce
U.S. Congress, Senate, Judiciary	United States Congress, Senate, Committee on the Judiciary

Aaron, Henry J., and William B. Schwartz. *The Painful Prescription: Rationing Hospital Care.* Washington, D.C.: Brookings Institution, 1984.

Abel-Smith, Brian. *A History of the Nursing Profession in Great Britain.* New York: Springer Publishing Co., 1960.

Abel-Smith, Brian. *The Hospitals, 1800–1948.* London: Heinemann, 1964.

Abel-Smith, Brian. "The Major Pattern of Financing and the Organization of Medical Services That Have Emerged in Other Countries." *Medical Care* 3 (1965): 33–40.

Abel-Smith, Brian. *Value for Money in Health Services.* London: Heinemann, 1976.

Abel-Smith, Brian, and Richard Titmuss. *The Cost of the National Health Service in England and Wales.* Cambridge: Cambridge University Press, 1956.

Abrams, Herbert L., and Barbara J. McNeil. "Medical Implications of Computed Tomography." *New England Journal of Medicine* 298 (Feb. 2, 1978): 255–61; (Feb. 9, 1978): 310–18.

Abt Associates, Inc. *Incentives and Decisions underlying Hospitals' Adoption and Utilization of Major Capital Equipment.* Boston: HRA Contract no. HSM110–73–513, September, 1975.

Aday, LuAnn, Ronald Anderson, and Gretchen V. Fleming. *Health Care in the U.S.: Equitable for Whom?* Beverly Hills, Calif.: Sage Publications, 1980.

Aiken, Michael, and Jerald Hage. "The Organic Organization and Innovation." *Sociology* 5 (Jan. 1971): 63–82.

Alderson, M. R. "Social Class and the Health Service." *Medical Officer* 124 (1970): 50–52.

Alford, Robert R. *Health Care Politics: Ideological and Interest Group Barriers to Reform.* Chicago: University of Chicago Press, 1975.

Alford, Robert R. "The Political Economy of Health Care Dynamics without Change." *Politics and Society* 2 (Winter 1972): 127–64.

Alford, Robert R., and Roger Friedland. *Powers of Theory: Capitalism, the State, and Democracy.* Cambridge: Cambridge University Press, 1985.

Amenta, E., E. Clemens, J. Olsen, S. Parikh, and T. Skocpol. "Theories of Social Policy and the Origins of Unemployment Insurance in Five American States." Paper presented before the Social Science History Association, Toronto, 1984.

American College of Surgeons. *Surgery in the United States: A Summary Report of the Study on Surgical Services in the United States.* Chicago: American College of Surgeons and the American Surgical Association, 1975.

Anderson, Ronald, et al. *Two Decades of Health Services: Social Survey Trends in Use and Expenditure.* Cambridge, Mass.: Ballinger Publishing Co., 1976.

Anderson, Odin W. *Blue Cross since 1929: Accountability and the Public Trust.* Cambridge, Mass.: Ballinger Publishing Co., 1975.

Anderson, Odin W. "Compulsory Medical Care Insurance, 1910–1950." *Annals of the American Academy of Politics and Social Science* 273 (Jan. 1951): 106–13.

Anderson, Odin W. *Health Care: Can There Be Equity? The United States, Sweden, and England.* New York: John Wiley & Sons, 1972.

Anderson, Odin W. "Health Insurance in the United States, 1910–1920." *Journal of the History of Medicine and Allied Sciences* 5 (Autumn 1950): 363–95.

Anderson, Odin W. *The Uneasy Equilibrium: Private and Public Financing of Health Services in the United States, 1875–1965.* New Haven, Conn.: College and University Press, 1968.

Anderson, Odin W., and Jacob J. Feldman. "Distribution of Patients Hospitalized for Surgery in the U.S. from July, 1952 to July 1953." *Bulletin of the American College of Surgeons* 43 (Sept.–Oct. 1958): 236–41.

Anderson, Odin W., and Jacob J. Feldman. *Family Medical Costs and Voluntary Health Insurance: A Nationwide Survey.* New York: Blackiston Division, McGraw-Hill Book Co., 1956.

Anderson, Odin W., Terry E. Herold, Bruce W. Butler, Claire H. Kohrman, and Ellen M. Morrison. *HMO Development: Patterns and Prospects.* Chicago: Pluribus Press, 1985.

Anlyan, William G., et al., ed. *The Future of Medical Education.* Durham, N.C.: Duke University Press, 1973.

Arrow, Kenneth. "Uncertainty and the Welfare Economics of Medical Care." *American Economic Review* 53 (1963): 1950.

Atwater, Edward C. " 'Making Fewer Mistakes': A History of Students and Patients." *Bulletin of the History of Medicine* 57 (1983): 165–87.

Auster, Richard, Irving Leveson, and Deborah Sarachek. "The Production of Health: An Exploratory Study." *Journal of Human Resources* 4 (Fall 1969): 411–36.

Ayers, Gwendolyn. *England's First State Hospitals and the Metropolitan Asylums Board, 1867–1930.* London: Wellcome Institute of the History of Medicine, 1971.

Baker, Stephen R. "The Diffusion of High Technology Medical Innovation: The Computed Tomography Scanner Example." *Social Science and Medicine* 13D (Nov. 1979): 155–62.

Banta, H. David. "The Diffusion of the Computed Tomography (CT) Scanner in the United States." *International Journal of Health Services* 10 (1980): 251–69.

Barton, Richard Thomas. "Sources of Medical Morals." *Journal of the American Medical Association* 193 (1965): 133–38.

Beeson, Paul B. "McKeown's *The Role of Medicine*: A Clinician's Reaction." *Milbank Memorial Fund Quarterly* 55 (Summer 1977): 365–71.

Beeson, Paul B. "Some Good Features of the British National Health Services." *Journal of Medical Education* 49 (Jan. 1974): 43–49.

Beeson, Paul B. "The Ways of American Clinical Medicine in America since WW II." *Man and Medicine* 1 (Autumn 1975): 65–79.

Belknap, Ivan, and John G. Steinle. *The Community and Its Hospitals: A Comparative Analyses.* Syracuse: Syracuse University Press, 1963.

Bellot, H. Hale. *University College, London, 1826–1926.* London: University of London Press, 1929.

Ben-David, Joseph. "Scientific Productivity and Academic Organization in Nineteenth-Century Medicine." *American Sociological Review* 25 (1960): 828–43.

Ben-David, Joseph. *The Scientist's Role in Society: A Comparative Study.* Englewood Cliffs, N.J.: Prentice-Hall, 1971.

Bendick, Marc, Jr. "Education as a Three-Sector Industry." Ph.D. diss., University of Wisconsin, Madison, 1975.

Berlant, Jeffrey L. *Profession and Monopoly: A Study of Medicine in the United States and Great Britain.* Berkeley and Los Angeles: University of California Press, 1975.

Berliner, Howard S. "A Larger Perspective on the Flexner Report." *International Journal of Health Services* 5, no. 4 (1975): 573–92.

Berliner, Howard S. "Philanthropic Foundations and Scientific Medicine." Ph.D. diss., Johns Hopkins University, 1977.

Berliner, Howard S. *A System of Scientific Medicine: Philanthropic Foundations in the Flexner Era.* New York: Travistock Publications, 1986.

Berliner, Robert W., and Thomas J. Kennedy. "National Expenditures for Biomedical Research." *Journal of Medical Education* 45 (Sept. 1970): 666–78.

Beveridge, Sir William. *Social Insurance and Allied Services.* New York: Macmillan, 1942.

Bicknell, W. J., and J. Van Wyck. "Certificate-of-Need: The Massachusetts Experience: January 1974–June 1979." Mimeograph, 1979.

Billings, John S. "Literature and Institutions." In Edward H. Clarke, et al., *A Century of American Medicine.* Philadelphia: Lea Publishing, 1876.

Björkman, James W., "Politicizing Medicine and Medicalizing Politics: Physician Power in the United States." In Giorgio Freddi and James W. Björkman, eds., *Controlling Medical Professionals: The Comparative Politics of Health Governance.* London: Sage Publications, forthcoming.

Blackstone, Erwin A. "The Condition of Surgery: An Analysis of the American College of Surgeons and the American Surgical Association's Report on the Status of Surgery." *Milbank Memorial Fund Quarterly* 55 (Fall 1977): 429–54.

Blackstone, Erwin A. "Misallocation of Medical Resources: The Problem of Excessive Surgery." *Public Policy* 22 (Summer 1974): 329–52.

Blagg, Christopher R., and Belding H. Scribner. "Dialysis: Medical, Psychological, and Economic Problems Unique to the Dialysis Patient." In Barry M. Brenner and Floyd C. Rector, eds., *The Kidney,* vol. 2. Philadelphia: W. B. Saunders Co., 1976.

Block, Fred. "Beyond Relative Autonomy: State Managers as Historical Subjects." In Ralph Miliband and John Saville, eds., *Socialist Register.* London: Merlin Press, 1980.

Bluemle, Lewis W., Jr. "Dialysis." In Maurice B. Strauss and Louis G. Welt, eds., *Diseases of the Kidney.* Boston: Little, Brown & Co., 1971.

Bonner, Thomas N. *American Doctors and German Universities.* Lincoln: University of Nebraska Press, 1963.

Bonner, Thomas N. *The Kansas Doctor: A Century of Pioneering.* Lawrence: University of Kansas Press, 1959.

Bonner, Thomas N. *Medicine in Chicago.* New York: Stratford Press, 1957.

Bordley, James, and A. McGehee Harvey. *Two Centuries of American Medicine 1776–1976.* Philadelphia: W. B. Saunders Co., 1976.

Bowles, Samuel, and Herbert Gintis. *Schooling in Capitalist America: Changing Prospects in Western Society.* New York: John Wiley & Sons, 1976.

Boyden, S. V., ed. *The Impact of Civilization on the Biology of Man.* Toronto: University of Toronto Press, 1970.

Brand, Jeanne L. *Doctors and the State.* Baltimore: Johns Hopkins Press, 1965.

Braun, Percy. "The Cost, Condition and Results of Hospital Relief in London." *Journal of the Royal Statistical Society* 72 (Mar. 1909): 1–30.

Brearley, Paul. *The Social Context of Health Care.* London: Martin Robertson, 1978.

Brend, William. *Health and the State.* London: Constable & Co., 1917.

"British Medical Journal Reports Provincial Infirmaries." *British Medical Journal* 1 (June 1, 1895): 1231–32.

Brooks, Harvey. "The Physical Sciences: Bellwether of Science Policy." In James A Shannon, ed., *Science and the Evolution of Public Policy.* New York: Rockefeller University Press, 1973.

Brooks, Harvey. "The Problem of Research Priorities." *Daedalus* 107 (Spring 1978): 171–90.

Brown, J. H. U. *The Politics of Health Care.* Cambridge, Mass.: Ballinger Publishing Co., 1978.

Brown, Lawrence D. "The Formation of Federal Health Care Policy." *Bulletin of the New York Academy of Medicine* 54 (1978): 45–58.

Brown, Lawrence D. *Politics and Health Care Organization: HMOs as Federal Policy.* Washington, D.C.: Brookings Institution, 1983.

Brown, Richard E. *Rockefeller Medicine Men.* Berkeley and Los Angeles: University of California Press, 1979.

Bruce, Maurice. *The Coming of the Welfare State.* New York: Schocken Books, 1966.

Bunker, John P. "When Doctors Disagree." *New York Review of Books* 27, no. 7 (Apr. 25, 1985): 7–12.

Bunker, John P. "Surgical Manpower." *New England Journal of Medicine* 282 (Jan. 15, 1970): 135–44.

Bunker, John P., and John E. Wennberg. "Operation Rates, Mortality Statistics and the Quality of Life." *New England Journal of Medicine* 289 (Dec. 6, 1973): 1249–51.

Burdett, Henry C. *Burdett's Hospital Annual and Yearbook of Philanthropy.* (An annual yearbook published under various titles over the next several decades.)

Burkitt, Denis P. "Epidemiology of Cancer of the Colon and Rectum." *Cancer* 28 (July 1971): 3–13.

Burrow, James G. *AMA, Voice of American Medicine.* Baltimore: Johns Hopkins Press, 1963.

Burrow, James G. *Organized Medicine in the Progressive Era: The Move toward Monopoly.* Baltimore: Johns Hopkins University Press, 1977.

Cameron, H. C. *Mr. Guy's Hospital 1726–1948.* London: Longmans, Green & Co., 1954.

Cameron, Stewart. *Kidney Diseases: The Facts.* London: Oxford University Press, 1981.

Campbell, Walter J. "The Emergency Health Care Environment: Selected Issues." In Cotton M. Lindsay, ed., *The Pharmaceutical Industry.* New York: John Wiley & Sons, 1978.

Cardwell, Donald S. L. *The Organization of Science in England.* London: Heinemann, 1957.

Carlson, Rick. *The End of Medicine.* New York: John Wiley & Sons, 1975.

Carnoy, Martin. *The State and Political Theory.* Princeton: Princeton University Press, 1984.

Carter, C. O., and John Peel, ed., *Equalities and Inequalities in Health.* New York: Academic Press, 1976.

Cartwright, Ann. *Human Relations and Hospital Care.* London: Routledge & Kegan Paul, 1964.

Cartwright, Ann. *Patients and Their Doctors.* London: Routledge & Kegan Paul, 1967.

Cartwright, Ann, and M. O'Brien. "Social Class Variations in Health Care and in the Nature of General Practitioner Consultations." In M. Stacey, ed., *The Soci-*

ology of the National Health Service. Sociological Review Monograph, Keele, Eng.: Keele University Press, 1976.

Chapman, Carleton B. "The Flexner Report by Abraham Flexner." *Daedalus* 103 (Winter 1974): 105–17.

Chesney, Alan M. *The Johns Hopkins Hospital and the Johns Hopkins University School of Medicine: A Chronicle.* Vol. 2, 1893–1905. Baltimore: Johns Hopkins Press, 1958.

Chesney, Alan M. *The Johns Hopkins Hospital and the Johns Hopkins University School of Medicine: A Chronicle.* Vol. 3, 1905–1914. Baltimore: Johns Hopkins Press, 1963.

Christianson, Jon B., and Walter McClure. "Competition in the Delivery of Medical Care." *New England Journal of Medicine* 30 (Oct. 11, 1979): 812–18.

Clark, George. *A History of the Royal College of Physicians of London.* 2 vols. Oxford: At the Clarendon Press, 1964–66.

Cochrane, A. L. *Effectiveness and Efficiency: Random Reflections on Health Services.* London: Nuffield Provincial Hospitals Trust, 1972.

Coggeshall, Lowell T. *Planning for Medical Progress through Education.* Evanston, Ill.: Association of American Medical Colleges, 1965.

Cole, Jonathan R., and Stephen Cole. "The Ortego Hypothesis." *Science* 178 (Oct. 27, 1972): 368–75.

Collins, Elizabeth, and Rudolph Klein. "Equity and the NHS: Self-Reported Morbidity." *British Medical Journal* 281 (Oct. 25, 1980): 1111–15.

Commission on Public-General Hospitals, *The Future of the Public-General Hospital: An Agenda for Transition.* Chicago: Hospital Research and Educational Trust, 1978.

Committee on the Costs of Medical Care. *The Final Report of the Committee on the Costs of Medical Care.* Chicago: University of Chicago Press, 1932.

Cooper, Michael H. "Economics of Need: The Experience of the British Health Service." In Mark Perlman, ed., *The Economics of Health and Medical Care.* New York: John Wiley & Sons, 1974.

Cooper, Michael H. *Prices and Profits in the Pharmaceutical Industry.* London: Pergamon Press, 1966.

Cooper, Michael H. *Rationing Health Care.* New York: John Wiley & Sons, 1975.

Cooper, Michael H., and A. J. Cooper. *International Price Comparisons: A Study of the Prices of Pharmaceuticals in the United Kingdom and Eight Other Countries.* London: National Economic Development Office, 1972.

Corner, George W. *A History of the Rockefeller Institute, 1901–1953.* New York: Rockefeller Institute Press, 1964.

Corwin, E. H. L. *The American Hospital.* New York: Commonwealth Fund, 1946.

Cronin, James E. *Labour and Society in Britain 1918–1979.* London: Batsford Academic, 1984.

Cronin, James E., and Jonathan Schneer, eds. *Social Conflict and the Political Order in Modern Britain.* New Brunswick, N.J.: Rutgers University Press, 1982.

Culyer, A. J. *Need and the National Health Service.* London: Martin Robertson, 1976.

Culyer, Anthony, Alan Maynard, and Alan Williams. "An Essay on Motes and Beams: An Appraisal of Alternative Mechanisms for the Provision of Health

Care." Paper presented before Conference on Health Care sponsored by American Enterprise Institute for Public Policy Research, Sept. 1980.

Cuthbert, M. F. "Developments in the United Kingdom Drug Regulatory System." In P. E. Lucchelli, N. Benjamin, and V. Bachini, eds., *Rationality of Drug Development.* New York: American Elsevier Publishing Co., 1976.

Davis, Karen. (a) "Economic Theories of Behavior in Nonprofit, Private Hospitals." *Economic Theories of Behavior* 24 (Winter 1972): 1–13.

Davis, Karen. (b) "Rising Hospital Costs: Possible Causes and Cures." *Bulletin of the New York Academy of Medicine* 48 (Dec. 1972): 1354–71.

Davis, Karen. "Theories of Hospital Inflation: Some Empirical Evidence." *Journal of Human Resources* 8 (1974): 181–201.

Davis, Karen. (a) "Equal Treatment and Unequal Benefits: The Medicare Program." *Milbank Memorial Fund Quarterly* 53 (Fall 1975): 449–88.

Davis, Karen. (b) *National Health Insurance: Benefits, Costs and Consequences.* Washington, D.C.: Brookings Institution, 1975.

Davis, Karen. (a) "Achievements and Problems of Medicaid." *Public Health Reports* 91 (July–Aug. 1976): 313–16.

Davis, Karen. (b) "A Decade of Policy Developments in Providing Health Care for Low-Income Families." In Robert Haveman, ed., *A Decade of Federal Antipoverty Programs: Achievements, Failures, and Lessons.* New York: Academic Press, 1976.

Davis, Karen. (c) "Medicaid Payments and Utilization of Medical Services by the Poor." *Inquiry* 13 (June 1976): 122–35.

Davis, Karen, and Cathy Schoen. *Health and the War on Poverty: A Ten-Year Appraisal.* Washington, D.C.: Brookings Institution, 1978.

Davis, Michael M., Jr. *Clinics, Hospitals and Health Centers.* New York: Committee on Dispensary Development of the United Hospital Fund of New York, 1927.

Davis, Michael M., Jr., and Andrew R. Warner. *Dispensaries: Their Management and Development.* New York: Macmillan, 1918.

Derbyshire, Robert C. *Medical Licensure and the Discipline in the United States.* Baltimore: Johns Hopkins Press, 1969.

Diehl, Harold S., et al. "Medical Education in Great Britain." *Journal of the American Medical Association* 44 (1950): 32–51.

Doll, R. "The Geographical Distribution of Cancer." *British Journal of Cancer,* Mar. 23, 1969, pp. 1–8.

Domhoff, G. William. *The Higher Circles: The Governing Class in America.* New York: Vintage Books, 1971.

Donabedian, Avedis. *Benefits in Medical Care Programs.* Cambridge, Mass.: Harvard University Press, 1976.

Drew, Elizabeth. "The Health Syndicate: Washington's Noble Conspirators." *Atlantic Monthly* 220 (Dec. 1967): 75–82.

Dubos, René. *Man, Medicine and Environment.* New York: Frederick A. Praeger, 1968.

Dunham, Andrew R., and Theodore Marmor. "Federal Policy and Health: Recent Trends and Differing Perspectives." In Theodor J. Lowi and Alan Stone, eds., *Nationalizing Government: Public Polices in America.* Beverly Hills, Calif.: Sage Publications, 1978.

Dunlop, Derrick. "The British System of Drug Regulation." In Richard Landau, ed., *Regulating New Drugs*, 230–37. Chicago: University of Chicago Press, 1973.

Eckstein, Harry. *The English Health Services*. Cambridge, Mass.: Harvard University Press, 1958.

Eckstein, Harry. "The Politics of the British Medical Association." *Political Quarterly* 26 (1955): 345–59.

Eckstein, Harry. *Pressure Group Politics*. London: George Allen & Unwin, 1960.

Ehrenreich, Barbara, and John Ehrenreich. *The American Health Empire: Power, Profits and Politics*. New York: Vintage Books, 1971.

Eliot, Charles. *Harvard Memories*. Cambridge, Mass.: Harvard University Press, 1923.

Ellwood, Paul N., and Michael E. Herbert. "Health Care: Should Industry Buy It or Sell It?" *Harvard Business Review* 51 (July–Aug. 1973): 99–107.

Ellwood, Paul M., and Earl Hoagberg. "Problems of the Public Hospital." *Hospitals* 44 (July 1, 1970): 47–52.

English, Manuel L. "Budgeting for National Health Expenditures: The British System." *World Hospitals* 12 (1976): 164–71.

Enthoven, Alain C. (a) "Consumer-Choice Health Plan." *New England Journal of Medicine* 298 (Mar. 23, 1978): 650–68; (Mar. 30, 1978): 709–20.

Enthoven Alain C. (b) "Shattuck Lecture—Cutting Cost without Cutting the Quality of Care." *New England Journal of Medicine* 298 (June 1, 1978): 1229–38.

Enthoven, Alain C. *Health Plan: The Only Practical Solution to the Soaring Cost of Medical Care*. Reading, Mass.: Addison-Wesley Publishing Co., 1980.

Epstein, F. H. "The Epidemiology of Coronary Heart Disease: A Review." *Journal of Chronic Diseases* 18 (1965): 735–74.

Evans, P. B., D. Rueschemeyer, and Theda Skocpol. *Bringing the State Back In*. New York: Cambridge University Press, 1985.

Evans, Robert G. "Supplier-Induced Demand: Some Empirical Evidence and Implications." In Mark Perlman, ed., *The Economics of Health and Medical Care*. New York: John Wiley & Sons, 1974.

Evens, Ronald G. "The Economics of Computed Tomography: Comparison with Other Health Care Costs." *Radiology* 136 (Aug. 1980): 509–10.

Falk, I. S., et al. *The Incidence of Illness and the Receipt and Costs of Medical Care among Representative Families in Twelve Consecutive Months during 1928–1931*. Committee on the Costs of Medical Care, report 26. Chicago: University of Chicago Press, 1933.

Feder, Judith, Jack Hadley, and Ross Mullner. "Falling through the Cracks: Poverty, Insurance Coverage, and Hospital Care for the Poor, 1980 and 1982." *Health and Society* 62, no. 4 (1984): 544–66.

Feder, Judith, Jack Hadley, and Ross Mullner. "Poor People and Poor Hospitals: Implications for Public Policy." *Journal of Health Politics, Policy and Law* 9 (Summer 1984): 237–50.

Falkner, Frank. ed. *Advisory Conferences on Key Issues in Infant Mortality*. Washington, D.C.: GPO, 1969.

Feinbaum, Robert. "The Doctor and the Public: A Case Study of Professional Politics." Ph.D. diss., University of California, Berkeley, 1970.

Feldstein, Martin S. "The High Cost of Hospitals and What to Do about It." *Public Interest* 48 (1977): 40–54.

Feldstein, Martin S. *Economic Analysis for Health Service Efficiency.* Amsterdam: North-Holland Publishing Co., 1967.

Felstein, Martin S. "Hospital Cost Inflation: A Study of Nonprofit Price Dynamics." *American Economic Review* 61 (1971): 853–72.

Feldstein, Martin S. *The Rising Cost of Hospital Care.* Washington, D.C.: Information Resources Press, 1971.

Feldstein, Martin S. "The Rising Price of Physicians Services." *Review of Economics and Statistics* 52 (1970): 121–33.

Feldstein, Martin S. "Developments in Health Service Administration and Financial Control." *Medical Care* 1 (May 1963): 171–77.

Felstein, Martin S., and B. Friedman. "Tax Subsidies, the Rational Demand for Insurance and the Health Care Crisis." Discussion Paper no. 382. Cambridge, Mass.: Harvard Institute for Economic Research, 1947.

Feldstein, Martin M., and Amy Taylor. *The Rapid Rise of Hospital Costs.* Washington, D.C.: Executive Office of the President, Council on Wage and Price Stability, Jan. 1977.

Fisher, Donald. "The Impact of American Foundations on the Development of British University Education, 1900–1939." Ph.D. diss., University of California, Berkeley, 1977.

Fisher, Donald. "The Rockefeller Foundation and the Development of Scientific Medicine in Great Britain." *Minerva* 16 (Spring 1978): 20–41.

Fleming, Donald. *William H. Welch and the Rise of Modern Medicine.* Boston: Little, Brown & Co., 1954.

Flexner, Abraham. *Medical Education: A Comparative Study.* New York: Macmillan, 1925.

Flexner, Abraham. *Medical Education in Europe.* New York: Carnegie Foundation, 1912.

Flexner, Abraham. *Medical Education in the United States and Canada.* Boston: Merrymount Press, 1910.

Flexner, Simon, and James Thomas Flexner. *William Henry Welch and the Heroic Age of American Medicine.* New York: Viking Press, 1941.

Foner, Eric. "Why Is There No Socialism in the United States?" *History Workshop Journal* 17 (Spring 1984): 57–80.

Forsyth, Gordon. *Doctors and State Medicine: A Study of the British Health.* London: Pittman Medical, 1966.

Fowler, William. "Smallpox Vaccination Laws, Regulations, and Court Decisions." *Public Health Reports,* Supplement no. 60, 1–74. Washington, D.C.: GPO, 1927.

Fox, Daniel M. *Economists and Health Care.* New York: Prodist, 1979.

Fox, Peter D. "Options for National Health Insurance: An Overview." *Policy Analysis* 3, no. 1 (1977): 1–25.

Fox, Renee C., and Judith P. Swazey. *The Courage to Fail.* Chicago: University of Chicago Press, 1974.

Frech, H.E., III. "The Long-Lost Free Market in Health Care: Government Regulation of Medicine." Paper presented before the Conference on Health Care sponsored by American Enterprise Institute for Public Policy Research, Sept. 1980.

Fredrickson, Donald S. "Health and the Search for New Knowledge." In John H. Knowles, ed., *Doing Better and Feeling Worse: Health in the United States.* New York: W. W. Norton & Co., 1977.

Freidson, Eliot. *The Hospital in Modern Society.* London: Collier Macmillan, 1963.

Freidson, Eliot. *Profession of Medicine.* New York: Dodd, Mead & Co. 1973.

Friedman, Milton, and Simon Kuznets. *Income from Independent Professional Practice.* New York: National Bureau of Economic Research, 1945.

Fuchs, Victor R. (a) "Some Economic Aspects of Mortality in Developed Countries." In Mark Perlman, ed., *The Economics of Health and Medical Care.* New York: John Wiley & Sons, 1974.

Fuchs, Victor R. (b) *Who Shall Live?* New York: Basic Books, 1974.

Fuchs, Victor R. "Economics, Health, and Post-Industrial Society." *Milbank Memorial Fund Quarterly* 57 (Spring 1979): 153–82.

Fuchs, Victor R. *Essays in the Economics of Health and Medical Care.* New York: Columbia University Press for the National Bureau of Economic Research, 1972.

Fuchs, Victor R. *The Healthy Economy.* Cambridge, Mass.: Harvard University Press, 1986.

Gaston, Jerry. *The Reward System in British and American Science.* New York: John Wiley & Sons, 1978.

Geijerstam, Gunnar. "Low Birth Weight and Prenatal Mortality." *Public Health Reports* 84 (Nov. 11, 1969): 939–48.

Geison, Gerald L. *Michael Foster and the Cambridge School of Physiology.* Princeton: Princeton University Press, 1978.

Gempel, P. A., G. H. Harris, and R. G. Evens. *Comparative Cost Analysis: Computed Tomography versus Alternative Diagnostic Procedures, 1977 and 1980.* Cambridge, Mass.: Arthur D. Little, 1977.

Gilbert, Bentley B. *The Evolution of National Insurance in Great Britain.* London: Joseph, 1966.

Gill, D. G. "The British National Health Service: Professional Determinants of Administrative Structure." *International Journal of Health Services* 1 (1971): 342–52.

Ginsburg, Paul B., and Daniel M. Koretz. *The Effect of PSROs on Health Care Costs: Current Findings and Future Evaluations.* Washington, D.C.: Congressional Budget Office, 1979.

Ginzberg, Eli. *The Limits of Health Reform: The Search for Realism.* New York: Basic Books, 1977.

Glaser, William A. *Paying the Doctor.* Baltimore: Johns Hopkins Press, 1970.

Glaser, William A. *Paying the Doctor under National Health Insurance: Foreign Lessons for the United States.* Columbia University, Dec. 1975.

Golding, A. M. B., and D. Tosey. "The Cost of High-Technology Medicine." *Lancet,* July 26, 1980, pp. 195–97.

Goldsmith, Jeff C. *Can Hospitals Survive?* Homewood, Ill.: Dow Jones–Irwin, 1981.

Goodman, John C. (a) *National Health Care in Great Britain: Lessons for the U.S.A.* Dallas: Fisher Institute, 1980.

Goodman, John C. (b) *The Regulation of Medical Care: Is the Price Too High?* San Francisco: Cato Institute, 1980.

Gortmaker, Steven. (a) "The Effects of Prenatal Care upon the Health of the Newborn." *American Journal of Public Health* 69 (July 1979): 653–60.

Gortmaker, Steven. (b) "Poverty and Infant Mortality in the United States." *American Sociological Review* 44 (Apr. 1979): 280–97.

Gortmaker, Steven. "Stratification, Health Care and Infant Mortality in the United States." Ph.D. diss., University of Wisconsin, Madison, 1977.

Gould, George M. "Charity Organization and Medicine: The President's Address." *Bulletin of the American Academy of Medicine* 1 (1894): 547–48.

Grabowski, Henry G. *Drug Regulation and Innovation: Empirical Evidence and Policy Options.* Washington, D.C.: American Enterprise Institute for Public Policy Research, 1976.

Grabowski, Henry G., and John M. Vernon. "New Studies on Market Definition, Concentration, Theory of Supply, Entry, and Promotion." In Robert I. Chien, ed., *Issues in Pharmaceutical Economics*, 29–52. Lexington, Mass.: Lexington Books, 1979.

Graham-Smith, D. G. "Problems Facing a Regulatory Authority." In J. F. Cavalla, ed., *Risk-Benefit Analysis in Drug Research.* Lancaster, Eng.: MTP Press, 1981.

Great Britain. Central Office of Information. Reference Division. *Health Services in Britain.* London: HMSO, 1974.

Great Britain. Department of Health and Social Security. *Health and Personal Social Service Statistics.* London: HMSO, 1972.

Great Britain. Ministry of Health. *Annual Report of the Ministry of Health for the Year 1967.* London HMSO, 1968.

Great Britain. Ministry of Health. *Hospital Survey.* London: HMSO, 1945–46.

Great Britain. Ministry of Health. *Postgraduate Medical Education and the Specialties.* London: HMSO, 1962.

Great Britain. Ministry of Health. Consultative Council on Medical and Allied Services (Dawson Committee). *Interim Report on the Future Provision of Medical and Allied Services.* Cmd. 693. London: HMSO, 1920.

Great Britain. Ministry of Health. Inter-departmental Committee on Medical Schools. *Report* (Goodenough Report) London: HMSO, 1944.

Great Britain. Ministry of Health. Voluntary Hospitals Committee (Cave Committee). *Interim Report.* Cmd. 1206. London: HMSO, 1921.

Great Britain. Office of Population Censuses and Surveys. *Decennial Census, 1891–1971.* London: HMSO.

Great Britain. Office of Population Censuses and Surveys. *Occupational Mortality: The Registrar General's Decennial Supplement for England and Wales, 1970–72.* London: HMSO, 1978.

Great Britain. Office of Population Censuses and Surveys. Social Survey Division. *The General Household Survey: Introductory Report.* London: HMSO, 1973.

Great Britain. Parliamentary Papers (Commons). *Report of the Royal Commission on National Health Insurance.* Cmd. 2596. London: HMSO, 1928.

Great Britain. Parliamentary Papers (Commons). *Report of the Royal Commission on the Poor Laws.* London: HMSO, 1909.

Great Britain. Parliamentary Papers (Lords). *Report of the Committee on Metropolitan Hospitals.* Vols. 12, 13, 14, 1890–1892. Shannon: Irish University Press, 1970.

Great Britain. Registrar General. *Reports, 1891–1971.* London: HMSO.

Great Britain. Registrar General. *Statistical Reviews of England and Wales for the Year 1971.* London: HMSO, 1971.

Great Britain. Royal Commission on Medical Education. *Report, 1965–1968.* Cmd. 3569. London: HMSO, 1968.

Great Britain. Royal Commission on National Health Insurance. *Report.* London: HMSO 1926.

Great Britain. Royal Commission on the National Health Service. *Report.* London: HMSO, 1979.

Great Britain. Royal Commission on University Education in London. *Fifth Report of the Commissioners,* appendix. Cmd. 6312. London: HMSO, 1912.

Great Britain. Royal Commission on University Education in London. *Third Report of the Commissioners.* Cmd. 5910. London: HMSO, 1911.

Great Britain. Royal Commission on Workman's Compensation. *Report.* Cmd. 6588. London: HMSO, 1944–45.

Green, Ronald M. "*Beyond the Role of Medicine:* McKeown as a Medical Philosopher." *Milbank Memorial Fund Quarterly* 55 (Summer 1977): 389–403.

Greenberg, Daniel S. *The Politics of Pure Science.* New York: New American Library, 1967.

Gregory, Janet. *Patients' Attitudes to the Hospital Services.* Royal Commission on the National Health Service Research Paper No. 5. London: HMSO, 1978.

Grob, Gerald N. *The State and the Mentally Ill.* Chapel Hill: University of North Carolina Press, 1966.

Grossman, Michael. *The Demand for Health: A Theoretical and Empirical Investigation.* New York: Columbia University Press for the National Bureau of Economic Research, 1972.

Grossman, Michael. "The Correlation Between Health and Schooling." In N. E. Terleckyj, ed., *Household Production and Consumption.* New York: Columbia University Press, 1976.

Grossman, Michael, and Steven Jacobowitz. "Variations in Infant Mortality Rates among Counties of the United States: The Roles of Public Policy and Programs." *Demography* 18 (Nov. 1981): 695–713.

Grove, Robert D., and Alice M. Hetzel. *Vital Statistics Rates in the United States 1940–1960.* Washington, D.C.: National Center for Health Statistics, 1968.

Guralnick, Lillian. *Mortality by Occupation and Cause of Death among Men Twenty to Sixty-four Years of Age: United States, 1950.* Vital Statistics: Special Reports, no. 53. Washington, D.C.: GPO, 1963.

Hage, Jerald. *Theories of Organizations: Form, Process, and Transformation.* New York: John Wiley & Sons, 1980.

Hage, Jerald, and Michael Aiken. *Social Change in Complex Organizations.* New York: Random House, 1970.

Hage, Jerald, and J. Rogers Hollingsworth. "The First Steps toward the Integration of Social Theory and Social Policy." *Annals of the American Academy of Political and Social Science* 434 (Nov. 1977): 1–23.

Hanneman, Robert, and J. Rogers Hollingsworth. "Modeling and Simulation in Historical Inquiry." *Historical Methods* 17 (Summer 1984): 150–63.

Harper, Alfred E. "Dietary Goals: A Skeptical View." *American Journal of Clinical Nutrition* 31 (Feb. 1978): 310–21.

Harper, Alfred E. " 'Healthy People': Critique of the Nutrition Segments of the Surgeon General's Report on Health Promotion and Disease Prevention." *American Journal of Clinical Nutrition* 33 (July 1980): 1703–12.

Harrell, George R. "Osler's Practice." *Bulletin of the History of Medicine* 47 (Nov.-Dec. 1973): 545–68.

Harris, R. W. *National Health Insurance in Great Britain 1911–1946.* London: George Allen & Unwin, 1946.

Hart, Julian Tudor. (a) "Primary Care in the Industrial Areas of Britain." *International Journal of Health Services* 2 (Aug. 1972): 349–65.

Hart, Julian Tudor. (b) "Reform and Reaction in Medical Care." *International Journal of Health Services* 2 (1972): 567–74.

Hart, Julian Tudor. "Bevan and the Doctors." *Lancet,* Nov. 24, 1973, pp. 1196–97.

Hart, Julian Tudor. "The Inverse Care Law." *Lancet,* Feb. 27, 1971, pp. 405–12.

Hart, Julian Tudor. "McKeown's *The Role of Medicine*: Advancing Backwards." *Milbank Memorial Fund Quarterly* 55 (Summer 1977): 383–88.

Havighurst, Clark C. "Controlling Health Care Costs." *Journal of Health Politics, Policy and Law* 1 (Winter 1977): 471–98.

Havighurst, Clark C. "Health Maintenance Organizations and the Market for Health Services." *Law and Contemporary Problems* 35 (1970): 716–95.

Havighurst, Clark C. *Public Utility Regulation for Hospitals: The Relevance of Experience in Other Related Industries.* Washington, D.C.: Booz, Allen & Hamilton, 1973.

Havighurst, Clark C., and James F. Blumstein. "Coping With Quality/Cost Trade-Offs in Medical Care: The Role of PSROs." *Northwestern University Law Review* 70 (1976): 6–68.

Health Care Financing Review 1 (Summer 1979): 22.

Hearnshaw, F. J. C. *The Centenary History of King's College, London, 1828–1928.* London: Harrop, 1929.

Heclo, H. *Modern Social Politics in Britain and Sweden.* New Haven, Conn.: Yale University Press, 1974.

Heidenheimer, Arnold J., and John Layson. "Approaches toward Universality and Recourse to Selectivity in American and European Social Policies: The Longer View." Paper prepared for the Conference on Universal Versus Income-Tested Transfer Programs, sponsored by the Institute for Research on Poverty, University of Wisconsin, Madison, Mar. 1979 (Political Science Paper no. 20).

Herbert, S. Mervyn. *Britain's Health.* Harmondsworth, Eng.: Penguin Books, 1939.

Herman, Tom. "When Medicare Stops." *Wall Street Journal,* June 18, 1979.

Hertzler, Arthur. *The Horse and Buggy Doctor.* New York: Harper & Brothers, 1938.

Hirschfield, Daniel S. *The Lost Reform: The Campaign for Compulsory Health Insurance in the United States from 1932 to 1943.* Cambridge, Mass.: Harvard University Press, 1970.

Hogarth, James. *The Payment of the General Practitioner.* New York: Pergamon Press, 1963.

Holahan, James. *Financing Health Care for the Poor: The Medicaid Experience.* Lexington, Mass.: Lexington Books, 1975.

Holland, Walter. "McKeown's *The Role of Medicine*: A View from Social Medicine." *Milbank Memorial Fund Quarterly* 55 (Summer 1977): 379–82.

Hollingsworth, J. Rogers. "Inequality in Levels of Health in England and Wales, 1891–1971." *Journal of Health and Social Behavior* 22 (Sept. 1981): 268–83.

Hollingsworth, J. Rogers. "Perspectives on Inequality in Education and Health in Great Britain and the United States." Paper presented before the Comparative and International Education Society, Toronto, Feb. 1976.

Hollingsworth, J. Rogers. "The Political-Structural Basis for Economic Performance." *Annals of the American Academy of Political and Social Science* 459 (Jan. 1982): 28–45.

Hollingsworth, J. Rogers, and Jerald Hage. "Social Costs and Benefits of Health and Educational Policies in Four Western Countries." Paper presented before the American Historical Association, Dec. 1974.

Hollingsworth, J. Rogers, Jerald Hage, and Robert Hanneman. (a) "The Impact of the Organization of Health Delivery Systems on Health Efficiency: A Comparative Analysis of the United States, France, and Great Britain." Paper presented before the American Sociological Association, San Francisco, Sept. 1978.

Hollingsworth, J. Rogers, Jerald Hage, and Robert Hanneman. (b) "Social Structure and the Diffusion of Medical Innovations in the United States, Great Britain, Sweden, and France." Paper presented before the World Congress of Sociology, Uppsala, Aug. 1978.

Hollingsworth, J. Rogers, and Robert Hanneman. *Centralization and Power in Social Delivery Systems: The Cases of England, Wales, and the United States.* Boston: Kluwer-Nijhoff Publishing Co., 1983.

Hollingsworth, J. Rogers, and Robert Hanneman. "Centralization in Health and Education Delivery Systems: British and American Experience." Paper presented before the American Political Science Association, New York, Sept. 1978.

Hollingsworth, J. Rogers, and R. A. Hanneman. "Working-Class Power and the Political Economy of Western Capitalist Societies." *Comparative Social Research* 5 (1982): 61–80.

Hollingsworth, J. Rogers, and Ellen Jane Hollingsworth. "Differences between Voluntary and Public Organizations: The Behavior of Hospitals in England and Wales." *Journal of Health Politics, Policy and Law* 10 (Summer 1985): 371–97.

Hollingsworth, J. Rogers, and Ellen Jane Hollingsworth. "A Study of Voluntary, For-Profit, and Public Sector Organizations: The Case of American Hospitals." Forthcoming.

Hollingsworth, J. Rogers, and Ellen Jane Hollingsworth. "Voluntary and Public Hospitals in England and Wales." Working Paper no. 75. New Haven, Conn.: Yale University Program on Non-Profit Organizations, 1983.

Hollingsworth, J. Rogers, et al. "The Structure and Performance of Medical Deliv-

ery Systems: The Cases of France, Great Britain, Sweden, and the United States."
Forthcoming.

Hollis, Ernest V. *Philanthropic Foundations and Higher Education*. New York:
Columbia University Press, 1938.

Honigsbaum, Frank. *The Division in British Medicine: A History of the Separation of General Practice from Hospital Care, 1911–1968*. New York: St. Martin's
Press, 1979.

Huebscher, Julian. "Surgeons and Operations." *New England Journal of Medicine*
282 (May 7, 1970): 1106.

Illich, Ivan. *Medical Nemesis: The Expropriation of Health*. New York: Pantheon
Books, 1976.

Jacobs, Philip. "A Survey of Economic Models of Hospitals." *Inquiry* 10 (June
1974): 83–97.

Jencks, Christopher, et al. *Inequality: A Reassessment of the Effect of Family and
Schooling in America*. New York: Basic Books, 1972.

Jewkes, John, and Sylvia Jewkes. *The Genesis of the British National Health Services*. Oxford: Basil Blackwell & Mott, 1961.

Johnson, Robert F., and Kenneth H. Wildrick. " 'State of the Art' Review of the
Impact of Chemotherapy on the Care of Patients with Tuberculosis." *American
Review of Respiratory Disease* 109 (1974): 636–64.

Jones, Francis Avery, and Mary McCarthy. "Understanding Waiting Lists."
Lancet, July 1, 1978, pp. 34–36.

Jones, Philip R. *Doctors and the B.M.A.: A Case Study in Collective Action*.
Westmead, Eng.: Gower Publishing Co., 1981.

Jones, R. J. *Atherosclerosis: Proceedings of the Second International Symposium*.
New York: Springer Publishing Co., 1970.

Joskow, Paul. "Alternative Regulatory Mechanisms for Controlling Hospital
Costs." Paper presented before the Conference on Health Care sponsored by
American Enterprise Institute for Public Policy Research, Sept. 1980.

Journal of the American Medical Association 62 (Apr. 25, June 6, June 13, 1914);
63 (Jan. 30, Dec. 11, 1915); 80 (Dec. 3, 1932).

Karl, Barry D., and Stanley N. Katz. "The American Private Philanthropic Foundation and the Public Sphere, 1890–1930." *Minerva* 19 (Summer 1981): 236–70.

Katz, Sidney, et. al. "Measuring the Health Status of Populations." In *Health Status Indices*. Chicago: Hospital Research and Education Trust, 1973.

Katznelson, Ira. "Working-Class Formation and the State: Nineteenth-Century
England in American Perspective." In Evans, Rueschemeyer, and Skocpol,
Bringing the State Back In. New York: Cambridge University Press, 1985.

Kaufman, Martin. *American Medical Education: The Formative Years 1765–1910*.
Westport, Conn.: Greenwood Press, 1976.

Kelman, Sander. "The Social Nature of the Definition Problem in Health." *International Journal of Health Services* 5 (1975): 625–41.

Kessner, David et al. "Infant Death: An Analyses by Maternal Risk and Health
Care." In *Contrasts in Health Status*. Washington, D.C.: Institute of Medicine,
National Academy of Sciences, 1973.

Kett, Joseph. *The Formation of the American Medical Profession*. New Haven,
Conn.: Yale University Press, 1968.

Keyfitz, Nathan. "What Difference Would It Make If Cancer Were Eradicated? An Examination of the Taeuber Paradox." *Demography* 14 (Nov. 1977): 411–18.

King, Lester S. "Development of Medical Ethics." *New England Journal of Medicine* 258 (Mar. 6, 1958): 480–86.

Kitagawa, Evelyn, and Philip M. Hauser. *Differential Mortality in the United States.* Cambridge, Mass.: Harvard University Press, 1973.

Klarman, Herbert. *The Economics of Health.* New York: Columbia University Press, 1965.

Klarman, Herbert. *Empirical Studies in Health Economics.* Baltimore: Johns Hopkins Press, 1970.

Klein, Rudolf. (a) "The NHS and the Theater of Inadequacy." *University Quarterly* 37 (Summer 1983): 201–15.

Klein, Rudolf. (b) *The Politics of the National Health Service.* London: Longman, 1983.

Klein, Rudolf. "Ideology, Class, and the National Health Service." *Journal of Health Politics, Policy and Law* 4 (Fall 1979): 464–90.

Klein, Rudolf. "Models of Man and Models of Policy: Reflections on Exit, Voice and Loyalty." *Milbank Memorial Fund Quarterly* 58 (Summer 1980): 416–29.

Knowles, John H., ed. *Doing Better and Feeling Worse: Health in the United States.* New York: W. W. Norton & Co., 1977.

Knowles, John H. "Medical Education and the Rationalization of Health Services." In John H. Knowles, ed., *Views of Medical Education and Medical Care,* 81, 82. Cambridge, Mass.: Harvard University Press, 1968.

Kohler, Robert E. "Discovery and Using Biomedical Knowledge: The Achievements of the United Kingdom, Medical Research Council." *Minerva* 16 (Autumn 1978): 445–52.

Kohler, Robert E. "The Management of Science: The Experience of Warren Weaver and the Rockefeller Foundation Program in Molecular Biology." *Minerva* 14 (Autumn 1976): 279–306.

Konold, Donald E. *A History of American Medical Ethics 1847–1912.* New York: Book Craftsman Associates, 1962.

Larrabee, Eric. *The Benevolent and Necessary Institution: The New York Hospital, 1771–1971.* Garden City, N.Y.: Doubleday, 1971.

Larson, E. B., et al. "Computed Tomography of the Brain in Patients with Cerebrovascular Disease: Impact of a New Technology on Patient Care." *American Journal of Roentgenology* 113 (1978): 35–40.

Larson, Magali Sarfatti. *The Rise of Professionalism: A Sociological Analysis.* Berkeley and Los Angeles: University of California Press, 1977.

Lave, Judith R., and Lester B. Lave. *The Hospital Construction Act: An Evaluation of the Hill-Burton Program, 1948–1973.* Washington, D.C.: American Enterprise Institute for Public Policy Research, 1974.

Law, Sylvia. *Blue Cross: What Went Wrong?* New Haven, Conn.: Yale University Press, 1974.

Leavitt, Judith Walzer. *The Healthiest City: Milwaukee and the Politics of Health Reform.* Princeton: Princeton University Press, 1982.

Leavitt, Judith Walzer, and Ronald L. Numbers, eds. *Sickness and Health in*

America: Readings in the History of Medicine and Public Health. Madison: University of Wisconsin Press, 1978.

Lee, Maw Lin. "A Conspicuous Production Theory of Hospital Behavior." *Southern Economic Journal* 38 (July 1971): 48–58.

Lefcowitz, Myron J. "Poverty and Health: A Re-examination." *Inquiry* 10 (1973): 3–13.

LeGrand, Julian. "The Distribution of Public Expenditure: The Case of Health Care." *Economica* 45 (May 1978): 125–48.

Letourmy, A. "Some Aspects of the Relationships between Mortality, Environmental Conditions, and Medical Care." In Norman T. J. Bailey and Mark Thompson, eds., *Systems Aspects of Health Planning: Proceedings of the IIASA Conference.* Amsterdam: North-Holland Publishing Co., 1975.

Levy, Hermann. *National Health Insurance, A Critical Study.* Cambridge: Cambridge University Press, 1944.

Levy, Robert I. "The Decline in Cardiovascular Disease Mortality." *Annual Review of Public Health* 2 (1981): 49–70.

Liebenau, Jonathan. "Industrial R and D in Pharmaceutical Firms in the Early Twentieth Century." *Business History* 26 (November 1984): 329–46.

Liebenau, Jonathan. "Medical Science and Medical Industry, 1890–1929." Ph.D. diss., University of Pennsylvania, 1981.

Lindbloom, Charles. "The Science of 'Muddling Through.' " *Public Administration Review* 19 (Spring 1959): 79–88.

Lindsey, Almont. *Socialized Medicine in England and Wales: The National Health Service, 1948–1961.* Chapel Hill: University of North Carolina Press, 1962.

Lippard, Vernon W. *A Half-Century of American Medical Education: 1920–1970.* New York: Josiah Macy, Jr. Foundation, 1974.

Little, Ernest Muirhead. *History of the British Medical Association 1832–1932.* London: British Medical Association Press, 1932.

Ludmerer, Kenneth M. *Learning to Heal: The Development of American Medical Education.* New York: Basic Books, 1986.

Ludmerer, Kenneth M. "Reform at Harvard Medical School, 1869–1909." *Bulletin of the History of Medicine* 55 (1981): 343–70.

Luft, Harold S. *Health Maintenance Organizations: Dimensions of Performance.* New York: John Wiley & Sons, 1981.

Luft, Harold S. "How Do Health-Maintenance Organizations Achieve Their 'Savings'?—Rhetoric and Evidence." *New England Journal of Medicine* 298 (June 15, 1978): 1336–43.

Lynaugh, Joan E. "The Community Hospitals of Kansas City, Missouri, 1870–1915." Ph.D. diss., University of Kansas, 1982.

McCleary, G. F. *The Early History of the Infant Welfare Movement.* London: H. K. Lewis & Co., 1933.

McCleary, G. F. *National Health Insurance.* London: H. K. Lewis & Co., 1932.

McKeown, Thomas. *Medicine in Modern Society.* London: George Allen & Unwin, 1975.

McKeown, Thomas. *The Modern Rise of Population.* New York: Academic Press, 1976.

McKeown, Thomas. *The Role of Medicine: Dream, Mirage, or Nemesis?* London: Nuffield Provincial Hospitals Trust, 1976.

McKeown, Thomas, and R. G. Brown. "Medical Evidence Related to English Population Changes in the Eighteenth Century." *Population Studies* 9 (Nov. 1955): 119–41.

McKeown, Thomas, and R. G. Record. "An Interpretation of the Decline of Mortality in England and Wales during the Twentieth Century." *Population Studies* 29 (1975): 391–422.

McKeown, Thomas, and R. G. Record. "Reasons for the Decline of Mortality in England and Wales during the Nineteenth Century." *Population Studies* 16 (1967): 94–122.

McKinlay, John B. "Epidemiological and Political Determinants of Social Policies regarding the Public Health." *Social Science and Medicine* 13A (1979): 541–58.

McKinlay, John B., and Sonja M. McKinlay. "The Questionable Contribution of Medicine Measures to the Decline of Mortality in the United States in the Twentieth Century." *Milbank Memorial Fund Quarterly* 55 (Summer 1977): 405–28.

McNeill, William H. *Plagues and Peoples.* New York: Anchor Press, 1976.

McNerney, Walter J. "Control of Health-Care Costs in the 1980's." *New England Journal of Medicine* 303 (Nov. 6, 1980): 1088–95.

McNerney, Walter J., and study staff. *Hospital and Medical Economics.* 2 vols. Chicago: Hospital Research and Educational Trust, 1962.

McVail, John C. *Report to the Royal Commission on the Poor Laws and Relief of Distress on Poor Law Medical Relief.* Cmd. 4573, 1909, vol. 42. London: HMSO.

Markowitz, Gerald, and David Rosner. "Doctors and Crisis." *American Quarterly* 25 (Mar. 1973): 83–107.

Marmor, Theodore R. *The Politics of Medicare.* London: Routledge & Kegan Paul, 1970.

Marmor, Theodore R. "The Policies of National Health Insurance: Analysis and Prescription." *Policy Analysis* 3 (Winter 1977): 25–48.

Marmor, Theodore R., and Jon B. Christianson. *Health Care Policy: A Political Economy Approach.* Beverly Hills, Calif.: Sage Publications, 1982.

Mayer, Jack A. "Health Care Competition: Are Tax Incentives Enough?" Paper presented before the Conference on Health Care sponsored by American Enterprise Institute for Public Policy Research, Sept. 1980.

Mead, Lawrence M. (a) "Health Policy: The Need for Governance." *Annals of the American Academy of Political and Social Science* 434 (Nov. 1977): 39–57.

Mead, Lawrence M. (b) *Institutional Analysis: An Approach to Implementation Problems in Medicaid.* Washington, D.C.: Urban Institute, 1977.

Mechanic, David. "Assumptions Underlying Cost-Containment Philosophies: Strategies for Medical Care." Research and Analytic Report Series. Home Economics Research Center/Center for Medical Sociology and Health Services Research, University of Wisconsin, Madison, 1977.

Mechanic, David. "The Comparative Studies of Health Care Delivery Systems." *Annual Review of Sociology* 1 (1975): 43–65.

Mechanic, David. *Politics, Medicine, and Social Science.* New York: John Wiley & Sons, 1974.

Mechanic, David. *Public Expectations and Public Health.* New York: John Wiley & Sons, 1972.

Medical News 83 (Oct. 3, 1903): 661.

Mellanby, K. "The Disorganization of Scientific Research." *Minerva* 12 (1974): 67.

Mencher, S. *Private Practice in Britain.* London: G. Bell & Sons, 1967.

Millis, John S. "The Graduate Education of Physicians." *New England Journal of Medicine* 276 (May 18, 1967): 1103.

Millis, John S. *A Rational Public Policy for Medical Education and Its Financing.* New York: National Fund for Medical Education, 1971.

Monsma, George N., Jr. "Marginal Revenue and the Demand for Physicians' Services." In Herbert E. Klarman, ed., *Empirical Studies in Health Economic.* Baltimore: Johns Hopkins Press, 1970.

Moore, Benjamin, and Charles A. Parker. "The Case for a State Medical Service Re-stated." *Lancet,* July 20, 1918, pp. 85–87.

Morone, James A., and A. B. Dunham. "The Emerging Autonomy of the State: Health Politics and the Hospital Industry." Paper presented before the American Political Science Association, Chicago, Sept. 1983.

Morone, James A., and A. B. Dunham. "Slouching towards National Health Insurance: The New Health Care Politics." *Yale Journal on Regulation* 2, no. 2 (1985): 263–91.

Morone, James, and A. B. Dunham. "The Waning of Professional Dominance: DRGs and the Hospital." *Health Affairs* 3 (1984): 73–86.

Morone, James A., and T. R. Marmor. "Representing Consumer Interests: The Case of American Health Planning." *Ethics* 91 (Apr. 1981): 431–50.

Morris, J. N. "Social Inequalities Undiminished." *Lancet,* Jan. 23, 1979, pp. 87–90.

Moulin, L. "The Nobel Prizes for the Sciences: An Essay in Sociological Analysis." *British Journal of Sociology* 6 (1955): 246–63.

Murray, D. Stark. *Why a National Health Service? The Part Played by the Socialist Medical Association.* London: Pemberton Publishing Co., 1971.

Mulkay, M. J. "The Sociology of Science in Britain." In Robert K. Merton and Jerry Gaston, eds., *The Sociology of Science in Europe.* Carbondale: Southern Illinois University Press, 1977.

Murtaugh, Joseph S. "Biomedical Sciences." In James A. Shannon, ed., *Science and the Evolution of Public Policy.* New York: Rockefeller University Press, 1973.

Narain, Francis, et al. *Evaluations Bibliometrics: The Use of Publications and Citation Analyses in the Evaluation of Scientific Activity.* Cherry Hill, N.J.: Computer Horizons, 1976.

Navarro, Vincente. *Class Struggle, the State, and Medicine: An Historical and Contemporary Analysis of the Medical Sector in Great Britain.* New York: Proclist, 1978.

Navarro, Vincente. (a) "Social Class, Political Power, and the State and Their Implications in Medicine." *Social Science and Medicine* 10 (1976): 437–56.

Navarro, Vincente. (b) "The Underdevelopment of Health in Working America: Causes, Consequences, and Possible Solutions." *American Journal of Public Health* 66 (1976): 538–47.

Navarro, Vincente. "Work, Ideology, and Science: The Case of Medicine." *Social Science and Medicine* 14C (1980): 191–203.

Newhouse, Joseph P., and Lindy J. Friedlander. *The Relationship between Medical Resources and Measures of Health: Some Additional Evidence.* Santa Monica, Calif.: Rand Corporation, 1977.

Newman, Charles. *The Evolution of Medical Education in the Nineteenth Century.* London: Oxford University Press, 1957.

Newman, George. "Some Notes on Medical Education in England." Great Britain. Parliamentary Papers (Commons), 1918, vol. 19, Cmd. 9124.

Norwood, William Frederick. *Medical Education in the United States Before the Civil War.* Philadelphia: University of Pennsylvania Press, 1944.

Numbers, Ronald L. *Almost Persuaded: American Physicians and Compulsory Health Insurance, 1912–1920.* Baltimore: Johns Hopkins University Press, 1978.

Numbers, Ronald L., ed. *The Education of American Physicians.* Berkeley and Los Angeles: University of California Press, 1980.

O'Connor, James. *The Fiscal Crisis of the State.* New York: St. Martin's Press, 1973.

Offe, Claus. "Advanced Capitalism and the Welfare State." *Politics and Society,* Summer 1972, 472–88.

Offe, Claus. "Structural Problems of the Capitalist State: Class Rule and the Political System. On the Selectiveness of Political Institutions." In Klaus Von Beyme, ed., *German Political Studies.* Vol. 1. Beverly Hills, Calif.: Sage Publications, 1974.

Offe, Claus. "The Theory of the Capitalist State and the Problem of Policy Formation." In Leon Lindberg, ed., *Stress and Contradiction in Modern Capitalism.* Lexington, Mass.: D. C. Heath, 1975.

Office of Health Economics. *End Stage Renal Failure.* London: Office of Health Economics, 1980.

Office of Health Economics. *Expenditures on Medical Research.* London: Office of Health Economics, 1974.

Office of Health Economics. *Renal Failure: A Priority in Health?* London: Office of Health Economics, 1978.

Oliver, D. O., and P. J. Morris. "The Organization and Results of an Integrated Home Dialysis and Transplant Service." In A. M. Davison, ed., *Dialysis Review.* London: Pitman Medical, 1978.

Olson, Mancur. *A New Approach to the Economics of Health Care.* Washington, D.C.: American Enterprise Institute for Public Policy Research, 1981.

Olson, Mancur. *The Rise and Decline of Nations: Economic Growth, Stagflation, and Social Rigidities.* New Haven, Conn.: Yale University Press, 1982.

Organization for Economic Cooperation and Development. *Reviews of National Science Policy: United Kingdom and Germany.* Paris: OECD, 1967.

Orloff, Ann S. "The Politics of Pensions: A Comparative Analysis of the Origins of Pensions and Old Age Insurance in Canada, Great Britain, and the United States." Ph.D. diss., Princeton University, 1985.

Orloff, Ann S., and Theda Skocpol. "Why Not Equal Protection? Explaining the Politics of Public Social Spending in Britain, 1900–1911 and the United States, 1880s–1920." *American Sociological Review* 49 (Dec. 1984): 726–50.

Parish, H. J. *Victory with Vaccines: The Story of Immunization.* Edinburgh: E. and S. Livingston, 1968.

Parker, Julia, et al. "Health." In A. H. Halsey, ed., *Trends in British Society since 1900.* London: Macmillan, 1972.

Patent-Term Extension and the Pharmaceutical Industry. Washington, D.C.: GPO, 1981.

Perlman, Mark. *The Economics of Health and Medical Care.* New York: John Wiley & Sons, 1974.

Perrow, Charles. "Goals and Power Structures: A Historical Case Study." In Eliot Freidson, ed., *The Hospital in Modern Society.* New York: Free Press of Glencoe, 1963.

Perrow, Charles. "Hospitals: Technology, Structure and Goals." In James G. March, ed., *Handbook of Organizations.* Chicago: Rand McNally, 1965.

Petersdorf, Robert G. "The Evolution of Departments of Medicine." *New England Journal of Medicine* 303 (Aug. 28, 1980): 489–96.

Peterson, Jeanne M. *The Medical Profession in Mid-Victorian London.* Berkeley and Los Angeles: University of California Press, 1978.

Pinker, Robert. *English Hospital Statistics, 1861–1938.* London: Heinemann, 1966.

Political and Economic Planning, *Report on the British Health Services.* London: Political and Economic Planning, 1937.

Powles, John. "On the Limitations of Modern Man." *Science, Medicine, and Man* 1 (1973): 1–30.

Poynter, F. N. L., ed. *The Evolution of Medical Practice in Britain.* London: Pitman Medical, 1961.

President's Science Advisory Committee. Panel on Biological and Medical Science. *Scientific and Educational Basis for Improving Health.* Washington, D.C.: GPO, 1972.

Price, Derek John de Solla. *Little Science, Big Science.* New York: Columbia University Press, 1963.

Price, Don K. "Endless Frontier of Bureaucratic Morass." *Daedalus* 107 (Spring 1978): 75–92.

Proceedings of the European Dialysis and Transplant Association, vol. 16, 1978.

Prottas, Jeffrey, et al. "Cross-National Differences in Dialysis Rates." *Health Care Financing Review* 4 (Mar. 1983): 91–103.

Rayack, Elton. (a) "The American Medical Association and the Development of Voluntary Insurance, Part I." *Social and Economic Administration* 1 (Apr. 1967): 3–24.

Rayack, Elton. (b) "The American Medical Association and the Development of Voluntary Insurance, Part II." *Social and Economic Administration* 1 (July 1967): 29–54.

Rayack, Elton. (c) *Professional Power and American Medicine: The Economics of the American Medical Association.* Cleveland, Ohio: World Publishing Co., 1967.

Relman, Arnold S. "The New Medical-Industrial Complex." *New England Journal of Medicine* 303 (Oct. 23, 1980): 963–70.

Revans, John, and Gordon McLachlan. *Postgraduate Medical Education.* Nuffield Provincial Hospitals Trust, 1967.

Reverby, Susan, and David Rosner. *Health Care in America.* Philadelphia: Temple University Press, 1979.

Robert Wood Johnson Foundation. *Updated Report on Access to Health Care for the American People.* Princeton: Robert Wood Johnson Foundation, 1983.

Robson, John. "The NHS Company Inc.? The Social Consequences of the Professional Dominance in the National Health Service." *International Journal of Health Services* 3 (1973): 413–26.

Rockefeller Foundation. History, vol. 17. Rockefeller Foundation Archives, Rockefeller Archives Center, North Tarrytown, N.Y.

Roemer, Milton I. "Bed Supply and Hospital Utilization: A Natural Experiment." *Hospitals* 35 (1961): 36–42.

Roemer, Milton I. "Hospital Utilization and the Supply of Physicians." *Journal of the American Medical Association* 178 (Dec. 1961): 933–39.

Roemer, Milton I., and M. Shain. *Hospital Utilization under Insurance.* Chicago: American Hospital Association, 1959.

Rogers, David E. "The Challenge of Primary Care." In John Knowles, ed., *Doing Better and Feeling Worse: Health in the United States.* New York: W. W. Norton & Co., 1977.

Rogers, David E. "Medical Academe and the Problems of Primary Care." *Journal of Medical Education* 50 (Dec. 1975): 171–81.

Rogers, David E. "On Preparing Academic Health Centers for the Very Different 1980s." *Journal of Medical Education* 55 (Jan. 1980): 1–12.

Rogers, David E., and Robert J. Blendon. "The Academic Medical Center: A Stressed American Institution." *New England Journal of Medicine* 298 (Apr. 27, 1978): 940–50.

Rogers, David E., and Robert J. Blendon. "The Changing American Health Scene." *Journal of the American Medical Association* 237 (Apr. 18, 1977): 1710–14.

Rose, Geoffrey. "Epidemiology of Ischaemic Heart Disease." *British Journal of Hospital Medicine* 8 (1972): 285–88.

Rosen, George. "The Bacteriological, Immunologic, and Chemotherapeutic Period, 1875–1950." *Bulletin of the New York Academy of Medicine* 42 (1964): 483–94.

Rosen, George. "Disease, Debility and Death." In H. Dyos and M. Wolff, eds., *The Victorian City: Images and Realities.* London: Routledge & Kegan Paul, 1973.

Rosen, George. "The Efficiency Criterion in Medical Care, 1900–1920." *Bulletin of the History of Medicine* 50 (1976): 28–44.

Rosen, George. "The Evolution of Social Medicine." In Howard Freeman, et al., *Handbook of Medical Sociology.* Englewood Cliffs, N.J.: Prentice-Hall, 1972.

Rosen, George. *A History of Public Health.* New York: M. D. Publications, 1958.

Rosen, George. "Patterns of Health Research in the U.S., 1900–1960." *Bulletin of the History of Medicine* 39, no. 3 (May-June 1965): 201–21.

Rosen, George. *The Specialization of Medicine, with Particular Reference to Ophthalmology.* New York: Froben Press, 1944.

Rosenberg, Charles. (a) "And Heal the Sick: The Hospital and the Patient in Nineteenth-Century America." *Journal of Social History* 10 (Summer 1977): 428–47.

Rosenberg, Charles (b) "The Therapeutic Revolution: Medicine, Meaning and Social Change in Nineteenth-Century America." *Perspectives in Biology and Medicine* 20 (1977): 485–516.

Rosenberg, Charles E. (a) "Henry Newell Martin." In *Dictionary of Scientific Biography*, vol. 9. New York: Charles Scribners Sons, 1974.

Rosenberg, Charles E. (b) "Social Class and Medical Care in Nineteenth-Century America: The Rise and Fall of the Dispensary." *Journal of the History of Medicine* 29 (1974): 32–54.

Rosenberg, Charles E. "From Almshouse to Hospital: The Shaping of Philadelphia General Hospital." *Health and Society* 60 (1982): 108–54.

Rosenberg, Charles E. "Inward Vision and Outward Glance: The Shaping of the American Hospital." *Bulletin of the History of Medicine* 53 (1979): 346–91.

Rosenberg, Charles E. "The Practice of Medicine in New York a Century Ago." *Bulletin of the History of Medicine* 41 (1967): 223–53.

Rosenkrantz, Barbara. *Public Health and the State.* Cambridge, Mass.: Harvard University Press, 1972.

Rosner, David. "Business at the Bedside: Health Care in Brooklyn, 1890–1915." In Susan Reverby and David Rosner, eds., *Health Care in America.* Philadelphia: Temple University Press, 1979.

Rosner, David. "Gaining Control: Reform, Reimbursement, and Politics in New York's Community Hospitals, 1890–1915." *American Journal of Public Health* 70 (1980): 533–42.

Rosner, David. *A Once Charitable Enterprise: Hospitals and Health Care in Brooklyn and New York, 1885–1915.* Cambridge: Cambridge University Press, 1982.

Ross, James S. *The National Health Service in Great Britain.* London: Oxford University Press, 1952.

Ross, Richard S. "Ischemic Heart Disease: An Overview." *American Journal of Cardiology* 36 (1975): 496–505.

Rothstein, William G. *American Physicians in the Nineteeth Century.* Baltimore: Johns Hopkins Press, 1972.

Rowntree, B. Seebohm. *Poverty: A Study of Town Life.* London: Macmillan, 1908.

Royal College of Physicians. *Smoking and Health Now.* London: Pitman Medical, 1971.

Russell, Louise B. *Is Prevention Better Than Cure?* Washington, D.C.: Brookings Institution, 1986.

Rutkow, I. M., and G. D. Zuidema. "Unnecessary Surgery: An Update." *Surgery*, Nov. 1978.

Salkever, D. C., and T. W. Brice. "The Impact of Certificate-of-Need Controls on Hospital Investment." *Milbank Memorial Fund Quarterly* 54 (Spring 1976): 185–213.

Schwartz, Jerome L. "Early History of Prepaid Medical Care Plans." *Bulletin of the History of Medicine* 39 (1965): 450–75.

Science and Government Report 4 (Dec. 1974): 1–3.

Science Indicators 1978. Washington, D.C.: GPO, 1978.

Serbein, Oscar N., Jr. *Paying for Medical Care in the United States.* New York: Columbia University Press, 1953.

Shannon, James A. "The Advancement of Medical Research: A Twenty-Year View of the Role of National Institutes on Health." *Journal of Medical Education* 42 (Feb. 1967): 97–108.

Shannon, James A., ed. *Science and the Evolution of Public Policy.* New York: Rockefeller University Press, 1973.

Sharpey-Shafer, E. A. "Developments of Physiology." *Nature* 104 (1919): 207–8.

Sheldrake, Peter. "Trends in Medical Education in Great Britain." *Journal of Medical Education* 51 (1976): 558–64.

Shryock, Richard H. (a) *American Medical Research Past and Present.* New York: Commonwealth Fund, 1947.

Shryock, Richard. (b) *The Development of Modern Medicine: An Interpretation of the Social and Scientific Factors Involved.* New York: Knopf, 1947.

Shryock, R. H. *Medical Licensing in America 1650–1965.* Baltimore: Johns Hopkins Press, 1967.

Sigerist, Henry. "An Outline of the Development of the Hospital." *Bulletin of the History of Medicine* 4 (July 1936): 573–81.

Simpson, J., et al. *Customs and Practices in Medical Care: A Comparative Study of Two Hospitals in Arbroath, Scotland, and Waterville, Maine.* London: Oxford University Press, 1978.

Skocpol, Theda. "Political Response to Capitalist Crisis: Neo-Marxist Theories of the State and the Case of the New Deal." *Politics and Society* 10 (1981): 155–201.

Skocpol, Theda, and J. Ikenberry. "The Political Formation of the American Welfare State in Historical and Comparative Perspective." *Comparative Social Research* 6 (1983): 87–147.

Sloan, Frank A. "Rate Regulation as a Strategy for Hospital Cost Control: Evidence from the Last Decade." *Milbank Memorial Fund Quarterly* 61 (1983): 195–221.

Sloan, Frank A., and B. Steinwald. "Effects of Regulation on Hospital Costs and Input Use." *Journal of Law and Economics,* Apr. 1980, 81–109.

Somers, Anne, and Herman Somers. *Health and Health Care.* Germantown, Md.: Aspen Systems Corp., 1977.

Somers, Herman, and Anne Somers. *Doctors, Patients, and Health Insurance.* New York: Doubleday & Co., Anchor Books, 1962.

Spicer, C. C., and L. Lipworth. *Regional and Social Factors in Infant Mortality.* Medical and Population Studies, no. 19. London: HMSO, 1966.

Spivak, Jonathan. "Private Health Care in Britain." *Wall Street Journal,* Aug. 21, 1979.

Stamler, J., et al., eds. *The Epidemiology of Hypertension.* New York: Grune & Stratton, 1967.

Starr, Paul. "Medicine, Economy and Society in Nineteeth-Century America." *Journal of Social History* 10 (1976): 588–607.

Starr, Paul. *The Social Transformation of American Medicine.* New York: Basic Books, 1982.

Steele, John Charles. "The Charitable Aspects of Medical Relief." *Journal of the Royal Statistical Society* 55 (1891): 263–99.

'Steinwald, Bruce, and Duncan Neuhauser. "The Role of the Proprietary Hospital." *Law and Contemporary Problems* 35 (1970): 817–38.

Steinwald, Bruce, and Frank A. Sloan. "Regulatory Approaches to Hospital Cost Containment: A Synthesis of the Empirical Evidence." Paper presented before the Conference on Health Care sponsored by American Enterprise Institute for Public Policy Research, Sept. 1980.

Stern, Bernhard. *American Medical Practice in the Perspectives of a Century.* New York: Commonwealth Fund, 1945.

Stern, Bernhard. *Society and Medical Progress.* Princeton: Princeton University Press, 1941.

Stevens, Rosemary. *American Medicine and the Public Interest.* New Haven, Conn.: Yale University Press, 1971.

Stevens, Rosemary. "The Evolution of the Health-Care Systems in the United States and the United Kingdom: Similarities and Differences." In *Priorities for the Use of Resources in Medicine.* Fogarty International Center Proceedings. Bethesda, Md.: U.S. Department of Health, Education, and Welfare, 1976.

Stevens, Rosemary A. "Graduate Medical Education: A Continuing History." *Journal of Medical Education* 53 (1978): 1–18.

Stevens, Rosemary. *Medical Practice in Modern England: The Impact of Specialization and State Medicine.* New Haven, Conn.: Yale University Press, 1966.

Stevens, Robert, and Rosemary Stevens. *Welfare Medicine in America: A Case Study of Medicaid.* New York: Free Press, 1974.

Steward, F., and G. Wibberley. "Drug Innovation—What's Slowing It Down?" *Nature* 284 (1980): 118–20.

Stone, Deborah. "The Political Meaning of Medical Ideas." Paper presented before the American Political Science Association, Sept. 1983.

Strickland, Stephen P. *Politics, Science and Dread Disease.* Cambridge, Mass.: Harvard University Press, 1972.

Sullivan, Daniel F. "Conceptual Problems in Developing an Index of Health." In *Vital and Health Statistics.* Series 2, no. 17. Washington, D.C.: National Center for Health Statistics, 1966.

Sullivan, Sean, with Polly M. Ehrenhaft. *Managing Health Care Costs: Private Sector Innovations.* Washington, D.C.: American Enterprise Institute for Public Policy Research, 1984.

Sulvetta, Margaret. *Public Hospital Provision of Care to the Poor and Financial Status.* Washington, D.C.: Urban Institute, 1985.

Symposium on Medical Research Systems in Europe. *Medical Research in Europe.* New York: Elsevier, North Holland, 1973.

Temin, Peter. *Taking Your Medicine: Drug Regulation in the United States.* Cambridge, Mass.: Harvard University Press, 1980.

Terry, Charles, and Mildred Pellens. *The Opium Problem.* New York: Committee on Drug Addiction/Bureau of Social Hygiene, 1928.

Thomas, A. Landsborough. *Half a Century of Medical Research.* 2 vols. London: HMSO, 1973, 1975.

Thomas, Lewis. "On the Limitations of Modern Medicine." In John H. Knowles, ed., *Doing Better and Feeling Worse: Health in the United States*. New York: W. W. Norton & Co., 1977.

Thomas, Lewis. "On the Science and Technology of Medicine." In John H. Knowles, ed., *Doing Better and Feeling Worse: Health in the United States*. New York: W. W. Norton & Co., 1977.

Thomas, Lewis. *The Youngest Science: Notes of a Medicine-Watcher*. New York: Viking Press, 1983.

Titmuss, Richard M. *Birth, Poverty and Wealth*. London: Hamish Hamilton Medical Books, 1943.

Titmuss, Richard M. *Essays on the Welfare State*. Boston: Beacon Press, 1958.

Titmuss, Richard M. *Problems of Social Policy*. London: H.M.S.O. and Longmans, Green & Co., 1950.

Townsend, Peter. *The Last Refuge: A Survey of Residential Institutions and Homes for the Aged in England and Wales*. London: Routledge & Kegan Paul, 1962.

Townsend, Peter, and Nick Davidson, eds. *Inequalities in Health: The Black Report*. London: Penguin Books, 1982.

Turner, Thomas Bourne. *Heritage of Excellence*. Baltimore: Johns Hopkins University Press, 1974.

Turner, Thomas Bourne. *The Johns Hopkins Medical School, 1957–1968*. Baltimore: Johns Hopkins Press, 1969.

United Nations. *Demographic Yearbook*. New York: United Nations Department of International Economic and Social Affairs, Statistical Office, various years.

United States Commissioner of Education. *Report of the U.S. Commissioner of Education, 1914*. Washington, D.C.: GPO, 1915.

United States Comptroller General. *Report to the Congress. FDA's Approach to Reviewing Over-the-Counter Drugs Is Reasonable, but Progress Is Slow*. Gaithersburg, Md.: General Accounting Office, 1982.

United States Congress. House. Committee on Interstate and Foreign Commerce. *Conflicts of Interest on Blue Shield Boards of Directors*. Washington, D.C.: GPO, Dec. 1978.

United States Congress. House. Committee on Interstate and Foreign Commerce. Subcommittee on Oversight and Investigations. *Cost and Quality of Health Care: Unnecessary Surgery*. Washington, D.C.: GPO, Jan. 1976.

United States Congress. House. Committee on Interstate and Foreign Commerce. Subcommittee on Oversight and Investigations. *Hearings on Getting Ready for National Health Insurance: Unnecessary Surgery*. Washington, D.C.: 1975.

United States Congress. House. Committee on Ways and Means. Subcommittee on Health. *Hearings on Medicare End-State Renal Disease*, Apr. 25, 1977 (Washington, D.C.: GPO, 1978).

United States Congress. House. Select Committee on Aging. *A Staff Study*. Washington, D.C.: GPO, Nov. 28, 1979.

United States Congress. Office of Technology Assessment. *Policy Implications of the Computed Tomography (CT) Scanner*. Washington, D.C.: GPO, 1978.

United States Congress. Senate. Committee on Finance. *Hearings on Medicare and Medicaid*. Washington, D.C.: GPO, 1969.

United States Congress. Senate. Committee on the Judiciary. *Examination of the Pharmaceutical Industry, 1973–74.*

United States Congress. Senate. Committee on the Judiciary. *Hearings on the Regulation of Drug Research and Development by the Food and Drug Administration,* 1974.

United States Congress. Senate. Committee on Labor and Public Welfare. Subcommittee on Health. *Hearings.* Dec. 18–19, 1973. Washington, D.C.: GPO, 1973.

United States Congress. Senate. Committee on Labor and Public Welfare. Subcommittee on Health. *Hearings: Examination of the Pharmaceutical Industry.* Washington, D.C.: GPO, 1968.

United States Congress. Senate. Special Committee on Aging. *Developments in Aging.* Washington, D.C.: GPO, 1976.

United States Congress. Senate. Special Committee on Aging. Subcommittee on Long-Term Care. *Nursing Home Care in the United States: Failure in Public Policy,* 1975.

United States Congress. Senate. Specal Committee on Aging. Subcommittee on Long-Term Care. *Nursing Home Care in the United States: Failure in Public Policy—Introductory Report.* Washington, D.C.: GPO, 1974.

United States Congress. Senate. Select Committee on Small Business. Subcommittee on Monopoly. *Competitive Problems in the Drug Industry,* 1973.

United States Department of Commerce. Bureau of the Census. (a) *Historical Statistics of the United States.* Washington, D.C.: GPO, 1979.

United States Department of Commerce. Bureau of the Census. (b) *Vital Statistics of the United States, 1975.* Hyattsville, Md.: National Center for Health Statistics, 1979.

United States Department of Commerce. Bureau of the Census. *1900 Census Reports.* Vol. 3, *Vital Statistics,* pt. I, "Analysis and Rate Tables." Washington, D.C.: Bureau of the Census, 1902.

United States Department of Commerce. Bureau of the Census. *Report on Vital and Social Statistics in the United States at the Eleventh Census.* Part I, "Analysis and Rate Tables." Washington, D.C.: GPO, 1896.

United States Department of Commerce. Bureau of the Census. *Statistical Abstract of the United States, 1981.* Washington, D.C.: Bureau of the Census, 1981.

United States Department of Commerce. Bureau of the Census. *Vital Statistics of the United States* (Annual Reports). Washington, D.C.: GPO.

United States Department of Health, Education, and Welfare. *Health Services for American Indians.* Public Health Service Publication no. 531. Washington, D.C.: GPO, 1957.

United States Department of Health, Education, and Welfare. *Healthy People: The Surgeon General's Report on Health Promotion and Disease Prevention.* Public Health Service Publication no. 79–55071A. Washington, D.C.: GPO, 1979.

United States Department of Health, Education, and Welfare. National Center for Health Statistics. *Infant Mortality Rates: Socioeconomic Factors.* Series 22, no. 14. Washington, D.C.: GPO, 1972.

Virchow, Rudolf. *Die Einheitsbestrebungen in der wissenschaftlichen Medicin.* Berlin: G. Reimer, 1849, 48.

Virchow, Rudolf. "Die offentliche Gesundheilspflege," *Medicinische Reform*, Aug. 5, 1848, 21–22.

Vladeck, Bruce C. *Unloving Care: The Nursing Home Tragedy*. New York: Basic Books, 1980.

Vogel, Morris J. "Boston's Hospitals, 1870–1930: A Social History." Ph.D. diss., University of Chicago, 1975.

Vogel, Morris J. *The Invention of the Modern Hospital: Boston, 1870–1930*. Chicago: University of Chicago Press, 1980.

Vogel, Morris J. "The Transformation of the American Hospital, 1850–1920." In Susan Reverby and David Rosner, eds., *Health Care in America*. Philadelphia: Temple University Press, 1979.

Vogt, T. M. "Risk Assessment and Health Hazard Appraisal." *Annual Review of Public Health* 2 (1981): 31–47.

Waddington, Ivan. "The Development of Medical Ethics. *Medical History* 19 (Jan. 1975): 36–45.

Waite, Frederick. *The Story of a Country Medical College*. Montpelier: Vermont Historical Society, 1945.

Walker, Norman. "The Medical Professor in the United States." *Edinbrugh Medical Journal* 37 (1891): 240–41.

Walters, Vivienne. *Class Inequality and Health Care*. London: Croom Helm, 1980.

Wardell, William M. (a) "British and American Awareness of Some New Therapeutic Drugs." *Clinical Pharmacology and Therapeutics* 14 (Nov.-Dec. 1973): 1022–34.

Wardell, William M. (b) "Introduction of New Therapeutic Drugs in the United States and Great Britain: An International Comparison." *Clinical Pharmacology and Therapeutics* 14 (Sept.-Oct. 1973): 773–90.

Wardell, William M. "Developments in the Introduction of New Drugs in the United States and Britain, 1971–1974." In Robert B. Helms, ed., *Drug Development and Marketing*. Washington, D.C.: American Enterprise Institute for Public Policy Research, 1975.

Wardell, William M. "The History of Drug Discovery, Development, and Regulation." In Robert I. Chien, ed., *Issues in Pharmaceutical Economics*. Lexington, Mass.: Lexington Books, 1979.

Wardell, William M. "The Impact of Regulation on New Drug Development." In Robert I. Chien, ed., *Issues in Pharmaceutical Economics*. Lexington, Mass.: Lexington Books, 1979.

Wardell, William M. "Therapeutic Implications of the Drug Lag." *Clinical Pharmacology and Therapeutics* 15 (Jan. 1974): 73–96.

Wardell, William M., and Louis Lasagna. *Regulations and Drug Development*. Washington, D.C.: American Enterprise Institute for Public Policy Research, 1975.

Warner, Amos G. *American Charities*. 1904. Reprint. New York: Arno Press, 1971.

Watkin, Brian. *Documents on Health and Social Services: 1834 to the Present Day*. London: Methuen & Co., 1975.

Watkin, Brian. *The National Health Service: The First Phase, 1948–1974 and After*. London: George Allen & Unwin, 1978.

Watson, James D. *The Double Helix.* New York: New American Library, 1969.

Webb, Sidney, and Beatrice Webb. *The State and the Doctor.* London: Longmans, Green & Co., 1910.

Weinstein, Louis. "Infectious Disease: Retrospect and Reminiscence." *Journal of Infectious Diseases* 129 (Apr. 1974): 480–92.

Weisbrod, Burton A. *The Voluntary Nonprofit Sector.* Lexington, Mass.: Lexington Books, 1977.

Weiss, Robert, et al. "Trends in Health-Insurance Operating Expenses." *New England Journal of Medicine* 287 (Sept. 28, 1972): 638–39.

West, Kelly M., and John Kalbfleisch. "Influence of Nutritional Factors on Prevalence of Diabetes." *Diabetes* 20 (1971): 99–108.

West, P. A. "Allocation and Equity in the Public Sector." *Applied Economics* 5 (1973): 153–66.

Wheeler, John Brooks. *Memoirs of a Small-Town Surgeon.* Garden City, N.Y.: Stokes, 1933.

Whittet, T. D. "Drug Control in Britain: From World War I to the Medicines Act of 1968." In John B. Blake, ed., *Safeguarding the Public: Historical Aspects of Medical Drug Control.* Baltimore: Johns Hopkins Press, 1970.

Widgery, David. "Unions and Strikes in the National Health Service in Britain." *International Journal of Health Services* 6 (1976): 301–8.

Winter, Jay, ed. *The Working Class in Modern British History.* Cambridge: Cambridge University Press, 1983.

Woodbury, Robert Morse. *Causal Factors in Infant Mortalilty.* U.S. Department of Labor, Children's Bureau Publication 142. Washington, D.C.: 1925.

Worthington, Nancy L., and Paula A. Piro. "The Effects of Hospital Rate-Setting Programs on Volumes of Hospital Services: A Preliminary Analysis." *Health Care Financing Review* 41 (December 1982): 47–65.

Wortzman, George, and Richard Holgate. "Reappraisal of the Cost-Effectiveness of Computed Tomography in a Government-Sponsored Health Care System." *Radiology* 130 (Jan. 1979): 257–61.

Young, Harvey. *The Toadstool Millionares.* Princeton: Princeton University Press, 1961.

Zechhauser, Richard, and Christopher Zook. "Failures to Control Health Costs: Departures from First Principles." Paper presented before the Conference on Health Care sponsored by American Enterprise Institute for Public Policy Research, Sept. 1980.

Index

Abel-Smith, Brian, xi

Access: facilities by interest-group power, 63; novelty of universal, 63; social class, 44. *See also* Equality of access in Britain; Equality of access in U.S.

Advisory Board for Medical Specialties, 106

American Association of Labor Legislation, 112, 113

American College of Physicians, 103

American College of Surgeons, 114; effects of, 102; as precedent, 102; requirements of, for membership, 102

American Hospital Association, 114, 117, 118

American Medical Association (AMA), 95, 102, 117, 118, 228; on federal aid to medical schools, 228; and financial security, 95; importance in policy, 113; and insurance, position on, 115; motives of, in changing education, 89; national health insurance stance, 113; opposition of, to private insurance, 113; role of, in education change, 89

Anderson, Odin, xi

Authority, levels of: functions of, 253; participation in, 253; proliferation of, 253

Beeson, Paul, 229, 231, 232

Bellevue Hospital, 68

Ben-David, Joseph, 37

Berliner, Howard S., 93, 96

Bevan, Aneurin, 51, 60, 61; goals of, 61; strategy of, 61

Beveridge Report, 49

Billings, John Shaw, on improving education, 89

Blue Cross: features of, 114; growth of, 115

Blue Shield, 115

Blumberg, Baruch S., 237

Boards of certification, 105–6

British Medical Association (BMA), 21, 30, 51; and NHI reform, position on, 46

Burkitt, Dennis P., 270

Business spirit in U.S., 66

Cancer, 270

Cancer research, 237

Capitalist class, 3–10, 28, 242–47; alliance of, with medical profession, 89–96; cleavage of, over costs, 274; influence of, xii

Carnegie Foundation, 224

Cave Commission, 45

Centralization, 129; autonomy of state, 136; change in, 250; change in levels of, 250; compared in different countries, 186, 188; constrains performance, 247; cost, 134; cost containment, 132; cost effects, 249; definition of, 134, 248; degree of participation, 252; dimensions, 188; distribution of resources, 184; effect of, on performance, 248; effects of, on costs, 134; effects of mixed pattern, 134; equality effects, 250; equality of access, 184, 188; innovation and, 248–49; low-income groups, 251; measured, 183; medical services in, 134; power strategy, 250; provider power, 251; shaping interest groups, 253; standardization, 249; system in England and Wales, 3; trade-offs, 248; U.S. lack of, 3; variation in, 136

Centralized decision-making, factors influencing, 251

Certificate of need, 154

Charity, indiscriminate, 100

Children's Bureau, 193

Chronic care, 272

Class structure. *See* Capitalist class; Working class

Clinical medicine and biomedicine, literature compared, 233

Coggeshall Report, 107

College of Physicians and Surgeons, 68

Committee on the Safety of Drugs, 169, 172

Comparative analysis, reasons for, xii

Comprehensive approach, 273

Computed tomography scanner, 151, 178–80

Consultants in England and Wales, 8, 9, 34–35, 48, 51, 55–58

responsibility increased, 79; services in, 79, 80; sources of revenue, 80; stigma in, 79; tax income, 79; teaching in, 80
Public sector health services in England and Wales, 25: fragmentation of care, 25; groups covered, 25; programs developed prior to World War II, 24; for school-children, 25

Quality of medical systems compared, 108–9, 229, 231–32, 235, 264

Regional equality in England and Wales: distribution of beds, 201; distribution of doctors and nurses, 199; inequalities, 201; pre–World War II inequalities, 200; specialist redistribution, 200
Regional equality in U.S.: alternative ex-planation, 201; change in 1940–1970, 201; federal programs, variance in, 202; Medicaid variance in, 202; resources, variance in, 201; variation remains, 201
Regional mortality in England and Wales: contrast of, with U.S., 203–5; distribu-tion of resources, 205; reduction in, 204
Regional mortality in U.S., 203–5
Research funds: coordination of, 232; ex-tent of, 232; number of sources, 232
Residency programs in U.S.: decentralized, 105; hospital growth and, 105; in hospi-tals, 105; privatization of system, 107; role of, in delivering services, 105; role of university-affiliated hospital, 107; vari-able quality of, 104. *See also* Specializa-tion
Retrospective reimbursement in U.S., 150–51
Rockefeller, John D., 92, 93, 237
Rockefeller Foundation, 89–96, 218, 224; and Nobel prize winners, 235
Rockefeller Institute for Medical Research: as model, 93; training, 92
Rosenberg, Charles, xi
Rosner, David, 71, 77
Royal College of Physicians, 21, 35
Royal College of Surgeons, 21, 35
Royal Commission on National Health In-surance, 46

Size: and decentralization, 254; system change, 254

Skocpol, Theda, 124
Smith, Adam, 132
Social and environmental medicine, 95, 237, 272
Social heterogeneity, and cleavage and consumer power, 255
Socialist Medical Association, 44, 46
South, Medicaid in, 203
Specialists in U.S.: function of, 63; number of, 63
Specialization, 122, 129; apprenticelike, 107; certification and, 103; decentralized, 103; hospitalization and, 104; hospital training, 106; internship and, 103; options for training, 103; spiraling phenomenon, 104; and technology, 136; in U.S., 101–2
Specialized hospitals in England and Wales, 10
Starr, Paul, xi, 75, 77
State, 122, 124; autonomy, 5, 124, 274; autonomy in shaping system, xii; and cost control, 124; increased influence of, 125; as mediator among interest groups, 5
State Medical Service Association, plans for reform, 44, 46
Status of medical profession, 32
Statutory Medicines Commission, 172
Stevens, Rosemary, xi, 95, 102, 119, 263
Structure of medical systems: changes in twentieth century, 241; differences in U.S. and Britain, 241
Style of life, 274
Style of research funding compared, 235
Subnational systems, linked to national systems, 257
Supportive medicine, 271, 273
Surgery: and certification in U.S., 109; ex-cess, 109; and fee for service, 110; inci-dence of, 108; need for rationing, 109; view of, 108
System change, potential for, 273

Tax subsidy: costs of, 151; effects of, 152; size of, 151
Technology: affected by group power and centralization, 255; chronic disease and, 271; complexity of, 186; costs, 136; de-mand, 136, 183; effect of, on structure, 42; efficacy, 184, 186; expenditures as in-dicator, 186; government role in, 136;

Technology (*continued*)
hospitalization as indicator, 186; inability to manage, 255; indicators, 186; levels of health, 184; logic, 255; specialists as indicator, 186; twentieth-century change in, 184
Tension, among doctors, 12
Theory construction: basis for, xii; method for, xii; presentation of, xii
Theory structure and performance, 241
Thomas, Lewis, 268
Trade-offs, 131, 182; in performance, 130

Utilization: review, 157; third-party payers, 135

Virchow, Rudolph, 32, 96
Vogel, Morris, xi
Voluntary hospitals in England and Wales: beds for paying patients, 9; BMA efforts to limit outpatients, 30; cases admitted, 9; charity, 7, 30; cost increase, 9; cottage hospitals, 30; and "deserving poor," 7; and elite, continued influences of, 9; financial strain between world wars, 29; fund-raising, 29; insurance, 29; maldistribution of, 30; and middle and upper classes, 30; outpatient clinic services, 11; outpatient services between world wars, 30; Parliamentary aid, 29; patient payments increase, 29; private paying beds, 29; reliance of, on fees, 9; rivalry of, with general practitioners, 30; source of in-

come, 7; 29; specialization, turn toward, 11; technology, 9, 29
Voluntary hospitals in U.S., 74; dependence on paying patients, 77; "deserving poor," 75; early services of, 75; effect of ethnic and religious ties on, 78; era of construction of, 75; ethnic and religious, 75, 76; patients admitted, 75; paying patients of, 77; persistance of, 77; philanthropists and, 75; philanthropy for, limits of, 77; public role in, 76; purpose for founding, 75; in southeast, 76; technology changes services of, 77

Wardell, William, 172
Watson, James, 220
Wealth: policy and revenue levels, 256; revenue sources, 256
Wellcome Trust, 220
White paper: features, 50; general practitioners' attitude toward, 51; new medical system proposed, 49; objections to, 50; wide support for, 50
Whitley Councils, 148
Workhouses: dreadful conditions of, 16; inadequate staff of, 16; patients in, 16; sick ward in, 16
Working class, 42, 63, 121; compared in U.S. and in England and Wales, 4; influence of, xii; limited influence of, on medical education, 31; preferences of, 245; World War II, effect of, on medical delivery system change, 48